ANATOMY OF CRITICISM

Four Essays

ORIGINALLY PUBLISHED BY PRINCETON UNIVERSITY PRESS

Anatomy of Criticism

FOUR ESSAYS

by NORTHROP FRYE

ATHENEUM, NEW YORK

1967

Publication of this book has been aided by a
grant from The Council of Humanities,
Princeton University, and the Class of 1932
Lectureship.

Published by Atheneum
Reprinted by arrangement with Princeton University Press
Copyright © 1957 by Princeton University Press
All rights reserved
Printed in the United States of America by
The Murray Printing Company, Forge Village, Massachusetts
Bound by The Colonial Press, Inc., Clinton, Massachusetts
Published in Canada by McClelland & Stewart Ltd.
First Atheneum Printing December 1965
Second Printing June 1966
Third Printing October 1966
Fourth Printing January 1967
Fifth Printing September 1967

HELENAE UXORI

PREFATORY STATEMENTS AND
ACKNOWLEDGMENTS

THIS book forced itself on me while I was trying to write something else, and it probably still bears the marks of the reluctance with which a great part of it was composed. After completing a study of William Blake (*Fearful Symmetry*, 1947), I determined to apply the principles of literary symbolism and Biblical typology which I had learned from Blake to another poet, preferably one who had taken these principles from the critical theories of his own day, instead of working them out by himself as Blake did. I therefore began a study of Spenser's *Faerie Queene*, only to discover that in my beginning was my end. The introduction to Spenser became an introduction to the theory of allegory, and that theory obstinately adhered to a much larger theoretical structure. The basis of argument became more and more discursive, and less and less historical and Spenserian. I soon found myself entangled in those parts of criticism that have to do with such words as "myth," "symbol," "ritual," and "archetype," and my efforts to make sense of these words in various published articles met with enough interest to encourage me to proceed further along these lines. Eventually the theoretical and the practical aspects of the task I had begun completely separated. What is here offered is pure critical theory, and the omission of all specific criticism, even, in three of the four essays, of quotation, is deliberate. The present book seems to me, so far as I can judge at present, to need a complementary volume concerned with practical criticism, a sort of morphology of literary symbolism.

I am grateful to the J. S. Guggenheim Memorial Foundation for a Fellowship (1950-1951) which gave me leisure and freedom to deal with my Protean subject at the time when it stood in the greatest need of both.

I am also grateful to the Class of 1932 of Princeton University, and to the Committee of the Special Program in the Humanities at Princeton, for providing me with a most stimulating term of work, in the course of which a good deal of the present book took its final shape. This book contains the substance of the four public lectures delivered in Princeton in March 1954.

The "Polemical Introduction" is a revised version of "The

Function of Criticism at the Present Time," *University of Toronto Quarterly*, October 1949, also reprinted in *Our Sense of Identity*, ed. Malcolm Ross, Toronto, 1954. The first essay is a revised and expanded version of "Towards a Theory of Cultural History," *University of Toronto Quarterly*, July 1953. The second essay incorporates the material of "Levels of Meaning in Literature," *Kenyon Review*, Spring 1950; of "Three Meanings of Symbolism," *Yale French Studies* No. 9 (1952); of "The Language of Poetry," *Explorations* 4 (Toronto, 1955); and of "The Archetypes of Literature," *Kenyon Review*, Winter 1951. The third essay contains the material of "The Argument of Comedy," *English Institute Essays* 1948, Columbia University Press, 1949; of "Characterization in Shakespearean Comedy," *Shakespeare Quarterly*, July 1953; of "Comic Myth in Shakespeare," *Transactions of the Royal Society of Canada* (Section II), June 1952; and of "The Nature of Satire," *University of Toronto Quarterly*, October 1944. The fourth essay contains the material of "Music in Poetry," *University of Toronto Quarterly*, January 1942; of "A Conspectus of Dramatic Genres," *Kenyon Review*, Autumn 1951; of "The Four Forms of Prose Fiction," *Hudson Review*, Winter 1950; and of "Myth as Information," *Hudson Review*, Summer 1954. I am greatly obliged to the courtesy of the editors of the above-mentioned periodicals, the Columbia University Press, and the Royal Society of Canada, for permission to reprint this material. I have also transplanted a few sentences from other articles and reviews of mine, all from the same periodicals, when they appeared to fit the present context.

For my further obligations, all that can be said here, and is not less true for being routine, is that many of the virtues of this book are due to others: the errors of fact, taste, logic, and proportion are poor things, but my own.

N. F.

Victoria College
University of Toronto

Contents

CONTENTS

ANATOMY OF CRITICISM

Four Essays

Polemical Introduction

THIS BOOK consists of "essays," in the word's original sense of a trial or incomplete attempt, on the possibility of a synoptic view of the scope, theory, principles, and techniques of literary criticism. The primary aim of the book is to give my reasons for believing in such a synoptic view; its secondary aim is to provide a tentative version of it which will make enough sense to convince my readers that *a* view, of the kind that I outline, is attainable. The gaps in the subject as treated here are too enormous for the book ever to be regarded as presenting *my* system, or even my theory. It is to be regarded rather as an interconnected group of suggestions which it is hoped will be of some practical use to critics and students of literature. Whatever is of no practical use to anybody is expendable. My approach is based on Matthew Arnold's precept of letting the mind play freely around a subject in which there has been much endeavor and little attempt at perspective. All the essays deal with criticism, but by criticism I mean the whole work of scholarship and taste concerned with literature which is a part of what is variously called liberal education, culture, or the study of the humanities. I start from the principle that criticism is not simply a part of this larger activity, but an essential part of it.

The subject-matter of literary criticism is an art, and criticism is evidently something of an art too. This sounds as though criticism were a parasitic form of literary expression, an art based on pre-existing art, a second-hand imitation of creative power. On this theory critics are intellectuals who have a taste for art but lack both the power to produce it and the money to patronize it, and thus form a class of cultural middlemen, distributing culture to society at a profit to themselves while exploiting the artist and increasing the strain on his public. The conception of the critic as a parasite or artist *manqué* is still very popular, especially among artists. It is sometimes reinforced by a dubious analogy between the creative and the procreative functions, so that we hear about the "impotence" and "dryness" of the critic, of his hatred for genuinely creative people, and so on. The golden age of anti-critical criticism was the latter part of the nineteenth century, but some of its prejudices are still around.

However, the fate of art that tries to do without criticism is

3

instructive. The attempt to reach the public directly through "popular" art assumes that criticism is artificial and public taste natural. Behind this is a further assumption about natural taste which goes back through Tolstoy to Romantic theories of a spontaneously creative "folk." These theories have had a fair trial; they have not stood up very well to the facts of literary history and experience, and it is perhaps time to move beyond them. An extreme reaction against the primitive view, at one time associated with the "art for art's sake" catchword, thinks of art in precisely the opposite terms, as a mystery, an initiation into an esoterically civilized community. Here criticism is restricted to ritual masonic gestures, to raised eyebrows and cryptic comments and other signs of an understanding too occult for syntax. The fallacy common to both attitudes is that of a rough correlation between the merit of art and the degree of public response to it, though the correlation assumed is direct in one case and inverse in the other.

One can find examples which appear to support both these views; but it is clearly the simple truth that there is no real correlation either way between the merits of art and its public reception. Shakespeare was more popular than Webster, but not because he was a greater dramatist; Keats was less popular than Montgomery, but not because he was a better poet. Consequently there is no way of preventing the critic from being, for better or worse, the pioneer of education and the shaper of cultural tradition. Whatever popularity Shakespeare and Keats have *now* is equally the result of the publicity of criticism. A public that tries to do without criticism, and asserts that it knows what it wants or likes, brutalizes the arts and loses its cultural memory. Art for art's sake is a retreat from criticism which ends in an impoverishment of civilized life itself. The only way to forestall the work of criticism is through censorship, which has the same relation to criticism that lynching has to justice.

There is another reason why criticism has to exist. Criticism can talk, and all the arts are dumb. In painting, sculpture, or music it is easy enough to see that the art shows forth, but cannot *say* anything. And, whatever it sounds like to call the poet inarticulate or speechless, there is a most important sense in which poems are as silent as statues. Poetry is a *disinterested* use of words: it does not address a reader directly. When it does so, we usually feel that the poet has some distrust in the capacity of readers and critics to

4

interpret his meaning without assistance, and has therefore dropped into the sub-poetic level of metrical talk ("verse" or "doggerel") which anybody can learn to produce. It is not only tradition that impels a poet to invoke a Muse and protest that his utterance is involuntary. Nor is it strained wit that causes Mr. MacLeish, in his famous *Ars Poetica*, to apply the words "mute," "dumb," and "wordless" to a poem. The artist, as John Stuart Mill saw in a wonderful flash of critical insight, is not heard but overheard. The axiom of criticism must be, not that the poet does not know what he is talking about, but that he cannot talk about what he knows. To defend the right of criticism to exist at all, therefore, is to assume that criticism is a structure of thought and knowledge existing in its own right, with some measure of independence from the art it deals with.

The poet may of course have some critical ability of his own, and so be able to talk about his own work. But the Dante who writes a commentary on the first canto of the *Paradiso* is merely one more of Dante's critics. What he says has a peculiar interest, but not a peculiar authority. It is generally accepted that a critic is a better judge of the *value* of a poem than its creator, but there is still a lingering notion that it is somehow ridiculous to regard the critic as the final judge of its meaning, even though in practice it is clear that he must be. The reason for this is an inability to distinguish literature from the descriptive or assertive writing which derives from the active will and the conscious mind, and which is primarily concerned to "say" something.

Part of the critic's reason for feeling that poets can be properly assessed only after their death is that they are then unable to presume on their merits as poets to tease him with hints of inside knowledge. When Ibsen maintains that *Emperor and Galilean* is his greatest play and that certain episodes in *Peer Gynt* are not allegorical, one can only say that Ibsen is an indifferent critic of Ibsen. Wordsworth's Preface to the *Lyrical Ballads* is a remarkable document, but as a piece of Wordsworthian criticism nobody would give it more than about a B plus. Critics of Shakespeare are often supposed to be ridiculed by the assertion that if Shakespeare were to come back from the dead he would not be able to appreciate or even understand their criticism. This in itself is likely enough: we have little evidence of Shakespeare's interest in criticism, either of himself or of anyone else. Even if there were

5

such evidence, his own account of what he was trying to do in *Hamlet* would no more be a definitive criticism of that play, clearing all its puzzles up for good, than a performance of it under his direction would be a definitive performance. And what is true of the poet in relation to his own work is still more true of his opinion of other poets. It is hardly possible for the critical poet to avoid expanding his own tastes, which are intimately linked to his own practice, into a general law of literature. But criticism has to be based on what the whole of literature actually does: in its light, whatever any highly respected writer thinks literature in general ought to do will show up in its proper perspective. The poet speaking as critic produces, not criticism, but documents to be examined by critics. They may well be valuable documents: it is only when they are accepted as directives for criticism that they are in any danger of becoming misleading.

The notion that the poet necessarily is or could be the definitive interpreter of himself or of the theory of literature belongs to the conception of the critic as a parasite or jackal. Once we admit that the critic has his own field of activity, and that he has autonomy within that field, we have to concede that criticism deals with literature in terms of a specific conceptual framework. The framework is not that of literature itself, for this is the parasite theory again, but neither is it something outside literature, for in that case the autonomy of criticism would again disappear, and the whole subject would be assimilated to something else.

This latter gives us, in criticism, the fallacy of what in history is called determinism, where a scholar with a special interest in geography or economics expresses that interest by the rhetorical device of putting his favorite study into a causal relationship with whatever interests him less. Such a method gives one the illusion of explaining one's subject while studying it, thus wasting no time. It would be easy to compile a long list of such determinisms in criticism, all of them, whether Marxist, Thomist, liberal-humanist, neo-Classical, Freudian, Jungian, or existentialist, substituting a critical attitude for criticism, all proposing, not to find a conceptual framework for criticism within literature, but to attach criticism to one of a miscellany of frameworks outside it. The axioms and postulates of criticism, however, have to grow out of the art it deals with. The first thing the literary critic has to do is to read literature, to make an inductive survey of his own field and let his critical principles shape themselves solely out of his knowledge of that field. Critical principles cannot be taken over ready-made from theology, philosophy, politics, science, or any combination of these.

To subordinate criticism to an externally derived critical attitude is to exaggerate the values in literature that can be related to the external source, whatever it is. It is all too easy to impose on literature an extra-literary schematism, a sort of religio-political color-filter, which makes some poets leap into prominence and others show up as dark and faulty. All that the disinterested critic can do with such a color-filter is to murmur politely that it shows things in a new light and is indeed a most stimulating contribution to criticism. Of course such filtering critics usually imply, and often believe, that they are letting their literary experience speak for itself and are holding their other attitudes in reserve, the coincidence between their critical valuations and their religious or political views being silently gratifying to them but not explicitly forced on the reader. Such independence of criticism from prejudice, however, does not invariably occur even with those who best understand criticism. Of their inferiors the less said the better.

If it is insisted that we cannot criticize literature until we have acquired a coherent philosophy of life with its center of gravity in something else, the existence of criticism as a separate subject is still being denied. But there is another possibility. If criticism exists, it must be an examination of literature in terms of a conceptual framework derivable from an inductive survey of the literary field. The word "inductive" suggests some sort of scientific procedure. What if criticism is a science as well as an art? Not a "pure" or "exact" science, of course, but these phrases belong to a nineteenth-century cosmology which is no longer with us. The writing of history is an art, but no one doubts that scientific principles are involved in the historian's treatment of evidence, and that the presence of this scientific element is what distinguishes history from legend. It may also be a scientific element in criticism which distinguishes it from literary parasitism on the one hand, and the superimposed critical attitude on the other. The presence of science in any subject changes its character from the casual to the causal, from the random and intuitive to the systematic, as well as safeguarding the integrity of that subject from external invasions. However, if there are any readers for whom the word "scientific" conveys emotional overtones of unimaginative barbarism, they may substitute "systematic" or "progressive" instead.

It seems absurd to say that there *may* be a scientific element in criticism when there are dozens of learned journals based on the assumption that there is, and hundreds of scholars engaged in a scientific procedure related to literary criticism. Evidence is examined scientifically; previous authorities are used scientifically; fields are investigated scientifically; texts are edited scientifically. Prosody is scientific in structure; so is phonetics; so is philology. Either literary criticism is scientific, or all these highly trained and intelligent scholars are wasting their time on some kind of pseudo-science like phrenology. Yet one is forced to wonder whether scholars realize the implications of the fact that their work is scientific. In the growing complication of secondary sources one misses that sense of consolidating progress which belongs to a science. Research begins in what is known as "background," and one would expect it, as it goes on, to start organizing the foreground as well. Telling us what we should know about literature ought to fulfil itself in telling us something about what it is. As soon as it comes to this point, scholarship seems to be dammed by some kind of barrier, and washes back into further research projects.

So to "appreciate" literature and get more direct contact with it, we turn to the public critic, the Lamb or Hazlitt or Arnold or Sainte-Beuve who represents the reading public at its most expert and judicious. It is the task of the public critic to exemplify how a man of taste uses and evaluates literature, and thus show how literature is to be absorbed into society. But here we no longer have the sense of an impersonal body of consolidating knowledge. The public critic tends to episodic forms like the lecture and the familiar essay, and his work is not a science, but another kind of literary art. He has picked up his ideas from a pragmatic study of literature, and does not try to create or enter into a theoretical structure. In Shakespearean criticism we have a fine monument of Augustan taste in Johnson, of Romantic taste in Coleridge, of Victorian taste in Bradley. The ideal critic of Shakespeare, we feel, would avoid the Augustan, Romantic, and Victorian limitations and prejudices respectively of Johnson, Coleridge, and Bradley. But we have no clear notion of progress in the criticism of Shakespeare, or of how a critic who read all his predecessors could, as a result, become anything better than a monument of contemporary taste, with all *its* limitations and prejudices.

In other words, there is as yet no way of distinguishing what is genuine criticism, and therefore progresses toward making the whole of literature intelligible, from what belongs only to the history of taste, and therefore follows the vacillations of fashionable prejudice. I give an example of the difference between the two which amounts to a head-on collision. In one of his curious, brilliant, scatter-brained footnotes to *Munera Pulveris*, John Ruskin says:

> Of Shakspeare's names I will afterwards speak at more length; they are curiously—often barbarously—mixed out of various traditions and languages. Three of the clearest in meaning have been already noticed. Desdemona—"$\delta\upsilon\sigma\delta\alpha\iota\mu\text{ov}\acute{\iota}\alpha$,"*miserable fortune*—is also plain enough. Othello is, I believe, "the careful"; all the calamity of the tragedy arising from the single flaw and error in his magnificently collected strength. Ophelia, "serviceableness," the true, lost wife of Hamlet, is marked as having a Greek name by that of her brother Laertes; and its signification is once exquisitely alluded to in that brother's last word of her, where her gentle preciousness is opposed to the uselessness of the churlish clergy:—"A *ministering* angel shall my sister be, when thou liest howling."

On this passage Matthew Arnold comments as follows:

> Now, really, what a piece of extravagance all that is! I will not say that the meaning of Shakspeare's names (I put aside the question as to the correctness of Mr. Ruskin's etymologies) has no effect at all, may be entirely lost sight of; but to give it that degree of prominence is to throw the reins to one's whim, to forget all moderation and proportion, to lose the balance of one's mind altogether. It is to show in one's criticism, to the highest excess, the note of provinciality.

Now whether Ruskin is right or wrong, he is attempting genuine criticism. He is trying to interpret Shakespeare in terms of a conceptual framework which belongs to the critic alone, and yet relates itself to the plays alone. Arnold is perfectly right in feeling that this is not the sort of material that the public critic can directly use. But he does not seem even to suspect the existence

9

of a systematic criticism as distinct from the history of taste. Here it is Arnold who is the provincial. Ruskin has learned his trade from the great iconological tradition which comes down through Classical and Biblical scholarship into Dante and Spenser, both of whom he had studied carefully, and which is incorporated in the medieval cathedrals he had pored over in such detail. Arnold is assuming, as a universal law of nature, certain "plain sense" critical axioms which were hardly heard of before Dryden's time and which can assuredly not survive the age of Freud and Jung and Frazer and Cassirer.

What we have so far is, on one side of the "study of literature," the work of the scholar who tries to make it possible, and on the other side the work of the public critic who assumes that it exists. In between is "literature" itself, a game preserve where the student wanders with his native intelligence his only guide. The assumption seems to be that the scholar and the public critic are connected by a common interest in literature alone. The scholar lays down his materials outside the portals of literature: like other offerings brought to unseen consumers, a good deal of such scholarship seems to be the product of a rather touching faith, sometimes only a hope that some synthetizing critical Messiah of the future will find it useful. The public critic, or the spokesman of the imposed critical attitude, is apt to make only a random and haphazard use of this material, often in fact to treat the scholar as Hamlet did the grave-digger, ignoring everything he throws out except an odd skull which he can pick up and moralize about.

Those who are concerned with the arts are often asked questions, not always sympathetic ones, about the use or value of what they are doing. It is probably impossible to answer such questions directly, or at any rate to answer the people who ask them. Most of the answers, such as Newman's "liberal knowledge is its own end," merely appeal to the experience of those who have had the right experience. Similarly, most "defenses of poetry" are intelligible only to those well within the defenses. The basis of critical apologetics, therefore, has to be the actual experience of art, and for those concerned with literature, the first question to answer is not "What use is the study of literature?" but, "What follows from the fact that it is possible?"

Everyone who has seriously studied literature knows that the mental process involved is as coherent and progressive as the study of science. A precisely similar training of the mind takes place, and a similar sense of the unity of the subject is built up. If this unity comes from literature itself, then literature itself must be shaped like a science, which contradicts our experience of it; or it must derive some informing power from an ineffable mystery at the heart of being, which seems vague; or the mental benefits alleged to be derived from it are imaginary, and are really derived from other subjects studied incidentally in connection with it.

This is as far as we can get on the assumption that the scholar and the man of taste are connected by nothing more than a common interest in literature. If this assumption is true, the high percentage of sheer futility in all criticism should be honestly faced, for the percentage can only increase with its bulk, until criticizing becomes, especially for university teachers, merely an automatic method of acquiring merit, like turning a prayer-wheel. But it is only an unconscious assumption—at least, I have never seen it stated as a doctrine—and it would certainly be convenient if it turned out to be nonsense. The alternative assumption is that scholars and public critics are directly related by an intermediate form of criticism, a coherent and comprehensive theory of literature, logically and scientifically organized, some of which the student unconsciously learns as he goes on, but the main principles of which are as yet unknown to us. The development of such a criticism would fulfil the systematic and progressive element in research by assimilating its work into a unified structure of knowledge, as other sciences do. It would at the same time establish an authority within criticism for the public critic and the man of taste.

We should be careful to realize what the possibility of such an intermediate criticism implies. It implies that at no point is there any direct learning of literature itself. Physics is an organized body of knowledge about nature, and a student of it says that he is learning physics, not nature. Art, like nature, has to be distinguished from the systematic study of it, which is criticism. It is therefore impossible to "learn literature": one learns about it in a certain way, but what one learns, transitively, is the criticism of literature. Similarly, the difficulty often felt in "teaching literature" arises from the fact that it cannot be done: the criticism of literature is all that can be directly taught. Literature is not a subject of study, but an object of study: the fact that it consists of words, as we have seen, makes us confuse it with the talking verbal disciplines. The libraries reflect our confusion by cataloguing criticism as one of the subdivisions of literature. Criticism, rather, is to art what history is to action and philosophy to wisdom: a verbal imitation of a human productive power which in itself does not speak. And just as there is nothing which the philosopher cannot consider philosophically, and nothing which the historian cannot consider historically, so the critic should be able to construct and dwell in a conceptual universe of his own. This critical universe seems to be one of the things implied in Arnold's conception of culture.

I am not, therefore, saying that literary criticism at present must be doing the wrong thing and ought to be doing something else. I am saying that it should be possible to get a comprehensive view of what it actually is doing. It is necessary that scholars and public critics should continue to make their contributions to criticism. It is not necessary that the thing they contribute to should be invisible, as the coral island is invisible to the polyp. In the study of literary scholarship the student becomes aware of an undertow carrying him away from literature. He finds that literature is the central division of the humanities, flanked on one side by history and on the other by philosophy. As literature is not itself an organized structure of knowledge, the critic has to turn to the conceptual framework of the historian for events, and to that of the philosopher for ideas. Asked what he is working on, the critic will invariably say that he is working on Donne, or Shelley's thought, or the 1640-1660 period, or give some other answer implying that history, philosophy, or literature itself is the conceptual basis of his criticism. In the unlikely event that he was concerned with the theory of criticism, he would say that he was working on a "general" topic. It is clear that the absence of systematic criticism has created a power vacuum, and all the neighboring disciplines have moved in. Hence the prominence of the Archimedes fallacy mentioned above: the notion that if we plant our feet solidly enough in Christian or democratic or Marxist values we shall be able to lift the whole of criticism at once with a dialectic crowbar. But if the varied interests of critics could be related to a central expanding pattern of systematic comprehension, this undertow would disappear, and they would be seen as converging on criticism instead of running away from it.

One proof that a systematic comprehension of a subject actually exists is the ability to write an elementary textbook expounding its fundamental principles. It would be interesting to see what such a book on criticism would contain. It would not start with a clear answer to the first question of all: "What is literature?" We have no real standards to distinguish a verbal structure that is literary from one that is not, and no idea what to do with the vast penumbra of books that may be claimed for literature because they are written with "style," or are useful as "background," or have simply got into a university course of "great books." We then discover that we have no word, corresponding to "poem" in poetry or "play" in drama, to describe a work of literary art. It is all very well for Blake to say that to generalize is to be an idiot, but when we find ourselves in the cultural situation of savages who have words for ash and willow and no word for tree, we wonder if there is not such a thing as being *too* deficient in the capacity to generalize.

So much for page one of our handbook. Page two would be the place to explain what seems the most far-reaching of literary facts, the distinction in rhythm between verse and prose. But it appears that a distinction which anyone can make in practice cannot be made as yet by any critic in theory. We continue to riffle through the blank pages. The next thing to do is to outline the primary categories of literature, such as drama, epic, prose fiction, and the like. This at any rate is what Aristotle assumed to be the obvious first step in criticism. We discover that the critical theory of genres is stuck precisely where Aristotle left it. The very word "genre" sticks out in an English sentence as the unpronounceable and alien thing it is. Most critical efforts to handle such generic terms as "epic" and "novel" are chiefly interesting as examples of the psychology of rumor. Thanks to the Greeks, we can distinguish tragedy from comedy in drama, and so we still tend to assume that each is the half of drama that is not the other half. When we come to deal with such forms as the masque, opera, movie, ballet, puppet-play, mystery-play, morality, commedia dell' arte, and Zauberspiel, we find ourselves in the position of the Renaissance doctors who refused to treat syphilis because Galen said nothing about it.

The Greeks hardly needed to develop a classification of prose forms. We do, but have never done so. We have, as usual, no word for a work of prose fiction, so the word "novel" does duty for everything, and thereby loses its only real meaning as the name of a genre. The circulating-library distinction between fiction and non-fiction, between books which are about things admitted not to be true and books which are about everything else, is apparently exhaustive enough for critics. Asked what form of prose fiction *Gulliver's Travels* belongs to, there are few critics who, if they could give the answer "Menippean satire," would regard it as knowledge essential for dealing with the book, although some notion of what a novel is is surely a prerequisite for dealing with a serious novelist. Other prose forms are even worse off. Western literature has been more influenced by the Bible than by any other book, but with all his respect for "sources," the critic knows little more about that influence than the fact that it exists. Biblical typology is so dead a language now that most readers, including scholars, cannot construe the superficial meaning of any poem which employs it. And so on. If criticism could ever be conceived as a coherent and systematic study, the elementary principles of which could be explained to any intelligent nineteen-year-old, then, from the point of view of such a conception, no critic now knows the first thing about criticism. What critics now have is a mystery-religion without a gospel, and they are initiates who can communicate, or quarrel, only with one another.

A theory of criticism whose principles apply to the whole of literature and account for every valid type of critical procedure is what I think Aristotle meant by poetics. Aristotle seems to me to approach poetry as a biologist would approach a system of organisms, picking out its genera and species, formulating the broad laws of literary experience, and in short writing as though he believed that there is a totally intelligible structure of knowledge attainable about poetry which is not poetry itself, or the experience of it, but poetics. One would imagine that, after two thousand years of post-Aristotelian literary activity, his views on poetics, like his views on the generation of animals, could be re-examined in the light of fresh evidence. Meanwhile, the opening words of the *Poetics*, in the Bywater translation, remain as good an introduction to the subject as ever, and describe the kind of approach that I have tried to keep in mind for myself:

> Our subject being poetry, I propose to speak not only of the art in general but also of its species and their respective capacities; of the structure of plot required for a good poem; of the number and nature of the constituent parts of a poem; and likewise of

any other matters in the same line of inquiry. Let us follow the natural order and begin with the primary facts.

Of course literature is only one of many arts, but this book is compelled to avoid the treatment of aesthetic problems outside of poetics. Every art, however, needs its own critical organization, and poetics will form a part of aesthetics as soon as aesthetics becomes the unified criticism of all the arts instead of whatever it is now.

Sciences normally begin in a state of naive induction: they tend first of all to take the phenomena they are supposed to interpret as data. Thus physics began by taking the immediate sensations of experience, classified as hot, cold, moist, and dry, as fundamental principles. Eventually physics turned inside out, and discovered that its real function was rather to explain what heat and moisture were. History began as chronicle; but the difference between the old chronicler and the modern historian is that to the chronicler the events he recorded were also the *structure* of his history, whereas the historian sees these events as historical phenomena, to be connected within a conceptual framework not only broader but different in shape from them. Similarly each modern science has had to take what Bacon calls (though in another context) an inductive leap, occupying a new vantage ground from which it can see its former data as new things to be explained. As long as astronomers regarded the movements of heavenly bodies as the structure of astronomy, they naturally regarded their own point of view as fixed. Once they thought of movement as itself explicable, a mathematical theory of movement became the conceptual framework, and so the way was cleared for the heliocentric solar system and the law of gravitation. As long as biology thought of animal and vegetable forms of life as constituting its subject, the different branches of biology were largely efforts of cataloguing. As soon as it was the existence of forms of life themselves that had to be explained, the theory of evolution and the conceptions of protoplasm and the cell poured into biology and completely revitalized it.

It occurs to me that literary criticism is now in such a state of naive induction as we find in a primitive science. Its materials, the masterpieces of literature, are not yet regarded as phenomena to be explained in terms of a conceptual framework which criticism alone possesses. They are still regarded as somehow constituting the framework or structure of criticism as well. I suggest that it is time for criticism to leap to a new ground from which it can discover what the organizing or containing forms of its conceptual framework are. Criticism seems to be badly in need of a coordinating principle, a central hypothesis which, like the theory of evolution in biology, will see the phenomena it deals with as parts of a whole.

The first postulate of this inductive leap is the same as that of any science: the assumption of total coherence. Simple as this assumption appears, it takes a long time for a science to discover that it is in fact a totally intelligible body of knowledge. Until it makes this discovery, it has not been born as an individual science but remains an embryo within the body of some other subject. The birth of physics from "natural philosophy" and of sociology from "moral philosophy" will illustrate the process. It is also approximately true that the modern sciences have developed in the order of their closeness to mathematics. Thus physics and astronomy began to assume their modern form in the Renaissance, chemistry in the eighteenth century, biology in the nineteenth, and the social sciences in the twentieth. If criticism is a science, it is clearly a social science, and if it is developing only in our day, the fact is at least not an anachronism. Meanwhile, the myopia of specialization remains an inseparable part of naive induction. From such a perspective, "general" questions are humanly impossible to deal with, because they involve "covering" a frighteningly large field. The critic is in the position of a mathematician who has to deal with numbers so large that it would keep him scribbling digits until the next ice age even to write them out in their conventional form as integers. Critic and mathematician alike will have somehow to invent a less cumbersome notation.

Naive induction thinks of literature entirely in terms of the enumerative bibliography of literature: that is, it sees literature as a huge aggregate or miscellaneous pile of discrete "works." Clearly, if literature is nothing more than this, any systematic mental training based on it becomes impossible. Only one organizing principle has so far been discovered in literature, the principle of chronology. This supplies the magic word "tradition," which means that when we see the miscellaneous pile strung out along a chronological line, some coherence is given it by sheer sequence. But even tradition does not answer all our questions. Total literary history gives us a glimpse of the possibility of seeing literature as a complication of a relatively restricted and simple group of formulas that can be studied in primitive culture. We next realize that the relation of later literature to these primitive formulas is by no means purely one of complication, as we find the primitive formulas reappearing in the greatest classics—in fact there seems to be a general tendency on the part of great classics to revert to them. This coincides with a feeling we have all had: that the study of mediocre works of art remains a random and peripheral form of critical experience, whereas the profound masterpiece draws us to a point at which we seem to see an enormous number of converging patterns of significance. We begin to wonder if we cannot see literature, not only as complicating itself in time, but as spread out in conceptual space from some kind of center that criticism could locate.

It is clear that criticism cannot be a systematic study unless there is a quality in literature which enables it to be so. We have to adopt the hypothesis, then, that just as there is an order of nature behind the natural sciences, so literature is not a piled aggregate of "works," but an order of words. A belief in an order of nature, however, is an inference from the intelligibility of the natural sciences; and if the natural sciences ever completely demonstrated the order of nature they would presumably exhaust their subject. Similarly, criticism, if a science, must be totally intelligible, but literature, as the order of words which makes the science possible, is, so far as we know, an inexhaustible source of new critical discoveries, and would be even if new works of literature ceased to be written. If so, then the search for a limiting principle in literature in order to discourage the development of criticism is mistaken. The absurd quantum formula of criticism, the assertion that the critic should confine himself to "getting out" of a poem exactly what the poet may vaguely be assumed to have been aware of "putting in," is one of the many slovenly illiteracies that the absence of systematic criticism has allowed to grow up. This quantum theory is the literary form of what may be called the fallacy of premature teleology. It corresponds, in the natural sciences, to the assertion that a phenomenon is as it is because Providence in its inscrutable wisdom made it so. That is, the critic is assumed to have no conceptual framework: it is simply his job to take a poem into which a poet has diligently stuffed a specific number of beauties or effects, and complacently extract them one by one, like his prototype Little Jack Horner.

The first step in developing a genuine poetics is to recognize and get rid of meaningless criticism, or talking about literature in a way that cannot help to build up a systematic structure of knowledge. This includes all the sonorous nonsense that we so often find in critical generalities, reflective comments, ideological perorations, and other consequences of taking a large view of an unorganized subject. It includes all lists of the "best" novels or poems or writers, whether their particular virtue is exclusiveness or inclusiveness. It includes all casual, sentimental, and prejudiced value-judgments, and all the literary chit-chat which makes the reputations of poets boom and crash in an imaginary stock exchange. That wealthy investor Mr. Eliot, after dumping Milton on the market, is now buying him again; Donne has probably reached his peak and will begin to taper off; Tennyson may be in for a slight flutter but the Shelley stocks are still bearish. This sort of thing cannot be part of any systematic study, for a systematic study can only progress: whatever dithers or vacillates or reacts is merely leisure-class gossip. The history of taste is no more a part of the *structure* of criticism than the Huxley-Wilberforce debate is a part of the structure of biological science.

I believe that if this distinction is maintained and applied to the critics of the past, what they have said about real criticism will show an astonishing amount of agreement, in which the outlines of a coherent and systematic study will begin to emerge. In the history of taste, where there are no facts, and where all truths have been, in Hegelian fashion, split into half-truths in order to sharpen their cutting edges, we perhaps do feel that the study of literature is too relative and subjective ever to make any consistent sense. But as the history of taste has no organic connection with criticism, it can easily be separated. Mr. Eliot's essay *The Function of Criticism* begins by laying down the principle that the existing monuments of literature form an ideal order among themselves, and are not simply collections of the writings of individuals. This is criticism, and very fundamental criticism. Much of this book attempts to annotate it. Its solidity is indicated by its consistency with a hundred other statements that could be collected from the better critics of all ages. There follows a rhetorical debate which makes tradition and its opposite into personified and contending forces, the former dignified with the titles of Catholic and Classical, the latter ridiculed by the epithet "Whiggery." This is the sort of thing that makes for confusion until we realize how easy it is to snip it off and throw it away. The debate is maintained against Mr. Middleton Murry, who is spoken of approvingly because "he is aware that there are definite positions to be taken, and that now and then one must actually reject something and select something else." There are no definite positions to be taken in chemistry or philology, and if there are any to be taken in criticism, criticism is not a field of genuine learning. For in any field of genuine learning, the only sensible response to the challenge "stand" is Falstaff's "so I do, against my will." One's "definite position" is one's weakness, the source of one's liability to error and prejudice, and to gain adherents to a definite position is only to multiply one's weakness like an infection.

The next step is to realize that criticism has a great variety of neighbors, and that the critic must enter into relations with them in any way that guarantees his own independence. He may want to know something of the natural sciences, but he need waste no time in emulating their methods. I understand that there is a Ph.D. thesis somewhere which displays a list of Hardy's novels in the order of the percentages of gloom they contain, but one does not feel that that sort of procedure should be encouraged. The critic may want to know something of the social sciences, but there can be no such thing as, for instance, a sociological "approach" to literature. There is no reason why a sociologist should not work exclusively on literary material, but if he does he should pay no attention to literary values. In his field Horatio Alger and the writer of the Elsie books may well be more important than Hawthorne or Melville, and a single issue of the *Ladies' Home Journal* worth all of Henry James. The critic is similarly under no obligation to sociological values, as the social conditions favorable to the production of great art are not necessarily those at which the social sciences aim. The critic may need to know something of religion, but by theological standards an orthodox religious poem will give a more satisfactory expression of its content than a heretical one: this makes nonsense in criticism, and there is nothing to be gained by confusing the standards of the two subjects.

Literature has been always recognized to be a marketable product, its producers being the creative writers and its consumers the culti-

vated readers, with the critics at their head. From this point of
view the critic is, in the metaphor of our opening page, the mid-
dleman. He has some wholesaler's privileges, such as free review
copies, but his function, as distinct from the bookseller's, is essentially a form of consumer's research. I recognize a second division
of labor in literature, which, like other forms of mental construction, has a theory and a practice. The practitioner of literature and
the producer of literature are not quite the same, though they
overlap a good deal; the theorist of literature and the consumer
of literature are not the same at all, even when they co-exist in
the same man. The present book assumes that the theory of literature is as primary a humanistic and liberal pursuit as its practice.
Hence, although it takes certain literary values for granted, as
fully established by critical experience, it is not directly concerned
with value-judgements. This fact needs explanation, as the value-
judgement is often, and perhaps rightly for all I know, regarded as
the distinguishing feature of the humanistic and liberal pursuit.

Value-judgements are subjective in the sense that they can be
indirectly but not directly communicated. When they are fashionable or generally accepted, they look objective, but that is all. The
demonstrable value-judgement is the donkey's carrot of literary
criticism, and every new critical fashion, such as the current fashion
for elaborate rhetorical analysis, has been accompanied by a belief
that criticism has finally devised a definitive technique for separating the excellent from the less excellent. But this always turns out
to be an illusion of the history of taste. Value-judgements are
founded on the study of literature; the study of literature can never
be founded on value-judgements. Shakespeare, we say, was one
of a group of English dramatists working around 1600, and also
one of the great poets of the world. The first part of this is a
statement of fact, the second a value-judgement so generally accepted as to pass for a statement of fact. But it is not a statement
of fact. It remains a value-judgement, and not a shred of systematic
criticism can ever be attached to it.

There are two types of value-judgements, comparative and positive. Criticism founded on comparative values falls into two main
divisions, according to whether the work of art is regarded as a product or as a possession. The former develops biographical criticism,
which relates the work of art primarily to the man who wrote it. The

latter we may call tropical criticism, and it is primarily concerned with the contemporary reader. Biographical criticism concerns itself largely with comparative questions of greatness and personal authority. It regards the poem as the oratory of its creator, and it feels most secure when it knows of a definite, and preferably heroic, personality behind the poetry. If it cannot find such a personality, it may try to project one out of rhetorical ectoplasm, as Carlyle does in his essay on Shakespeare as a "heroic" poet. Tropical criticism deals comparatively with style and craftsmanship, with complexity of meaning and figurative assimilation. It tends to dislike and belittle the oratorical poets, and it can hardly deal at all with heroic personality. Both are essentially rhetorical forms of criticism, as one deals with the rhetoric of persuasive speech and the other with the rhetoric of verbal ornament, but each distrusts the other's kind of rhetoric.

Rhetorical value-judgements are closely related to social values, and are usually cleared through a customs-house of moral metaphors: sincerity, economy, subtlety, simplicity, and the like. But because poetics is undeveloped, a fallacy arises from the illegitimate extension of rhetoric into the theory of literature. The invariable mark of this fallacy is the selected tradition, illustrated with great clarity in Arnold's "touchstone" theory, where we proceed from the intuition of value represented by the touchstone to a system of ranking poets in classes. The practice of comparing poets by weighing their lines (no new invention, as it was ridiculed by Aristophanes in *The Frogs*) is used by both biographical and tropical critics, mainly in order to deny first-class rating to those in favor with the opposite group.

When we examine the touchstone technique in Arnold, however, certain doubts arise about his motivation. The line from *The Tempest*, "In the dark backward and abysm of time," would do very well as a touchstone line. One feels that the line "Yet a tailor might scratch her where'er she did itch" somehow would not do, though it is equally Shakespearean and equally essential to the same play. (An extreme form of the same kind of criticism would, of course, deny this and insist that the line had been interpolated by a vulgar hack.) Some principle is clearly at work here which is much more highly selective than a purely critical experience of the play would be.

Arnold's "high seriousness" evidently is closely connected with the view that epic and tragedy, because they deal with ruling-class figures and require the high style of decorum, are the aristocrats of literary forms. All his Class One touchstones are from, or judged by the standards of, epic and tragedy. Hence his demotion of Chaucer and Burns to Class Two seems to be affected by a feeling that comedy and satire should be kept in their proper place, like the moral standards and the social classes which they symbolize. We begin to suspect that the literary value-judgements are projections of social ones. Why does Arnold *want* to rank poets? He says that we increase our admiration for those who manage to stay in Class One after we have made it very hard for them to do so. This being clearly nonsense, we must look further. When we read "in poetry the distinction between excellent and inferior . . . is of paramount importance . . . because of the high destinies of poetry," we begin to get a clue. We see that Arnold is trying to create a new scriptural canon out of poetry to serve as a guide for those social principles which he wants culture to take over from religion.

The treatment of criticism as the application of a social attitude is a natural enough result of what we have called the power vacuum in criticism. A systematic study alternates between inductive experience and deductive principles. In criticism rhetorical analysis provides some of the induction, and poetics, the theory of criticism, should be the deductive counterpart. There being no poetics, the critic is thrown back on prejudice derived from his existence as a social being. For prejudice is simply inadequate deduction, as a prejudice in the mind can never be anything but a major premise which is mostly submerged, like an iceberg.

It is not hard to see prejudice in Arnold, because his views have dated: it is a little harder when "high seriousness" becomes "maturity," or some other powerful persuader of more recent critical rhetoric. It is harder when the old question of what books one would take to a desert island emerges from parlor games, where it belongs, into an expensive library alleged to constitute the scriptural canon of democratic values. Rhetorical value-judgements usually turn on questions of decorum, and the central conception of decorum is the difference between high, middle, and low styles. These styles are suggested by the class structure of society, and criticism, if it is not to reject half the facts of literary experience, obviously has to look at art from the standpoint of an ideally classless society. Arnold himself points this out when he says that "culture seeks to do away with classes." Every deliberately constructed hierarchy of values in literature known to me is based on a concealed social, moral, or intellectual analogy. This applies whether the analogy is conservative and Romantic, as it is in Arnold, or radical, giving the top place to comedy, satire, and the values of prose and reason, as it is in Bernard Shaw. The various pretexts for minimizing the communicative power of certain writers, that they are obscure or obscene or nihilistic or reactionary or what not, generally turn out to be disguises for a feeling that the views of decorum held by the ascendant social or intellectual class ought to be either maintained or challenged. These social fixations keep changing, like a fan turning in front of a light, and the changing inspires the belief that posterity eventually discovers the whole truth about art.

A selective approach to tradition, then, invariably has some ultra-critical joker concealed in it. There is no question of accepting the whole of literature as the basis of study, but a tradition (or, of course, "the" tradition) is abstracted from it and attached to contemporary social values, being then used to document those values. The hesitant reader is invited to try the following exercise. Pick three big names at random, work out the eight possible combinations of promotion and demotion (on a simplified, or two-class, basis) and defend each in turn. Thus if the three names picked were Shakespeare, Milton, and Shelley, the agenda would run:

1. Demoting Shelley, on the ground that he is immature in technique and profundity of thought compared to the others.

2. Demoting Milton, on the ground that his religious obscurantism and heavy doctrinal content impair the spontaneity of his utterance.

3. Demoting Shakespeare, on the ground that his detachment from ideas makes his dramas a reflection of life rather than a creative attempt to improve it.

4. Promoting Shakespeare, on the ground that he preserves an integrity of poetic vision which in the others is obfuscated by didacticism.

5. Promoting Milton, on the ground that his penetration of the highest mysteries of faith raises him above Shakespeare's unvarying worldliness and Shelley's callowness.

6. Promoting Shelley, on the ground that his love of freedom

speaks to the heart of modern man more immediately than poets who accepted outworn social or religious values.

7. Promoting all three (for this a special style, which we may call the peroration style, should be used).

8. Demoting all three, on the ground of the untidiness of English genius when examined by French or Classical or Chinese standards.

The reader may sympathize with some of these "positions," as they are called, more than with others, and so be seduced into thinking that one of them must be right, and that it is important to decide which one it is. But long before he has finished his assignment he will realize that the whole procedure involved is an anxiety neurosis prompted by a moral censor, and is totally devoid of content. Of course, in addition to the moralists, there are poets who regard only those other poets as authentic who sound like themselves; there are critics who enjoy making religious, anti-religious, or political campaigns with toy soldiers labelled "Milton" or "Shelley" more than they enjoy studying poetry; there are students who have urgent reasons for making as much edifying reading as possible superfluous. But a conspiracy even of all these still does not make criticism.

The social dialectics applied externally to criticism, then, are, *within criticism*, pseudo-dialectics, or false rhetoric. It remains to try to define the true dialectic of criticism. On this level the biographical critic becomes the historical critic. He develops from hero-worship towards total and indiscriminate acceptance: there is nothing "in his field" that he is not prepared to read with interest. From a purely historical point of view, however, cultural phenomena are to be read in their own context without contemporary application. We study them as we do the stars, seeing their interrelationships but not approaching them. Hence historical criticism needs to be complemented by a corresponding activity growing out of tropical criticism.

We may call this ethical criticism, interpreting ethics not as a rhetorical comparison of social facts to predetermined values, but as the consciousness of the presence of society. As a critical category this would be the sense of the real presence of culture in the community. Ethical criticism, then, deals with art as a communication from the past to the present, and is based on the conception of the total and simultaneous possession of past culture. An exclusive devotion to it, ignoring historical criticism, would lead to a naive translation of all cultural phenomena into our own terms without regard to their original character. As a counterweight to historical criticism, it is designed to express the contemporary impact of all art, without selecting a tradition. Every new critical fashion has increased the appreciation of some poets and depreciated others, as the increase of interest in the metaphysical poets tended to depreciate the Romantics about twenty-five years ago. On the ethical level we can see that every increase of appreciation has been right, and every decrease wrong: that criticism has no business to react against things, but should show a steady advance toward undiscriminating catholicity. Oscar Wilde said that only an auctioneer could be equally appreciative of all kinds of art: he had of course the public critic in mind, but even the public critic's job of getting the treasures of culture into the hands of the people who want them is largely an auctioneer's job. And if this is true of him, it is *a fortiori* true of the scholarly critic.

The dialectic axis of criticism, then, has as one pole the total acceptance of the data of literature, and as the other the total acceptance of the potential values of those data. This is the real level of culture and of liberal education, the fertilizing of life by learning, in which the systematic progress of scholarship flows into a systematic progress of taste and understanding. On this level there is no itch to make weighty judgements, and none of the ill effects which follow the debauchery of judiciousness, and have made the word critic a synonym for an educated shrew. Comparative estimates of value are really inferences, most valid when silent ones, from critical practice, not expressed principles guiding its practice. The critic will find soon, and constantly, that Milton is a more rewarding and suggestive poet to work with than Blackmore. But the more obvious this becomes, the less time he will want to waste in belaboring the point. For belaboring the point is all he can do: any criticism motivated by a desire to establish or prove it will be merely one more document in the history of taste. There is doubtless much in the culture of the past which will always be of comparatively slight value to the present. But the difference between redeemable and irredeemable art, being based on the *total* experience of criticism, can never be theoretically formulated. There are too many Cinderellas among the poets, too many stones rejected from one fashionable building that have become heads of the next corner.

There may, then, be such things as rules of critical procedure, and laws, in the sense of the patterns of observed phenomena, of literary practice. All efforts of critics to discover rules or laws in the sense of moral mandates telling the artist what he ought to do, or have done, to be an authentic artist, have failed. "Poetry," said Shelley, "and the art which professes to regulate and limit its powers, cannot subsist together." There is no such art, and there never has been. The substitution of subordination and value-judgement for coordination and description, the substitution of "all poets should" for "some poets do," is only a sign that all the relevant facts have not yet been considered. Critical statements with "must" or "should" in their predicates are either pedantries or tautologies, depending on whether they are taken seriously or not. Thus a dramatic critic may wish to say "all plays must have unity of action." If he is a pedant, he will then try to define unity of action in specific terms. But creative power is versatile, and he is sure to find himself sooner or later asserting that some perfectly reputable dramatist, whose effectiveness on the stage has been proved over and over again, does not exhibit the unity of action he has defined, and is consequently not writing what he regards as plays at all. The critic who attempts to apply such principles in a more liberal or more cautious spirit will soon have to broaden his conceptions to the point, not of course of saying, but of trying to conceal the fact that he is saying, "all plays that have unity of action must have unity of action," or, more simply and more commonly, "all good plays must be good plays."

Criticism, in short, and aesthetics generally, must learn to do what ethics has already done. There was a time when ethics could take the simple form of comparing what man does with what he ought to do, known as the good. The "good" invariably turned out to be whatever the author of the book was accustomed to and found sanctioned by his community. Ethical writers now, though they still have values, tend to look at their problems rather differently. But a procedure which is hopelessly outmoded in ethics is still in vogue among writers on aesthetic problems. It is still possible for a critic to define as authentic art whatever he happens to like, and to go on to assert that what he happens not to like is, in terms of that definition, not authentic art. The argument has the great advantage of being irrefutable, as all circular arguments are, but it is shadow and not substance.

The odious comparisons of greatness, then, may be left to take care of themselves, for even when we feel obliged to assent to them they are still only unproductive platitudes. The real concern of the evaluating critic is with positive value, with the goodness, or perhaps the genuineness, of the poem rather than with the greatness of its author. Such criticism produces the direct value-judgement of informed good taste, the proving of art on the pulses, the disciplined response of a highly organized nervous system to the impact of poetry. No critic in his senses would try to belittle the importance of this; nevertheless there are some caveats even here. In the first place, it is superstition to believe that the swift intuitive certainty of good taste is infallible. Good taste follows and is developed by the study of literature; its precision results from knowledge, but does not produce knowledge. Hence the accuracy of any critic's good taste is no guarantee that its inductive basis in literary experience is adequate. This may still be true even after the critic has learned to base his judgements on his experience of literature and not on his social, moral, religious, or personal anxieties. Honest critics are continually finding blind spots in their taste: they discover the possibility of recognizing a valid form of poetic experience without being able to realize it for themselves.

In the second place, the positive value-judgement is founded on a direct experience which is central to criticism yet forever excluded from it. Criticism can account for it only in critical terminology, and that terminology can never recapture or include the original experience. The original experience is like the direct vision of color, or the direct sensation of heat or cold, that physics "explains" in what, from the point of view of the experience itself, is a quite irrelevant way. However disciplined by taste and skill, the experience of literature is, like literature itself, unable to speak. "If I feel physically as if the top of my head were taken off," said Emily Dickinson, "I know this is poetry." This remark is perfectly sound, but it relates only to criticism as experience. The reading of literature should, like prayer in the Gospels, step out of the talking world of criticism into the private and secret presence of literature. Otherwise the reading will not be a genuine literary experience, but a mere reflection of critical conventions, memories, and prejudices. The presence of incommunicable experience in the center of criticism will always keep criticism an art, as long as the critic recognizes that criticism comes out of it but cannot be built on it.

Thus, though the normal development of a critic's taste is toward greater tolerance and catholicity, still criticism as knowledge is one thing, and value-judgements informed by taste are another. The attempt to bring the direct experience of literature into the structure of criticism produces the aberrations of the history of taste already dealt with. The attempt to reverse the procedure and bring criticism into direct experience will destroy the integrity of both. Direct experience, even if it is concerned with something already read hundreds of times, still tries to be a new and fresh experience each time, which is clearly impossible if the poem itself has been replaced by a critical view of the poem. To bring my own view that criticism as knowledge should constantly progress and reject nothing into direct experience would mean that the latter should progress toward a general stupor of satisfaction with everything written, which is not quite what I have in mind.

Finally, the skill developed from constant practice in the direct experience of literature is a special skill, like playing the piano, not the expression of a general attitude to life, like singing in the shower. The critic has a subjective background of experience formed by his temperament and by every contact with words he has made, including newspapers, advertisements, conversations, movies, and whatever he read at the age of nine. He has a specific skill in responding to literature which is no more like this subjective background, with all its private memories, associations, and arbitrary prejudices, than reading a thermometer is like shivering. Again, there is no one of critical ability who has not experienced intense and profound pleasure from something simultaneously with a low critical valuation of what produced it. There must be several dozen critical and aesthetic theories based on the assumption that subjective pleasure and the specific response to art are, or develop from, or ultimately become, the same thing. Yet every cultivated person who is not suffering from advanced paranoia knows that they are constantly distinct. Or, again, the ideal value may be quite different from the actual one. A critic may spend a thesis, a book, or even a life work on something that he candidly admits to be third-rate, simply because it is connected with something else that he thinks sufficiently important for his pains. No critical theory known to me takes any real account of the different systems of valuation implied by one of the most common practices of criticism.

Now that we have swept out our interpreter's parlor in the spirit of the law, and raised the dust, we shall try it again with whatever unguents of revelation we may possess. It should hardly be necessary to point out that my polemic has been written in the first person plural, and is quite as much a confession as a polemic. It is clear, too, that a book of this kind can only be offered to a reader who has enough sympathy with its aims to overlook, in the sense not of ignoring but of seeing past, whatever strikes him as inadequate or simply wrong. I am convinced that if we wait for a fully qualified critic to tackle the subjects of these essays, we shall wait a long time. In order to keep the book within the bounds that would make it possible to write and publish it, I have proceeded deductively, and been rigorously selective in examples and illustrations. The deductiveness does not extend further than tactical method, and so far as I know there is no principle in the book which is claimed as a perfect major premise, without exceptions or negative instances. Such expressions as "normally," "usually," "regularly," or "as a rule" are thickly strewn throughout. An objection of the "what about so-and-so?" type may always be made by the reader without necessarily destroying statements based on collective observations, and there are many questions of the "where would you put so-and-so?" type that cannot be answered by the present writer.

Still, the schematic nature of this book is deliberate, and is a feature of it that I am unable, after long reflection, to apologize for. There is a place for classification in criticism, as in any other discipline which is more important than an elegant accomplishment of some mandarin caste. The strong emotional repugnance felt by many critics toward any form of schematization in poetics is again the result of a failure to distinguish criticism as a body of knowledge from the direct experience of literature, where every act is unique, and classification has no place. Whenever schematization appears in the following pages, no importance is attached to the schematic form itself, which may be only the result of my own lack of ingenuity. Much of it, I expect, and in fact hope, may be mere scaffolding, to be knocked away when the building is in better shape. The rest of it belongs to the systematic study of the formal causes of art.

FIRST ESSAY

Historical Criticism: Theory of Modes

First Essay

HISTORICAL CRITICISM: THEORY OF MODES

FICTIONAL MODES: INTRODUCTION

In the second paragraph of the *Poetics* Aristotle speaks of the differences in works of fiction which are caused by the different elevations of the characters in them. In some fictions, he says, the characters are better than we are, in others worse, in still others on the same level. This passage has not received much attention from modern critics, as the importance Aristotle assigns to goodness and badness seems to indicate a somewhat narrowly moralistic view of literature. Aristotle's words for good and bad, however, are *spoudaios* and *phaulos*, which have a figurative sense of weighty and light. In literary fictions the plot consists of somebody doing something. The somebody, if an individual, is the hero, and the something he does or fails to do is what he can do, or could have done, on the level of the postulates made about him by the author and the consequent expectations of the audience. Fictions, therefore, may be classified, not morally, but by the hero's power of action, which may be greater than ours, less, or roughly the same. Thus:

1. If superior in *kind* both to other men and to the environment of other men, the hero is a divine being, and the story about him will be a *myth* in the common sense of a story about a god. Such stories have an important place in literature, but are as a rule found outside the normal literary categories.

2. If superior in *degree* to other men and to his environment, the hero is the typical hero of *romance*, whose actions are marvellous but who is himself identified as a human being. The hero of romance moves in a world in which the ordinary laws of nature are slightly suspended: prodigies of courage and endurance, unnatural to us, are natural to him, and enchanted weapons, talking animals, terrifying ogres and witches, and talismans of miraculous power violate no rule of probability once the postulates of romance have been established. Here we have moved from myth, properly so called, into legend, folk tale, *märchen*, and their literary affiliates and derivatives.

3. If superior in degree to other men but not to his natural en-

vironment, the hero is a leader. He has authority, passions, and powers of expression far greater than ours, but what he does is subject both to social criticism and to the order of nature. This is the hero of the *high mimetic* mode, of most epic and tragedy, and is primarily the kind of hero that Aristotle had in mind.

4. If superior neither to other men nor to his environment, the hero is one of us: we respond to a sense of his common humanity, and demand from the poet the same canons of probability that we find in our own experience. This gives us the hero of the *low mimetic* mode, of most comedy and of realistic fiction. "High" and "low" have no connotations of comparative value, but are purely diagrammatic, as they are when they refer to Biblical critics or Anglicans. On this level the difficulty in retaining the word "hero," which has a more limited meaning among the preceding modes, occasionally strikes an author. Thackeray thus feels obliged to call *Vanity Fair* a novel without a hero.

5. If inferior in power or intelligence to ourselves, so that we have the sense of looking down on a scene of bondage, frustration, or absurdity, the hero belongs to the *ironic* mode. This is still true when the reader feels that he is or might be in the same situation, as the situation is being judged by the norms of a greater freedom.

Looking over this table, we can see that European fiction, during the last fifteen centuries, has steadily moved its center of gravity down the list. In the pre-medieval period literature is closely attached to Christian, late Classical, Celtic, or Teutonic myths. If Christianity had not been both an imported myth and a devourer of rival ones, this phase of Western literature would be easier to isolate. In the form in which we possess it, most of it has already moved into the category of romance. Romance divides into two main forms: a secular form dealing with chivalry and knight-errantry, and a religious form devoted to legends of saints. Both lean heavily on miraculous violations of natural law for their interest as stories. Fictions of romance dominate literature until the cult of the prince and the courtier in the Renaissance brings the high mimetic mode into the foreground. The characteristics of this mode are most clearly seen in the genres of drama, particularly tragedy, and national epic. Then a new kind of middle-class culture introduces the low mimetic, which predominates in English literature from Defoe's time to the end of the nineteenth century. In French literature it begins and ends about fifty years earlier. During the last hundred years, most serious fiction has tended increasingly to be ironic in mode.

Something of the same progression may be traced in Classical literature too, in a greatly foreshortened form. Where a religion is mythological and polytheistic, where there are promiscuous incarnations, deified heroes and kings of divine descent, where the same adjective "godlike" can be applied either to Zeus or to Achilles, it is hardly possible to separate the mythical, romantic, and high mimetic strands completely. Where the religion is theological, and insists on a sharp division between divine and human natures, romance becomes more clearly isolated, as it does in the legends of Christian chivalry and sanctity, in the Arabian Nights of Mohammedanism, in the stories of the judges and thaumaturgic prophets of Israel. Similarly, the inability of the Classical world to shake off the divine leader in its later period has much to do with the abortive development of low mimetic and ironic modes that got barely started with Roman satire. At the same time the establishing of the high mimetic mode, the developing of a literary tradition with a consistent sense of an order of nature in it, is one of the great feats of Greek civilization. Oriental fiction does not, so far as I know, get very far away from mythical and romantic formulas.

We shall here deal chiefly with the five epochs of Western literature, as given above, using Classical parallels only incidentally. In each mode a distinction will be useful between naive and sophisticated literature. The word naive I take from Schiller's essay on naive and sentimental poetry: I mean by it, however, primitive or popular, whereas in Schiller it means something more like Classical. The word sentimental also means something else in English, but we do not have enough genuine critical terms to dispense with it. In quotation marks, therefore, "sentimental" refers to a later re-creation of an earlier mode. Thus Romanticism is a "sentimental" form of romance, and the fairy tale, for the most part, a "sentimental" form of folk tale. Also there is a general distinction between fictions in which the hero becomes isolated from his society, and fictions in which he is incorporated into it. This distinction is expressed by the words "tragic" and "comic" when they refer to aspects of plot in general and not simply to forms of drama.

TRAGIC FICTIONAL MODES

Tragic stories, when they apply to divine beings, may be called

35

Dionysiac. These are stories of dying gods, like Hercules with his poisoned shirt and his pyre, Orpheus torn to pieces by the Bacchantes, Balder murdered by the treachery of Loki, Christ dying on the cross and marking with the words "Why hast thou forsaken me?" a sense of his exclusion, as a divine being, from the society of the Trinity.

The association of a god's death with autumn or sunset does not, in literature, necessarily mean that he is a god "of" vegetation or the sun, but only that he is a god capable of dying, whatever his department. But as a god is superior to nature as well as to other men, the death of a god appropriately involves what Shakespeare, in *Venus and Adonis*, calls the "solemn sympathy" of nature, the word solemn having here some of its etymological connections with ritual. Ruskin's pathetic fallacy can hardly be a fallacy when a god is the hero of the action, as when the poet of *The Dream of the Rood* tells us that all creation wept at the death of Christ. Of course there is never any real fallacy in making a purely imaginative alignment between man and nature, but the use of "solemn sympathy" in a piece of more realistic fiction indicates that the author is trying to give his hero some of the overtones of the mythical mode. Ruskin's example of a pathetic fallacy is "the cruel, crawling foam" from Kingsley's ballad about a girl drowned in the tide. But the fact that the foam is so described gives to Kingsley's Mary a faint coloring of the myth of Andromeda.

The same associations with sunset and the fall of the leaf linger in romance, where the hero is still half a god. In romance the suspension of natural law and the individualizing of the hero's exploits reduce nature largely to the animal and vegetable world. Much of the hero's life is spent with animals, or at any rate the animals that are incurable romantics, such as horses, dogs, and falcons, and the typical setting of romance is the forest. The hero's death or isolation thus has the effect of a spirit passing out of nature, and evokes a mood best described as elegiac. The elegiac presents a heroism unspoiled by irony. The inevitability in the death of Beowulf, the treachery in the death of Roland, the malignancy that compasses the death of the martyred saint, are of much greater emotional importance than any ironic complications of hybris and hamartia that may be involved. Hence the elegiac is often accompanied by a diffused, resigned, melancholy sense of the passing of time, of the old order changing and yielding to a new one: one thinks of Beowulf looking, while he is dying, at the great stone monuments of the eras of history that vanished before him. In a very late "sentimental" form the same mood is well caught in Tennyson's *Passing of Arthur*.

Tragedy in the central or high mimetic sense, the fiction of the fall of a leader (he has to fall because that is the only way in which a leader can be isolated from his society), mingles the heroic with the ironic. In elegiac romance the hero's mortality is primarily a natural fact, the sign of his humanity; in high mimetic tragedy it is also a social and moral fact. The tragic hero has to be of a properly heroic size, but his fall is involved both with a sense of his relation to society and with a sense of the supremacy of natural law, both of which are ironic in reference. Tragedy belongs chiefly to the two indigenous developments of tragic drama in fifth-century Athens and seventeenth-century Europe from Shakespeare to Racine. Both belong to a period of social history in which an aristocracy is fast losing its effective power but still retains a good deal of ideological prestige.

The central position of high mimetic tragedy in the five tragic modes, balanced midway between godlike heroism and all-too-human irony, is expressed in the traditional conception of catharsis. The words pity and fear may be taken as referring to the two general directions in which emotion moves, whether towards an object or away from it. Naive romance, being closer to the wish-fulfilment dream, tends to absorb emotion and communicate it internally to the reader. Romance, therefore, is characterized by the acceptance of pity and fear, which in ordinary life relate to pain, as forms of pleasure. It turns fear at a distance, or terror, into the adventurous; fear at contact, or horror, into the marvellous, and fear without an object, or dread (*Angst*) into a pensive melancholy. It turns pity at a distance, or concern, into the theme of chivalrous rescue; pity at contact, or tenderness, into a languid and relaxed charm, and pity without an object (which has no name but is a kind of animism, or treating everything in nature as though it had human feelings) into creative fantasy. In sophisticated romance the characteristics peculiar to the form are less obvious, especially in tragic romance, where the theme of inevitable death works against the marvellous, and often forces it into the background. In *Romeo and Juliet,* for instance, the marvellous survives only in Mercutio's speech on Queen Mab. But this play is marked as closer to romance than

37

the later tragedies by the softening influences that work in the opposite direction from catharsis, draining off the irony, so to speak, from the main characters.

In high mimetic tragedy pity and fear become, respectively, favorable and adverse moral judgement, which are relevant to tragedy but not central to it. We pity Desdemona and fear Iago, but the central tragic figure is Othello, and our feelings about him are mixed. The particular thing called tragedy that happens to the tragic hero does not depend on his moral status. If it is causally related to something he has done, as it generally is, the tragedy is in the inevitability of the consequences of the act, not in its moral significance as an act. Hence the paradox that in tragedy pity and fear are raised and cast out. Aristotle's hamartia or "flaw," therefore, is not necessarily wrongdoing, much less moral weakness: it may be simply a matter of being a strong character in an exposed position, like Cordelia. The exposed position is usually the place of leadership, in which a character is exceptional and isolated at the same time, giving us that curious blend of the inevitable and the incongruous which is peculiar to tragedy. The principle of the hamartia of leadership can be more clearly seen in naive high mimetic tragedy, as we get it in *The Mirror for Magistrates* and similar collections of tales based on the theme of the wheel of fortune.

In low mimetic tragedy, pity and fear are neither purged nor absorbed into pleasures, but are communicated externally, as sensations. In fact the word "sensational" could have a more useful meaning in criticism if it were not merely an adverse value-judgement. The best word for low mimetic or domestic tragedy is, perhaps, pathos, and pathos has a close relation to the sensational reflex of tears. Pathos presents its hero as isolated by a weakness which appeals to our sympathy because it is on our own level of experience. I speak of a hero, but the central figure of pathos is often a woman or a child (or both, as in the death-scenes of Little Eva and Little Nell), and we have a whole procession of pathetic female sacrifices in English low mimetic fiction from Clarissa Harlowe to Hardy's Tess and James's Daisy Miller. We notice that while tragedy may massacre a whole cast, pathos is usually concentrated on a single character, partly because low mimetic society is more strongly individualized.

Again, in contrast to high mimetic tragedy, pathos is increased by the inarticulateness of the victim. The death of an animal is usually pathetic, and so is the catastrophe of defective intelligence that is frequent in modern American literature. Wordsworth, who as a low mimetic artist was one of our great masters of pathos, makes his sailor's mother speak in a flat, dumpy, absurdly inadequate style about her efforts to salvage her son's clothes and "other property"— or did before bad criticism made him spoil his poem. Pathos is a queer ghoulish emotion, and some failure of expression, real or simulated, seems to be peculiar to it. It will always leave a fluently plangent funeral elegy to go and batten on something like Swift's memoir of Stella. Highly articulate pathos is apt to become a factitious appeal to self-pity, or tear-jerking. The exploiting of fear in the low mimetic is also sensational, and is a kind of pathos in reverse. The terrible figure in this tradition, exemplified by Heathcliff, Simon Legree, and the villains of Dickens, is normally a ruthless figure strongly contrasted with some kind of delicate virtue, generally a helpless victim in his power.

The root idea of pathos is the exclusion of an individual on our own level from a social group to which he is trying to belong. Hence the central tradition of sophisticated pathos is the study of the isolated mind, the story of how someone recognizably like ourselves is broken by a conflict between the inner and outer world, between imaginative reality and the sort of reality which is established by a social consensus. Such tragedy may be concerned, as it often is in Balzac, with a mania or obsession about rising in the world, this being the central low mimetic counterpart of the fiction of the fall of the leader. Or it may deal with the conflict of inner and outer life, as in *Madame Bovary* and *Lord Jim,* or with the impact of inflexible morality on experience, as in Melville's *Pierre* and Ibsen's *Brand.* The type of character involved here we may call by the Greek word *alazon,* which means impostor, someone who pretends or tries to be something more than he is. The most popular types of *alazon* are the *miles gloriosus* and the learned crank or obsessed philosopher.

We are most familiar with such characters in comedy, where they are looked at from the outside, so that we see only the social mask. But the *alazon* may be one aspect of the tragic hero as well: the touch of *miles gloriosus* in Tamburlaine, even in Othello, is unmistakable, as is the touch of the obsessed philosopher in Faustus and Hamlet. It is very difficult to study a case of obsession, or even hypocrisy, from the inside, in a dramatic medium: even Tartuffe, as far as his dramatic function is concerned, is a study of parasitism rather than hypocrisy. The analysis of obsession belongs more naturally to prose fiction or to a semi-dramatic medium like the Browning monologue. For all the differences in technique and attitude, Conrad's Lord Jim is a lineal descendant of the *miles gloriosus*, of the same family as Shaw's Sergius or Synge's playboy, who are parallel types in a dramatic and comic setting. It is, of course, quite possible to take the *alazon* at his own valuation: this is done for instance by the creators of the inscrutable gloomy heroes in Gothic thrillers, with their wild or piercing eyes and their dark hints of interesting sins. The result as a rule is not tragedy so much as the kind of melodrama which may be defined as comedy without humor. When it rises out of this, we have a study of obsession presented in terms of fear instead of pity: that is, the obsession takes the form of an unconditioned will that drives its victim beyond the normal limits of humanity. One of the clearest examples is Heathcliff, who plunges through death itself into vampirism; but there are many others, ranging from Conrad's Kurtz to the mad scientists of popular fiction.

The conception of irony meets us in Aristotle's *Ethics*, where the *eiron* is the man who deprecates himself, as opposed to the *alazon*. Such a man makes himself invulnerable, and, though Aristotle disapproves of him, there is no question that he is a predestined artist, just as the *alazon* is one of his predestined victims. The term irony, then, indicates a technique of appearing to be less than one is, which in literature becomes most commonly a technique of saying as little and meaning as much as possible, or, in a more general way, a pattern of words that turns away from direct statement or its own obvious meaning. (I am not using the word ironic itself in any unfamiliar sense, though I am exploring some of its implications.)

The ironic fiction-writer, then, deprecates himself and, like Socrates, pretends to know nothing, even that he is ironic. Complete objectivity and suppression of all explicit moral judgements are essential to his method. Thus pity and fear are not raised in ironic art: they are reflected to the reader from the art. When we try to isolate the ironic as such, we find that it seems to be simply the attitude of the poet as such, a dispassionate construction of a literary form, with all assertive elements, implied or expressed, eliminated. Irony, as a mode, is born from the low mimetic; it takes life exactly as it finds it. But the ironist fables without moralizing, and has no object but his subject. Irony is naturally a sophisticated mode, and the chief difference between sophisticated and naive irony is that the naive ironist calls attention to the fact that he is being ironic, whereas sophisticated irony merely states, and lets the reader add the ironic tone himself. Coleridge, noting an ironic comment in Defoe, points out how Defoe's subtlety could be made crude and obvious simply by over-punctuating the same words with italics, dashes, exclamation points, and other signs of being oneself aware of irony.

Tragic irony, then, becomes simply the study of tragic isolation as such, and it thereby drops out the element of the special case, which in some degree is in all the other modes. Its hero does not necessarily have any tragic hamartia or pathetic obsession: he is only somebody who gets isolated from his society. Thus the central principle of tragic irony is that whatever exceptional happens to the hero should be causally out of line with his character. Tragedy is intelligible, not in the sense of having any pat moral to go with it, but in the sense that Aristotle had in mind when he spoke of discovery or recognition as essential to the tragic plot. Tragedy is intelligible because its catastrophe is plausibly related to its situation. Irony isolates from the tragic situation the sense of arbitrariness, of the victim's having been unlucky, selected at random or by lot, and no more deserving of what happens to him than anyone else would be. If there is a reason for choosing him for catastrophe, it is an inadequate reason, and raises more objections than it answers.

Thus the figure of a typical or random victim begins to crystallize in domestic tragedy as it deepens in ironic tone. We may call this typical victim the *pharmakos* or scapegoat. We meet a *pharmakos* figure in Hawthorne's Hester Prynne, in Melville's Billy Budd, in Hardy's Tess, in the Septimus of *Mrs. Dalloway*, in stories of persecuted Jews and Negroes, in stories of artists whose genius makes them Ishmaels of a bourgeois society. The *pharmakos* is neither innocent nor guilty. He is innocent in the sense that what happens to him is far greater than anything he has done provokes, like the mountaineer whose shout brings down an avalanche. He is guilty in the sense that he is a member of a guilty society, or living in a world where such injustices are an inescapable part of existence.

The two facts do not come together; they remain ironically apart. The *pharmakos*, in short, is in the situation of Job. Job can defend himself against the charge of having done something that makes his catastrophe morally intelligible; but the success of his defense makes it morally unintelligible.

Thus the incongruous and the inevitable, which are combined in tragedy, separate into opposite poles of irony. At one pole is the inevitable irony of human life. What happens to, say, the hero of Kafka's *Trial* is not the result of what he has done, but the end of what he is, which is an "all too human" being. The archetype of the inevitably ironic is Adam, human nature under sentence of death. At the other pole is the incongruous irony of human life, in which all attempts to transfer guilt to a victim give that victim something of the dignity of innocence. The archetype of the incongruously ironic is Christ, the perfectly innocent victim excluded from human society. Halfway between is the central figure of tragedy, who is human and yet of a heroic size which often has in it the suggestion of divinity. His archetype is Prometheus, the immortal titan rejected by the gods for befriending men. The Book of Job is not a tragedy of the Promethean type, but a tragic irony in which the dialectic of the divine and the human nature works itself out. By justifying himself as a victim of God, Job tries to make himself into a tragic Promethean figure, but he does not succeed.

These references may help to explain something that might otherwise be a puzzling fact about modern literature. Irony descends from the low mimetic: it begins in realism and dispassionate observation. But as it does so, it moves steadily towards myth, and dim outlines of sacrificial rituals and dying gods begin to reappear in it. Our five modes evidently go around in a circle. This reappearance of myth in the ironic is particularly clear in Kafka and in Joyce. In Kafka, whose work, from one point of view, may be said to form a series of commentaries on the Book of Job, the common contemporary types of tragic irony, the Jew, the artist, Everyman, and a kind of sombre Chaplin clown, are all found, and most of these elements are combined, in a comic form, in Joyce's Shem. However, ironic myth is frequent enough elsewhere, and many features of ironic literature are unintelligible without it. Henry James learned his trade mainly from the realists and naturalists of the nineteenth century, but if we were to judge, for example, the story called *The Altar of the Dead* purely by low mimetic standards, we should have to call it a tissue of improbable coincidence, in-adequate motivation, and inconclusive resolution. When we look at it as ironic myth, a story of how the god of one person is the *pharmakos* of another, its structure becomes simple and logical.

COMIC FICTIONAL MODES

The theme of the comic is the integration of society, which usually takes the form of incorporating a central character into it. The mythical comedy corresponding to the death of the Dionysiac god is Apollonian, the story of how a hero is accepted by a society of gods. In Classical literature the theme of acceptance forms part of the stories of Hercules, Mercury, and other deities who had a probation to go through, and in Christian literature it is the theme of salvation, or, in a more concentrated form, of assumption: the comedy that stands just at the end of Dante's *Commedia*. The mode of romantic comedy corresponding to the elegiac is best de-scribed as idyllic, and its chief vehicle is the pastoral. Because of the social interest of comedy, the idyllic cannot equal the intro-version of the elegiac, but it preserves the theme of escape from society to the extent of idealizing a simplified life in the country or on the frontier (the pastoral of popular modern literature is the Western story). The close association with animal and vegetable nature that we noted in the elegiac recurs in the sheep and pleasant pastures (or the cattle and ranches) of the idyllic, and the same easy connection with myth recurs in the fact that such imagery is often used, as it is in the Bible, for the theme of salvation.

The clearest example of high mimetic comedy is the Old Comedy of Aristophanes. The New Comedy of Menander is closer to the low mimetic, and through Plautus and Terence its formulas were handed down to the Renaissance, so that there has always been a strongly low mimetic bias to social comedy. In Aristophanes there is usually a central figure who constructs his (or her) own society in the teeth of strong opposition, driving off one after another all the people who come to prevent or exploit him, and eventually achieving a heroic triumph, complete with mistresses, in which he is sometimes assigned the honors of a reborn god. We notice that just as there is a catharsis of pity and fear in tragedy, so there is a catharsis of the corresponding comic emotions, which are sympathy and ridicule, in Old Comedy. The comic hero will get his triumph whether what he has done is sensible or silly, honest or rascally.

Thus Old Comedy, like the tragedy contemporary with it, is a blend of the heroic and the ironic. In some plays this fact is partly concealed by Aristophanes' strong desire to get his own opinion of what the hero is doing into the record, but his greatest comedy, *The Birds*, preserves an exquisite balance between comic heroism and comic irony.

New Comedy normally presents an erotic intrigue between a young man and a young woman which is blocked by some kind of opposition, usually paternal, and resolved by a twist in the plot which is the comic form of Aristotle's "discovery," and is more manipulated than its tragic counterpart. At the beginning of the play the forces thwarting the hero are in control of the play's society, but after a discovery in which the hero becomes wealthy or the heroine respectable, a new society crystallizes on the stage around the hero and his bride. The action of the comedy thus moves towards the incorporation of the hero into the society that he naturally fits. The hero himself is seldom a very interesting person: in conformity with low mimetic decorum, he is ordinary in his virtues, but socially attractive. In Shakespeare and in the kind of romantic comedy that most closely resembles his there is a development of these formulas in a more distinctively high mimetic direction. In the figure of Prospero we have one of the few approaches to the Aristophanic technique of having the whole comic action projected by a central character. Usually Shakespeare achieves his high mimetic pattern by making the struggle of the repressive and the desirable societies a struggle between two levels of existence, the former like our own world or worse, the latter enchanted and idyllic. This point will be dealt with more fully later.

For the reasons given above the domestic comedy of later fiction carries on with much the same conventions as were used in the Renaissance. Domestic comedy is usually based on the Cinderella archetype, the kind of thing that happens when Pamela's virtue is rewarded, the incorporation of an individual very like the reader into the society aspired to by both, a society ushered in with a happy rustle of bridal gowns and banknotes. Here again, Shakespearean comedy may marry off eight or ten people of approximately equal dramatic interest, just as a high mimetic tragedy may kill the same number, but in domestic comedy such diffusion of sexual energy is more rare. The chief difference between high and low mimetic comedy, however, is that the resolution of the latter more frequently involves a social promotion. More sophisticated writers of low mimetic comedy often present the same success-story formula with the moral ambiguities that we have found in Aristophanes. In Balzac or Stendhal a clever and ruthless scoundrel may achieve the same kind of success as the virtuous heroes of Samuel Smiles and Horatio Alger. Thus the comic counterpart of the *alazon* seems to be the clever, likeable, unprincipled *picaro* of the picaresque novel.

In studying ironic comedy we must start with the theme of driving out the *pharmakos* from the point of view of society. This appeals to the kind of relief we are expected to feel when we see Jonson's Volpone condemned to the galleys, Shylock stripped of his wealth, or Tartuffe taken off to prison. Such a theme, unless touched very lightly, is difficult to make convincing, for the reasons suggested in connection with ironic tragedy. Insisting on the theme of social revenge on an individual, however great a rascal he may be, tends to make him look less involved in guilt and the society more so. This is particularly true of characters who have been trying to amuse either the actual or the internal audience, and who are the comic counterparts of the tragic hero as artist. The rejection of the entertainer, whether fool, clown, buffoon, or simpleton, can be one of the most terrible ironies known to art, as the rejection of Falstaff shows, and certain scenes in Chaplin.

In some religious poetry, for example at the end of the *Paradiso*, we can see that literature has an upper limit, a point at which an imaginative vision of an eternal world becomes an experience of it. In ironic comedy we begin to see that art has also a lower limit in actual life. This is the condition of savagery, the world in which comedy consists of inflicting pain on a helpless victim, and tragedy in enduring it. Ironic comedy brings us to the figure of the scape-goat ritual and the nightmare dream, the human symbol that concentrates our fears and hates. We pass the boundary of art when this symbol becomes existential, as it does in the black man of a lynching, the Jew of a pogrom, the old woman of a witch hunt, or anyone picked up at random by a mob, like Cinna the poet in *Julius Caesar*. In Aristophanes the irony sometimes edges very close to mob violence because the attacks are personal: one thinks of all the easy laughs he gets, in play after play, at the pederasty of Cleisthenes or the cowardice of Cleonymus. In Aristophanes the word *pharmakos* means simply scoundrel, with no nonsense about

45

it. At the conclusion of *The Clouds*, where the poet seems almost to be summoning a lynching party to go and burn down Socrates' house, we reach the comic counterpart of one of the greatest masterpieces of tragic irony in literature, Plato's *Apology*.

But the element of *play* is the barrier that separates art from savagery, and playing at human sacrifice seems to be an important theme of ironic comedy. Even in laughter itself some kind of deliverance from the unpleasant, even the horrible, seems to be very important. We notice this particularly in all forms of art in which a large number of auditors are simultaneously present, as in drama, and, still more obviously, in games. We notice too that playing at sacrifice has nothing to do with any historical descent from sacrificial ritual, such as has been suggested for Old Comedy. All the features of such ritual, the king's son, the mimic death, the executioner, the substituted victim, are far more explicit in Gilbert and Sullivan's *Mikado* than they are in Aristophanes. There is certainly no evidence that baseball has descended from a ritual of human sacrifice, but the umpire is quite as much of a *pharmakos* as if it had: he is an abandoned scoundrel, a greater robber than Barabbas; he has the evil eye; the supporters of the losing team scream for his death. At play, mob emotions are boiled in an open pot, so to speak; in the lynching mob they are in a sealed furnace of what Blake would call moral virtue. The gladiatorial combat, in which the audience has the actual power of life and death over the people who are entertaining them, is perhaps the most concentrated of all the savage or demonic parodies of drama.

The fact that we are now in an ironic phase of literature largely accounts for the popularity of the detective story, the formula of how a man-hunter locates a *pharmakos* and gets rid of him. The detective story begins in the Sherlock Holmes period as an intensification of low mimetic, in the sharpening of attention to details that makes the dullest and most neglected trivia of daily living leap into mysterious and fateful significance. But as we move further away from this we move toward a ritual drama around a corpse in which a wavering finger of social condemnation passes over a group of "suspects" and finally settles on one. The sense of a victim chosen by lot is very strong, for the case against him is only plausibly manipulated. If it were really inevitable, we should have tragic irony, as in *Crime and Punishment*, where Raskolnikoff's crime is so interwoven with his character that there can be no question of any "whodunit" mystery. In the growing brutality of the crime story (a brutality protected by the convention of the form, as it is conventionally impossible that the man-hunter can be mistaken in believing that one of his suspects is a murderer), detection begins to merge with the thriller as one of the forms of melodrama. In melodrama two themes are important: the triumph of moral virtue over villainy, and the consequent idealizing of the moral views assumed to be held by the audience. In the melodrama of the brutal thriller we come as close as it is normally possible for art to come to the pure self-righteousness of the lynching mob.

We should have to say, then, that all forms of melodrama, the detective story in particular, were advance propaganda for the police state, in so far as that represents the regularizing of mob violence, if it were possible to take them seriously. But it seems not to be possible. The protecting wall of play is still there. Serious melodrama soon gets entangled with its own pity and fear: the more serious it is, the more likely it is to be looked at ironically by the reader, its pity and fear seen as sentimental drivel and owlish solemnity, respectively. One pole of ironic comedy is the recognition of the absurdity of naive melodrama, or, at least, of the absurdity of its attempt to define the enemy of society as a person outside that society. From there it develops toward the opposite pole, which is true comic irony or satire, and which defines the enemy of society as a spirit within that society. Let us arrange the forms of ironic comedy from this point of view.

Cultivated people go to a melodrama to hiss the villain with an air of condescension: they are making a point of the fact that they cannot take his villainy seriously. We have here a type of irony which exactly corresponds to that of two other major arts of the ironic age, advertising and propaganda. These arts pretend to address themselves seriously to a subliminal audience of cretins, an audience that may not even exist, but which is assumed to be simple-minded enough to accept at their face value the statements made about the purity of a soap or a government's motives. The rest of us, realizing that irony never says precisely what it means, take these arts ironically, or, at least, regard them as a kind of ironic game. Similarly, we read murder stories with a strong sense of the unreality of the villainy involved. Murder is doubtless a serious crime, but if private murder really were a major threat to

47

our civilization it would not be relaxing to read about it. We may compare the abuse showered on the pimp in Roman comedy, which was similarly based on the indisputable ground that brothels are immoral.

The next step is an ironic comedy addressed to the people who can realize that murderous violence is less an attack on a virtuous society by a malignant individual than a symptom of that society's own viciousness. Such a comedy would be the kind of intellectual-ized parody of melodramatic formulas represented by, for instance, the novels of Graham Greene. Next comes the ironic comedy directed at the melodramatic spirit itself, an astonishingly per-sistent tradition in all comedy in which there is a large ironic admixture. One notes a recurring tendency on the part of ironic comedy to ridicule and scold an audience assumed to be hankering after sentiment, solemnity, and the triumph of fidelity and ap-proved moral standards. The arrogance of Jonson and Congreve, the mocking of bourgeois sentiment in Goldsmith, the parody of melodramatic situations in Wilde and Shaw, belong to a consistent tradition. Molière had to please his king, but was not tempera-mentally an exception. To comic drama one may add the ridicule of melodramatic romance in the novelists, from Fielding to Joyce.

Finally comes the comedy of manners, the portrayal of a chat-tering-monkey society devoted to snobbery and slander. In this kind of irony the characters who are opposed to or excluded from the fictional society have the sympathy of the audience. Here we are close to a parody of tragic irony, as we can see in the appalling fate of the relatively harmless hero of Evelyn Waugh's *A Handful of Dust*. Or we may have a character who, with the sympathy of the author or audience, repudiates such a society to the point of deliberately walking out of it, becoming thereby a kind of *phar-makos* in reverse. This happens for instance at the conclusion of Aldous Huxley's *Those Barren Leaves*. It is more usual, however, for the artist to present an ironic deadlock in which the hero is regarded as a fool or worse by the fictional society, and yet impresses the real audience as having something more valuable than his society has. The obvious example, and certainly one of the greatest, is Dostoievsky's *The Idiot*, but there are many others. *The Good Soldier Schweik*, *Heaven's My Destination* and *The Horse's Mouth* are instances that will give some idea of the range of the theme.

What we have said about the return of irony to myth in tragic

modes thus holds equally well for comic ones. Even popular literature appears to be slowly shifting its center of gravity from murder
stories to science fiction—or at any rate a rapid growth of science
fiction is certainly a fact about contemporary popular literature.
Science fiction frequently tries to imagine what life would be like
on a plane as far above us as we are above savagery; its setting is
often of a kind that appears to us as technologically miraculous.
It is thus a mode of romance with a strong inherent tendency to
myth.

The conception of a sequence of fictional modes should do
something, let us hope, to give a more flexible meaning to some of
our literary terms. The words "romantic" and "realistic," for instance, as ordinarily used, are relative or comparative terms: they
illustrate tendencies in fiction, and cannot be used as simply descriptive adjectives with any sort of exactness. If we take the sequence De Raptu Proserpinae, The Man of Law's Tale, Much
Ado About Nothing, Pride and Prejudice, An American Tragedy,
it is clear that each work is "romantic" compared to its successors
and "realistic" compared to its predecessors. On the other hand,
the term "naturalism" shows up in its proper perspective as a
phase of fiction which, rather like the detective story, though in a
very different way, begins as an intensification of low mimetic, an
attempt to describe life exactly as it is, and ends, by the very logic
of that attempt, in pure irony. Thus Zola's obsession with ironic
formulas gave him a reputation as a detached recorder of the
human scene.

The difference between the ironic tone that we may find in low
mimetic or earlier modes and the ironic structure of the ironic
mode itself is not hard to sense in practice. When Dickens, for
instance, uses irony the reader is invited to share in the irony,
because certain standards of normality common to author and
reader are assumed. Such assumptions are a mark of a relatively
popular mode: as the example of Dickens indicates, the gap between serious and popular fiction is narrower in low mimetic than
in ironic writing. The literary acceptance of relatively stable social
norms is closely connected with the reticence of low mimetic as
compared to ironic fiction. In low mimetic modes characters are
usually presented as they appear to others, fully dressed and with
a large section of both their physical lives and their inner mono-

logue carefully excised. Such an approach is entirely consistent with the other conventions involved.

If we were to make this distinction the basis of a comparative value-judgement, which would, of course, be a moral value-judgement disguised as a critical one, we should be compelled either to attack low mimetic conventions for being prudish and hypocritical and leaving too much of life out, or to attack ironic conventions for not being wholesome, healthy, popular, reassuring, and sound, like the conventions of Dickens. As long as we are concerned simply to distinguish between the conventions, we need only remark that the low mimetic is one step more heroic than the ironic, and that low mimetic reticence has the effect of making its characters, on the average, more heroic, or at least more dignified, than the characters in ironic fiction.

We may also apply our scheme to the principles of selection on which a writer of fiction operates. Let us take, as a random example, the use of ghosts in fiction. In a true myth there can obviously be no consistent distinction between ghosts and living beings. In romance we have real human beings, and consequently ghosts are in a separate category, but in a romance a ghost as a rule is merely one more character: he causes little surprise because his appearance is no more marvellous than many other events. In high mimetic, where we are within the order of nature, a ghost is relatively easy to introduce because the plane of experience is above our own, but when he appears he is an awful and mysterious being from what is perceptibly another world. In low mimetic, ghosts have been, ever since Defoe, almost entirely confined to a separate category of "ghost stories." In ordinary low mimetic fiction they are inadmissible, "in complaisance to the scepticism of a reader," as Fielding puts it, a skepticism which extends only to low mimetic conventions. The few exceptions, such as *Wuthering Heights*, go a long way to prove the rule—that is, we recognize a strong influence of romance in *Wuthering Heights*. In some forms of ironic fiction, such as the later works of Henry James, the ghost begins to come back as a fragment of a disintegrating personality.

Once we have learned to distinguish the modes, however, we must then learn to recombine them. For while one mode constitutes the underlying tonality of a work of fiction, any or all of the other four may be simultaneously present. Much of our sense of the subtlety of great literature comes from this modal counterpoint. Chaucer is a medieval poet specializing mainly in romance, whether sacred or secular. Of his pilgrims, the knight and the parson clearly present the norms of the society in which he functions as a poet, and, as we have them, the *Canterbury Tales* are contained by these two figures, who open and close the series. But to overlook Chaucer's mastery of low mimetic and ironic techniques would be as wrong as to think of him as a modern novelist who got into the Middle Ages by mistake. The tonality of *Antony and Cleopatra* is high mimetic, the story of the fall of a great leader. But it is easy to look at Mark Antony ironically, as a man enslaved by passion; it is easy to recognize his common humanity with ourselves; it is easy to see in him a romantic adventurer of prodigious courage and endurance betrayed by a witch; there are even hints of a superhuman being whose legs bestrid the ocean and whose downfall is a conspiracy of fate, explicable only to a soothsayer. To leave out any of these would oversimplify and belittle the play. Through such an analysis we may come to realize that the two essential facts about a work of art, that it is contemporary with its own time and that it is contemporary with ours, are not opposed but complementary facts.

Our survey of fictional modes has also shown us that the mimetic tendency itself, the tendency to verisimilitude and accuracy of description, is one of two poles of literature. At the other pole is something that seems to be connected both with Aristotle's word *mythos* and with the usual meaning of myth. That is, it is a tendency to tell a story which is in origin a story about characters who can do anything, and only gradually becomes attracted toward a tendency to tell a plausible or credible story. Myths of gods merge into legends of heroes; legends of heroes merge into plots of tragedies and comedies; plots of tragedies and comedies merge into plots of more or less realistic fiction. But these are change of social context rather than of literary form, and the constructive principles of story-telling remain constant through them, though of course they adapt to them. Tom Jones and Oliver Twist are typical enough as low mimetic characters, but the birth-mystery plots in which they are involved are plausible adaptations of fictional formulas that go back to Menander, and from Menander to Euripides' *Ion*, and from Euripides to legends like those of Perseus and Moses. We note in passing that imitation of nature in fiction produces, not truth or reality, but plausibility, and plausibility varies in weight from a mere perfunctory concession in a myth or folk tale to a kind of censor principle in a naturalistic novel. Reading forward in history, therefore, we may think of our romantic, high mimetic and low mimetic modes as a series of *displaced* myths, *mythoi* or plot-formulas progressively moving over towards the opposite pole of verisimilitude, and then, with irony, beginning to move back.

THEMATIC MODES

Aristotle lists six aspects of poetry: three of them, melody, diction, and spectacle, form a group by themselves, and we shall consider them in due course. The other three are *mythos* or plot, *ethos*, which includes both characters and setting, and *dianoia* or "thought." The literary works we have so far been considering are works of fiction in which the plot is, as Aristotle called it, the "soul" or shaping principle, and the characters exist primarily as functions of the plot. But besides the internal fiction of the hero and his society, there is an external fiction which is a relation between the writer and the writer's society. Poetry may be as completely absorbed in its internal characters as it is in Shakespeare, or in Homer, where the poet himself simply points to his story and disappears, the second word of the *Odyssey*, *moi*, being all we get of him in that poem. But as soon as the poet's personality appears on the horizon, a relation with the reader is established which cuts across the story, and which may increase until there is no story at all apart from what the poet is conveying to his reader.

In such genres as novels and plays the internal fiction is usually of primary interest; in essays and in lyrics the primary interest is in *dianoia*, the idea or poetic thought (something quite different, of course, from other kinds of thought) that the reader gets from the writer. The best translation of *dianoia* is, perhaps, "theme," and literature with this ideal or conceptual interest may be called thematic. When a reader of a novel asks, "How is this story going to turn out?" he is asking a question about the plot, specifically about that crucial aspect of the plot which Aristotle calls discovery or *anagnorisis*. But he is equally likely to ask, "What's the *point* of this story?" This question relates to *dianoia*, and indicates that themes have their elements of discovery just as plots do.

It is easy to say that some literary works are fictional and others thematic in their main emphasis. But clearly there is no such thing as *a* fictional or *a* thematic work of literature, for all four ethical elements (ethical in the sense of relating to character), the hero, the hero's society, the poet and the poet's readers, are always at least potentially present. There can hardly be a work of literature without some kind of relation, implied or expressed, between its creator and its auditors. When the audience the poet had in mind is superseded by posterity, the relation changes, but it still holds. On the other hand, even in lyrics and essays the writer is to some extent a fictional hero with a fictional audience, for if the element of fictional projection disappeared completely, the writing would become direct address, or straight discursive writing, and cease to be literature. A poet sending a love poem to his lady complaining of her cruelty has stereoscoped his four ethical elements into two, but the four are still there.

Hence every work of literature has both a fictional and a thematic aspect, and the question of which is more important is often simply a matter of opinion or emphasis in interpretation. We have cited Homer as the very type of impersonal fiction writer, but the main emphasis of Homeric criticism, down to about 1750 at least, has been overwhelmingly thematic, concerned with the *dianoia* or ideal of leadership implicit in the two epics. *The History of Tom Jones, a Foundling*, is a novel named after its plot; *Sense and Sensibility* is named after its theme. But Fielding has as strong a thematic interest (revealed chiefly in the introductory chapters to the different books) as Jane Austen has in telling a good story. Both novels are strongly fictional in emphasis compared to *Uncle Tom's Cabin* or *The Grapes of Wrath*, where the plot exists primarily to illustrate the themes of slavery and migratory labor respectively. They in their turn are fictional in emphasis compared to *The Pilgrim's Progress*, and *The Pilgrim's Progress* is fictional in emphasis compared to an essay of Montaigne. We note that as we move from fictional to thematic emphasis, the element represented by the term *mythos* tends to mean increasingly "narrative" rather than "plot."

When a work of fiction is written or interpreted thematically, it becomes a parable or illustrative fable. All formal allegories have, *ipso facto*, a strong thematic interest, though it does not follow, as is often said, that any thematic criticism of a work of fiction will turn it into an allegory (though it may and does allegorize, as we shall see). Genuine allegory is a structural element in literature: it has to be there, and cannot be added by critical interpretation alone.

Again, nearly every civilization has, in its stock of traditional myths, a particular group which is thought of as more serious, more authoritative, more educational and closer to fact and truth than the rest. For most poets of the Christian era who have used both the Bible and Classical literature, the latter has not stood on the same plane of authority as the former, although they are equally mythological as far as literary criticism is concerned. This distinction of canonical and apocryphal myth, which can be found even in primitive societies, gives to the former group a particular thematic importance.

We have now to see how our sequence of modes works out in the thematic aspect of literature. We shall have to confine ourselves here more strictly to Western literature, as the foreshortening process that we noticed in Classical fiction is even more marked on the thematic side.

In fiction, we discovered two main tendencies, a "comic" tendency to integrate the hero with his society, and a "tragic" tendency to isolate him. In thematic literature the poet may write as an individual, emphasizing the separateness of his personality and the distinctness of his vision. This attitude produces most lyrics and essays, a good deal of satire, epigrams, and the writing of "eclogues" or occasional pieces generally. The frequency of the moods of protest, complaint, ridicule, and loneliness (whether bitter or serene) in such works may perhaps indicate a rough analogy to the tragic modes of fiction. Or the poet may devote himself to being a spokesman of his society, which means, as he is not addressing a second society, that a poetic knowledge and expressive power which is latent or needed in his society comes to articulation in him.

Such an attitude produces poetry which is educational in the broadest sense: epics of the more artificial or thematic kind, didactic poetry and prose, encyclopaedic compilations of myth, folklore, and legend like those of Ovid and Snorri, where, though the stories themselves are fictional, the arrangement of them and the motive for collecting them is thematic. In poetry which is educational in this sense, the social function of the poet figures prominently as a theme. If we call the poetry of the isolated individual a "lyric" and the poetry of the social spokesman an "epic" tendency (in

54

comparison to the more "dramatic" fictions of internal characters) we shall perhaps gain some preliminary conception of them. But it is obvious that we are not here using these terms in any generic sense, and as they certainly should be used in a generic sense, we shall drop them at once and substitute "episodic" and "encyclopaedic" instead. That is, when the poet communicates as an individual, his forms tend to be discontinuous; when he communicates as a professional man with a social function, he tends to seek more extended patterns.

On the mythical plane there is more legend than evidence, but it is clear that the poet who sings about gods is often considered to be singing as one, or as an instrument of one. His social function is that of an inspired oracle; he is frequently an ecstatic, and we hear strange stories of his powers. Orpheus could draw trees after him; the bards and ollaves of the Celtic world could kill their enemies with their satire; the prophets of Israel foretold the future. The poet's visionary function, his proper work as a poet, is on this plane to reveal the god for whom he speaks. This usually means that he reveals the god's will in connection with a specific occasion, when he is consulted as an oracle in a state of "enthusiasm" or divine possession. But in time the god in him reveals his nature and history as well as his will, and so a larger pattern of myth and ritual is built up out of a series of oracular pronouncements. We can see this very clearly in the emergence of the Messiah myth from the oracles of the Hebrew prophets. The Koran is one clear historical instance at the beginning of the Western period of the mythical mode in action. Authentic examples of oracular poetry are so largely pre- and extra-literary that they are difficult to isolate. For more recent examples, such as the ecstatic oracles which are said to be an important aspect of the culture of the Plains Indians, we have to depend on anthropologists.

Two principles of some importance are already implicit in our argument. One is a conception of a total body of vision that poets as a whole class are entrusted with, a total body tending to incorporate itself in a single encyclopaedic form, which can be attempted by one poet if he is sufficiently learned or inspired, or by a poetic school or tradition if the culture is sufficiently homogeneous. We note that traditional tales and myths and histories have a strong tendency to stick together and form encyclopaedic aggregates, especially when they are in a conventional metre, as they usually are. Some such process as this has been postulated for the Homeric epics, and in the Prose Edda the themes of the fragmentary lays of the Elder Edda are organized into a connected prose sequence. The Biblical histories obviously developed in a similar way, and in India, where the process of transmission was more relaxed, the two traditional epics, the Mahabharata and the Ramayana, apparently went on distending themselves for centuries, like pythons swallowing sheep. The expansion of *The Romaunt of the Rose* into an encyclopaedic satire by a second author is a medieval example. In the Finnish *Kalevala* everything that is unified or continuous about the poem is a nineteenth-century reconstruction. It does not follow that the *Kalevala*, considered as a single epic, is a fake: on the contrary, what follows is that the material of the *Kalevala* is the sort of material that lends itself readily to such reconstruction. In the mythical mode the encyclopaedic form is the sacred scripture, and in the other modes we should expect to find encyclopaedic forms which constitute a series of increasingly human *analogies* of mythical or scriptural revelation.

The other principle is that while there may be a great variety of episodic forms in any mode, in each mode we may attach a special significance to the particular episodic form that seems to be the germ out of which the encyclopaedic forms develop. In the mythical mode this central or typical episodic product is the oracle. The oracle develops a number of subsidiary forms, notably the commandment, the parable, the aphorism, and the prophecy. Out of these, whether strung loosely together as they are in the Koran or carefully edited and arranged as they are in the Bible, the scripture or sacred book takes shape. The Book of Isaiah, for example, can be analyzed into a mass of separate oracles, with three major foci, so to speak, one mainly pre-exilic, one exilic and one post-exilic. The "higher critics" of the Bible are not literary critics, and we have to make the suggestion ourselves that the Book of Isaiah is in fact the unity it has always been traditionally taken to be, a unity not of authorship but of theme, and that theme in epitome the theme of the Bible as a whole, as the parable of Israel lost, captive, and redeemed.

In the period of romance, the poet, like the corresponding hero, has become a human being, and the god has retreated to the sky. His function now is primarily to remember. Memory, said Greek myth at the beginning of its historical period, is the mother of the Muses, who inspire the poets, but no longer in the same degree that the god inspires the oracle—though the poets clung to the connection as long as they could. In Homer, in the perhaps more primitive Hesiod, in the poets of the heroic age of the North, we can see the kind of thing the poet had to remember. Lists of kings and foreign tribes, myths and genealogies of gods, historical traditions, the proverbs of popular wisdom, taboos, lucky and unlucky days, charms, the deeds of the tribal heroes, were some of the things that came out when the poet unlocked his word-hoard. The medieval minstrel with his repertory of memorized stories and the clerical poet who, like Gower or the author of the *Cursor Mundi*, tries to get everything he knows into one vast poem or poetic testament, belong in the same category. The encyclopaedic knowledge in such poems is regarded sacramentally, as a human analogy of divine knowledge.

The age of romantic heroes is largely a nomadic age, and its poets are frequently wanderers. The blind wandering minstrel is traditional in both Greek and Celtic literature; Old English poetry expresses some of the bleakest loneliness in the language; troubadours and Goliardic satirists roam over Europe in the Middle Ages; Dante himself was an exile. Or, if the poet stays where he is, it is poetry that travels: folk tales follow the trade routes; ballads and romances return from the great fairs; or Malory, writing in England, tells his readers what the "French book" says that has come to his hand. Of all fictions, the marvellous journey is the one formula that is never exhausted, and it is this fiction that is employed as a parable in the definitive encyclopaedic poem of the mode, Dante's *Commedia*. Poetry in this mode is an agent of catholicity, whether Hellenic in one age or Roman Christian in another.

Its typical episodic theme is perhaps best described as the theme of the boundary of consciousness, the sense of the poetic mind as passing from one world to another, or as simultaneously aware of both. The poem of exile, the lay of the *Widsith* or wayfarer who may be a wandering minstrel, a rejected lover, or a nomadic satirist, normally contrasts the worlds of memory and of experience. The poem of vision, conventionally dated on a May morning, contrasts the worlds of experience and dream. The poem of revelation through female or divine grace contrasts the old dispensation with the *vita nuova*. In the opening lines of the *Inferno* the affinity of the great encyclopaedic poem with both the poem of exile and the poem of vision is clearly marked.

The high mimetic period brings in a society more strongly established around the court and capital city, and a centripetal perspective replaces the centrifugal one of romance. The distant goals of the quest, the Holy Grail or the City of God, modulate into symbols of convergence, the emblems of prince, nation, and national faith. The encyclopaedic poems of this period, *The Faerie Queene, The Lusiad, Jerusalem Delivered, Paradise Lost,* are national epics unified by patriotic and religious ideas. The reasons for the exceptional role of the political elements in *Paradise Lost* are familiar, and constitute no real difficulty in seeing it as a national epic. Along with *The Pilgrim's Progress,* it also constitutes a kind of introduction to English low mimetic, being in one of its essential aspects the story of Everyman. Such thematic epics are as a rule recognizably different in emphasis from narratives where the primary interest is in telling the story, as in most epic poetry of the heroic age, most Icelandic sagas and Celtic romances, and, in the Renaissance period, in the greater part of *Orlando Furioso,* though Renaissance critics showed that it was quite possible to interpret Ariosto thematically.

The central episodic theme of the high mimetic is the theme of cynosure or centripetal gaze, which, whether addressed to mistress, friend, or deity, seems to have something about it of the court gazing upon its sovereign, the court-room gazing upon the orator, or the audience gazing upon the actor. For the high mimetic poet is pre-eminently a courtier, a counsellor, a preacher, a public orator or a master of decorum, and the high mimetic is the period in which the settled theatre comes into its own as the chief medium of fictional forms. In Shakespeare the control of decorum is so great that his personality disappears behind it altogether, but this is unlikely to happen with a dramatist who has a strong thematic interest, like Ben Jonson. As a rule the high mimetic poet tends to think of his function in relation to social or divine leadership, the theme of leadership being at the center of his normal fictional mode. The courtier-poet devotes his learning to the court and his life to courtesy: the function of his education is the service of his prince and the climax of it is courtly love, conceived as the fulfilling of the gaze upon beauty in the union with it. The religious poet may transfer this imagery to the spiritual life, as the English metaphysicals often do, or he may find his centripetal images in the liturgy. Jesuit poetry of the seventeenth century, and its English counterpart in Crashaw, have a unique quality of iconic intensity: Herbert, too, draws his reader step by step into a visible "temple."

The literary Platonism of the high mimetic period is of a kind appropriate to the mode. Most of the Renaissance humanists show a strong sense of the importance of symposium and dialogue, the social and educational aspects respectively of an elite culture. There is also a widespread assumption that the *dianoia* of poetry represents a form, pattern, ideal, or model in nature. "Nature's world is brazen," says Sidney: "the poets only deliver a golden." He makes it clear that this golden world is not something separated from nature but is "in effect a second nature": a unification of fact, or example, with model, or precept. What is usually called the "neo-Classical" in art and criticism is chiefly, in our terms, a sense of poetic *dianoia* as a manifestation of the true form of nature, the true form being assumed to be ideal.

With the low mimetic, where fictional forms deal with an intensely individualized society, there is only one thing for an analogy of myth to become, and that is an act of individual creation. The typical result of this is "Romanticism," a thematic development which to a considerable extent turns away from contemporary forms of fiction and develops its own contrasting kind. The qualities necessary to create *Hyperion* and the qualities necessary to create *Pride and Prejudice*, though contemporary, seem curiously opposed to each other, as though there were a sharper division between fictional and thematic in the low mimetic than in other modes. To some extent this is true, for a sense of contrast between subjective and objective, mental state and outward condition, individual and social or physical data, is characteristic of the low mimetic. In this age the thematic poet becomes what the fictional hero was in the age of romance, an extraordinary person who lives in a higher and more imaginative order of experience than that of nature. He creates his own world, a world which reproduces many of the characteristics of fictional romance already touched on. The Romantic poet's mind is normally in a state of pantheistic rapport with nature, and seems curiously invulnerable to the assaults of real evil. A tendency, also paralleled in the earlier fictional romance, to transmute pain and terror into a form of pleasure is reflected in the sadism and diabolic imagery of the "Romantic agony." The encyclopaedic tendency of this period is toward the construction of mythological epics in which the myths represent psychological or subjective states of mind. *Faust*, especially in the second part, is the most nearly definitive example; the prophecies of Blake and the mythological poems of Keats and Shelley are the best known English representatives.

The thematic poet of this period is interested in himself, not necessarily out of egotism, but because the basis of his poetic skill is individual, and hence genetic and psychological. He uses biological metaphors; he contrasts the organic with the dead or mechanical; he thinks socially in terms of a biological difference between the genius and the ordinary man, and genius to him is a fertile seed among abortive ones. He confronts nature directly, as an individual, and, in contrast to most of his predecessors, is apt to think of literary tradition as a second-hand substitute for personal experience. Like the hero of low mimetic comedy, the Romantic poet is often socially aggressive: the possession of creative genius confers authority, and its social impact is revolutionary. Romantic critics often develop theories of poetry as the rhetoric of personal greatness. The central episodic theme is the analysis or presentation of the subjective mental state, a theme usually taken to be typical of the literary movements accompanying Rousseau and Byron. The Romantic poet finds it much easier than his predecessors to be at once individual in content and attitude and continuous in form. The fact that so many of Wordsworth's shorter poems could be absorbed into the *Prelude*, in much the way in which primitive lays stick together to form epics, represents a technical innovation of some significance.

The poets who succeed the Romantics, the poets of French *symbolisme* for example, begin with the ironic gesture of turning away from the world of the market-place, with all its blurred sounds and imprecise meanings: they renounce rhetoric, moral judgement, and all other idols of the tribe, and devote their entire energy to the poet's literal function as a maker of poems. We said that the ironic fiction-writer is influenced by no considerations except craftsmanship, and the thematic poet in the ironic age thinks of himself more as a craftsman than as a creator or "unacknowledged legislator." That is, he makes the minimum claim for his personality and the maximum for his art—a contrast which underlies Yeats's theory of the poetic mask. At his best he is a dedicated spirit, a saint or anchorite of poetry. Flaubert, Rilke, Mallarmé, Proust, were all in their very different ways "pure" artists. Hence the central episodic theme is the theme of the pure but transient vision, the aesthetic or timeless moment, Rimbaud's *illumination*, Joyce's epiphany, the *Augenblick* of modern German thought, and the kind of non-didactic revelation implied in such terms as *symbolisme* and imagism.

The comparison of such instants with the vast panorama unrolled by history ("temps perdu") is the main theme of the encyclopaedic tendency. In Proust the repetitions of certain experiences at widely scattered intervals create these timeless moments out of time; in *Finnegans Wake* the whole of history itself is presented as a single gigantic anti-epiphany. On a smaller but still encyclopaedic scale, Eliot's *The Waste Land* and Virginia Woolf's last and most profound book, *Between the Acts*, have in common (a fact more striking because they have nothing else in common) a sense of contrast between the course of a whole civilization and the tiny flashes of significant moments which reveal its meaning. And just as the Romantic poet found it possible to write as an individual in continuous forms, so the ironic mode is rationalized by critical theories of the essential discontinuity of poetry. The paradoxical technique of the poetry which is encyclopaedic and yet discontinuous, the technique of *The Waste Land* and of Ezra Pound's *Cantos*, is, like its direct opposite in Wordsworth, a technical innovation heralding a new mode.

Details of the same technique fit the general pattern of thematic irony. The ironic method of saying one thing and meaning something rather different is incorporated in Mallarmé's doctrine of the avoidance of direct statement. The practice of cutting out predication, of simply juxtaposing images without making any assertions about their relationship, is consistent with the effort to avoid oratorical rhetoric. The same is true of the elimination of apostrophes and similar devices for including some mimesis of direct address. One study has even demonstrated a substantial increase in the use of the definite article in the ironic mode, a use said to be linked with the implicit sense of an initiated group aware of a real meaning behind an ironically baffling exterior.

The return of irony to myth that we noted in fiction is paralleled by some tendencies of the ironic craftsman to return to the oracular. This tendency is often accompanied by cyclical theories of history which help to rationalize the idea of a return, the appearance of such theories being a typical phenomenon of the ironic mode. We have Rimbaud and his "dérèglement de tous les sens" designed to make himself a reincarnation of the Prometheus who brought the divine fire to man and to restore the old mythical connection between the manic and the mantic. We have Rilke and his lifetime of tense listening to an oracular voice within him. We have Nietzsche proclaiming the advent of a new divine power in man, a proclamation which is somewhat confused by including a theory of identical recurrence. We have Yeats telling us that the Western cycle is nearly over and that a new Classical one, with Leda and the swan taking the place of the dove and the virgin, is about to begin. We have Joyce and his Viconian theory of history which sees our own age as a frustrated apocalypse followed instantly by a return to a period before Tristram.

As for the inferences which may be made from the above survey, one is clearly that many current critical assumptions have a limited historical context. In our day an ironic provincialism, which looks everywhere in literature for complete objectivity, suspension of moral judgements, concentration on pure verbal craftsmanship, and similar virtues, is in the ascendant. A Romantic provincialism, which looks everywhere for genius and evidences of great personality, is more old-fashioned, but it is still around. The high mimetic mode also had its pedants, some of them still trying to apply canons of ideal form in the eighteenth and even the nineteenth centuries. The suggestion made here is that no set of critical standards derived from only one mode can ever assimilate the whole truth about poetry.

There may be noticed a general tendency to react most strongly against the mode immediately preceding, and, to a lesser extent, to return to some of the standards of the modal grandfather. Thus the humanists of the high mimetic age were in general contemptuous of the "fablers and loud lyars," as Spenser's E.K. calls them, who produced medieval romance. But, as we can see in Sidney, they were never tired of justifying poetry by referring to the social importance of the original mythical phase. They tended to think of themselves as secular oracles of the order of nature, responding to the occasions of public affairs like the oracular poets, within a context of social and natural law. The Romantics, the thematic poets of the low mimetic period, set their faces against their predecessors' methods of following nature, and went back to the mode of romance.

The Romantic standards, in English literature, were in the main carried on by the Victorians, indicating a continuity of mode; the long anti-Romantic revolt that began around 1900 (several decades earlier in French literature) indicated a shift to the ironic. In the new mode the fondness for the small closely-knit group, the sense of the esoteric, and the nostalgia for the aristocratic that has produced such very different phenomena as the royalism of Eliot, the fascism of Pound, and the cult of chivalry in Yeats, are all in a way part of a reversion to high mimetic standards. The sense of the poet as courtier, of poetry as the service of a prince, of the supreme importance of the symposium or elite group, are among the high mimetic conceptions reflected in twentieth-century literature, especially in the poetry of the *symboliste* tradition from Mallarmé to George and Rilke. The exceptions to this tendency are sometimes less exceptional than they seem. The Fabian Society, when Bernard Shaw first joined it, was a group esoteric enough to satisfy Yeats himself: after Fabian socialism became a mass movement, Shaw turned into what became at length unmistakably a frustrated royalist.

Again, we may note that each period of Western culture has made a conspicuous use of the Classical literature nearest to it in mode: romanticized versions of Homer in the Middle Ages; Virgilian epic, Platonic symposium, and Ovidian courtly love in the high mimetic; Roman satire in the low mimetic; the products of the latest possible period of Latin in the ironic phase of Huysmans' À *Rebours*.

We saw in our survey of fictional modes that the poet never imitates "life" in the sense that life becomes anything more than the content of his work. In every mode he imposes the same kind of mythical form on his content, but makes different adaptations of it. In thematic modes, similarly, the poet never imitates thought except in the same sense of imposing a literary form on his thought. The failure to understand this produces a fallacy to which we may give the general term "existential projection." Suppose a writer finds that he is most successful with tragedies. His works will inevitably be full of gloom and catastrophe, and in his final scenes there will be characters standing around making remarks about the sternness of necessity, the vicissitudes of fortune, and the ineluctability of fate. Such sentiments are part of the *dianoia* of tragedy; but a writer who specializes in tragedy may well come to feel that they speak for the profoundest of all philosophies, and begin to emit similar utterances himself when asked what his own philosophy of life is. On the other hand, a writer whose specialty is comedy and happy endings will have *his* characters standing around at the end talking about the beneficence of providence, the miracles that come when we least expect them, the spirit of thankfulness and joy which we all ought to feel for the mercies of life.

It is natural, then, for tragedy and comedy to throw their shadows, so to speak, into philosophy and shape there a philosophy of fate and a philosophy of providence respectively. Thomas Hardy and Bernard Shaw both flourished around 1900 and both were interested in evolution. Hardy did better with tragedy, and saw evolution in terms of a stoical meliorism, a Schopenhauerian immanent will, and an activity of "chance" or "hap" in which any individual life may be expendable. Shaw, who wrote comedies, saw evolution as creative, leading to revolutionary politics, the advent of a Superman, and to whatever metabiology is. But it is obvious that Hardy and Shaw are not substantial philosophers, and they must stand or fall by their achievements in poetry, fiction, and drama.

Similarly, each mode of literature develops its own existential projection. Mythology projects itself as theology: that is, a mythopoeic poet usually accepts some myths as "true" and shapes his poetic structure accordingly. Romance peoples the world with fantastic, normally invisible personalities or powers: angels, demons, fairies, ghosts, enchanted animals, elemental spirits like those in *The Tempest* and *Comus*. Dante wrote in this mode, but not speculatively: he accepted the spiritual beings recognized by Christian doctrine, and concerns himself with no others. But for a late poet interested in the techniques of romance—Yeats, for instance— the question of whether and which of these mysterious creatures "really exist" is likely to project itself. The high mimetic projects mainly a quasi-Platonic philosophy of ideal forms, like the love and beauty of Spenser's hymns or the virtues of *The Faerie Queene*, and the low mimetic mainly a philosophy of genesis and organism, like that of Goethe, which finds unity and development in everything. The existential projection of irony is, perhaps, existentialism itself; and the return of irony to myth is accompanied, not only by the cyclical theories of history mentioned above, but, in a later stage, by a widespread interest in sacramental philosophy and dogmatic theology.

Mr. Eliot distinguishes between the poet who creates a philosophy for himself, and the poet who takes over one that he finds to hand, and advances the view that the latter course is better, or at least safer, for most poets. The distinction is fundamentally a distinction between the practice of the thematic poets of the low mimetic and of the ironic modes. Such poets as Blake, Shelley, Goethe, and Victor Hugo were compelled by the conventions of their mode to present the conceptual aspect of their imagery as self-generated; the poets of the last century have different conventions and different compulsions. But if the view taken here of the relation of form to content in poetry is sound, then no matter which he does the poet will still have much the same technical problems to face.

Ever since Aristotle criticism has tended to think of literature as *essentially* mimetic, and as divided between a "high" form of epic and tragedy dealing with ruling-class figures, and a "low" form confined to comedy and satire and more concerned with characters like ourselves. The larger scheme set forth in this chapter will, it is hoped, afford a useful background against which to relate the different and apparently contradictory remarks of Plato about poetry. *Phaedrus* deals largely with poetry as myth, and forms a commentary on Plato's treatment of myth; *Ion*, which is centered on the figure of a minstrel or rhapsode, sets forth both the encyclopaedic and the memorial conceptions of poetry which are typical of the romantic mode; the *Symposium*, which introduces Aristophanes, adopts the high mimetic canons which are probably nearest to Plato's own views. The famous discussion at the end of the *Republic* then falls into its place as a polemic against the *low* mimetic element in poetry, and in the *Cratylus* we are introduced to the ironic techniques of ambiguity, verbal association, paronomasia, and the apparatus now being revived by criticism to deal with the poetry of the ironic mode—the criticism which, by a further refinement of irony, is called "new" criticism.

Again, the difference in emphasis that we have described as fictional and thematic corresponds to a distinction between two views of literature that has run all through the history of criticism. These two views are the aesthetic and the creative, the Aristotelian and the Longinian, the view of literature as product and the view of literature as process. For Aristotle, the poem is a *techne* or aesthetic artifact: he is, as a critic, mainly interested in the more objective fictional forms, and his central conception is catharsis. Catharsis implies the detachment of the spectator, both from the work of art itself and from the author. The phrase "aesthetic distance" is generally accepted now in criticism, but it is almost a tautology: wherever there is aesthetic apprehension there is emotional and intellectual detachment. The principles of catharsis in other fictional forms than tragedy, such as comedy or satire, were not worked out by Aristotle, and have therefore never been worked out since.

In the thematic aspect of literature, the external relation between author and reader becomes more prominent, and when it does, the emotions of pity and terror are involved or contained rather than purged. In catharsis the emotions are purged by being attached to objects; where they are involved with the response they are unattached and remain prior conditions in the mind. We have noticed that terror without an object, as a condition of mind prior to being afraid *of* anything, is now conceived as *Angst* or anxiety, a somewhat narrow term for a feeling that extends from the pleasure of *Il Penseroso* to the pain of the *Fleurs du Mal*. In the general area of pleasure comes the conception of the sublime, in which austerity, gloom, grandeur, melancholy, or even menace are a source of romantic or penseroso feelings.

Similarly, we defined pity without an object as an imaginative animism which finds human qualities everywhere in nature, and includes the "beautiful," traditionally the corresponding term to the sublime. The beautiful has the same relation to the diminutive that the sublime has to bigness, and is closely related to the sense of the intricate and exquisite. The fairies of English folklore become Shakespeare's Mustard-Seed and Drayton's Pigwiggen, and Yeats's animism is linked to his sense of "many ingenious lovely things," and to his image of the toy bird in *Sailing to Byzantium*.

66

Just as catharsis is the central conception of the Aristotelian approach to literature, so ecstasis or absorption is the central conception of the Longinian approach. This is a state of identification in which the reader, the poem, and sometimes, at least ideally, the poet also, are involved. We say reader, because the Longinian conception is primarily that of a thematic or individualized response: it is more useful for lyrics, just as the Aristotelian one is more useful for plays. Sometimes, however, the normal categories of approach are not the right ones. In *Hamlet*, as Mr. Eliot has shown, the amount of emotion generated by the hero is too great for its objects; but surely the correct conclusion to draw from this fine insight is that *Hamlet* is best approached as a tragedy of *Angst* or of melancholy as a state in itself, rather than purely as an Aristotelian imitation of an action. On the other hand, the lack of emotional involvement in *Lycidas* has been thought by some, including Johnson, to be a failure in that poem, but surely the correct conclusion is that *Lycidas*, like *Samson Agonistes*, should be read in terms of catharsis with all passion spent.

SECOND ESSAY

Ethical Criticism: Theory of Symbols

Second Essay

ETHICAL CRITICISM: THEORY OF SYMBOLS

INTRODUCTION

OF THE PROBLEMS arising from the lack of a technical vocabulary of poetics, two demand special attention. The fact, already mentioned, that there is no word for a work of literary art is one that I find particularly baffling. One may invoke the authority of Aristotle for using "poem" in this sense, but usage declares that a poem is a composition in metre, and to speak of *Tom Jones* as a poem would be an abuse of ordinary language. One may discuss the question whether great works of prose deserve to be called poetry in some more extended sense, but the answer can only be a matter of taste in definitions. The attempt to introduce a value-judgement into a definition of poetry (e.g., "What, after all, do we mean by a poem—that is, something worthy of the name of poem?") only adds to the confusion. So of course does the antique snobbery about the superiority of metre which has given "prosy" the meaning of tedious and "prosaic" the meaning of pedestrian. As often as I can, I use "poem" and its relatives by synecdoche, because they are short words; but where synecdoche would be confusing, the reader will have to put up with such cacophonous jargon as "hypothetical verbal structure" and the like.

The other matter concerns the use of the word "symbol," which in this essay means any unit of any literary structure that can be isolated for critical attention. A word, a phrase, or an image used with some kind of special reference (which is what a symbol is usually taken to mean) are all symbols when they are distinguishable elements in critical analysis. Even the letters a writer spells his words with form part of his symbolism in this sense: they would be isolated only in special cases, such as alliteration or dialect spellings, but we are still aware that they symbolize sounds. Criticism as a whole, in terms of this definition, would begin with, and largely consist of, the systematizing of literary symbolism. It follows that other words must be used to classify the different types of symbolism.

For there must be different types: the criticism of literature can hardly be a simple or one-level activity. The more familiar one is

71

with a great work of literature, the more one's understanding of it grows. Further, one has the feeling of growing in the understanding of the work itself, not in the number of things one can attach to it. The conclusion that a work of literary art contains a variety or sequence of meanings seems inescapable. It has seldom, however, been squarely faced in criticism since the Middle Ages, when a precise scheme of literal, allegorical, moral, and anagogic meanings was taken over from theology and applied to literature. Today there is more of a tendency to consider the problem of literary meaning as subsidiary to the problems of symbolic logic and semantics. In what follows I try to work as independently of the latter subjects as I can, on the ground that the obvious place to start looking for a theory of literary meaning is in literature.

The principle of manifold or "polysemous" meaning, as Dante calls it, is not a theory any more, still less an exploded superstition, but an established fact. The thing that has established it is the simultaneous development of several different schools of modern criticism, each making a distinctive choice of symbols in its analysis. The modern student of critical theory is faced with a body of rhetoricians who speak of texture and frontal assaults, with students of history who deal with traditions and sources, with critics using material from psychology and anthropology, with Aristotelians, Coleridgians, Thomists, Freudians, Jungians, Marxists, with students of myths, rituals, archetypes, metaphors, ambiguities, and significant forms. The student must either admit the principle of polysemous meaning, or choose one of these groups and then try to prove that all the others are less legitimate. The former is the way of scholarship, and leads to the advancement of learning; the latter is the way of pedantry, and gives us a wide choice of goals, the most conspicuous today being fantastical learning, or myth criticism, contentious learning, or historical criticism, and delicate learning, or "new" criticism.

Once we have admitted the principle of polysemous meaning, we can either stop with a purely relative and pluralistic position, or we can go on to consider the possibility that there is a finite number of valid critical methods, and that they can all be contained in a single theory. It does not follow that all meanings can be arranged, as the medieval four-level scheme implies, in a hierarchical sequence, in which the first steps are comparatively elementary and apprehension gets more subtle and rarefied as one goes on. The term "level" is used here only for convenience, and should not be taken as indicating any belief on my part in a series of degrees of critical initiation. Again, there is a general reservation to be made about the conception of polysemous meaning: the meaning of a literary work forms a part of a larger whole. In the previous essay we saw that meaning or *dianoia* was one of three elements, the other two being *mythos* or narrative and *ethos* or characterization. It is better to think, therefore, not simply of a sequence of meanings, but of a sequence of contexts or relationships in which the whole work of literary art can be placed, each context having its characteristic *mythos* and *ethos* as well as its *dianoia* or meaning. I call these contexts or relationships "phases."

LITERAL AND DESCRIPTIVE PHASES: SYMBOL AS MOTIF AND AS SIGN

Whenever we read anything, we find our attention moving in two directions at once. One direction is outward or centrifugal, in which we keep going outside our reading, from the individual words to the things they mean, or, in practice, to our memory of the conventional association between them. The other direction is inward or centripetal, in which we try to develop from the words a sense of the larger verbal pattern they make. In both cases we deal with symbols, but when we attach an external meaning to a word we have, in addition to the verbal symbol, the thing represented or symbolized by it. Actually we have a series of such representations: the verbal symbol "cat" is a group of black marks on a page representing a sequence of noises representing an image or memory representing a sense experience representing an animal that says meow. Symbols so understood may here be called *signs*, verbal units which, conventionally and arbitrarily, stand for and point to things outside the place where they occur. When we are trying to grasp the context of words, however, the word "cat" is an element in a larger body of meaning. It is not primarily a symbol "of" anything, for in this aspect it does not represent, but connects. We can hardly even say that it represents a part of the author's intention in putting it there, for the author's intention ceases to exist as a separate factor as soon as he has finished revising. Verbal elements understood inwardly or centripetally, as parts of a verbal structure, are, as symbols, simply and literally verbal elements, or units of a verbal structure. (The word "literally" should be kept

73

in mind.) We may, borrowing a term from music, call such elements *motifs*.

These two modes of understanding take place simultaneously in all reading. It is impossible to read the word "cat" in a context without some representational flash of the animal so named; it is impossible to see the bare sign "cat" without wondering what context it belongs to. But verbal structures may be classified according to whether the *final* direction of meaning is outward or inward. In descriptive or assertive writing the final direction is outward. Here the verbal structure is intended to represent things external to it, and it is valued in terms of the accuracy with which it does represent them. Correspondence between phenomenon and verbal sign is truth; lack of it is falsehood; failure to connect is tautology, a purely verbal structure that cannot come out of itself.

In all literary verbal structures the final direction of meaning is inward. In literature the standards of outward meaning are secondary, for literary works do not pretend to describe or assert, and hence are not true, not false, and yet not tautological either, or at least not in the sense in which such a statement as "the good is better than the bad" is tautological. Literary meaning may best be described, perhaps, as hypothetical, and a hypothetical or assumed relation to the external world is part of what is usually meant by the word "imaginative." This word is to be distinguished from "imaginary," which usually refers to an assertive verbal structure that fails to make good its assertions. In literature, questions of fact or truth are subordinated to the primary literary aim of producing a structure of words for its own sake, and the sign-values of symbols are subordinated to their importance as a structure of interconnected motifs. Wherever we have an autonomous verbal structure of this kind, we have literature. Wherever this autonomous structure is lacking, we have language, words used instrumentally to help human consciousness do or understand something else. Literature is a specialized form of language, as language is of communication.

The reason for producing the literary structure is apparently that the inward meaning, the self-contained verbal pattern, is the field of the responses connected with pleasure, beauty, and interest. The contemplation of a detached pattern, whether of words or not, is clearly a major source of the sense of the beautiful, and of the pleasure that accompanies it. The fact that interest is most easily aroused by such a pattern is familiar to every handler of words, from the poet to the after-dinner speaker who digresses from an assertive harangue to present the self-contained structure of verbal inter-relationships known as a joke. It often happens that an originally descriptive piece of writing, such as the histories of Fuller and Gibbon, survives by virtue of its "style," or interesting verbal pattern, after its value as a representation of facts has faded.

The old precept that poetry is designed to delight and instruct sounds like an awkward hendiadys, as we do not usually feel that a poem does two different things to us, but we can understand it when we relate it to these two aspects of symbolism. In literature, what entertains is prior to what instructs, or, as we may say, the reality-principle is subordinate to the pleasure-principle. In assertive verbal structures the priority is reversed. Neither factor can, of course, ever be eliminated from any kind of writing.

One of the most familiar and important features of literature is the absence of a controlling aim of descriptive accuracy. We should, perhaps, like to feel that the writer of a historical drama knew what the historical facts of his theme were, and that he would not alter them without good reason. But that such good reasons may exist in literature is not denied by anyone. They seem to exist only there: the historian selects his facts, but to suggest that he had manipulated them to produce a more symmetrical structure would be grounds for libel. Some other types of verbal structures, such as theology and metaphysics, are declared by some to be centripetal in final meaning, and hence to be tautological ("purely verbal"). I have no opinion on this, except that in literary criticism theology and metaphysics must be treated as assertive, because they are outside literature, and everything that influences literature from without creates a centrifugal movement in it, whether it is directed toward the nature of absolute being or advice on the raising of hops. It is clear, too, that the proportion between the sense of being pleasantly entertained and the sense of being instructed, or awakened to reality, will vary in different forms of literature. The sense of reality is, for instance, far higher in tragedy than in comedy, as in comedy the logic of events normally gives way to the audience's desire for a happy ending.

The apparently unique privilege of ignoring facts has given the poet his traditional reputation as a licensed liar, and explains why so many words denoting literary structure, "fable," "fiction," "myth," and the like, have a secondary sense of untruth, like the

Norwegian word *digter* which is said to mean liar as well as poet. But, as Sir Philip Sidney remarked, "the poet never affirmeth," and therefore does not lie any more than he tells the truth. The poet, like the pure mathematician, depends, not on descriptive truth, but on conformity to his hypothetical postulates. The appearance of a ghost in *Hamlet* presents the hypothesis "let there be a ghost in *Hamlet*." It has nothing to do with whether ghosts exist or not, or whether Shakespeare or his audience thought they did. A reader who quarrels with postulates, who dislikes *Hamlet* because he does not believe that there are ghosts or that people speak in pentameters, clearly has no business in literature. He cannot distinguish fiction from fact, and belongs in the same category as the people who send cheques to radio stations for the relief of suffering heroines in soap operas. We may note here, as the point will be important later, that the accepted postulate, the contract agreed on by the reader before he can start reading, is the same thing as a convention.

The person who cannot be brought to understand literary convention is often said to be "literal-minded." But as "literal" surely ought to have some connection with letters, it seems curious to use the phrase "literal-minded" for imaginative illiterates. The reason for the anomaly is interesting, and important to our argument. Traditionally, the phrase "literal meaning" refers to descriptive meaning that is free from ambiguity. We usually say that the word cat "means literally" a cat when it is an adequate sign for a cat, when it stands in a simple representative relation to the animal that says meow. This sense of the term literal comes down from medieval times, and may be due to the theological origin of critical categories. In theology, the literal meaning of Scripture is usually the historical meaning, its accuracy as a record of facts or truths. Dante says, commenting on the verse in the Psalms, "When Israel went out of Egypt," "considering the letter only, the exodus of the Israelites to Palestine in the time of Moses is what is signified to us (*significatur nobis*)." The word "signified" shows that the literal meaning here is the simplest kind of descriptive or representational meaning, as it would still be to a Biblical "literalist."

But this conception of literal meaning as simple descriptive meaning will not do at all for literary criticism. An historical event cannot be literally anything but an historical event; a prose narrative describing it cannot be literally anything but a prose narrative.

The literal meaning of Dante's own *Commedia* is not historical, not at any rate a *simple* description of what "really happened" to Dante. And if a poem cannot be literally anything but a poem, then the literal basis of meaning in poetry can only be its letters, its inner structure of interlocking motifs. We are always wrong, in the context of criticism, when we say "this poem means literally"— and then give a prose paraphrase of it. All paraphrases abstract a secondary or outward meaning. Understanding a poem literally means understanding the whole of it, as a poem, and as it stands. Such understanding begins in a complete surrender of the mind and senses to the impact of the work as a whole, and proceeds through the effort to unite the symbols toward a simultaneous perception of the unity of the structure. (This is a *logical* sequence of critical elements, the *integritas, consonantia,* and *claritas* of Stephen's argument in Joyce's *Portrait.* I have no idea what the psychological sequence is, or whether there is a sequence—I suppose there would not be in a *Gestalt* theory.) Literal understanding occupies the same place in criticism that observation, the direct exposure of the mind to nature, has in the scientific method. "Every poem must necessarily be a perfect unity," says Blake: this, as the wording implies, is not a statement of fact about all existing poems, but a statement of the hypothesis which every reader adopts in first trying to comprehend even the most chaotic poem ever written.

Some principle of recurrence seems to be fundamental to all works of art, and this recurrence is usually spoken of as rhythm when it moves along in time, and as pattern when it is spread out in space. Thus we speak of the rhythm of music and the pattern of painting. But a slight increase of sophistication will soon start us talking about the pattern of music and the rhythm of painting. The inference is that all arts possess both a temporal and a spatial aspect, whichever takes the lead when they are presented. The score of a symphony may be studied all at once, as a spread-out pattern: a painting may be studied as the track of an intricate dance of the eye. Works of literature also move in time like music and spread out in images like painting. The word narrative or *mythos* conveys the sense of movement caught by the ear, and the word meaning or *dianoia* conveys, or at least preserves, the sense of simultaneity caught by the eye. We *listen to* the poem as it moves from beginning to end, but as soon as the whole of it is in our minds at once we "see" what it means. More exactly, this response is not simply to *the* whole *of* it, but to *a* whole *in* it: we have a vision of meaning or *dianoia* whenever any simultaneous apprehension is possible.

Now as a poem is literally a poem, it belongs, in its literal context, to the class of things called poems, which in their turn form part of the larger class known as works of art. The poem from this point of view presents a flow of sounds approximating music on one side, and an integrated pattern of imagery approximating the pictorial on the other. Literally, then, a poem's narrative is its rhythm or movement of words. If a dramatist writes a speech in prose, and then rewrites it in blank verse, he has made a strategic rhythmical change, and therefore a change in the literal narrative. Even if he alters "came a day" to "a day came" he has still made a tiny alteration of sequence, and so, literally, of his rhythm and narrative. Similarly, a poem's meaning is literally its pattern or integrity as a verbal structure. Its words cannot be separated and attached to sign-values: all possible sign-values of a word are absorbed into a complexity of verbal relationships.

The word's meaning is therefore, from the centripetal or inward-meaning point of view, variable or ambiguous, to use a term now familiar in criticism, a term which, significantly enough, is pejorative when applied to assertive writing. The word "wit" is said to be employed in Pope's *Essay on Criticism* in nine different senses. In assertive writing, such a semantic theme with variations could produce nothing but hopeless muddle. In poetry, it indicates the ranges of meanings and contexts that a word may have. The poet does not equate a word with a meaning; he establishes the functions or powers of words. But when we look at the symbols of a poem as verbal *signs*, the poem appears in a different context altogether, and so do its narrative and meaning. Descriptively, a poem is not primarily a work of art, but primarily a *verbal* structure or set of representative words, to be classed with other verbal structures like books on gardening. In this context narrative means the relation of the order of words to events resembling the events in "life" outside; meaning means the relation of its pattern to a body of assertive propositions, and the conception of symbolism involved is the one which literature has in common, not with the arts, but with other structures in words.

A considerable amount of abstraction enters at this stage. When we think of a poem's narrative as a description of events, we no longer think of the narrative as literally embracing every word and letter. We think rather of a sequence of gross events, of the obvious and externally striking elements in the word-order. Similarly, we think of meaning as the kind of discursive meaning that a prose paraphrase of the poem might reproduce. Hence a parallel abstraction comes into the conception of symbolism. On the literal level, where the symbols are motifs, any unit whatever, down to the letters, may be relevant to our understanding. But only large and striking symbols are likely to be treated critically as signs: nouns and verbs, and phrases built up out of important words. Prepositions and conjunctions are almost pure connectives. A dictionary, which is primarily a table of conventional sign-values, can tell us nothing about such words unless we already understand them.

So literature in its descriptive context is a body of hypothetical verbal structures. The latter stand between the verbal structures that describe or arrange actual events, or histories, and those that describe or arrange actual ideas or represent physical objects, like the verbal structures of philosophy and science. The relation of the spatial to the conceptual world is one that we obviously cannot examine here; but from the point of view of literary criticism, descriptive writing and didactic writing, the representation of natural objects and of ideas, are simply two different branches of centrifugal meaning. We may use the word "plot" or "story" for the sequence of gross events, and the connection of story with history is indicated in its etymology. But it is more difficult to use "thought," or even "thought-content," for the representational aspect of pattern, or gross meaning, because "thought" also describes what we are here trying to distinguish it from. Such are the problems of a vocabulary of poetics.

The literal and the descriptive phases of symbolism are, of course, present in every work of literature. But we find (as we shall also find with the other phases) that each phase has a particularly close relationship to a certain kind of literature, and to a certain type of critical procedure as well. Literature deeply influenced by the descriptive aspect of symbolism is likely to tend toward the realistic in its narrative and toward the didactic or descriptive in its meaning. Its prevailing rhythm will be the prose of direct speech, and its main effort will be to give as clear and honest an impression of external reality as is possible with a hypothetical structure. In the documentary naturalism generally associated with such names as

79

Zola and Dreiser, literature goes about as far as a representation of life, to be judged by its accuracy of description rather than by its integrity as a structure of words, as it could go and still remain literature. Beyond this point, the hypothetical or fictional element in literature would begin to dissolve. The limits of literary expression of this type are, of course, very wide, and nearly all the great empire of realistic poetry, drama, and prose fiction lies well within them. But we notice that the great age of documentary naturalism, the nineteenth century, was also the age of Romantic poetry, which, by concentrating on the process of imaginative creation, indicated a feeling of tension between the hypothetical and the assertive elements in literature.

This tension finally snaps off in the movement generally called *symbolisme*, a term which we expand here to take in the whole tradition which develops with a broad consistency through Mallarmé and Rimbaud to Valéry in France, Rilke in Germany, and Pound and Eliot in England. In the theory of *symbolisme* we have the complement to extreme naturalism, an emphasis on the literal aspect of meaning, and a treatment of literature as centripetal verbal pattern, in which elements of direct or verifiable statement are subordinated to the integrity of that pattern. The conception of "pure" poetry, or evocative verbal structure injured by assertive meaning, was a minor by-product of the same movement. The great strength of *symbolisme* was that it succeeded in isolating the hypothetical germ of literature, however limited it may have been in its earlier stages by its tendency to equate this isolation with the entire creative process. All its characteristics are solidly based on its conception of poetry as concerned with the centripetal aspect of meaning. Thus the achieving of an acceptable theory of literal meaning in criticism rests on a relatively recent development in literature.

Symbolisme, as expressed for instance in Mallarmé, maintains that the representational answer to the question "what does this mean?" should not be pressed in reading poetry, for the poetic symbol means primarily itself in relation to the poem. The unity of a poem, then, is best apprehended as a unity of mood, a mood being a phase of emotion, and emotion being the ordinary word for the state of mind directed toward the experiencing of pleasure or the contemplating of beauty. And as moods are not long sustained, literature, for *symbolisme*, is essentially discontinuous, longer poems being held together only by the use of the grammatical structures more appropriate to descriptive writing. Poetic images do not state or point to anything, but, by pointing to each other, they suggest or evoke the mood which informs the poem. That is, they express or articulate the mood. The emotion is not chaotic or inarticulate: it merely would have remained so if it had not turned into a poem, and when it does so, it *is* the poem, not something else still behind it. Nevertheless the words suggest and evoke are appropriate, because in *symbolisme* the word does not echo the thing but other words, and hence the immediate impact *symbolisme* makes on the reader is that of incantation, a harmony of sounds and the sense of a growing richness of meaning unlimited by denotation.

Some philosophers who assume that all meaning is descriptive meaning tell us that, as a poem does not describe things rationally, it must be a description of an emotion. According to this the literal core of poetry would be a *cri de coeur*, to use the elegant expression, the direct statement of a nervous organism confronted with something that seems to demand an emotional response, like a dog howling at the moon. *L'Allegro* and *Il Penseroso* would be respectively, according to this theory, elaborations of "I feel happy" and "I feel pensive." We have found, however, that the real core of poetry is a subtle and elusive verbal pattern that avoids, and does not lead to, such bald statements. We notice too that in the history of literature the riddle, the oracle, the spell, and the kenning are more primitive than a presentation of subjective feelings. The critics who tell us that the basis of poetic expression is irony, or a pattern of words that turns away from obvious (i.e., descriptive) meaning, are much closer to the facts of literary experience, at least on the literal level. The literary structure is ironic because "what it says" is always different in kind or degree from "what it means." In discursive writing what is said tends to approximate, ideally to become identified with, what is meant.

The criticism as well as the creation of literature reflects the distinction between literal and descriptive aspects of symbolism. The type of criticism associated with research and learned journals treats the poem as a verbal document, to be related as fully as possible to the history and the ideas that it reflects. The poem is most valuable to this kind of criticism when it is most explicit and descriptive, and when its core of imaginative hypothesis can be most easily separated. (Note that I am speaking of a kind of criticism, not of a kind of critic.) What is now called "new criticism," on the other hand, is largely criticism based on the conception of a poem as literally a poem. It studies the symbolism of a poem as an ambiguous structure of interlocking motifs; it sees the poetic pattern of meaning as a self-contained "texture," and it thinks of the external relations of a poem as being with the other arts, to be approached only with the Horatian warning of *favete linguis*, and not with the historical or the didactic. The word texture, with its overtones of a complicated surface, is a most expressive one for this approach. These two aspects of criticism are often thought of as antithetical, as were, in the previous century, the corresponding groups of writers. They are of course complementary, not antithetical, but still the difference in emphasis between them is important to grasp before we go on to try to resolve the antithesis in a third phase of symbolism.

FORMAL PHASE: SYMBOL AS IMAGE

We have now established a new sense of the term "literal meaning" for literary criticism, and have also assigned to literature, as one of its subordinate aspects of meaning, the ordinary descriptive meaning that works of literature share with all other structures of words. But it seems unsatisfactory to stop with this quizzical antithesis between delight and instruction, ironic withdrawal from reality and explicit connection with it. Surely, it will be said, we have overlooked the essential unity, in works of literature, expressed by the commonest of all critical terms, the word form. For the usual associations of "form" seem to combine these apparently contradictory aspects. On the one hand, form implies what we have called the literal meaning, or unity of structure; on the other, it implies such complementary terms as content and matter, expressive of what it shares with external nature. The poem is not natural in form, but it relates itself naturally to nature, and so, to quote Sidney again, "doth grow in effect a second nature."

Here we reach a more unified conception of narrative and meaning. Aristotle speaks of *mimesis praxeos*, an imitation of an action, and it appears that he identifies this *mimesis praxeos* with *mythos*. Aristotle's greatly abbreviated account here needs some reconstruction. Human action (*praxis*) is primarily imitated by histories, or verbal structures that describe specific and particular actions. A

82

mythos is a secondary imitation of an action, which means, not that it is at two removes from reality, but that it describes typical actions, being more philosophical than history. Human thought (*theoria*) is primarily imitated by discursive writing, which makes specific and particular predications. A *dianoia* is a secondary imitation of thought, a *mimesis logou*, concerned with typical thought, with the images, metaphors, diagrams, and verbal ambiguities out of which specific ideas develop. Poetry is thus more historical than philosophy, more involved in images and examples. For it is clear that all verbal structures with meaning are verbal imitations of that elusive psychological and physiological process known as thought, a process stumbling through emotional entanglements, sudden irrational convictions, involuntary gleams of insight, rationalized prejudices, and blocks of panic and inertia, finally to reach a completely incommunicable intuition. Anyone who imagines that philosophy is not a verbal imitation of this process, but the process itself, has clearly not done much thinking.

The form of a poem, that to which every detail relates, is the same whether it is examined as stationary or as moving through the work from beginning to end, just as a musical composition has the same form when we study the score as it has when we listen to the performance. The *mythos* is the *dianoia* in movement; the *dianoia* is the *mythos* in stasis. One reason why we tend to think of literary symbolism solely in terms of meaning is that we have ordinarily no word for the *moving* body of imagery in a work of literature. The word form has normally two complementary terms, matter and content, and it perhaps makes some distinction whether we think of form as a shaping principle or as a containing one. As shaping principle, it may be thought of as narrative, organizing temporally what Milton called, in an age of more exact terminology, the "matter" of his song. As containing principle it may be thought of as meaning, holding the poem together in a simultaneous structure.

The literary standards generally called "Classical" or "neo-Classical," which prevailed in Western Europe from the sixteenth to the eighteenth centuries, have the closest affinity with this formal phase. Order and clarity are particularly emphasized: order because of the sense of the importance of grasping a central form, and clarity because of the feeling that this form must not dissolve or withdraw into ambiguity, but must preserve a continuous relation-

83

ship to the nature which is its own content. It is the attitude characteristic of "humanism" in the historical sense, an attitude marked on the one hand by a devotion to rhetoric and verbal craftsmanship, and on the other by a strong attachment to historical and ethical affairs.

Writers typical of the formal phase—Ben Jonson for instance—are sure that they are in contact with reality and that they follow nature, yet the effect they produce is quite different from the descriptive realism of the nineteenth century, the difference being largely in the conception of imitation involved. In formal imitation, or Aristotelian mimesis, the work of art does not reflect external events and ideas, but exists between the example and the precept. Events and ideas are now aspects of its content, not external fields of observation. Historical fictions are not designed to give insight into a period of history, but are exemplary; they illustrate action, and are ideal in the sense of manifesting the universal form of human action. (The vagaries of language make "exemplary" the adjective for both example and precept.) Shakespeare and Jonson were keenly interested in history, yet their plays seem timeless; Jane Austen did not write historical fiction, yet, because she represents a later and more externalized method of following nature, the picture she gives of Regency society has a specific historical value.

A poem, according to Hamlet, who, though speaking of acting, is following a conventional Renaissance line of poetics, holds the mirror up to nature. We should be careful to notice what this implies: the poem is not itself a mirror. It does not merely reproduce a shadow of nature; it causes nature to be reflected in its containing form. When the formal critic comes to deal with symbols, therefore, the units he isolates are those which show an analogy of proportion between the poem and the nature which it imitates. The symbol in this aspect may best be called the image. We are accustomed to associate the term "nature" primarily with the external physical world, and hence we tend to think of an image as primarily a replica of a natural object. But of course both words are far more inclusive: nature takes in the conceptual or intelligible order as well as the spatial one, and what is usually called an "idea" may be a poetic image also.

One could hardly find a more elementary critical principle than the fact that the events of a literary fiction are not real but hypothetical events. For some reason it has never been consistently understood that the ideas of literature are not real propositions, but verbal formulas which imitate real propositions. The *Essay on Man* does not expound a system of metaphysical optimism founded on the chain of being: it uses such a system as a model on which to construct a series of hypothetical statements which are more or less useless as propositions, but inexhaustibly rich and suggestive when read in their proper context as epigrams. As epigrams, as solid, resonant, centripetal verbal structures, they may apply pointedly to millions of human situations which have nothing to do with metaphysical optimism. Wordsworth's pantheism, Dante's Thomism, Lucretius' Epicureanism, all have to be read in the same way, as do Gibbon or Macaulay or Hume when they are read for style instead of subject-matter.

Formal criticism begins with an examination of the imagery of a poem, with a view to bringing out its distinctive pattern. The recurring or most frequently repeated images form the tonality, so to speak, and the modulating, episodic and isolated images relate themselves to this in a hierarchic structure which is the critical analogy to the proportions of the poem itself. Every poem has its peculiar spectroscopic band of imagery, caused by the requirements of its genre, the predilections of its author, and countless other factors. In *Macbeth*, for instance, the images of blood and of sleeplessness have a thematic importance, as is very natural for a tragedy of murder and remorse. Hence in the line "Making the green one red," the colors are of different thematic intensities. Green is used incidentally and for contrast; red, being closer to the *key* of the play as a whole, is more like the repetition of a tonic chord in music. The opposite would be true of the contrast between red and green in Marvell's *The Garden*.

The form of the poem is the same whether it is studied as narrative or as meaning, hence the structure of imagery in *Macbeth* may be studied as a pattern derived from the text, or as a rhythm of repetition falling on an audience's ear. There is a vague notion that the latter method produces a simpler result, and may therefore be used as a commonsense corrective to the niggling subtleties of textual study. The analogy of music again may be helpful. The average audience at a symphony knows very little about sonata form, and misses practically all the subtleties detected by an analysis of the score; yet those subtleties are really there, and as the audience can hear everything that is being played, it gets them

85

all as part of a linear experience; the awareness is less conscious, but not less real. The same is true of the response to the imagery of a highly concentrated poetic drama.

The analysis of recurrent imagery is, of course, one of the chief techniques of rhetorical or "new" criticism as well: the difference is that formal criticism, after attaching the imagery to the central form of the poem, renders an aspect of the form into the propositions of discursive writing. Formal criticism, in other words, is commentary, and commentary is the process of translating into explicit or discursive language what is implicit in the poem. Good commentary naturally does not read ideas into the poem; it reads and translates what is there, and the evidence that it is there is offered by the study of the structure of imagery with which it begins. The sense of tact, of the desirability of not pushing a point of interpretation "too far," is derived from the fact that the proportioning of emphasis in criticism should normally bear a rough analogy to the proportioning of emphasis in the poem.

The failure to make, in practice, the most elementary of all distinctions in literature, the distinction between fiction and fact, hypothesis and assertion, imaginative and discursive writing, produces what in criticism has been called the "intentional fallacy," the notion that the poet has a primary intention of conveying meaning to a reader, and that the first duty of a critic is to recapture that intention. The word intention is analogical: it implies a relation between two things, usually a conception and an act. Some related terms show this duality even more clearly: to "aim at" something means that a target and a missile are being brought into alignment. Hence such terms properly belong only to discursive writing, where the correspondence of a verbal pattern with what it describes is of primary importance. But a poet's primary concern is to produce a work of art, and hence his intention can only be expressed by some kind of tautology.

In other words, a poet's intention is centripetally directed. It is directed towards putting words together, not towards aligning words with meanings. If we had the privilege of Gulliver in Glubbdubdrib to call up the ghost of, say, Shakespeare, to ask him what he meant by such and such a passage, we could only get, with maddening iteration, the same answer: "I meant it to form part of the play." One may pursue the centripetal intention as far as genre, as a poet intends to produce, not simply a poem, but a certain kind of poem. In reading, for instance, *Zuleika Dobson* as a description of life in Oxford, we should be well advised to allow for ironic intention. One has to assume, as an essential heuristic axiom, that the work as produced constitutes the definitive record of the writer's intention. For many of the flaws which an inexperienced critic thinks he detects, the answer "But it's supposed to be that way" is sufficient. All other statements of intention, however fully documented, are suspect. The poet may change his mind or mood; he may have intended one thing and done another, and then rationalized what he did. (A cartoon in a *New Yorker* of some years back hit off this last problem beautifully: it depicted a sculptor gazing at a statue he had just made and remarking to a friend: "Yes, the head is too large. When I put it in exhibition I shall call it 'The Woman with the Large Head.'") If intention is still thought to be apparent in the poem itself, the poem is being regarded as incomplete, like a freshman's essay where the reader has continually to speculate about what the author may have had in his mind. If the author has been dead for centuries, such speculation cannot get us very far, however irresistibly it may suggest itself.

What the poet meant to say, then, is, literally, the poem itself; what he meant to say in any given passage is, in its literal meaning, part of the poem. But literal meaning, we have seen, is variable and ambiguous. The reader may be dissatisfied with the ghost of Shakespeare's answer: he may feel that Shakespeare, unlike, say, Mallarmé, is a poet he can trust, and that he also meant his passage to be intelligible in itself (i.e., have descriptive or rephrasable meaning). Doubtless he did, but the relationship of the passage to the rest of the play creates myriads of new meanings for it. Just as a vivid sketch of a cat by a good draughtsman may contain in a few crisp lines the entire feline experience of everyone who looks at it, so the powerfully constructed pattern of words that we know as *Hamlet* may contain an amount of meaning which the vast and constantly growing library of criticism on the play cannot begin to exhaust. Commentary, which translates the implicit into the explicit, can only isolate the aspect of meaning, large or small, which is appropriate or interesting for certain readers to grasp at a certain time. Such translation is an activity with which the poet has very little to do. The relation in bulk between commentary and a sacred book, such as the Bible or the Vedic hymns, is even more striking, and indicates that when a poetic structure attains a certain degree of concentration or social recognition, the amount of commentary it will carry is infinite. This fact is in itself no more incredible than the fact that a scientist can state a law illustrated by more phenomena than he could ever observe or count, and there is no occasion for wondering, like the yokels in Goldsmith, how one small poet's head can carry the amount of wit, wisdom, instruction, and significance that Shakespeare and Dante have given the world.

Still there is a genuine mystery in art, and a real place for wonder. In *Sartor Resartus* Carlyle distinguishes extrinsic symbols, like the cross or the national flag, which are without value in themselves but are signs or indicators of something existential, from intrinsic symbols, which include works of art. On this basis we may distinguish two kinds of mystery. (A third kind, the mystery which is a puzzle, a problem to be solved and annihilated, belongs to discursive thought, and has little to do with the arts, except in matters of technique.) The mystery of the unknown or unknowable essence is an extrinsic mystery, which involves art only when art is also made illustrative of something else, as religious art is to the person concerned primarily with worship. But the intrinsic mystery is that which remains a mystery in itself no matter how fully known it is, and hence is not a mystery separated from what is known. The mystery in the greatness of *King Lear* or *Macbeth* comes not from concealment but from revelation, not from something unknown or unknowable in the work, but from something unlimited in it.

It could be said, of course, that poetry is the product, not only of a deliberate and voluntary act of consciousness, like discursive writing, but of processes which are subconscious or preconscious or half-conscious or unconscious as well, whatever psychological metaphor one prefers. It takes a great deal of will power to write poetry, but part of that will power must be employed in trying to relax the will, so making a large part of one's writing involuntary. This is no doubt true, and it is also true that poetic technique, like all technique, is a habitual, and therefore an increasingly unconscious, skill. But I feel that literary data are in the long run only explicable within criticism, and I am reluctant to explain literary facts by psychological clichés. Still, it seems now almost impossible to avoid the term "creative," with all the biological analogies it suggests, when speaking of the arts. And creation, whether of God, man, or nature, seems to be an activity whose only intention is to abolish intention, to eliminate final dependence on or relation to something else, to destroy the shadow that falls between itself and its conception.

One wishes that literary criticism had a Samuel Butler to formulate some of the paradoxes involved in this parallel between the work of art and the organism. We can describe objectively what happens when a tulip blooms in spring and a chrysanthemum in autumn, but we cannot describe it from the inside of the plant, except by metaphors derived from human consciousness and ascribed to some agent like God or nature or environment or *élan vital*, or to the plant itself. It is projected metaphor to say that a flower "knows" when it is time for it to bloom, and of course to say that "nature knows" is merely to import a faded mother-goddess cult into biology. I can well understand that in their own field biologists would find such teleological metaphors both unnecessary and confusing, a fallacy of misplaced concreteness. The same would be true of criticism to the extent that criticism has to deal with imponderables other than consciousness or logically directed will. If one critic says that another has discovered a mass of subtleties in a poet of which that poet was probably quite unconscious, the phrase points up the biological analogy. A snowflake is probably quite unconscious of forming a crystal, but what it does may be worth study even if we are willing to leave its inner mental processes alone.

It is not often realized that all commentary is allegorical interpretation, an attaching of ideas to the structure of poetic imagery. The instant that any critic permits himself to make a genuine comment about a poem (e.g., "In *Hamlet* Shakespeare appears to be portraying the tragedy of irresolution") he has begun to allegorize. Commentary thus looks at literature as, in its formal phase, a potential allegory of events and ideas. The relation of such commentary to poetry itself is the source of the contrast which was developed by several critics of the Romantic period between "symbolism" and "allegory," symbolism here being used in the sense of thematically significant imagery. The contrast is between a "concrete" approach to symbols which begins with images of actual things and works outward to ideas and propositions, and an "abstract" approach which begins with the idea and then tries to find a concrete image to represent it. This distinction is valid enough in itself, but it has deposited a large terminal moraine of confusion in modern criticism, largely because the term allegory is very loosely employed for a great variety of literary phenomena.

We have actual allegory when a poet explicitly indicates the relationship of his images to examples and precepts, and so tries to indicate how a commentary on him should proceed. A writer is being allegorical whenever it is clear that he is saying "by this I *also* (*allos*) mean that." If this seems to be done continuously, we may say, cautiously, that what he is writing "is" an allegory. In *The Faerie Queene*, for instance, the narrative systematically refers to historical examples and the meaning to moral precepts, besides doing their own work in the poem. Allegory, then, is a contrapuntal technique, like canonical imitation in music. Dante, Spenser, Tasso, and Bunyan use it throughout: their works are the masses and oratorios of literature. Ariosto, Goethe, Ibsen, Hawthorne write in a *freistimmige* style in which allegory may be picked up and dropped again at pleasure. But even continuous allegory is still a structure of images, not of disguised ideas, and commentary has to proceed with it exactly as it does with all other literature, trying to see what precepts and examples are suggested by the imagery as a whole.

The commenting critic is often prejudiced against allegory without knowing the real reason, which is that continuous allegory prescribes the direction of his commentary, and so restricts its freedom. Hence he often urges us to read Spenser and Bunyan, for example, for the story alone and let the allegory go, meaning by that that he regards his own type of commentary as more interesting. Or else he will frame a definition of allegory that will exclude the poems he likes. Such a critic is often apt to treat all allegory as though it were naive allegory, or the translation of ideas into images.

Naive allegory is a disguised form of discursive writing, and belongs chiefly to educational literature on an elementary level: schoolroom moralities, devotional exempla, local pageants, and the like. Its basis is the habitual or customary ideas fostered by education and ritual, and its normal form is that of transient spectacle. Under the excitement of a particular occasion familiar ideas suddenly become sense experiences, and vanish with the occasion. The defeat of Sedition and Discord by Sound Government and Encouragement of Trade would be the right sort of theme for a pageant designed only to entertain a visiting monarch for half an hour. The apparatus of "mass media" and "audiovisual aids" plays a similar allegorical role in contemporary education. Because of this basis in spectacle, naive allegory has its center of gravity in the pictorial arts, and is most successful as art when recognized to be a form of occasional wit, as it is in the political cartoon. The more solemn and permanent naive allegories of official murals and statuary show a marked tendency to date.

At one extreme of commentary, then, there is the naive allegory so anxious to make its own allegorical points that it has no real literary or hypothetical center. When I say that naive allegory "dates," I mean that any allegory which resists a primary analysis of imagery—that is, an allegory which is simply discursive writing with an illustrative image or two stuck into it—will have to be treated less as literature than as a document in the history of ideas. When the author of II Esdras, for instance, introduces an allegorical vision of an eagle, and then says, "Behold, on the right side there arose one feather, which reigned over all the earth," it is clear that he is not sufficiently interested in his eagle as a poetic image to remain within the normal boundaries of literary expression. The basis of poetic expression is the metaphor, and the basis of naive allegory is the mixed metaphor.

Within the boundaries of literature we find a kind of sliding scale, ranging from the most explicitly allegorical, consistent with being literature at all, at one extreme, to the most elusive, anti-explicit and anti-allegorical at the other. First we meet the continuous allegories, like *The Pilgrim's Progress* and *The Faerie Queene*, and then the free-style allegories just mentioned. Next come the poetic structures with a large and insistent doctrinal interest, in which the internal fictions are exempla, like the epics of Milton. Then we have, in the exact center, works in which the structure of imagery, however suggestive, has an implicit relation only to events and ideas, and which includes the bulk of Shakespeare. Below this, poetic imagery begins to recede from example and precept and become increasingly ironic and paradoxical. Here the modern critic begins to feel more at home, the reason being that this type is more consistent with the modern literal view of art, the sense of the poem as withdrawn from explicit statement.

Several types of this ironic and anti-allegorical imagery are familiar. One is the typical symbol of the metaphysical school of the

Baroque period, the "conceit" or deliberately strained union of normally disparate things. The paradoxical techniques of metaphysical poetry are based on a sense of the breakdown of the internal relation of art and nature into an external one. Another is the substitute-image of *symbolisme*, part of a technique for suggesting or evoking things and avoiding the explicit naming of them. Still another is the kind of image described by Mr. Eliot as an objective correlative, the image that sets up an inward focus of emotion in poetry and at the same time substitutes itself for an idea. Still another, closely related to if not identical with the objective correlative, is the heraldic symbol, the central emblematic image which comes most readily to mind when we think of the word "symbol" in modern literature. We think, for example, of Hawthorne's scarlet letter, Melville's white whale, James's golden bowl, or Virginia Woolf's lighthouse. Such an image differs from the image of the formal allegory in that there is no continuous relationship between art and nature. In contrast to the allegorical symbols of Spenser, for instance, the heraldic emblematic image is in a paradoxical and ironic relation to both narrative and meaning. As a unit of meaning, it arrests the narrative; as a unit of narrative, it perplexes the meaning. It combines the qualities of Carlyle's intrinsic symbol with significance in itself, and the extrinsic symbol which points quizzically to something else. It is a technique of symbolism which is based on a strong sense of a lurking antagonism between the literal and the descriptive aspects of symbols, the same antagonism that made Mallarmé and Zola so extreme a contrast in nineteenth-century literature.

Below this we run into still more indirect techniques, such as private association, symbolism intended not to be fully understood, the deliberate spoofing of Dadaism, and kindred signs of another approaching boundary of literary expression. We should try to keep this whole range of possible commentary clearly in mind, so as to correct the perspective both of the medieval and Renaissance critics who assumed that all major poetry should be treated as far as possible as continuous allegory, and of the modern ones who maintain that poetry is essentially anti-allegorical and paradoxical.

What we have now is a conception of literature as a body of hypothetical creations which is not necessarily involved in the worlds of truth and fact, nor necessarily withdrawn from them, but which may enter into any kind of relationship to them, ranging from the most to the least explicit. We are strongly reminded of the relationship of mathematics to the natural sciences. Mathematics, like literature, proceeds hypothetically and by internal consistency, not descriptively and by outward fidelity to nature. When it is applied to external facts, it is not its truth but its applicability that is being verified. As I seem to have fastened on the cat for my semantic emblem in this essay, I note that this point comes out sharply in the discussion between Yeats and Sturge Moore over the problem of Ruskin's cat, the animal that was picked up and flung out of a window by Ruskin although it was not there. Anyone measuring his mind against an external reality has to fall back on an axiom of faith. The distinction between an empirical fact and an illusion is not a rational distinction, and cannot be logically proved. It is "proved" only by the practical and emotional necessity of assuming the distinction. For the poet, *qua* poet, this necessity does not exist, and there is no poetic reason why he should either assert or deny the existence of any cat, real or Ruskinian.

The conception of art as having a relation to reality which is neither direct nor negative, but potential, finally resolves the dichotomy between delight and instruction, the style and the message. "Delight" is not readily distinguishable from pleasure, and hence opens the way to that aesthetic hedonism we glanced at in the introduction, the failure to distinguish personal and impersonal aspects of valuation. The traditional theory of catharsis implies that the emotional response to art is not the raising of an actual emotion, but the raising and casting out of actual emotion on a wave of something else. We may call this something else, perhaps, exhilaration or exuberance: the vision of something liberated from experience, the response kindled in the reader by the transmutation of experience into mimesis, of life into art, of routine into play. At the center of liberal education something surely ought to get liberated. The metaphor of creation suggests the parallel image of birth, the emergence of a new-born organism into independent life. The ecstasy of creation and its response produce, on one level of creative effort, the hen's cackle; on another, the quality that the Italian critics called *sprezzatura* and that Hoby's translation of Castiglione calls "recklessness," the sense of buoyancy or release that accompanies perfect discipline, when we can no longer know the dancer from the dance.

It is impossible to understand the effect of what Milton called "gorgeous Tragedy" as producing a real emotion of gloom or sorrow. Aeschylus's *The Persians* and Shakespeare's *Macbeth* are certainly tragedies, but they are associated respectively with the victory of Salamis and the accession of James I, both occasions of national rejoicing. Some critics carry the theory of real emotion over into Shakespeare himself, and talk about a "tragic period," in which he is supposed to have felt dismal from 1600 to 1608. Most people, if they had just finished writing a play as good as *King Lear*, would be in a mood of exhilaration, and while we have no right to ascribe this mood to Shakespeare, it is surely the right way to describe our response to the play. On the other hand, it comes as something of a shock to realize that the blinding of Gloucester is primarily entertainment, the more so as the pleasure we get from it obviously has nothing to do with sadism. If any literary work is emotionally "depressing," there is something wrong with either the writing or the reader's response. Art seems to produce a kind of buoyancy which, though often called pleasure, as it is for instance by Wordsworth, is something more inclusive than pleasure. "Exuberance is beauty," said Blake. That seems to me a practically definitive solution, not only of the minor question of what beauty is, but of the far more important problem of what the conceptions of catharsis and ecstasis really mean.

Such exuberance is, of course, as much intellectual as it is emotional: Blake himself was willing to define poetry as "allegory addressed to the intellectual powers." We live in a world of threefold external compulsion: of compulsion on action, or law; of compulsion on thinking, or fact; of compulsion on feeling, which is the characteristic of all pleasure whether it is produced by the *Paradiso* or by an ice cream soda. But in the world of imagination a fourth power, which contains morality, beauty, and truth but is never subordinated to them, rises free of all their compulsions. The work of imagination presents us with a vision, not of the personal greatness of the poet, but of something impersonal and far greater: the vision of a decisive act of spiritual freedom, the vision of the recreation of man.

94

MYTHICAL PHASE: SYMBOL AS ARCHETYPE

In the formal phase the poem belongs neither to the class "art," nor to the class "verbal": it represents its own class. There are thus two aspects to its form. In the first place, it is unique, a *techne* or artifact, with its own peculiar structure of imagery, to be examined by itself without immediate reference to other things like it. The critic here begins with poems, not with a prior conception or definition of poetry. In the second place, the poem is one of a class of similar forms. Aristotle knows that *Oedipus Tyrannus* is in one sense not like any other tragedy, but he also knows that it belongs to the class called tragedy. We, who have experienced Shakespeare and Racine, can add the corollary that tragedy is something bigger than a phase of Greek drama. We may also find tragedy in literary works which are not dramas. To understand what tragedy is, therefore, takes us beyond the merely historical into the question of what an aspect of literature as a whole is. With this idea of the external relations of a poem with other poems, two considerations in criticism for the first time become important: convention and genre.

The study of genres is based on analogies in form. It is characteristic of documentary and historical criticism that it cannot deal with such analogies. It can trace influence with great plausibility, whether it exists or not, but confronted with a tragedy of Shakespeare and a tragedy of Sophocles, to be compared solely because they are both tragedies, the historical critic has to confine himself to general reflections about the seriousness of life. Similarly, nothing is more striking in rhetorical criticism than the absence of any consideration of genre: the rhetorical critic analyzes what is in front of him without much regard to whether it is a play, a lyric, or a novel. He may in fact even assert that there are no genres in literature. That is because he is concerned with his structure simply as a work of art, not as an artifact with a possible function. But there are many analogies in literature apart altogether from sources and influences (many of which, of course, are not analogous at all) and noticing such analogies forms a large part of our actual experience of literature, whatever its role so far in criticism.

The central principle of the formal phase, that a poem is an imitation of nature, is, though a perfectly sound one, still a principle which isolates the individual poem. And it is clear that any poem may be examined, not only as an imitation of nature, but as an imitation of other poems. Virgil discovered, according to Pope, that following nature was ultimately the same thing as following Homer. Once we think of a poem in relation to other poems, as a unit of poetry, we can see that the study of genres has to be founded on the study of convention. The criticism which can deal with such matters will have to be based on that aspect of symbolism which relates poems to one another, and it will choose, as its main field of operations, the symbols that link poems together. Its ultimate object is to consider, not simply *a* poem as *an* imitation of nature, but the order of nature as a whole as imitated by a corresponding order of words.

All art is equally conventionalized, but we do not ordinarily notice this fact unless we are unaccustomed to the convention. In our day the conventional element in literature is elaborately disguised by a law of copyright pretending that every work of art is an invention distinctive enough to be patented. Hence the conventionalizing forces of modern literature—the way, for instance, that an editor's policy and the expectation of his readers combine to conventionalize what appears in a magazine—often go unrecognized. Demonstrating the debt of A to B is merely scholarship if A is dead, but a proof of moral delinquency if A is alive. This state of things makes it difficult to appraise a literature which includes Chaucer, much of whose poetry is translated or paraphrased from others; Shakespeare, whose plays sometimes follow their sources almost verbatim; and Milton, who asked for nothing better than to steal as much as possible out of the Bible. It is not only the inexperienced reader who looks for a *residual* originality in such works. Most of us tend to think of a poet's real achievement as distinct from, or even contrasted with, the achievement present in what he stole, and we are thus apt to concentrate on peripheral rather than on central critical facts. For instance, the central greatness of *Paradise Regained*, as a poem, is not the greatness of the rhetorical decorations that Milton added to his source, but the greatness of the theme itself, which Milton *passes on* to the reader from his source. This conception of the great poet's being entrusted with the great theme was elementary enough to Milton, but violates most of the low mimetic prejudices about creation that most of us are educated in.

The underestimating of convention appears to be a result of, may even be a part of, the tendency, marked from Romantic times on, to think of the individual as ideally prior to his society. The view opposed to this, that the new baby is conditioned by a hereditary and environmental kinship to a society which already exists, has, whatever doctrines may be inferred from it, the initial advantage of being closer to the facts it deals with. The literary consequence of the second view is that the new poem, like the new baby, is born into an already existing order of words, and is typical of the structure of poetry to which it is attached. The new baby *is* his own society appearing once again as a unit of individuality, and the new poem has a similar relation to its poetic society.

It is hardly possible to accept a critical view which confuses the original with the aboriginal, and imagines that a "creative" poet sits down with a pencil and some blank paper and eventually produces a new poem in a special act of creation *ex nihilo*. Human beings do not create in that way. Just as a new scientific discovery manifests something that was already latent in the order of nature, and at the same time is logically related to the total structure of the existing science, so the new poem manifests something that was already latent in the order of words. Literature may have life, reality, experience, nature, imaginative truth, social conditions, or what you will for its *content*; but literature itself is not made out of these things. Poetry can only be made out of other poems; novels out of other novels. Literature shapes itself, and is not shaped externally: the *forms* of literature can no more exist outside literature than the forms of sonata and fugue and rondo can exist outside music.

All this was much clearer before the assimilation of literature to private enterprise concealed so many of the facts of criticism. When Milton sat down to write a poem about Edward King, he did not ask himself: "What can I find to say about King?" but "How does poetry require that such a subject should be treated?" The notion that convention shows a lack of feeling, and that a poet attains "sincerity" (which usually means articulate emotion) by disregarding it, is opposed to all the facts of literary experience and history. The origin of this notion is, again, the view that poetry is a description of emotion, and that its "literal" meaning is an assertion about the emotions held by the individual poet. But any serious study of literature soon shows that the real difference between the original and the imitative poet is simply that the former is more profoundly imitative. Originality returns to the origins of literature, as radicalism returns to its roots. The remark of Mr. Eliot that a good poet is more likely to steal than to imitate affords a more balanced view of convention, as it indicates that the poem is specifically involved with other poems, not vaguely with such abstractions as tradition or style. The copyright law, and the mores attached to it, make it difficult for a modern novelist to steal anything except his title from the rest of literature: hence it is often only in such titles as *For Whom the Bell Tolls*, *The Grapes of Wrath*, or *The Sound and the Fury*, that we can clearly see how much impersonal dignity and richness of association an author can gain by the communism of convention.

As with other products of divine activity, the father of a poem is much more difficult to identify than the mother. That the mother is always nature, the realm of the objective considered as a field of communication, no serious criticism can ever deny. But as long as the father of a poem is assumed to be the poet himself, we have once again failed to distinguish literature from discursive verbal structures. The discursive writer writes as an act of conscious will, and that conscious will, along with the symbolic system he employs for it, is set over against the body of things he is describing. But the poet, who writes creatively rather than deliberately, is not the father of his poem; he is at best a midwife, or, more accurately still, the womb of Mother Nature herself: her privates he, so to speak. The fact that revision is possible, that a poet can make changes in a poem not because he likes them better but because they are better, shows clearly that the poet has to give birth to the poem as it passes through his mind. He is responsible for delivering it in as uninjured a state as possible, and if the poem is alive, it is equally anxious to be rid of him, and screams to be cut loose from all the navel-strings and feeding-tubes of his ego.

The true father or shaping spirit of the poem is the form of the poem itself, and this form is a manifestation of the universal spirit of poetry, the "onlie begetter" of Shakespeare's sonnets who was not Shakespeare himself, much less that depressing ghost Mr. W. H., but Shakespeare's subject, the master-mistress of his passion. When a poet speaks of the *internal* spirit which shapes the poem, he is apt to drop the traditional appeal to female Muses and think of himself as in a feminine, or at least receptive, relation to some god or lord, whether Apollo, Dionysus, Eros, Christ, or (as in Milton) the Holy Spirit. Est *deus* in nobis, Ovid says:

'n modern times we may compare Nietzsche's remarks about his inspiration in *Ecce Homo*.

The problem of convention is the problem of how art can be communicable, for literature is clearly as much a technique of communication as assertive verbal structures are. Poetry, taken as a whole, is no longer simply an aggregate of artifacts imitating nature, but one of the activities of human artifice taken as a whole. If we may use the word "civilization" for this, we may say that our fourth phase looks at poetry as one of the techniques of civilization. It is concerned, therefore, with the social aspect of poetry, with poetry as the focus of a community. The symbol in this phase is the communicable unit, to which I give the name archetype: that is, a typical or recurring image. I mean by an archetype a symbol which connects one poem with another and thereby helps to unify and integrate our literary experience. And as the archetype is the communicable symbol, archetypal criticism is primarily concerned with literature as a social fact and as a mode of communication. By the study of conventions and genres, it attempts to fit poems into the body of poetry as a whole.

The repetition of certain common images of physical nature like the sea or the forest in a large number of poems cannot in itself be called even "coincidence," which is the name we give to a piece of design when we cannot find a use for it. But it does indicate a certain unity in the nature that poetry imitates, and in the communicating activity of which poetry forms part. Because of the larger communicative context of education, it is possible for a story about the sea to be archetypal, to make a profound imaginative impact, on a reader who has never been out of Saskatchewan. And when pastoral images are deliberately employed in *Lycidas*, for instance, merely because they are conventional, we can see that the convention of the pastoral makes us assimilate these images to other parts of literary experience.

We think first of the pastoral's descent from Theocritus, where the pastoral elegy first appears as a literary adaptation of the ritual of the Adonis lament, and through Theocritus to Virgil and the whole pastoral tradition to *The Shepheardes Calender* and beyond to *Lycidas* itself. Then we think of the intricate pastoral symbolism of the Bible and the Christian Church, of Abel and the twenty-third Psalm and Christ the Good Shepherd, of the ecclesiastical overtones of "pastor" and "flock," and of the link between the Classical

99

and Christian traditions in Virgil's Messianic Eclogue. Then we think of the extensions of pastoral symbolism into Sidney's *Arcadia*, *The Faerie Queene*, Shakespeare's forest comedies, and the like; then of the post-Miltonic development of pastoral elegy in Shelley, Arnold, Whitman, and Dylan Thomas; perhaps too of pastoral conventions in painting and music. In short, we can get a whole liberal education simply by picking up one conventional poem and following its archetypes as they stretch out into the rest of literature. An avowedly conventional poem like *Lycidas* urgently demands the kind of criticism that will absorb it into the study of literature as a whole, and this activity is expected to begin at once, with the first cultivated reader. Here we have a situation in literature more like that of mathematics or science, where the work of genius is assimilated to the whole subject so quickly that one hardly notices the difference between creative and critical activity.

If we do not accept the archetypal or conventional element in the imagery that links one poem with another, it is impossible to get any systematic mental training out of the reading of literature alone. But if we add to our desire to know literature a desire to know how we know it, we shall find that expanding images into conventional archetypes of literature is a process that takes place unconsciously in all our reading. A symbol like the sea or the heath cannot remain within Conrad or Hardy: it is bound to expand over many works into an archetypal symbol of literature as a whole. Moby Dick cannot remain in Melville's novel: he is absorbed into our imaginative experience of leviathans and dragons of the deep from the Old Testament onward. And what is true for the reader is *a fortiori* true of the poet, who learns very quickly that there is no singing school for his soul except the study of the monuments of its own magnificence.

In each phase of symbolism there is a point at which the critic is compelled to break away from the range of the poet's own knowledge. Thus the historical or documentary critic has sooner or later to call Dante a "medieval" poet, a notion unknown and unintelligible to Dante. In archetypal criticism, the poet's conscious knowledge is considered only so far as the poet may allude to or imitate other poets ("sources") or make a deliberate use of a convention. Beyond that, the poet's control over his poem stops with the poem. Only the archetypal critic can be concerned with its relationship to the rest of literature. But here again we have to distinguish between explicitly conventionalized literature, such as *Lycidas*, where the poet himself starts us off by referring to Theocritus, Virgil, Renaissance pastoralists, and the Bible, and literature which conceals or ignores its conventional links. The conception of copyright and the revolutionary nature of the low mimetic view of creation also extends to a general unwillingness on the part of authors of the copyright age to have their imagery studied conventionally, and in dealing with this period, most archetypes have to be established by critical inspection alone.

To give a random example, one very common convention of the nineteenth-century novel is the use of two heroines, one dark and one light. The dark one is as a rule passionate, haughty, plain, foreign or Jewish, and in some way associated with the undesirable or with some kind of forbidden fruit like incest. When the two are involved with the same hero, the plot usually has to get rid of the dark one or make her into a sister if the story is to end happily. Examples include *Ivanhoe, The Last of the Mohicans, The Woman in White, Ligeia, Pierre* (a tragedy because the hero chooses the dark girl, who is also his sister), *The Marble Faun*, and countless incidental treatments. A male version forms the symbolic basis of *Wuthering Heights*. This device is as much a convention as Milton's calling Edward King by a name out of Virgil's *Eclogues*, but it shows a confused, or, as we say, "unconscious" approach to conventions. Again, when we meet the images of a man, a woman, and a serpent in the ninth book of *Paradise Lost*, there is no doubt of their conventional links with similar figures in the Book of Genesis. In Hudson's *Green Mansions* the hero and heroine first meet over a serpent in a quasi-Paradisal setting: here the conventional nature of the imagery is a matter on which the author gives us no help. When a critic meets St. George the Redcross Knight in Spenser, bearing a red cross on a white ground, he has some idea what to do with this figure. When he meets a female in Henry James's *The Other House* called Rose Armiger with a white dress and a red parasol, he is, in the current slang, clueless. It is clear that a deficiency in contemporary education often complained of, the disappearance of a common cultural ground which makes a modern poet's allusions to the Bible or to Classical mythology fall with less weight than they should, has much to do with the decline in the explicit use of archetypes.

Whitman, as is well known, was a spokesman of an anti-archetypal view of literature, and urged the Muse to forget the matter of Troy and develop new themes. This is a low mimetic prejudice, and is consequently appropriate enough for Whitman, who is both right and wrong. He is wrong because the matter of Troy will always be, in the foreseeable future, an integral part of the Western cultural heritage, and hence references to Agamemnon in Yeats's *Leda* or Eliot's *Sweeney among the Nightingales* have as much cumulative power as ever for the properly instructed reader. But he is of course perfectly right in feeling that the *content* of poetry is normally an immediate and contemporary environment. He was right, being the kind of poet he was, in making the content of his own *When Lilacs Last in the Dooryard Bloomed* an elegy on Lincoln and not a conventional Adonis lament. Yet his elegy is, in its *form*, as conventional as *Lycidas*, complete with purple flowers thrown on coffins, a great star drooping in the west, imagery of "ever-returning spring" and all the rest of it. Poetry organizes the content of the world as it passes before the poet, but the forms in which that content is organized come out of the structure of poetry itself.

Archetypes are associative clusters, and differ from signs in being complex variables. Within the complex is often a large number of specific learned associations which are communicable because a large number of people in a given culture happen to be familiar with them. When we speak of "symbolism" in ordinary life we usually think of such learned cultural archetypes as the cross or the crown, or of conventional associations, as of white with purity or green with jealousy. As an archetype, green may symbolize hope or vegetable nature or a go sign in traffic or Irish patriotism as easily as jealousy, but the word green as a verbal sign always refers to a certain color. Some archetypes are so deeply rooted in conventional association that they can hardly avoid suggesting that association, as the geometrical figure of the cross inevitably suggests the death of Christ. A *completely* conventionalized art would be an art in which the archetypes, or communicable units, were essentially a set of esoteric signs. This can happen in the arts—for instance in some of the sacred dances of India—but it has not happened in Western literature yet, and the resistance of modern writers to having their archetypes "spotted," so to speak, is due to a natural anxiety to keep them as versatile as possible, not pinned down exclusively to one interpretation. A poet may be showing an esoteric tendency if he specifically points out one association, as Yeats does in his footnotes to some of his early poems. There are no *necessary* associations: there are some exceedingly obvious ones, such as the association of darkness with terror or mystery, but there are no intrinsic or inherent correspondences which must invariably be present. As we shall see later, there is a context in which the phrase "universal symbol" makes sense, but it is not this context. The stream of literature, however, like any other stream, seeks the easiest channels first: the poet who uses the expected associations will communicate more rapidly.

At one extreme of literature we have the pure convention, which a poet uses merely because it has often been used before in the same way. This is most frequent in naive poetry, in the fixed epithets and phrase-tags of medieval romance and ballad, in the invariable plots and character types of naive drama, and, to a lesser degree, in the *topoi* or rhetorical commonplaces which, like other ideas in literature, are so dull when stated as propositions, and so rich and variegated when they are used as structural principles in literature. At the other extreme we have the pure variable, where there is a deliberate attempt at novelty or unfamiliarity, and consequently a disguising or complicating of archetypes. Such techniques come very close to a distrust of communication itself as a function of literature. However, extremes meet, as Coleridge said, and anti-conventional poetry soon becomes a convention in its turn, to be explored by hardy scholars accustomed to the dreariness of literary bad lands. Between these extreme points conventions vary from the most explicit to the most indirect, along a scale parallel to the scale of allegory and paradox already dealt with. The two scales may be often confused or identified, but translating imagery into examples and precepts is a quite distinct process from following images into other poems.

Near the extreme of pure convention is translation, paraphrase, and the kind of use which Chaucer makes of Boccaccio in *Troilus* and *The Knight's Tale*. Next we come to deliberate and explicit convention, such as we have noted in *Lycidas*. Next comes paradoxical or ironic convention, including parody—often a sign that certain vogues in handling conventions are getting worn out. Then comes the attempt to reach originality through turning one's back on explicit convention, an attempt which results in implicit convention of the kind we detected in Whitman. Then comes a tendency to identify originality with "experimental" writing, based in our day on an analogy with scientific discovery, and which is frequently spoken of as "breaking with convention." And, of course, at every stage of literature, including this last one, there is a great deal of superficial and inorganic convention, producing the kind of writing that most students of literature prefer to keep in the middle distance: run-of-the-mill Elizabethan sonnets and love lyrics, Plautine comedy-formulas, eighteenth-century pastorals, nineteenth-century happy-ending novels, works of followers and disciples and schools and trends generally.

It is clear from all this that archetypes are most easily studied in highly conventionalized literature: that is, for the most part, naive, primitive, and popular literature. In suggesting the possibility of archetypal criticism, then, I am suggesting the possibility of extending the kind of comparative and morphological study now made of folk tales and ballads into the rest of literature. This should be more easily conceivable now that it is no longer fashionable to mark off popular and primitive literature from ordinary literature as sharply as we used to do. Also, we shall find that superficial literature, of the kind just spoken of, is of great value to archetypal criticism simply because it is conventional. If throughout this book I refer to popular fiction as frequently as to the greatest novels and epics, it is for the same reason that a musician attempting to explain the rudimentary facts about counterpoint would be more likely, at least at first, to illustrate from "Three Blind Mice" than from a complex Bach fugue.

Every phase of symbolism has its particular approach to narrative and to meaning. In the literal phase, narrative is a flow of significant sounds, and meaning an ambiguous and complex verbal pattern. In the descriptive phase, narrative is an imitation of real events, and meaning an imitation of actual objects or propositions. In the formal phase, poetry exists between the example and the precept. In the exemplary event there is an element of *recurrence*; in the precept, or statement about what ought to be, there is a strong element of *desire*, or what is called "wish-thinking." These elements of recurrence and desire come into the foreground in archetypal criticism, which studies poems as units of poetry as a whole and symbols as units of communication.

From such a point of view, the narrative aspect of literature is a recurrent act of symbolic communication: in other words a ritual. Narrative is studied by the archetypal critic as ritual or imitation of human action as a whole, and not simply as a *mimesis praxeos* or imitation of *an* action. Similarly, in archetypal criticism the significant content is the conflict of desire and reality which has for its basis the work of the dream. Ritual and dream, therefore, are the narrative and significant content respectively of literature in its archetypal aspect. The archetypal analysis of the plot of a novel or play would deal with it in terms of the generic, recurring, or conventional actions which show analogies to rituals: the weddings, funerals, intellectual and social initiations, executions or mock executions, the chasing away of the scapegoat villain, and so on. The archetypal analysis of the meaning or significance of such a work would deal with it in terms of the generic, recurring, or conventional shape indicated by its mood and resolution, whether tragic, comic, ironic, or what not, in which the relationship of desire and experience is expressed.

Recurrence and desire interpenetrate, and are equally important in both ritual and dream. In its archetypal phase, the poem imitates nature, not (as in the formal phase) nature as a structure or system, but nature as a cyclical process. The principle of recurrence in the rhythm of art seems to be derived from the repetitions in nature that make time intelligible to us. Rituals cluster around the cyclical movements of the sun, the moon, the seasons, and human life. Every crucial periodicity of experience: dawn, sunset, the phases of the moon, seed-time and harvest, the equinoxes and the solstices, birth, initiation, marriage, and death, get rituals attached to them. The pull of ritual is toward pure cyclical narrative, which, if there could be such a thing, would be automatic and unconscious repetition. In the middle of all this recurrence, however, is the central recurrent cycle of sleeping and waking life, the daily frustration of the ego, the nightly awakening of a titanic self.

The archetypal critic studies the poem as part of poetry, and poetry as part of the total human imitation of nature that we call civilization. Civilization is not merely an imitation of nature, but the process of making a total human form out of nature, and it is impelled by the force that we have just called desire. The desire for food and shelter is not content with roots and caves: it produces the human forms of nature that we call farming and architecture. Desire is thus not a simple response to need, for an animal may need food without planting a garden to get it, nor is it a simple response to want, or desire *for* something in particular. It is neither limited to nor satisfied by objects, but is the energy that leads human society to develop its own form. Desire in this sense is the social aspect of what we met on the literal level as emotion, an impulse toward expression which would have remained amorphous if the poem had not liberated it by providing the form of its expression. The form of desire, similarly, is liberated and made apparent by civilization. The efficient cause of civilization is work, and poetry in its social aspect has the function of expressing, as a verbal hypothesis, a vision of the goal of work and the forms of desire.

There is however a moral dialectic in desire. The conception of a garden develops the conception "weed," and building a sheepfold makes the wolf a greater enemy. Poetry in its social or archetypal aspect, therefore, not only tries to illustrate the fulfilment of desire, but to define the obstacles to it. Ritual is not only a recurrent act, but an act expressive of a dialectic of desire and repugnance: desire for fertility or victory, repugnance to drought or to enemies. We have rituals of social integration, and we have rituals of expulsion, execution, and punishment. In dream there is a parallel dialectic, as there is both the wish-fulfilment dream and the anxiety or nightmare dream of repugnance. Archetypal criticism, therefore, rests on two organizing rhythms or patterns, one cyclical, the other dialectic.

The union of ritual and dream in a form of verbal communication is myth. This is a sense of the term myth slightly different from that used in the previous essay. But, first, the sense is equally familiar, and the ambiguity not mine but the dictionary's; and, second, there is a real connection between the two senses which will become more apparent as we go on. The myth accounts for, and makes communicable, the ritual and the dream. Ritual, by itself, cannot account for itself: it is pre-logical, pre-verbal, and in a sense pre-human. Its attachment to the calendar seems to link human life to the biological dependence on the natural cycle which plants, and to some extent animals, still have. Everything in nature that we think of as having some analogy with works of art, like the flower or the bird's song, grows out of a synchronization between an organism and the rhythms of its natural environment, especially that of the solar year. With animals some expressions of synchronization, like the mating dances of birds, could almost be called rituals. Myth is more distinctively human, as the most intelligent partridge cannot tell even the most absurd story explaining why it drums in the mating season. Similarly, the dream, by itself, is a system of cryptic allusions to the dreamer's own life, not fully understood by him, or so far as we know of any real use to him. But in all dreams there is a mythical element which has a power of independent communication, as is obvious, not only in the stock example of Oedipus, but in any collection of folk tales. Myth, therefore, not only gives meaning to ritual and narrative to dream: it is the identification of ritual and dream, in which the former is seen to be the latter in movement. This would not be possible unless there were a common factor to ritual and dream which made one the social expression of the other; the investigation of this common factor we must leave for later treatment. All that we need to say here is that ritual is the archetypal aspect of *mythos* and dream the archetypal aspect of *dianoia*.

The same distinction in emphasis that we noted in the first essay between fictional and thematic literature recurs here. Some literary forms, such as drama, remind us with particular vividness of analogies to rituals, for the drama in literature, like the ritual in religion, is primarily a social or ensemble performance. Others, such as romance, suggest analogies to dreams. Ritual analogies are most easily seen, not in the drama of the educated audience and the settled theatre, but in naive or spectacular drama: in the folk play, the puppet show, the pantomime, the farce, the pageant, and their descendants in masque, comic opera, commercial movie, and revue. Dream analogies are best studied in naive romance, which includes the folk tales and fairy tales that are so closely related to dreams of wonderful wishes coming true, and to nightmares of ogres and witches. Naive drama and naive romance, of course, also interpenetrate. What naive drama dramatizes is usually some kind of romance, and the close relation of romance to ritual can be seen in the number of medieval romances that are linked to some part of the calendar, the winter solstice, a May morning, or a saint's eve; or else to some class ritual like the tournament. The fact that the archetype is primarily a *communicable* symbol largely accounts for the ease with which ballads and folk tales and mimes travel through the world, like so many of their heroes, over all barriers of language and culture. We come back here to the fact that literature most deeply influenced by the archetypal phase of symbolism impresses us as primitive and popular.

By these words I mean possessing the ability to communicate in time and space respectively. Otherwise they mean much the same thing. Popular art is normally decried as vulgar by the cultivated people of its time; then it loses favor with its original audience as a new generation grows up; then it begins to merge into the softer lighting of "quaint," and cultivated people become interested in it, and finally it begins to take on the archaic dignity of the primitive. This sense of the archaic recurs whenever we find great art using popular forms, as Shakespeare does in his last period, or as the Bible does when it ends in a fairy tale about a damsel in distress, a hero killing dragons, a wicked witch, and a wonderful city glittering with jewels. Archaism is a regular feature of all social uses of archetypes. Soviet Russia is very proud of its production of tractors, but it will be some time before the tractor replaces the sickle on the Soviet flag.

It is at this point that we must notice and avoid the fallacy of a theory of mythological contract. That is, there may be such a thing as a social contract in political theory, if we keep the discussion to observable facts about the present structure of society. But when these facts are attached to a fable about something that happened in a past too remote for any evidence to disturb the fabler's assertions, and we are told that once upon a time men surrendered or delegated or were tricked into surrendering their power, political theory has merely become one of Plato's indoctrinating lies. And because the only evidence for this remote event is its analogy to the present facts, the present facts are being compared with their own shadows. A precisely similar fabling process has taken place in the literary criticism concerned with myth, which has hardly yet emerged from its historical contract stage.

As the archetypal critic is concerned with ritual and dream, it is likely that he would find much of interest in the work done by contemporary anthropology in ritual, and by contemporary psychology in dreams. Specifically, the work done on the ritual basis of naive drama in Frazer's *Golden Bough*, and the work done on the dream basis of naive romance by Jung and the Jungians, are of most direct value to him. But the three subjects of anthropology, psychology, and literary criticism are not yet clearly separated, and the danger of determinism has to be carefully watched. To the

108

literary critic, ritual is the *content* of dramatic action, not the source or origin of it. *The Golden Bough* is, from the point of view of literary criticism, an essay on the ritual content of naive drama: that is, it reconstructs an archetypal ritual from which the structural and generic principles of drama may be logically, not chronologically, derived. It does not matter two pins to the literary critic whether such a ritual had any historical existence or not. It is very probable that Frazer's hypothetical ritual would have many and striking analogies to actual rituals, and collecting such analogies is part of his argument. But an analogy is not necessarily a source, an influence, a cause, or an embryonic form, much less an identity. The *literary* relation of ritual to drama, like that of any other aspect of human action to drama, is a relation of content to form only, not one of source to derivation.

The critic, therefore, is concerned only with the ritual or dream patterns which are actually in what he is studying, however they got there. The work of the Classical scholars who have followed Frazer's lead has produced a general theory of the spectacular or ritual content of Greek drama. *The Golden Bough* purports to be a work of anthropology, but it has had more influence on literary criticism than in its own alleged field, and it may yet prove to be really a work of literary criticism. If the ritual pattern is in the plays—and it is fact, not opinion, that one of the main themes of *Iphigeneia in Tauris*, for example, is human sacrifice—the critic need not take sides in the quite separate historical controversy over the ritual *origin* of Greek drama. Hence ritual, as the content of action, and more particularly of dramatic action, is something continuously latent in the order of words, and is quite independent of direct influence. Even in the nineteenth century, we find that the instant drama becomes primitive and popular, as it does in *The Mikado*, to repeat an example given before, back comes all Frazer's apparatus, the king's son, the mock sacrifice, the analogy with the festival of the Sacaea, and many other things that Gilbert knew and cared nothing about. It comes back because it is still the best way of holding an audience's attention, and the experienced dramatist knows it.

The prestige of documentary criticism, which deals entirely with sources and historical transmission, has misled some archetypal critics into feeling that all such ritual elements ought to be traced directly, like the lineage of royalty, as far back as a willing sus-

pension of disbelief will allow. The vast chronological gaps resulting are usually bridged by some theory of race memory, or by
some conspiratorial conception of history involving secrets jealously
guarded for centuries by esoteric cults or traditions. It is curious
that when archetypal critics hang on to a historical framework
they almost invariably produce some hypothesis of continuous de-
generation from a golden age lost in antiquity. Thus the prelude
to Thomas Mann's Joseph series traces back several of our central
myths to Atlantis, Atlantis being clearly more useful as an archetypal idea than as a historical one. When archetypal criticism revived in the nineteenth century with a vogue for sun myths, an
attempt was made to ridicule it by proving with equal plausibility
that Napoleon was a sun myth. The ridicule is effective only
against the historical distortion of the method. Archetypally, we
turn Napoleon into a sun myth whenever we speak of the rise of
his career, the zenith of his fame, or the eclipse of his fortunes.

Social and cultural history, which is anthropology in an extended sense, will always be a part of the context of criticism, and
the more clearly the anthropological and the critical treatments of
ritual are distinguished, the more beneficial their influence on
each other will be. The same is true of the relation of psychology
to criticism. The first and most striking unit of poetry larger than
the individual poem is the total work of the man who wrote the
poem. Biography will always be a part of criticism, and the biog-
rapher will naturally be interested in his subject's poetry as a personal document, recording his private dreams, associations, ambitions, and expressed or repressed desires. Studies of such matters
form an essential part of criticism. I am not of course speaking
of the silly ones, which simply project the author's own erotica,
in a rationalized clinical disguise, on his victim, but only of the
serious studies which are technically competent both in psychology
and in criticism, which are aware how much guesswork is involved
and how tentative all the conclusions must be.

Such an approach is easiest, and most rewarding, with what we
have called thematic writers of the low mimetic—that is, chiefly,
the Romantic poets, where the poet's own psychological processes
are often part of the theme. With other writers, say a dramatist
who is aware from the first word he writes that "They who live
to please must please to live," there is danger of making an unreal
abstraction of the poet from his literary community. Suppose a

critic finds that a certain pattern is repeated time and again in the plays of Shakespeare. If Shakespeare is unique or anomalous, or even exceptional, in using this pattern, the reason for his use of it may be at least partly psychological. If there were any evidence that he had persisted in using it when it failed to please an audience, the probability of a personal psychological element would be very high. But if we can find the same pattern in half a dozen of his contemporaries, we clearly have to allow for convention. And if we find it in a dozen dramatists of different ages and cultures, we have to allow for genre, for the structural requirements of drama itself. Now as a matter of fact we do find in Shakespeare's comedies that the same devices are used over and over, and it is the business of the literary critic to compare these devices with those of other dramatists, in a morphological study of comic form. Otherwise we shall deprive ourselves of the perfectly legitimate appreciation of the *scholarly* qualities of Shakespeare, of seeing in the repeated devices of his comedies a kind of Art of Fugue of comedy.

A psychologist examining a poem will tend to see in it what he sees in the dream, a mixture of latent and manifest content. For the literary critic the manifest content of the poem is its form, hence its latent content becomes simply its actual content, its *dianoia* or theme. And this *dianoia* on the archetypal level is a dream, a presentation of the conflict of desire and actuality. We seem to be going around in a circle, but not quite. For the critic, a problem appears which does not exist for a purely psychological analysis, the problem of communicable latent content, of intelligible dream, Plato's conception of art as a dream for awakened minds. For the psychologist all dream symbols are private ones, interpreted by the personal life of the dreamer. For the critic there is no such thing as private symbolism, or, if there is, it is his job to make sure that it does not remain so.

This problem is already present in Freud's treatment of *Oedipus Tyrannus* as a play which owes much of its power to the fact that it dramatizes the Oedipus complex. The dramatic and psychological elements can be linked without any reference to the personal life of Sophocles, of which we know nothing whatever. This emphasis on impersonal content has been developed by Jung and his school, where the communicability of archetypes is accounted for by a theory of a collective unconscious—an unnecessary hypothesis in literary criticism, so far as I can judge.

What we have found to be true of the writer's intention is also true of the audience's attention. Both are centripetally directed, and implications exist in the response to art as they do in the creation of it, implications of which the audience is not explicitly aware. Discrete conscious awareness can take in only a very few details of the complex of response. This state of things enabled Tennyson, for instance, to be praised for the chastity of his language and read for his powerful erotic sensuousness. It also makes it possible for a contemporary critic to draw on the fullest resources of modern knowledge in explicating a work of art without any real fear of anachronism.

For instance, *Le Malade Imaginaire* is a play about a man who, in seventeenth-century terms, including no doubt Molière's own terms, was not really sick but just thought he was. A modern critic might object that life is not so simple: that it is perfectly possible for a *malade imaginaire* to be a *malade véritable,* and that what is wrong with Argan is clearly an unwillingness to see his children grow up, an infantile regression which his wife—his second wife, incidentally—shows that she understands completely by coddling him and murmuring such phrases as "pauvre petit fils." Such a critic would find the clue to Argan's whole behavior in his unguarded remark after the scene with the little girl Louison (the erotic nature of which the critic would also notice): "Il n'y a plus d'enfants." Now whether this reading is right or wrong, it does not swerve from Molière's text, yet it tells us nothing about Molière himself. The play is generically a comedy; it must therefore end happily; Argan must therefore be brought to see some reason; his wife, whose dramatic function it is to keep him within his obsession, must therefore be "exposed" as inimical to him. The plot is a ritual moving toward a scapegoat rejection followed by a marriage, and the theme is a dream-pattern of irrational desire in conflict with reality.

Another essay in this book will be concerned with the details and practice of archetypal criticism: here we are concerned only with its place in the context of criticism as a whole. In its archetypal aspect, art is a part of civilization, and civilization we defined as the process of making a human form out of nature. The shape of this human form is revealed by civilization itself as it develops: its major components are the city, the garden, the farm, the sheepfold, and the like, as well as human society itself. An archetypal symbol is usually a natural object with a human meaning, and it forms part of the critical view of art as a civilized product, a vision of the goals of human work.

Such a vision is bound to idealize some aspects of civilization and ridicule or ignore others; in other words the social context of art is also the moral context. All artists have to come to terms with their communities: many artists, and many great ones, are content to be the spokesmen of them. But in terms of his moral significance, the poet reflects, and follows at a distance, what his community really achieves through its work. Hence the moral view of the artist is invariably that he ought to assist the work of his society by framing workable hypotheses, imitating human action and thought in such a way as to suggest realizable modes of both. If he does not do this, his hypotheses should at least be clearly labelled as playful or fantastic. Marxism takes more or less this view of art, and thereby repeats the argument reached at the end of the *Republic*. We are told there, if we follow the argument simply as it stands, that according to justice, or social work properly done, the painter's bed is an external imitation of the craftsman's bed. The artist, therefore, is confined either to reflecting or to escaping from the world that the true worker is realizing.

We have adopted the principle in this essay that the events and ideas of poetry are hypothetical imitations of history and discursive writing respectively, which in their turn are verbal imitations of action and thought. This principle brings us close to the view of poetry as a secondary imitation of reality. We are interpreting mimesis, however, not as a Platonic "recollection" but as an emancipation of externality into image, nature into art. From this point of view the work of art must be its own object: it cannot be ultimately descriptive of something, and can never be ultimately related to any other system of phenomena, standards, values, or final causes. All such external relations form part of the "intentional fallacy." Poetry is a vehicle for morality, truth, and beauty, but the poet does not aim at these things, but only at inner verbal strength. The poet *qua* poet intends only to write a poem, and as a rule it is not the artist, but the ego in the artist, who turns away from his proper work to go and chase these other seductive marshlights.

It is an elementary axiom in criticism that morally the lion lies down with the lamb. Bunyan and Rochester, Sade and Jane Austen, *The Miller's Tale* and *The Second Nun's Tale*, are all equally elements of a liberal education, and the only moral criterion to be applied to them is that of decorum. Similarly, the moral attitude taken by the poet in his work derives largely from the structure of that work. Thus the fact that *Le Malade Imaginaire* is a comedy is the only reason for making Argan's wife a hypocrite—she must be got rid of to make the play end happily.

The pursuit of beauty is much more dangerous nonsense than the pursuit of truth or goodness, because it affords a stronger temptation to the ego. Beauty, like truth and goodness, is a quality that may in one sense be predicated of all great art, but the deliberate attempt to beautify can, in itself, only weaken the creative energy. Beauty in art is like happiness in morals: it may accompany the act, but it cannot be the goal of the act, just as one cannot "pursue happiness," but only something else that may give happiness. Aiming at beauty produces, at best, the attractive: the quality of beauty represented by the word loveliness, a quality which depends on a carefully restricted choice of both subject and technique. A religious painter, for instance, can produce this quality only as long as churches keep commissioning Madonnas: if a church asks for a Crucifixion he must paint cruelty and horror instead.

When we speak of the human body as "beautiful," we usually mean the body of someone in good physical condition between eighteen and about thirty, and if Degas, for example, shows us pictures of thick-bottomed matrons squatting in hip baths, we interpret the shock to our propriety as an aesthetic judgement. Whenever the word beauty means loveliness or attractiveness, as it is bound to do whenever it is made the intention of art, it becomes reactionary: it tries to restrict either what the artist may choose for a subject or the method in which he may choose to treat it, and it marshals all the forces of prudery to keep him from expanding his vision beyond an arid and insipid pseudo-classicism. Ruskin spoiled many of his finest critical insights with this fallacy; Tennyson often hampered the vigor of his poetry by it, and in some of the lesser beauticians of the same period we can see clearly what the neurotic compulsion to beautify everything leads to. It

leads to an exaggerated cult of style, a technique of making everything in a work of art, even a drama, sound all alike, and like the
author, and like the author at his most impressive. Here again the
vanity of the ego has replaced the honest pride of the craftsman.

The formal or third phase of narrative and meaning, although
it includes the external relations of literature to events and ideas,
nevertheless brings us back ultimately to the aesthetic view of the
work of art as an object of contemplation, a *techne* designed for
ornament and pleasure rather than use. This view encourages us
to separate aesthetic objects from other kinds of artifacts and to
postulate an aesthetic experience different in kind from other
experiences. Corresponding to the bibliographical view of literature as the aggregate or pile of all the books and plays and poems
that have been written, we find the aesthetic view of criticism as a
discrete series of special (sometimes vaguely sacramental) appre-
hensions. There is no reason for not granting this view of literary
experience its own validity; one objects to it only when it excludes
other approaches.

The archetypal view of literature shows us literature as a total
form and literary experience as a part of the continuum of life,
in which one of the poet's functions is to visualize the goals of
human work. As soon as we add this approach to the other three,
literature becomes an ethical instrument, and we pass beyond
Kierkegaard's "Either/Or" dilemma between aesthetic idolatry
and ethical freedom, without any temptation to dispose of the
arts in the process. Hence the importance, after accepting the
validity of this view of literature, of rejecting the external goals of
morality, beauty, and truth. The fact that they are external makes
them ultimately idolatrous, and so demonic. But if no social, moral,
or aesthetic standard is in the long run externally determinative of
the value of art, it follows that the archetypal phase, in which art
is part of civilization, cannot be the ultimate one. We need still
another phase where we can pass from civilization, where poetry
is still useful and functional, to culture, where it is disinterested
and liberal, and stands on its own feet.

ANAGOGIC PHASE: SYMBOL AS MONAD

In tracing the different phases of literary symbolism, we have
been going up a sequence parallel to that of medieval criticism.
We have, it is true, established a different meaning for the word

115

"literal." It is our second or descriptive level that corresponds to the historical or literal one of the medieval scheme, or at any rate of Dante's version of it. Our third level, the level of commentary and interpretation, is the second or allegorical level of the Middle Ages. Our fourth level, the study of myths, and of poetry as a technique of social communication, is the third medieval level of moral and tropological meaning, concerned at once with the social and the figurative aspect of meaning. The medieval distinction between the allegorical as what one believes (*quid credas*) and the moral as what one does (*quid agas*) is also reflected in our conception of the formal phase as aesthetic or speculative and the archetypal phase as social and part of the continuum of work. We have now to see if we can establish a modern parallel to the medieval conception of anagogy or universal meaning.

Again, the reader may have noticed a parallelism gradually shaping up between the five modes of our first essay and the phases of symbolism in this one. Literal meaning, as we expounded it, has much to do with the techniques of thematic irony introduced by *symbolisme*, and with the view of many of the "new" critics that poetry is primarily (i.e., literally) an ironic structure. Descriptive symbolism, shown at its most uncompromising in the documentary naturalism of the nineteenth century, seems to bear a close connection with the low mimetic, and formal symbolism, most easily studied in Renaissance and neo-Classical writers, with the high mimetic. Archetypal criticism seems to find its center of gravity in the mode of romance, when the interchange of ballads, folk tales, and popular stories was at its easiest. If the parallel holds, then, the last phase of symbolism will still be concerned, as the previous one was, with the mythopoeic aspect of literature, but with myth in its narrower and more technical sense of fictions and themes relating to divine or quasi-divine beings and powers.

We have associated archetypes and myths particularly with primitive and popular literature. In fact we could almost define popular literature, admittedly in a rather circular way, as literature which affords an unobstructed view of archetypes. We can find this quality on every level of literature: in fairy tales and folk tales, in Shakespeare (in most of the comedies), in the Bible (which would still be a popular book if it were not a sacred one), in Bunyan, in Richardson, in Dickens, in Poe, and of course in a vast amount of ephemeral rubbish as well. We began this book by remarking that we cannot correlate popularity and value. But there is still the danger of reduction, or assuming that literature is *essentially* primitive and popular. This view had a great vogue in the nineteenth century, and is by no means dead yet, but if we were to adopt it we should cut off a third and most important source of supply for archetypal criticism.

We notice that many learned and recondite writers whose work requires patient study are explicitly mythopoeic writers. Instances include Dante and Spenser, and in the twentieth century embrace nearly all the "difficult" writers in both poetry and prose. Such work, when fictional, is often founded on a basis of naive drama (*Faust, Peer Gynt*) or naive romance (Hawthorne, Melville: one may compare the sophisticated allegories of Charles Williams and C. S. Lewis in our day, which are largely based on the formulas of the Boy's Own Paper). Learned mythopoeia, as we have it in the last period of Henry James and in James Joyce, for example, may become bewilderingly complex; but the complexities are designed to reveal and not to disguise the myth. We cannot assume that a primitive and popular myth has been swathed like a mummy in elaborate verbiage, which is the assumption that the fallacy of reduction would lead to. The inference seems to be that the learned and the subtle, like the primitive and the popular, tend toward a center of imaginative experience.

Knowing that *The Two Gentlemen of Verona* is an early Shakespeare comedy and *The Winter's Tale* a late one, the student would expect the later play to be more subtle and complex; he might not expect it to be more archaic and primitive, more suggestive of ancient myths and rituals. The later play is also more popular, though not popular of course in the sense of giving a lower-middle class audience what it thinks it wants. As a result of expressing the inner forms of drama with increasing force and intensity, Shakespeare arrived in his last period at the bedrock of drama, the romantic spectacle out of which all the more specialized forms of drama, such as tragedy and social comedy, have come, and to which they recurrently return. In the greatest moments of Dante and Shakespeare, in, say *The Tempest* or the climax of the *Purgatorio*, we have a feeling of converging significance, the feeling that here we are close to seeing what our whole literary experience has been about, the feeling that we have moved into the still center of the order of words. Criticism as knowledge, the criticism which is

117

compelled to keep on talking about the subject, recognizes the fact that there *is* a center of the order of words.

Unless there is such a center, there is nothing to prevent the analogies supplied by convention and genre from being an endless series of free associations, perhaps suggestive, perhaps even tantalizing, but never creating a real structure. The study of archetypes is the study of literary symbols as parts of a whole. If there are such things as archetypes at all, then, we have to take yet another step, and conceive the possibility of a self-contained literary universe. Either archetypal criticism is a will-o'-the-wisp, an endless labyrinth without an outlet, or we have to assume that literature is a total form, and not simply the name given to the aggregate of existing literary works. We spoke before of the mythical view of literature as leading to the conception of an order of nature as a whole being imitated by a corresponding order of words.

If archetypes are communicable symbols, and there is a center of archetypes, we should expect to find, at that center, a group of universal symbols. I do not mean by this phrase that there is any archetypal code book which has been memorized by all human societies without exception. I mean that some symbols are images of things common to all men, and therefore have a communicable power which is potentially unlimited. Such symbols include those of food and drink, of the quest or journey, of light and darkness, and of sexual fulfilment, which would usually take the form of marriage. It is inadvisable to assume that an Adonis or Oedipus myth is universal, or that certain associations, such as the serpent with the phallus, are universal, because when we discover a group of people who know nothing of such matters we must assume that they did know and have forgotten, or do know and won't tell, or are not members of the human race. On the other hand, they may be confidently excluded from the human race if they cannot understand the conception of food, and so any symbolism founded on food is universal in the sense of having an indefinitely extensive scope. That is, there are no limits to its intelligibility.

In the archetypal phase the work of literary art is a myth, and unites the ritual and the dream. By doing so it limits the dream: it makes it plausible and acceptable to a social waking consciousness. Thus as a moral fact in civilization, literature embodies a good deal of the spirit which in the dream itself is called the censor. But the censor stands in the way of the impetus of the dream.

When we look at the dream as a whole, we notice three things about it. First, its limits are not the real, but the conceivable. Second, the limit of the conceivable is the world of fulfilled desire emancipated from all anxieties and frustrations. Third, the universe of the dream is entirely within the mind of the dreamer.

In the anagogic phase, literature imitates the total dream of man, and so imitates the thought of a human mind which is at the circumference and not at the center of its reality. We see here the completion of the imaginative revolution begun when we passed from the descriptive to the formal phase of symbolism. There, the imitation of nature shifted from a reflection of external nature to a formal organization of which nature was the content. But in the formal phase the poem is still contained by nature, and in the archetypal phase the whole of poetry is still contained within the limits of the natural, or plausible. When we pass into anagogy, nature becomes, not the container, but the thing contained, and the archetypal universal symbols, the city, the garden, the quest, the marriage, are no longer the desirable forms that man constructs inside nature, but are themselves the forms of nature. Nature is now inside the mind of an infinite man who builds his cities out of the Milky Way. This is not reality, but it is the conceivable or imaginative limit of desire, which is infinite, eternal, and hence apocalyptic. By an apocalypse I mean primarily the imaginative conception of the whole of nature as the content of an infinite and eternal living body which, if not human, is closer to being human than to being inanimate. "The desire of man being infinite," said Blake, "the possession is infinite and himself infinite." If Blake is thought a prejudiced witness on this point, we may cite Hooker: "That there is somewhat higher than either of these two (sensual and intellectual perfection), no other proof doth need than the very process of man's desire, which being natural should be frustrate, if there were not some farther thing wherein it might rest at the length contented, which in the former it cannot do."

If we turn to ritual, we see there an imitation of nature which has a strong element of what we call magic in it. Magic seems to begin as something of a voluntary effort to recapture a lost rapport with the natural cycle. This sense of a deliberate recapturing of something no longer possessed is a distinctive mark of human ritual. Ritual constructs a calendar and endeavors to imitate the precise and sensitive accuracy of the movements of the heavenly bodies and the response of vegetation to them. A farmer must harvest his crop at a certain time of the year, but because he must do this anyway, harvesting itself is not precisely a ritual. It is the expression of a will to synchronize human and natural energies at that time which produces the harvest songs, harvest sacrifices, and harvest folk customs that we associate with ritual. But the impetus of the magical element in ritual is clearly toward a universe in which a stupid and indifferent nature is no longer the container of human society, but is contained by that society, and must rain or shine at the pleasure of man. We notice too the tendency of ritual to become not only cyclical but encyclopaedic, as already noted. In its anagogic phase, then, poetry imitates human action as total ritual, and so imitates the action of an omnipotent human society that contains all the powers of nature within itself.

Anagogically, then, poetry unites total ritual, or unlimited social action, with total dream, or unlimited individual thought. Its universe is infinite and boundless hypothesis: it cannot be contained within any actual civilization or set of moral values, for the same reason that no structure of imagery can be restricted to one allegorical interpretation. Here the *dianoia* of art is no longer a *mimesis logou*, but the Logos, the shaping word which is both reason and, as Goethe's Faust speculated, *praxis* or creative act. The *ethos* of art is no longer a group of characters within a natural setting, but a universal man who is also a divine being, or a divine being conceived in anthropomorphic terms.

The form of literature most deeply influenced by the anagogic phase is the scripture or apocalyptic revelation. The god, whether traditional deity, glorified hero, or apotheosized poet, is the central image that poetry uses in trying to convey the sense of unlimited power in a humanized form. Many of these scriptures are documents of religion as well, and hence are a mixture of the imaginative and the existential. When they lose their existential content they become purely imaginative, as Classical mythology did after the rise of Christianity. They belong in general, of course, to the mythical or theogonic mode. We see the relation to anagogy also in the vast encyclopaedic structure of poetry that seems to be a whole world in itself, that stands in its culture as an inexhaustible storehouse of imaginative suggestion, and seems, like theories of gravitation or relativity in the physical universe, to be applicable to, or have analogous connections with, every part of the literary universe. Such works are definitive myths, or complete organizations of archetypes. They include what in the previous essay we called analogies of revelation: the epics of Dante and Milton and their counterparts in the other modes.

But the anagogic perspective is not to be confined only to works that seem to take in everything, for the principle of anagogy is not simply that everything is the subject of poetry, but that anything may be the subject of a poem. The sense of the infinitely varied unity of poetry may come, not only explicitly from an apocalyptic epic, but implicitly from any poem. We said that we could get a whole liberal education by picking up one conventional poem, *Lycidas* for example, and following its archetypes through literature. Thus the center of the literary universe is whatever poem we happen to be reading. One step further, and the poem appears as a microcosm of all literature, an individual manifestation of the total order of words. Anagogically, then, the symbol is a monad, all symbols being united in a single infinite and eternal verbal symbol which is, as *dianoia*, the Logos, and, as *mythos*, total creative act. It is this conception which Joyce expresses, in terms of subject-matter, as "epiphany," and Hopkins, in terms of form, as "inscape."

If we look at *Lycidas* anagogically, for example, we see that the subject of the elegy has been identified with a god who personifies both the sun that falls into the western ocean at night and the vegetable life that dies in the autumn. In the latter aspect Lycidas is the Adonis or Tammuz whose "annual wound," as Milton calls it elsewhere, was the subject of a ritual lament in Mediterranean religion, and has been incorporated in the pastoral elegy since Theocritus, as the title of Shelley's *Adonais* shows more clearly. As a poet, Lycidas's archetype is Orpheus, who also died young, in much the same role as Adonis, and was flung into the water. As priest, his archetype is Peter, who would have drowned on the "Galilean lake" without the help of Christ. Each aspect of *Lycidas* poses the question of premature death as it relates to the life of man, of poetry, and of the Church. But all of these aspects are contained within the figure of Christ, the young dying god who is eternally alive, the Word that contains all poetry, the head and body of the Church, the good Shepherd whose pastoral world sees no winter, the Sun of righteousness that never sets, whose power can raise Lycidas, like Peter, out of the waves, as it redeems souls from the lower world, which Orpheus failed to do. Christ does not enter the poem as a character, but he pervades every line of it so completely that the poem, so to speak, enters him.

Anagogic criticism is usually found in direct connection with religion, and is to be discovered chiefly in the more uninhibited utterances of poets themselves. It comes out in those passages of Eliot's quartets where the words of the poet are placed within the context of the incarnate Word. An even clearer statement is in a letter of Rilke, where he speaks of the function of the poet as revealing a perspective of reality like that of an angel, containing all time and space, who is blind and looking into himself. Rilke's angel is a modification of the more usual god or Christ, and his statement is all the more valuable because it is explicitly not Christian, and illustrates the independence of the anagogic perspective, of the poet's attempt to speak from the circumference instead of from the center of reality, from the acceptance of any specific religion. Similar views are expressed or implied in Valéry's conception of a total intelligence which appears more fancifully in his figure of M. Teste; in Yeats's cryptic utterances about the artifice of eternity, and, in *The Tower* and elsewhere, about man as the creator of all creation as well as of both life and death; in Joyce's non-theological use of the theological term epiphany; in Dylan Thomas's exultant hymns to a universal human body. We may note in passing that the more sharply we distinguish the poetic and the critical functions, the easier it is for us to take seriously what great writers have said about their work.

The anagogic view of criticism thus leads to the conception of literature as existing in its own universe, no longer a commentary on life or reality, but containing life and reality in a system of verbal relationships. From this point of view the critic can no longer think of literature as a tiny palace of art looking out upon an inconceivably gigantic "life." "Life" for him has become the seed-plot of literature, a vast mass of potential literary forms, only a few of which will grow up into the greater world of the literary universe. Similar universes exist for all the arts. "We make to ourselves pictures of facts," says Wittgenstein, but by pictures he means representative illustrations, which are not pictures. Pictures as pictures are themselves facts, and exist only in a pictorial universe. "Tout, au monde," says Mallarmé, "existe pour aboutir à un livre."

So far we have been dealing with symbols as isolated units, but clearly the unit of relationship between two symbols, corresponding to the phrase in music, is of equal importance. The testimony of critics from Aristotle on seems fairly unanimous that this unit of relationship is the metaphor. And the metaphor, in its radical form, is a statement of identity of the "A is B" type, or rather, putting it into its proper hypothetical form, of the "let X be Y" type (letters altered for euphony). Thus the metaphor turns its back on ordinary descriptive meaning, and presents a structure which literally is ironic and paradoxical. In ordinary descriptive meaning, if A is B then B is A, and all we have really said is that A is itself. In the metaphor two things are identified while each retains its own form. Thus if we say "the hero was a lion" we identify the hero *with* the lion, while at the same time both the hero and the lion are identified *as* themselves. A work of literary art owes its unity to this process of identification *with*, and its variety, clarity, and intensity to identification *as*.

On the literal level of meaning, metaphor appears in its literal shape, which is simple juxtaposition. Ezra Pound, in explaining this aspect of metaphor, uses the illustrative figure of the Chinese ideogram, which expresses a complex image by throwing a group of elements together without predication. In Pound's famous blackboard example of such a metaphor, the two-line poem "In a Station of the Metro," the images of the faces in the crowd and the petals on the black bough are juxtaposed with no predicate of any kind connecting them. Predication belongs to assertion and descriptive meaning, not to the literal structure of poetry.

On the descriptive level we have the double perspective of the verbal structure and the phenomena to which it is related. Here meaning is "literal" in the common sense which we explained would not do for criticism, an unambiguous alignment of words and facts. Descriptively, then, all metaphors are similes. When we are writing ordinary discursive prose and use a metaphor, we are not asserting that A is B; we are "really" saying that A is in some respects comparable with B; and similarly when we are extracting the descriptive or paraphrasable meaning of a poem. "The hero was a lion," then, on the descriptive level, is a simile with the word "like" omitted for greater vividness, and to show more clearly that the analogy is only a hypothetical one. In Whitman's poem *Out of the Cradle Endlessly Rocking*, we find shadows "twining and twisting as if they were alive," and the moon swollen "as if with tears."

As there is no *poetic* reason why shadows should not be alive or the moon tearful, we may perhaps see in the cautious "as if" the working of a low mimetic discursive prose conscience.

On the formal level, where symbols are images or natural phenomena conceived as matter or content, the metaphor is an analogy of natural proportion. Literally, metaphor is juxtaposition; we say simply "A; B." Descriptively, we say "A is (like) B." But formally we say "A is as B." An analogy of proportion thus requires four terms, of which two have a common factor. Thus "the hero was a lion" means, as a form of expression which has nature for its internal content, that the hero is to human courage as the lion is to animal courage, courage being the factor common to the third and fourth terms.

Archetypally, where the symbol is an associative cluster, the metaphor unites two individual images, each of which is a specific representative of a class or genus. The rose in Dante's *Paradiso* and the rose in Yeats's early lyrics are identified *with* different things, but both stand for all roses—all poetic roses, of course, not all botanical ones. Archetypal metaphor thus involves the use of what has been called the concrete universal, the individual identified with its class, Wordsworth's "tree of many one." Of course there are no *real* universals in poetry, only poetic ones. All four of these aspects of metaphor are recognized in Aristotle's discussion of metaphor in the *Poetics*, though sometimes very briefly and elliptically.

In the anagogic aspect of meaning, the radical form of metaphor, "A is B," comes into its own. Here we are dealing with poetry in its totality, in which the formula "A is B" may be hypothetically applied to anything, for there is no metaphor, not even "black is white," which a reader has any right to quarrel with in advance. The literary universe, therefore, is a universe in which everything is potentially identical with everything else. This does not mean that any two things in it are separate and very similar, like peas in a pod, or in the slangy and erroneous sense of the word in which we speak of identical twins. If twins were really identical they would be the same person. On the other hand, a grown man feels identical with himself at the age of seven, although the two manifestations of this identity, the man and the boy, have very little in common as regards similarity or likeness. In form, matter, personality, time, and space, man and boy are quite unlike. This is the only type of image I can think of that illustrates the process of identifying two independent forms. All poetry, then, proceeds as though all poetic images were contained within a single universal body. Identity is the opposite of similarity or likeness, and total identity is not uniformity, still less monotony, but a unity of various things.

Finally, identification belongs not only to the structure of poetry, but to the structure of criticism as well, at least of commentary. Interpretation proceeds by metaphor as well as creation, and even more explicitly. When St. Paul interprets the story of Abraham's wives in Genesis, for instance, he says that Hagar "is" Mount Sinai in Arabia. Poetry, said Coleridge, is the identity of knowledge.

The universe of poetry, however, is a literary universe, and not a separate existential universe. Apocalypse means revelation, and when art becomes apocalyptic, it reveals. But it reveals only on its own terms, and in its own forms: it does not describe or represent a separate content of revelation. When poet and critic pass from the archetypal to the anagogic phase, they enter a phase of which only religion, or something as infinite in its range as religion, can possibly form an external goal. The poetic imagination, unless it disciplines itself in the particular way in which the imaginations of Hardy and Housman were disciplined, is apt to get claustrophobia when it is allowed to talk only about human nature and subhuman nature; and poets are happier as servants of religion than of politics, because the transcendental and apocalyptic perspective of religion comes as a tremendous emancipation of the imaginative mind. If men were compelled to make the melancholy choice between atheism and superstition, the scientist, as Bacon pointed out long ago, would be compelled to choose atheism, but the poet would be compelled to choose superstition, for even superstition, by its very confusion of values, gives his imagination more scope than a dogmatic denial of imaginative infinity does. But the loftiest religion, no less than the grossest superstition, comes to the poet, *qua* poet, only as the spirits came to Yeats, to give him metaphors for poetry.

The study of literature takes us toward seeing poetry as the imitation of infinite social action and infinite human thought, the mind of a man who is all men, the universal creative word which is all words. About this man and word we can, speaking as critics, say only one thing ontologically: we have no reason to suppose either that they exist or that they do not exist. We can call them divine if by divine we mean the unlimited or projected human.

But the critic, *qua* critic, has nothing to say for or against the affirmations that a religion makes out of these conceptions. If Christianity wishes to identify the infinite Word and Man of the literary universe with the Word of God, the person of Christ, the historical Jesus, the Bible or church dogma, these identifications may be accepted by any poet or critic without injury to his work— the acceptance may even clarify and intensify his work, depending on his temperament and situation. But they can never be accepted by poetry as a whole, or by criticism as such. The literary critic, like the historian, is compelled to treat every religion in the same way that religions treat each other, as though it were a human hypothesis, whatever else he may in other contexts believe it to be. The discussion of the universal Word at the opening of the Chhandogya Upanishad (where it is symbolized by the sacred word "Aum") is exactly as relevant and as irrelevant to literary criticism as the discussion at the opening of the Fourth Gospel. Coleridge was right in thinking that the "Logos" was the goal of his work as a critic, but not right in thinking that his poetic Logos would so inevitably be absorbed into Christ as to make literary criticism a kind of natural theology.

The total Logos of criticism by itself can never become an object of faith or an ontological personality. The conception of a total Word is the postulate that there is such a thing as an order of words, and that the criticism which studies it makes, or could make, complete sense. Aristotle's *Physics* leads to the conception of an unmoved first mover at the circumference of the physical universe. This, in itself, means essentially that physics *has* a universe. The systematic study of motion would be impossible unless all phenomena of motion could be related to unifying principles, and those in their turn to a total unifying principle of movement which is not itself merely another phenomenon of motion. If theology identifies Aristotle's unmoved mover with a creating God, that is the business of theology; physics as physics will be unaffected by it. Christian critics may see their total Word as an analogy of Christ, as medieval critics did, but as literature itself may be accompanied in culture by any religion, criticism must detach itself accordingly. In short, the study of literature belongs to the "humanities," and the humanities, as their name indicates, can take only the human view of the superhuman.

The close resemblance between the conceptions of anagogic

criticism and those of religion has led many to assume that they can only be related by making one supreme and the other subordinate. Those who choose religion, like Coleridge, will, like him, try to make criticism a natural theology; those who choose culture, like Arnold, will try to reduce religion to objectified cultural myth. But for the purity of each the autonomy of each must be guaranteed. Culture interposes, between the ordinary and the religious life, a total vision of possibilities, and insists on its totality —for whatever is excluded from culture by religion or state will get its revenge somehow. Thus culture's essential service to a religion is to destroy intellectual idolatry, the recurrent tendency in religion to replace the object of its worship with its present understanding and forms of approach to that object. Just as no argument in favor of a religious or political doctrine is of any value unless it is an intellectually honest argument, and so guarantees the autonomy of logic, so no religious or political myth is either valuable or valid unless it assumes the autonomy of culture, which may be provisionally defined as the total body of imaginative hypothesis in a society and its tradition. To defend the autonomy of culture in this sense seems to me the social task of the "intellectual" in the modern world: if so, to defend its subordination to a total synthesis of any kind, religious or political, would be the authentic form of the *trahison des clercs*.

Besides, it is of the essence of imaginative culture that it transcends the limits both of the naturally possible and of the morally acceptable. The argument that there is no room for poets in any human society which is an end in itself remains unanswerable even when the society is the people of God. For religion is also a social institution, and so far as it is one, it imposes limitations on the arts just as a Marxist or Platonic state would do. Christian theology is no less of a revolutionary dialectic, or indissoluble union of theory and social practice. Religions, in spite of their enlarged perspective, cannot as social institutions *contain* an art of unlimited hypothesis. The arts in their turn cannot help releasing the powerful acids of satire, realism, ribaldry, and fantasy in their attempt to dissolve all the existential concretions that get in their way. The artist often enough has to find that, as God says in *Faust,* he "muss als Teufel schaffen," which I suppose means rather more than that he has to work like the devil. Between religion's "this is" and poetry's "but suppose *this* is," there must always be some kind of tension, until the possible and the actual meet at infinity. Nobody wants a poet in the perfect human state, and, as even the poets tell us, nobody but God himself can tolerate a poltergeist in the City of God.

THIRD ESSAY

Archetypal Criticism: Theory of Myths

Third Essay

ARCHETYPAL CRITICISM: THEORY OF MYTHS

INTRODUCTION

IN THE ART of painting it is easy to see both structural and representational elements. A picture is normally a picture "of" something: it depicts or illustrates a "subject" made up of things analogous to "objects" in sense experience. At the same time there are present certain elements of pictorial design: what a picture represents is organized into structural patterns and conventions which are found only in pictures. The words "content" and "form" are often employed to describe these complementary aspects of painting. "Realism" connotes an emphasis on what the picture represents; stylization, whether primitive or sophisticated, connotes an emphasis on pictorial structure. Extreme realism of the illusive or *trompe l'œil* type is about as far as the painter can go in one kind of emphasis; abstract, or, more strictly, non-objective painting is about as far as he can go in the other direction. (The phrase "non-representational painting" seems to me illogical, a painting being itself a representation.) The illusive painter however cannot escape from pictorial conventions, and non-objective painting is still an imitative art in Aristotle's sense, and so we may say without much fear of effective contradiction that the whole art of painting lies within a combination of pictorial "form" or structure and pictorial "content" or subject.

For some reason the traditions of both practice and theory in Western painting have weighed down heavily on the imitative or representational end. Even from Classical painting we have inherited a number of depressing stories, of birds pecking painted grapes and the like, suggesting that Greek painters took their greatest pride in concocting *trompe l'œil* puzzles. The development of perspective painting in the Renaissance gave a great prestige to such skills, the suggesting of three dimensions in a two-dimensional medium being essentially a *trompe l'œil* device. An eavesdropper in a modern art gallery may easily discover the strength and persistence of the feeling that to achieve recognizable likeness in a subject, and to make this likeness the primary thing in his picture, is a moral obligation on the painter. A good deal of the freakishness of experimental movements in painting during the last half-century or so has been due to the energy of its revolt against the tyranny of the representational fallacy.

An original painter knows, of course, that when the public demands likeness to an object, it generally wants the exact opposite, likeness to the pictorial conventions it is familiar with. Hence when he breaks with these conventions, he is often apt to assert that he is nothing but an eye, that he merely paints what he sees as he sees it, and the like. His motive in talking such nonsense is clear enough: he wishes to say that painting is not merely facile decoration, and involves a difficult conquest of some very real spatial problems. But this may be freely admitted without agreeing that the formal cause of a picture is outside the picture, an assertion which would destroy the whole art if it were taken seriously. What he has actually done is to obey an obscure but profound impulse to revolt against the conventions established in his own day, in order to rediscover convention on a deeper level. By breaking with the Barbizon school, Manet discovered a deeper affinity with Goya and Velasquez; by breaking with the impressionists, Cézanne discovered a deeper affinity with Chardin and Masaccio. The possession of originality cannot make an artist unconventional; it drives him further into convention, obeying the law of the art itself, which seeks constantly to reshape itself from its own depths, and which works through its geniuses for metamorphosis, as it works through minor talents for mutation.

Music affords a refreshing contrast to painting in its critical theory. When perspective was discovered in painting, music might well have gone in a similar direction, but in fact the development of representational or "program" music has been severely restricted. Listeners may still derive pleasure from hearing external sounds cleverly imitated in music, but no one asserts that a composer is being a decadent or a charlatan if he fails to produce such imitations. Nor is it believed that these imitations are prior in importance to the forms of music itself, still less that they constitute those forms. The result is that the structural principles of music are clearly understood, and can be taught even to children.

Suppose, for example, that the present book were an introduction to musical theory instead of poetics. Then we could begin by isolating, from the range of audible sounds, the interval of the octave, and explain that the octave is divided into twelve theoretically equal semitones, forming a scale of twelve notes which contains potentially all the melodies and harmonies that the reader of the book will ordinarily hear. Then we could abstract the two points of repose in this scale, the major and minor common chords, and explain the system of twenty-four interlocking keys and the conventions of tonality which require that a piece should normally open and close in the same key. We could describe the basis of rhythm as an accentuation of every second or every third beat, and so on through the whole list of rudiments.

Such an outline would give a rational account of the structure of Western music from 1600 to 1900, and, in a qualified and more flexible but not essentially different form, of everything that the user of the book would be accustomed to call music. If we chose, we could lock up all the music outside the Western tradition in the solitary confinement of a prefatory chapter, before we got down to serious business. Someone might object that the system of equal temperament, in which C♯ and D♭ are the same note, is an arbitrary fiction. Another might object that a composer ought not to be tied down to so rigidly conventionalized a set of musical elements, and that the resources of expression in music ought to be as free as the air. A third might object that we are not talking about music at all: that while the Jupiter Symphony is in C major and Beethoven's Fifth is in C minor, explaining the difference between the two keys will give nobody any real notion of the difference between the two symphonies. All these objectors could be quite safely ignored. Our handbook would not give the reader a complete musical education, nor would it give an account of music as it exists in the mind of God or the practice of angels—but it would do for its purposes.

In this book we are attempting to outline a few of the grammatical rudiments of literary expression, and the elements of it that correspond to such musical elements as tonality, simple and compound rhythm, canonical imitation, and the like. The aim is to give a rational account of some of the structural principles of Western literature in the context of its Classical and Christian heritage. We are suggesting that the resources of verbal expression are limited, if that is the word, by the literary equivalents of rhythm and key, though that does not mean, any more than it means in music, that its resources are artistically exhaustible. We doubtless have objectors similar to those just imagined for music, saying that our categories are artificial, that they do not do justice to the variety of literature, or that they are not relevant to their own experiences in reading. However, the question of what the structural principles of literature actually are seems important enough to discuss; and, as literature is an art of words, it should be at least as easy to find words to describe them as to find such words as sonata or fugue in music.

In literature, as in painting, the traditional emphasis in both practice and theory has been on representation or "lifelikeness." When, for instance, we pick up a novel of Dickens, our immediate impulse, a habit fostered in us by all the criticism we know, is to compare it with "life," whether as lived by us or by Dickens's contemporaries. Then we meet such characters as Heep or Quilp, and, as neither we nor the Victorians have ever known anything much "like" these curious monsters, the method promptly breaks down. Some readers will complain that Dickens has relapsed into "mere" caricature (as though caricature were easy); others, more sensibly, simply give up the criterion of lifelikeness and enjoy the creation for its own sake.

The structural principles of painting are frequently described in terms of their analogues in plane geometry (or solid, by a further reach of analogy). A famous letter of Cézanne speaks of the approximation of pictorial form to the sphere and the cube, and the practice of abstract painters seems to confirm his point. Geometrical shapes are analogous only to pictorial forms, not by any means identical with them; the real structural principles of painting are to be derived, not from an external analogy with something else, but from the internal analogy of the art itself. The structural principles of literature, similarly, are to be derived from archetypal and anagogic criticism, the only kinds that assume a larger context of literature as a whole. But we saw in the first essay that, as the modes of fiction move from the mythical to the low mimetic and ironic, they approach a point of extreme "realism" or representative likeness to life. It follows that the mythical mode, the stories about gods, in which characters have the greatest possible power of action, is the most abstract and conventionalized of all literary modes, just as the corresponding modes in other arts—religious Byzantine painting, for example—show the highest degree of stylization in their structure. Hence the structural principles of literature are as closely related to mythology and comparative religion as those of painting are to geometry. In this essay we shall be using the symbolism of the Bible, and to a lesser extent Classical mythology, as a grammar of literary archetypes.

In the Egyptian tale of The Two Brothers, thought to be the source of the Potiphar's wife story in the Joseph legend, an elder brother's wife attempts to seduce an unmarried younger brother who lives with them, and, when he resists her, accuses him of attempting to rape her. The younger brother is then forced to run away, with the enraged elder brother in pursuit. So far, the incidents reproduce more or less credible facts of life. Then the younger brother prays to Ra for assistance, pleading the justice of his cause; Ra places a large lake between him and his brother, and, in a burst of divine exuberance, fills it full of crocodiles. This incident is no more a fictional episode than anything that has preceded it, nor is it less logically related than any other episode to the plot as a whole. But it has given up the external analogy to "life": this, we say, is the kind of thing that happens only in stories. The Egyptian tale has acquired, then, in its mythical episode, an abstractly literary quality; and, as the story-teller could just as easily have solved his little problem in a more "realistic" way, it appears that literature in Egypt, like the other arts, preferred a certain degree of stylization.

Similarly, a medieval saint with a huge decorated halo around his head may look like an old man, but the mythical feature, the halo, both imparts a more abstract structure to the painting and gives the saint the kind of appearance that one sees only in pictures. In primitive societies, a flourishing development in myth and folk tale usually accompanies a taste for geometrical ornament in the plastic arts. In our tradition we have a place for verisimilitude, for human experience skilfully and consistently imitated. The occasional hoaxes in which fiction is presented, or even accepted, as fact, such as Defoe's *Journal of the Plague Year* or Samuel Butler's *The Fair Haven*, correspond to *trompe l'œil* illusions in painting. At the other extreme we have myths, or abstract fictional designs in which gods and other such beings do whatever they like, which in practice means whatever the story-teller likes. The return of irony to myth that we noted in the first essay is contemporary with, and parallel to, abstraction, expressionism, cubism, and similar efforts in painting to emphasize the self-contained pictorial structure. Sixty years ago, Bernard Shaw stressed the social significance of the themes in Ibsen's plays and his own. Today,

Mr. Eliot calls our attention to the Alcestis archetype in *The Cocktail Party*, to the Ion archetype in *The Confidential Clerk*. The former is of the age of Manet and Degas; the latter of the age of Braque and Graham Sutherland.

We begin our study of archetypes, then, with a world of myth, an abstract or purely literary world of fictional and thematic design, unaffected by canons of plausible adaptation to familiar experience. In terms of narrative, myth is the imitation of actions near or at the conceivable limits of desire. The gods enjoy beautiful women, fight one another with prodigious strength, comfort and assist man, or else watch his miseries from the height of their immortal freedom. The fact that myth operates at the top level of human desire does not mean that it necessarily presents its world as attained or attainable by human beings. In terms of meaning or *dianoia*, myth is the same world looked at as an area or field of activity, bearing in mind our principle that the meaning or pattern of poetry is a structure of imagery with conceptual implications. The world of mythical imagery is usually represented by the conception of heaven or Paradise in religion, and it is apocalyptic, in the sense of that word already explained, a world of total metaphor, in which everything is potentially identical with everything else, as though it were all inside a single infinite body.

Realism, or the art of verisimilitude, evokes the response "How like that is to what we know!" When what is written is *like* what is known, we have an art of extended or implied simile. And as realism is an art of implicit simile, myth is an art of implicit metaphorical identity. The word "sun-god," with a hyphen used instead of a predicate, is a pure ideogram, in Pound's terminology, or literal metaphor, in ours. In myth we see the structural principles of literature isolated; in realism we see the *same* structural principles (not similar ones) fitting into a context of plausibility. (Similarly in music, a piece by Purcell and a piece by Benjamin Britten may not be in the least *like* each other, but if they are both in D major their tonality will be the same.) The presence of a mythical structure in realistic fiction, however, poses certain technical problems for making it plausible, and the devices used in solving these problems may be given the general name of *displacement*.

Myth, then, is one extreme of literary design; naturalism is the other, and in between lies the whole area of romance, using that term to mean, not the historical mode of the first essay, but the tendency, noted later in the same essay, to displace myth in a human direction and yet, in contrast to "realism," to conventionalize content in an idealized direction. The central principle of displacement is that what can be metaphorically identified in a myth can only be linked in romance by some form of simile: analogy, significant association, incidental accompanying imagery, and the like. In a myth we can have a sun-god or a tree-god; in a romance we may have a person who is significantly associated with the sun or trees. In more realistic modes the association becomes less significant and more a matter of incidental, even coincidental or accidental, imagery. In the dragon-killing legend of the St. George and Perseus family, of which more hereafter, a country under an old feeble king is terrorized by a dragon who eventually demands the king's daughter, but is slain by the hero. This seems to be a romantic analogy (perhaps also, in this case, a descendant) of a myth of a waste land restored to life by a fertility god. In the myth, then, the dragon and the old king would be identified. We can in fact concentrate the myth still further into an Oedipus fantasy in which the hero is not the old king's son-in-law but his son, and the rescued damsel the hero's mother. If the story were a private dream such identifications would be made as a matter of course. But to make it a plausible, symmetrical, and morally acceptable story a good deal of displacement is necessary, and it is only after a comparative study of the story type has been made that the metaphorical structure within it begins to emerge.

In Hawthorne's *The Marble Faun* the statue which gives the story that name is so insistently associated with a character named Donatello that a reader would have to be unusually dull or inattentive to miss the point that Donatello "is" the statue. Later on we meet a girl named Hilda, of singular purity and gentleness, who lives in a tower surrounded by doves. The doves are very fond of her; another character calls her his "dove," and remarks indicating some special affinity with doves are made about her by both author and characters. If we were to say that Hilda is a dove-goddess like Venus, identified with her doves, we should not be reading the story quite accurately in its own mode; we should be translating it into straight myth. But to recognize how close Hawthorne is to myth here is not unfair. That is, we recognize that *The Marble Faun* is not a typical low mimetic fiction: it is dominated by an interest that looks back to fictional romance and forward to the ironic mythical writers of the next century—to Kafka, for instance, or Cocteau. This interest is often called allegory, but probably Hawthorne himself was right in calling it romance. We can see how this interest tends toward abstraction in character-drawing, and if we know no other canons than low mimetic ones, we complain of this.

Or, again, we have, in myth, the story of Proserpine, who disappears into the underworld for six months of every year. The pure myth is clearly one of death and revival; the story as we have it is slightly displaced, but the mythical pattern is easy to see. The same structural element often recurs in Shakespearean comedy, where it has to be adapted to a roughly high mimetic level of credibility. Hero in *Much Ado* is dead enough to have a funeral song, and plausible explanations are postponed until after the end of the play. Imogen in *Cymbeline* has an assumed name and an empty grave, but she too gets some funeral obsequies. But the story of Hermione and Perdita is so close to the Demeter and Proserpine myth that hardly any serious pretence of plausible explanations is made. Hermione, after her disappearance, returns once as a ghost in a dream, and her coming to life from a statue, a displacement of the Pygmalion myth, is said to require an awakening of faith, even though, on one level of plausibility, she has not been a statue at all, and nothing has taken place except a harmless deception. We notice how much more abstractly mythical a thematic writer can be than a fictional one: Spenser's Florimell, for instance, disappears under the sea for the winter with no questions asked, leaving a "snowy lady" in her place and returning with a great outburst of spring floods at the end of the fourth book.

In the low mimetic, we recognize the same structural pattern of the death and revival of the heroine when Esther Summerson gets smallpox, or Lorna Doone is shot at her marriage altar. But we are getting closer to the conventions of realism, and although Lorna's eyes are "dim with death," we know that the author does not really mean death if he is planning to revive her. Here again it is interesting to compare *The Marble Faun*, where there is so much about sculptors and the relation of statues to living people that we almost expect some kind of denouement like that of *The Winter's Tale*. Hilda mysteriously disappears, and during her absence her lover, the sculptor Kenyon, digs out of the earth a statue that he associates with Hilda. After that Hilda returns, with a plausible reason eventually assigned for her absence, but not without some rather pointed and petulant remarks from Hawthorne himself to the effect that he has no interest in concocting plausible explanations, and that he wishes his reading public would give him a bit more freedom. Yet Hawthorne's inhibitions seem to be at least in part self-imposed, as we can see if we turn to Poe's *Ligeia*, where the straight mythical death and revival pattern is given without apology. Poe is clearly a more radical abstractionist than Hawthorne, which is one reason why his influence on our century is more immediate.

This affinity between the mythical and the abstractly literary illuminates many aspects of fiction, especially the more popular fiction which is realistic enough to be plausible in its incidents and yet romantic enough to be a "good story," which means a clearly designed one. The introduction of an omen or portent, or the device of making a whole story the fulfilment of a prophecy given at the beginning, is an example. Such a device suggests, in its existential projection, a conception of ineluctable fate or hidden omnipotent will. Actually, it is a piece of pure literary design, giving the beginning some symmetrical relationship with the end, and the only ineluctable will involved is that of the author. Hence we often find it even in writers not temperamentally much in sympathy with the portentous. In *Anna Karenina*, for instance, the death of the railway porter in the opening book is accepted by Anna as an omen for herself. Similarly, if we find portents and omens in Sophocles, they are there primarily because they fit the structure of his type of dramatic tragedy, and prove nothing about any clear-cut beliefs in fate held by either dramatist or audience.

We have, then, three organizations of myths and archetypal symbols in literature. First, there is undisplaced myth, generally concerned with gods or demons, and which takes the form of two contrasting worlds of total metaphorical identification, one desirable and the other undesirable. These worlds are often identified with the existential heavens and hells of the religions contemporary with such literature. These two forms of metaphorical organization we call the apocalyptic and the demonic respectively. Second, we have the general tendency we have called romantic, the tendency to suggest implicit mythical patterns in a world more closely associated with human experience. Third, we have the tendency of "realism" (my distaste for this inept term is reflected in the quotation marks) to throw the emphasis on content and representation rather than on the shape of the story. Ironic literature begins with realism and tends toward myth, its mythical patterns being as a rule more suggestive of the demonic than of the apocalyptic, though sometimes it simply continues the romantic tradition of stylization. Hawthorne, Poe, Conrad, Hardy and Virginia Woolf all provide examples.

In looking at a picture, we may stand close to it and analyze the details of brush work and palette knife. This corresponds roughly to the rhetorical analysis of the new critics in literature. At a little distance back, the design comes into clearer view, and we study rather the content represented: this is the best distance for realistic Dutch pictures, for example, where we are in a sense reading the picture. The further back we go, the more conscious we are of the organizing design. At a great distance from, say, a Madonna, we can see nothing but the archetype of the Madonna, a large centripetal blue mass with a contrasting point of interest at its center. In the criticism of literature, too, we often have to "stand back" from the poem to see its archetypal organization. If we "stand back" from Spenser's *Mutabilitie Cantoes*, we see a background of ordered circular light and a sinister black mass thrusting up into the lower foreground—much the same archetypal shape that we see in the opening of the Book of Job. If we "stand back" from the beginning of the fifth act of *Hamlet*, we see a grave opening on the stage, the hero, his enemy, and the heroine descending into it, followed by a fatal struggle in the upper world. If we "stand back" from a realistic novel such as Tolstoy's *Resurrection* or Zola's *Germinal*, we can see the mythopoeic designs indicated by those titles. Other examples will be given in what follows.

We proceed to give an account first of the structure of imagery, or *dianoia*, of the two undisplaced worlds, the apocalyptic and the demonic, drawing heavily on the Bible, the main source for undisplaced myth in our tradition. Then we go on to the two intermediate structures of imagery, and finally to the generic narratives or *mythoi* which are these structures of imagery in movement.

THEORY OF ARCHETYPAL MEANING (1):
APOCALYPTIC IMAGERY

Let us proceed according to the general scheme of the game of Twenty Questions, or, if we prefer, of the Great Chain of Being, the traditional scheme for classifying sense data.

The apocalyptic world, the heaven of religion, presents, in the first place, the categories of reality in the forms of human desire, as indicated by the forms they assume under the work of human civilization. The form imposed by human work and desire on the *vegetable* world, for instance, is that of the garden, the farm, the grove, or the park. The human form of the *animal* world is a world of domesticated animals, of which the sheep has a traditional priority in both Classical and Christian metaphor. The human form of the *mineral* world, the form into which human work transforms stone, is the city. The city, the garden, and the sheepfold are the organizing metaphors of the Bible and of most Christian symbolism, and they are brought into complete metaphorical identification in the book explicitly called the Apocalypse or Revelation, which has been carefully designed to form an undisplaced mythical conclusion for the Bible as a whole. From our point of view this means that the Biblical Apocalypse is our grammar of apocalyptic imagery.

Each of these three categories, the city, the garden, and the sheepfold, is, by the principle of archetypal metaphor dealt with in the previous essay, and which we remember is the concrete universal, identical with the others and with each individual within it. Hence the *divine* and *human* worlds are, similarly, identical with the sheepfold, city and garden, and the social and individual aspects of each are identical. Thus the apocalyptic world of the Bible presents the following pattern:

divine world	=	society of gods	= One God
human world	=	society of men	= One Man
animal world	=	sheepfold	= One Lamb
vegetable world	=	garden or park	= One Tree (of Life)
mineral world	=	city	= One Building, Temple, Stone

The conception "Christ" unites all these categories in identity: Christ *is* both the one God and the one Man, the Lamb of God, the tree of life, or vine of which we are the branches, the stone which the builders rejected, and the rebuilt temple which is identical with his risen body. The religious and poetic identifications differ in intention only, the former being existential and the latter metaphorical. In medieval criticism the difference was of little importance, and the word "figura," as applied to the identification of a symbol with Christ, usually implies both kinds.

Now let us expand this pattern a little. In Christianity the concrete universal is applied to the divine world in the form of the Trinity. Christianity insists that, whatever dislocations of customary mental processes may be involved, God *is* three persons and yet one God. The conceptions of person and substance represent a few of the difficulties in extending metaphor to logic. In pure metaphor, of course, the unity of God could apply to five or seventeen or a million divine persons as easily as three, and we may find the divine concrete universal in poetry outside the Trinitarian orbit. When Zeus remarks, at the beginning of the eighth book of the Iliad, that he can pull the whole chain of being up into himself whenever he likes, we can see that for Homer there was some conception of a double perspective in Olympus, where a group of squabbling deities may at any time suddenly compose into the form of a single divine will. In Virgil we first meet a malicious and spoiled Juno, but the comment of Aeneas to his men a few lines later on, "deus dabit his quoque finem," indicates that a similar double perspective existed for him. We may compare perhaps the Book of Job, where Job and his friends are much too devout for it ever to occur to them that Job could have suffered so as a result of a half-jocular bet between God and Satan. There is a sense in which they are right, and the information given to the reader about Satan in heaven wrong. Satan is dropped out of the end of the poem, and whatever rewritings may be responsible for this, it is still difficult to see how the final enlightenment of Job could ever have returned completely from the conception of a single divine will to the mood of the opening scene.

As for human society, the metaphor that we are all members of one body has organized most political theory from Plato to our own day. Milton's "A Commonwealth ought to be but as one huge Christian personage, one mighty growth, and stature of an honest man" belongs to a Christianized version of this metaphor, in which, as in the doctrine of the Trinity, the full metaphorical statement "Christ *is* God and Man" is orthodox, and the Arian and Docetic

142

statements in terms of simile or likeness condemned as heretical. Hobbes's *Leviathan*, with its original frontispiece depicting a number of mannikins inside the body of a single giant, has also some connection with the same type of identification. Plato's Republic, in which the reason, will, and desire of the individual appear as the philosopher-king, guards, and artisans of the state, is also founded on this metaphor, which in fact we still use whenever we speak of a group or aggregate of human beings as a "body."

In sexual symbolism, of course, it is still easier to employ the "one flesh" metaphor of two bodies made into the same body by love. Donne's *The Extasie* is one of the many poems organized on this image, and Shakespeare's *Phoenix and the Turtle* makes great play with the outrage done to the "reason" by such identity. Themes of loyalty, hero-worship, faithful followers, and the like also employ the same metaphor.

The animal and vegetable worlds are identified with each other, and with the divine and human worlds as well, in the Christian doctrine of transubstantiation, in which the essential human forms of the vegetable world, food and drink, the harvest and the vintage, the bread and the wine, *are* the body and blood of the Lamb who is also Man and God, and in whose body we exist as in a city or temple. Here again the orthodox doctrine insists on metaphor as against simile, and here again the conception of substance illustrates the struggles of logic to digest the metaphor. It is clear from the opening of the *Laws* that the symposium had something of the same communion symbolism for Plato. It would be hard to find a simpler or more vivid image of human civilization, where man attempts to surround nature and put it inside his (social) body, than the sacramental meal.

The conventional honors accorded the sheep in the animal world provide us with the central archetype of pastoral imagery, as well as with such metaphors as "pastor" and "flock" in religion. The metaphor of the king as the shepherd of his people goes back to ancient Egypt. Perhaps the use of this particular convention is due to the fact that, being stupid, affectionate, gregarious, and easily stampeded, the societies formed by sheep are most like human ones. But of course in poetry any other animal would do as well if the poet's audience were prepared for it: at the opening of the Brihadaranyaka Upanishad, for instance, the sacrificial horse, whose body contains the whole universe, is treated in the same way that a Christian poet

would treat the Lamb of God. Of birds, too, the dove has traditionally represented the universal concord or love both of Venus
and of the Christian Holy Spirit. Identifications of gods with animals or plants and of those again with human society form the
basis of totemic symbolism. Certain types of etiological folk tale,
the stories of how supernatural beings were turned into the animals
and plants that we know, represent an attentuated form of the
same type of metaphor, and survive as the "metamorphosis" archetype familiar from Ovid.

Similar flexibility is possible with vegetable images. Elsewhere
in the Bible the leaves or fruit of the tree of life are used as communion symbols in place of the bread and wine. Or the concrete
universal may be applied not simply to a tree but to a single fruit
or flower. In the West the rose has a traditional priority among
apocalyptic flowers: the use of the rose as a communion symbol in
the *Paradiso* comes readily to mind, and in the first book of *The
Faerie Queene* the emblem of St. George, a red cross on a white
ground, is connected not only with the risen body of Christ and
the sacramental symbolism which accompanies it, but with the
union of the red and white roses in the Tudor dynasty. In the East
the lotus or the Chinese "golden flower" often occupied the place
of the rose, and in German Romanticism the blue cornflower en-
joyed a brief vogue.

The identity of the human body and the vegetable world gives
us the archetype of Arcadian imagery, of Marvell's green world, of
Shakespeare's forest comedies, of the world of Robin Hood and
other green men who lurk in the forests of romance, these last the
counterparts in romance of the metaphorical myth of the tree-god.
In Marvell's *The Garden* we meet a further but still conventional
extension in the identification of the human soul with a bird sitting
in the branches of the tree of life. The olive tree and its oil has supplied another identification in the "anointed" ruler.

The city, whether called Jerusalem or not, is apocalyptically identical with a single building or temple, a "house of many mansions,"
of which individuals are "lively stones," to use another New Testament phrase. The human use of the inorganic world involves the
highway or road as well as the city with its streets, and the metaphor
of the "way" is inseparable from all quest-literature, whether explicitly Christian as in *The Pilgrim's Progress* or not. To this cate-

gory also belong geometrical and architectural images: the tower and the winding stairway of Dante and Yeats, Jacob's ladder, the ladder of the Neo-platonic love poets, the ascending spiral or cornucopia, the "stately pleasure dome" that Kubla Khan decreed, the cross and quincunx patterns which Browne sought in every corner of art and nature, the circle as the emblem of eternity, Vaughan's "ring of pure and endless light," and so on.

On the archetypal level proper, where poetry is an artifact of human civilization, nature is the container of man. On the anagogic level, man is the container of nature, and his cities and gardens are no longer little hollowings on the surface of the earth, but the forms of a human universe. Hence in apocalyptic symbolism we cannot confine man only to his two natural elements of earth and air, and, in going from one level to the other, symbolism must, like Tamino in *The Magic Flute*, pass the ordeals of water and fire. Poetic symbolism usually puts fire just above man's life in this world, and water just below it. Dante had to pass through a ring of fire and the river of Eden to go from the mountain of purgatory, which is still on the surface of our own world, to Paradise or the apocalyptic world proper. The imagery of light and fire surrounding the angels in the Bible, the tongues of flame descending at Pentecost, and the coal of fire applied to the mouth of Isaiah by the seraph, associates fire with a spiritual or angelic world midway between the human and the divine. In Classical mythology the story of Prometheus indicates a similar provenance for fire, as does the association of Zeus with the thunderbolt or fire of lightning. In short, heaven in the sense of the sky, containing the fiery bodies of sun, moon, and stars, is usually identified with, or thought of as the passage to, the heaven of the apocalyptic world.

Hence all our other categories can be identified with fire or thought of as burning. The appearance of the Judaeo-Christian deity in fire, surrounded by angels of fire (seraphim) and light (cherubim), needs only to be mentioned. The burning animal of the ritual of sacrifice, the incorporating of an animal body in a communion between divine and human worlds, modulates into all the imagery connected with the fire and smoke of the altar, ascending incense, and the like. The burning man is represented in the saint's halo and the king's crown, both of which are analogues of the sun-god: one may compare also the "burning babe" of Southwell's Christmas poem. The image of the burning bird appears in the legendary phoenix. The tree of life may also be a burning tree, the unconsumed burning bush of Moses, the candlestick of Jewish ritual, or the "rosy cross" of later occultism. In alchemy the vegetable, mineral, and water worlds are identified in its rose, stone, and elixir; flower and jewel archetypes are identified in the "jewel in the lotus" of the Buddhist prayer. The links between fire, intoxicating wine, and the hot red blood of animals are also common.

The identification of the *city* with fire explains why the city of God in the Apocalypse is presented as a glowing mass of gold and precious stones, each stone presumably burning with a hard gemlike flame. For in apocalyptic symbolism the fiery bodies of heaven, sun, moon, and stars, are all inside the universal divine and human body. The symbolism of alchemy is apocalyptic symbolism of the same type: the center of nature, the gold and jewels hidden in the earth, is eventually to be united to its circumference in the sun, moon, and stars of the heavens; the center of the spiritual world, the soul of man, is united to its circumference in God. Hence there is a close association between the purifying of the human soul and the transmuting of earth to gold, not only literal gold but the fiery quintessential gold of which the heavenly bodies are made. The golden tree with its mechanical bird in *Sailing to Byzantium* identifies vegetable and mineral worlds in a form reminiscent of alchemy.

Water, on the other hand, traditionally belongs to a realm of existence below human life, the state of chaos or dissolution which follows ordinary death, or the reduction to the inorganic. Hence the soul frequently crosses water or sinks into it at death. In apocalyptic symbolism we have the "water of life," the fourfold river of Eden which reappears in the City of God, and is represented in ritual by baptism. According to Ezekiel the return of this river turns the sea fresh, which is apparently why the author of Revelation says that in the apocalypse there is no more sea. Apocalyptically, therefore, water circulates in the universal body like the blood in the individual body. Perhaps we should say "is held within" instead of "circulates," to avoid the anachronism of connecting a knowledge of the circulation of the blood with Biblical themes. For centuries, of course, the blood was one of four "humors," or bodily liquids, just as the river of life was traditionally fourfold.

THEORY OF ARCHETYPAL MEANING (2):
DEMONIC IMAGERY

Opposed to apocalyptic symbolism is the presentation of the world that desire totally rejects: the world of the nightmare and the scapegoat, of bondage and pain and confusion; the world as it is before the human imagination begins to work on it and before any image of human desire, such as the city or the garden, has been solidly established; the world also of perverted or wasted work, ruins and catacombs, instruments of torture and monuments of folly. And just as apocalyptic imagery in poetry is closely associated with a religious heaven, so its dialectic opposite is closely linked with an existential hell, like Dante's *Inferno*, or with the hell that man creates on earth, as in *1984*, *No Exit*, and *Darkness at Noon*, where the titles of the last two speak for themselves. Hence one of the central themes of demonic imagery is parody, the mocking of the exuberant play of art by suggesting its imitation in terms of "real life."

The demonic divine world largely personifies the vast, menacing, stupid powers of nature as they appear to a technologically undeveloped society. Symbols of heaven in such a world tend to become associated with the inaccessible sky, and the central idea that crystallizes from it is the idea of inscrutable fate or external necessity. The machinery of fate is administered by a set of remote invisible gods, whose freedom and pleasure are ironic because they exclude man, and who intervene in human affairs chiefly to safeguard their own prerogatives. They demand sacrifices, punish presumption, and enforce obedience to natural and moral law as an end in itself. Here we are not trying to describe, for instance, the gods in Greek tragedy: we are trying to isolate the sense of human remoteness and futility in relation to the divine order which is only one element among others in most tragic visions of life, though an essential one in all. In later ages poets become much more outspoken about this view of divinity: Blake's Nobodaddy, Shelley's Jupiter, Swinburne's "supreme evil, God," Hardy's befuddled Will, and Housman's "brute and blackguard" are examples.

The demonic human world is a society held together by a kind of molecular tension of egos, a loyalty to the group or the leader which diminishes the individual, or, at best, contrasts his pleasure with his duty or honor. Such a society is an endless source of tragic dilemmas like those of Hamlet and Antigone. In the apocalyptic conception of human life we found three kinds of fulfilment: individual, sexual, and social. In the sinister human world one individual pole is the tyrant-leader, inscrutable, ruthless, melancholy, and with an insatiable will, who commands loyalty only if he is egocentric enough to represent the collective ego of his followers. The other pole is represented by the *pharmakos* or sacrificed victim, who has to be killed to strengthen the others. In the most concentrated form of the demonic parody, the two become the same. The ritual of the killing of the divine king in Frazer, whatever it may be in anthropology, is in literary criticism the demonic or undisplaced radical form of tragic and ironic structures.

In religion the spiritual world is a reality distinct from the physical world. In poetry the physical or actual is opposed, not to the spiritually existential, but to the hypothetical. We met in the first essay the principle that the transmutation of act into mime, the advance from acting out a rite to playing at the rite, is one of the central features of the development from savagery into culture. It is easy to see a mimesis of conflict in tennis and football, but, precisely for that very reason, tennis and football players represent a culture superior to the culture of student duellists and gladiators. The turning of literal act into play is a fundamental form of the liberalizing of life which appears in more intellectual levels as liberal education, the release of fact into imagination. It is consistent with this that the Eucharist symbolism of the apocalyptic world, the metaphorical identification of vegetable, animal, human, and divine bodies, should have the imagery of cannibalism for its demonic parody. Dante's last vision of human hell is of Ugolino gnawing his tormentor's skull; Spenser's last major allegorical vision is of Serena stripped and prepared for a cannibal feast. The imagery of cannibalism usually includes, not only images of torture and mutilation, but of what is technically known as *sparagmos* or the tearing apart of the sacrificial body, an image found in the myths of Osiris, Orpheus, and Pentheus. The cannibal giant or ogre of folk tales, who enters literature as Polyphemus, belongs here, as does a long series of sinister dealings with flesh and blood from the story of Thyestes to Shylock's bond. Here again the form described by Frazer as the historically original form is in literary criticism the radical demonic form. Flaubert's *Salammbo* is a study

148

of demonic imagery which was thought in its day to be archaeological but turned out to be prophetic.

The demonic erotic relation becomes a fierce destructive passion that works against loyalty or frustrates the one who possesses it. It is generally symbolized by a harlot, witch, siren, or other tantalizing female, a physical object of desire which is sought as a possession and therefore can never be possessed. The demonic parody of marriage, or the union of two souls in one flesh, may take the form of hermaphroditism, incest (the most common form), or homosexuality. The social relation is that of the mob, which is essentially human society looking for a *pharmakos*, and the mob is often identified with some sinister animal image such as the hydra, Virgil's Fama, or its development in Spenser's Blatant Beast.

The other worlds can be briefly summarized. The animal world is portrayed in terms of monsters or beasts of prey. The wolf, the traditional enemy of the sheep, the tiger, the vulture, the cold and earth-bound serpent, and the dragon are all common. In the Bible, where the demonic society is represented by Egypt and Babylon, the rulers of each are identified with monstrous beasts: Nebuchadnezzar turns into a beast in Daniel, and Pharaoh is called a river-dragon by Ezekiel. The dragon is especially appropriate because it is not only monstrous and sinister but fabulous, and so represents the paradoxical nature of evil as a moral fact and an eternal negation. In the Apocalypse the dragon is called "the beast that was, and is not, and yet is."

The vegetable world is a sinister forest like the ones we meet in *Comus* or the opening of the *Inferno*, or a heath, which from Shakespeare to Hardy has been associated with tragic destiny, or a wilderness like that of Browning's *Childe Roland* or Eliot's *Waste Land*. Or it may be a sinister enchanted garden like that of Circe and its Renaissance descendants in Tasso and Spenser. In the Bible the waste land appears in its concrete universal form in the tree of death, the tree of forbidden knowledge in Genesis, the barren fig-tree of the Gospels, and the cross. The stake, with the hooded heretic, the black man or the witch attached to it, is the burning tree and body of the infernal world. Scaffolds, gallows, stocks, pillories, whips, and birch rods are or could be modulations. The contrast of the tree of life and the tree of death is beautifully expressed in Yeats's poem *The Two Trees*.

The inorganic world may remain in its unworked form of deserts, rocks, and waste land. Cities of destruction and dreadful night belong here, and the great ruins of pride, from the tower of Babel to the mighty works of Ozymandias. Images of perverted work belong here too: engines of torture, weapons of war, armor, and images of a dead mechanism which, because it does not humanize nature, is unnatural as well as inhuman. Corresponding to the temple or One Building of the apocalypse, we have the prison or dungeon, the sealed furnace of heat without light, like the City of Dis in Dante. Here too are the sinister counterparts of geometrical images: the sinister spiral (the maelstrom, whirlpool, or Charybdis), the sinister cross, and the sinister circle, the wheel of fate or fortune. The identification of the circle with the serpent, conventionally a demonic animal, gives us the ouroboros, or serpent with its tail in its mouth. Corresponding to the apocalyptic way or straight road, the highway in the desert for God prophesied by Isaiah, we have in this world the labyrinth or maze, the image of lost direction, often with a monster at its heart like the Minotaur. The labyrinthine wanderings of Israel in the desert, repeated by Jesus when in the company of the devil (or "wild beasts," according to Mark), fit the same pattern. The labyrinth can also be a sinister forest, as in *Comus*. The catacombs are effectively used in the same context in *The Marble Faun*, and of course in a further concentration of metaphor, the maze would become the winding entrails inside the sinister monster himself.

The world of fire is a world of malignant demons like the will-o'-the-wisps, or spirits broken from hell, and it appears in this world in the form of the *auto da fe*, as mentioned, or such burning cities as Sodom. It is in contrast to the purgatorial or cleansing fire, like the fiery furnace in Daniel. The world of water is the water of death, often identified with spilled blood, as in the Passion and in Dante's symbolic figure of history, and above all the "unplumbed, salt, estranging sea," which absorbs all rivers in this world, but disappears in the apocalypse in favor of a circulation of fresh water. In the Bible the sea and the animal monster are identified in the figure of the leviathan, a sea-monster also identified with the social tyrannies of Babylon and Egypt.

THEORY OF ARCHETYPAL MEANING (3):
ANALOGICAL IMAGERY

Most imagery in poetry has of course to deal with much less extreme worlds than the two which are usually projected as the eternal unchanging worlds of heaven and hell. Apocalyptic imagery is appropriate to the mythical mode, and demonic imagery to the ironic mode in the late phase in which it returns to myth. In the other three modes these two structures operate dialectically, pulling the reader toward the metaphorical and mythical undisplaced core of the work. We should therefore expect three intermediate structures of imagery, corresponding roughly to the romantic, high mimetic, and low mimetic modes. We shall give little attention to high mimetic imagery, however, in order to preserve the simpler pattern of the romantic and "realistic" tendencies within the two undisplaced structures given at the beginning of this essay.

These three structures are less rigorously metaphorical, and are rather significant constellations of images, which, when found together, make up what is often called, somewhat helplessly, "atmosphere." The mode of romance presents an idealized world: in romance heroes are brave, heroines beautiful, villains villainous, and the frustrations, ambiguities, and embarrassments of ordinary life are made little of. Hence its imagery presents a human counterpart of the apocalyptic world which we may call the *analogy of innocence*. It is best known to us, not from the age of romance itself, but from later romanticizings: *Comus*, *The Tempest*, and the third book of *The Faerie Queene* in the Renaissance; Blake's songs of innocence and "Beulah" imagery, Keats's *Endymion* and Shelley's *Epipsychidion* in the Romantic period proper.

In the analogy of innocence the divine or spiritual figures are usually parental, wise old men with magical powers like Prospero, or friendly guardian spirits like Raphael before Adam's fall. Among the human figures children are prominent, and so is the virtue most closely associated with childhood and the state of innocence—chastity, a virtue which in this structure of imagery usually includes virginity. In *Comus* the Lady's chastity is, like Prospero's wisdom, associated with magic, as is the invincible chastity of Spenser's Britomart. It is easiest to associate with young women—Dante's Matelda and Shakespeare's Miranda are examples—but male chastity is important too, as the Grail romances show. Sir Galahad's remark in Tennyson about his purity of heart giving him tenfold strength is consistent with the imagery of the world he belongs in. Fire in the innocent world is usually a purifying symbol, a world of flame that none but the perfectly chaste can pass, as in Spenser's castle of Busirane, the refining fire at the top of Dante's purgatory, and the flaming sword that keeps the fallen Adam and Eve away from Paradise. In the story of the sleeping beauty, which belongs here, the wall of flame is replaced by one of thorns and brambles: Wagner's *Die Walküre*, however, retains the fire, to the discomposure of stage managers. The moon, the coolest and hence most chaste of all the fiery heavenly bodies, has a special importance for this world.

Of animals, the most obvious are the pastoral sheep and lambs, along with the horses and hounds of romance, in their gentler aspects of fidelity and devotion. The unicorn, the traditional emblem of chastity and the lover of virgins, has an honored place here; so does the dolphin, whose association with Arion makes him the innocent contrast to the devouring leviathan; and also, for its humility and submissiveness, a very different animal—the ass. The dramatic festival of the ass, no less than that of the Boy Bishop, belongs to this structure of imagery, and when Shakespeare put an ass's head in Fairyland he was not doing something unique, as Robinson's poem implies, but following a tradition that goes back to the transformed Lucius listening to the story of Cupid and Psyche in Apuleius. Birds, butterflies (for this is Psyche's world, and Psyche means butterfly), and spirits with their qualities, like Ariel and Hudson's Rima, are other naturalized denizens.

The paradisal garden and the tree of life belong in the apocalyptic structure, as we saw, but the garden of Eden itself, as presented in the Bible and Milton, belongs rather to this one, and Dante puts it just below his Paradiso. Spenser's Gardens of Adonis, from which the attendant spirit in *Comus* comes, are parallel, along with all the medieval developments of the theme of the *locus amoenus*. Of special significance is the symbol of the body of the Virgin as a *hortus conclusus*, derived from the Song of Songs. A romantic counterpart to the tree of life appears in the magician's life-giving wand, and such parallel symbols as the blossoming rod in *Tannhaüser*.

Cities are more alien to the pastoral and rural spirit of this world, and the tower and the castle, with an occasional cottage or hermitage, are the chief images of habitation. Water symbolism features chiefly fountains and pools, fertilizing rains, and an occasional stream separating a man from a woman and so preserving the chastity of each, like the river of Lethe in Dante. The opening rose-garden episode of *Burnt Norton* gives a brief but extraordinarily complete summary of the symbols of the analogy of innocence; one may also compare the second section of Auden's *Kairos and Logos*.

The innocent world is neither totally alive, like the apocalyptic one, nor mostly dead, like ours: it is an animistic world, full of elemental spirits. All the characters of *Comus* are elemental spirits except the Lady and her brothers, and the connections of Ariel with air-spirits, of Puck with fire-spirits (Burton says of fire-spirits that "we commonly call them Pucks"), and of Caliban with earth-spirits are clear enough. In Spenser we find Florimell and Marinell, whose names indicate that they are spirits of flowers and water, a Proserpine and an Adonis. Often, too, as in *Comus* and the *Nativity Ode*, innocent or unfallen nature, nature as a divinely sanctioned order, is represented by the inaudible harmony of the music of the spheres.

Just as the organizing ideas of romance are chastity and magic, so the organizing ideas of the high mimetic area seem to be love and form. And as the field of romantic images may be called an analogy of innocence, so the field of high mimetic imagery may be called an *analogy of nature and reason*. We find here the emphasis on cynosure or centripetal gaze, and the tendency to idealize the human representatives of the divine and the spiritual world, which are characteristic of the high mimetic. Divinity hedges the king and the Courtly Love mistress is a goddess; love of both is an educating and informing power which brings one into unity with the spiritual and divine worlds. The fire of the angelic world blazes in the king's crown and the lady's eyes. The animals are those of proud beauty: the eagle and the lion stand for the vision of the royal by the loyal, the horse and falcon for "chivalry" or the aristocracy on horseback; the peacock and the swan are the birds of cynosure, and the phoenix or unique fire-bird is a favorite poetic emblem, especially, in England, for Queen Elizabeth. Garden symbolism recedes into the background, as city symbolism does in romance; there are formal gardens in close association with buildings, but the idea of a garden *world* is still a romantic one. The magician's wand is metamorphosed into the royal sceptre, and the magic tree to the fluttering banner. The city is preeminently the capital city, with the court at its center and a series of initiatory degrees of approach within the court, climaxed by the royal "presence." We note that as we go down the modes an increasing number of poetic images are taken from actual social conditions of life. Water-symbolism centers on the disciplined river, in England the Thames which runs softly in Spenser and in neo-Classical rhythms in Denham, a river whose most appropriate ornament is the royal barge.

In the low mimetic area we enter a world that we may call the *analogy of experience*, and which bears a relation to the demonic world corresponding to the relation of the romantic innocent world to the apocalyptic one. Except for this potentially ironic connection, and except for a certain number of hieratic or specially indicated symbols like Hawthorne's scarlet letter and Henry James's golden bowl and ivory tower, the images are the ordinary images of experience, and need no further explanation here beyond a few comments about some particular features that may be of use. The organizing low mimetic ideas seem to be genesis and work. Divine and spiritual beings have little functional place in low mimetic fiction, and in thematic writing they are often deliberately rediscovered or treated as aesthetic surrogates. The advice is given to the unborn in *Erewhon* (apparently close to Butler's own view, as he repeats the idea in *Life and Habit*) that if there is a spiritual world, one should turn one's back on it and find it again in immediate work. The same doctrine of the rediscovery of faith through works may be found in Carlyle, Ruskin, Morris, and Shaw. In poets, even in explicitly sacramental ones, there are parallel tendencies. From many points of view there could hardly be a greater contrast than the contrast between the "motion and a spirit" discovered by Wordsworth in Tintern Abbey and the "chevalier" discovered by Hopkins in the windhover, yet the tendency to anchor a spiritual vision in an empirical psychological experience is common to both.

The low mimetic treatment of human society reflects, of course, Wordsworth's doctrine that the essential human situations, for the poet, are the common and typical ones. Along with this goes a good deal of parody of the idealization of life in romance, a parody that extends to religious and aesthetic experience. As for the animal world, Thomas Huxley's reference to the qualities that humanity shares with the ape and the tiger is a significantly low mimetic choice. The ape has always been *par excellence* the mimetic animal, and long before evolution he was specifically the imitator of man. The rise of evolution however suggested an analogy of proportion in which present man becomes the ape of his counterpart in the future, as in Nietzsche's *Zarathustra*. Huxley's coupling of the ape and the tiger recalls the popular belief in the implacable and invariable ferocity of both apes and "cavemen," a belief for which there seems to be little more evidence than for unicorns and phoenixes, but which, like them, shows a tendency to look at natural history from within the appropriate framework of poetic metaphors. The low mimetic is not a rich field for animal symbolism, but Huxley's ape and tiger recur in Kipling's *Jungle Book*, where the monkeys chatter in the tree-tops to no purpose, like intellectuals, while the human animal learns instead the dark predatory wisdom of the panther in the jungle below.

Gardens in the low mimetic give place to farms and the painful labor of the man with the hoe, the peasant or furze cutter who stands in Hardy as an image of man himself, "slighted and enduring." Cities take of course the shape of the labyrinthine modern metropolis, where the main emotional stress is on loneliness and lack of communication. And just as water symbolism in the world of innocence consists largely of fountains and running streams, so low mimetic imagery seeks Conrad's "destructive element" the sea, generally with some humanized leviathan or *bateau ivre* on it of any size from the Titanic in Hardy to the capsizable open boat which is, with an irony rare even in literature, a favorite image of Shelley. *Moby Dick* returns us to a more traditional form of the leviathan. The destroyer which appears at the end of H. G. Wells's *Tono-Bungay* is notable as coming from a low mimetic writer not much given to introducing hieratic symbols. Fire symbolism is often ironic and destructive, as in the fire which ends the action of *The Spoils of Poynton*. In the industrial age, however, Prometheus, who stole fire for man's use, is one of the favorite, if not the actual favorite, mythological figure among poets.

The relation of innocence and experience to apocalyptic and demonic imagery illustrates an aspect of displacement which we have so far said little about: displacement in the direction of the moral. The two dialectical structures are, radically, the desirable and the undesirable. Racks and dungeons belong in the sinister vision not because they are morally forbidden but because it is impossible to make them objects of desire. Sexual fulfilment, on the other hand, may be desired even if it is morally condemned. Civilization tends to try to make the desirable and the moral coincide. The student of comparative mythology occasionally turns up, in a primitive or ancient cult, a bit of uninhibited mythopoeia that makes him realize how completely all the higher religions have limited their apocalyptic visions to morally acceptable ones. A good deal of expurgation clearly lies behind the development of Jewish, Greek, and other mythologies; or, as Victorian students of myth used to say, a repulsive and grotesque barbarism has been purified by a growing ethical refinement. Egyptian mythology begins with a god who creates the world by masturbation—a logical enough way of symbolizing the process of creation *de Deo,* but not one that we should expect to find in Homer, to say nothing of the Old Testament. As long as poetry follows religion towards the moral, religious and poetic archetypes will be very close together, as they are in Dante. Under such influence apocalyptic sexual imagery, for instance, tends to become matrimonial or virginal; the incestuous, the homosexual, and the adulterous go on the demonic side. The quality in art that Aristotle called *spoudaios* and that Matthew Arnold translated as "high seriousness" results from this rapprochement of religion and poetry within a common moral framework.

But poetry continually tends to right its own balance, to return to the pattern of desire and away from the conventional and moral. It usually does this in satire, the genre which is furthest removed from "high seriousness," but not always. The moral and the desirable have many important and significant connections, but still morality, which comes to terms with experience and necessity, is one thing, and desire, which tries to escape from necessity, is quite another. Thus literature is as a rule less inflexible than morality, and it owes much of its status as a liberal art to that fact. The qualities that morality and religion usually call ribald, obscene, subversive, lewd, and blasphemous have an essential place in literature, but often they can achieve expression only through ingenious techniques of displacement.

The simplest of such techniques is the phenomenon that we may call "demonic modulation," or the deliberate reversal of the customary moral associations of archetypes. Any symbol at all takes its meaning primarily from its context: a dragon may be sinister in a medieval romance or friendly in a Chinese one; an island may be

Prospero's island or Circe's. But because of the large amount of learned and traditional symbolism in literature, certain secondary associations become habitual. The serpent, because of its role in the garden of Eden story, usually belongs on the sinister side of our catalogue in Western literature; the revolutionary sympathies of Shelley impel him to use an innocent serpent in *The Revolt of Islam*. Or a free and equal society may be symbolized by a band of robbers, pirates, or gypsies; or true love may be symbolized by the triumph of an adulterous liaison over marriage, as in most triangle comedy; by a homosexual passion (if it *is* true love that is celebrated in Virgil's second eclogue) or an incestuous one, as in many Romantics. In the nineteenth century, with demonic myth approaching, this kind of reversed symbolism is organized into all the patterns of the "Romantic agony," chiefly sadism, Prometheanism, and diabolism, which in some of the "decadents" seem to provide all the disadvantages of superstition with none of the advantages of religion. Diabolism is not however invariably a sophisticated development: Huckleberry Finn, for example, wins our sympathy and admiration by preferring hell with his hunted friend to the heaven of the white slave-owners' god. On the other hand, imagery traditionally demonic may be used for the starting-point of a movement of redemption, like the City of Destruction in *The Pilgrim's Progress*. Alchemical symbolism takes the ouroboros and the hermaphrodite (*res bina*), as well as the traditional romantic dragon, in this redemptive context.

Apocalyptic symbolism presents the infinitely desirable, in which the lusts and ambitions of man are identified with, adapted to, or projected on the gods. The art of the analogy of innocence, which includes most of the comic (in its happy-ending aspect), the idyllic, the romantic, the reverent, the panegyrical, the idealized, and the magical, is largely concerned with an attempt to present the desirable in human, familiar, attainable, and morally allowable terms. Much the same is true of the relation of the demonic world to the analogy of experience. Tragedy, for instance, is a vision of what does happen and must be accepted. To this extent it is a moral and plausible displacement of the bitter resentments that humanity feels against all obstacles to its desires. However malignant we may feel Athene to be in Sophocles' *Ajax*, the tragedy clearly implies that we must come to terms with her possession of power, even in our thoughts. A Christian who believed the Greek gods to be nothing but devils would, if he were criticizing a tragedy of Sophocles, make an undisplaced or demonic interpretation of it. Such an interpretation would bring out everything that Sophocles was trying *not* to say; but it could be a shrewd criticism of its latent or underlying demonic structure for all that. The same kind of interpretation would be equally possible for many passages of Christian poetry dealing with the just wrath of God, the demonic content of which is often a hated father-figure. In pointing out the latent apocalyptic or demonic patterns in a literary work, we should not make the error of assuming that this latent content is the *real* content hypocritically disguised by a lying censor. It is simply one factor which is relevant to a full critical analysis. It is often, however, the factor which lifts a work of literature out of the category of the merely historical.

THEORY OF MYTHOS: INTRODUCTION

The meaning of a poem, its structure of imagery, is a static pattern. The five structures of meaning we have given are, to use another musical analogy, the *keys* in which they are written and finally resolve; but narrative involves movement from one structure to another. The main area of such movement obviously has to be the three intermediate fields. The apocalyptic and demonic worlds, being structures of pure metaphorical identity, suggest the eternally unchanging, and lend themselves very readily to being projected existentially as heaven and hell, where there is continuous life but no *process* of life. The analogies of innocence and experience represent the adaptation of myth to nature: they give us, not *the* city and *the* garden at the final goal of human vision, but the process of building and planting. The fundamental form of process is cyclical movement, the alternation of success and decline, effort and repose, life and death which is the rhythm of process. Hence our seven categories of images may also be seen as different forms of rotary or cyclical movement. Thus:

1. In the divine world the central process or movement is that of the death and rebirth, or the disappearance and return, or the incarnation and withdrawal, of a god. This divine activity is usually identified or associated with one or more of the cyclical processes of nature. The god may be a sun-god, dying at night and reborn at dawn, or else with an annual rebirth at the winter solstice; or he

may be a god of vegetation, dying in autumn and reviving in spring, or (as in the birth stories of the Buddha) he may be an incarnate god going through a series of human or animal life-cycles. As a god is almost by definition immortal, it is a regular feature of all such myths that the dying god is reborn as the same person. Hence the mythical or abstract structural principle of the cycle is that the continuum of identity in the individual life from birth to death is extended from death to rebirth. To this pattern of identical recurrence, the death and revival of the same individual, all other cyclical patterns are as a rule assimilated. The assimilation can be of course much closer in Eastern culture, where the doctrine of reincarnation is generally accepted, than in the West.

2. The fire-world of heavenly bodies presents us with three important cyclical rhythms. Most obvious is the daily journey of the sun-god across the sky, often thought of as guiding a boat or chariot, followed by a mysterious passage through a dark underworld, sometimes conceived as the belly of a devouring monster, back to the starting point. The solstitial cycle of the solar year supplies an extension of the same symbolism, incorporated in our Christmas literature. Here there is more emphasis on the theme of a newborn light threatened by the powers of darkness. The lunar cycle has been on the whole of less importance to Western poetry in historic times, whatever its prehistoric role. But its crucial sequence of old moon, "interlunar cave," and new moon may be the source, as it is clearly a close analogy, of the three-day rhythm of death, disappearance, and resurrection which we have in our Easter symbolism.

3. The human world is midway between the spiritual and the animal, and reflects that duality in its cyclical rhythms. Closely parallel to the solar cycle of light and darkness is the imaginative cycle of waking and of dreaming life. This cycle underlies the antithesis of the imagination of experience and of innocence already dealt with. For the human rhythm is the opposite of the solar one: a titanic libido wakes when the sun sleeps, and the light of day is often the darkness of desire. Then again, in common with animals, man exhibits the ordinary cycle of life and death, in which there is generic but not individual rebirth.

4. It is rare, in literature as in life, to find even a domesticated animal peacefully living through its full span of life to reach a final *nunc dimittis*. The exceptions, such as Odysseus' dog, are appropriate to the theme of *nostos* or full close of a cyclical movement. Ani-

mal lives, and human lives similarly subject to the order of nature, suggest more frequently the *tragic* process of life cut off violently by accident, sacrifice, ferocity, or some overriding need, the continuity which flows on after the tragic act being something other than the life itself.

5. The vegetable world supplies us of course with the annual cycle of seasons, often identified with or represented by a divine figure which dies in the autumn or is killed with the gathering of the harvest and the vintage, disappears in winter, and revives in spring. The divine figure may be male (Adonis) or female (Proserpine), but the symbolic structures resulting differ somewhat.

6. Poets, like critics, have generally been Spenglerians, in the sense that in poetry, as in Spengler, civilized life is frequently assimilated to the organic cycle of growth, maturity, decline, death, and rebirth in another individual form. Themes of a golden or heroic age in the past, of a millennium in the future, of the wheel of fortune in social affairs, of the *ubi sunt* elegy, of meditations over ruins, of nostalgia for a lost pastoral simplicity, of regret or exultation over the collapse of an empire, belong here.

7. Water-symbolism has also its own cycle, from rains to springs, from springs and fountains to brooks and rivers, from rivers to the sea or the winter snow, and back again.

These cyclical symbols are usually divided into four main phases, the four seasons of the year being the type for four periods of the day (morning, noon, evening, night), four aspects of the water-cycle (rain, fountains, rivers, sea or snow), four periods of life (youth, maturity, age, death), and the like. We find a great number of symbols from phases one and two in Keats's *Endymion*, and of symbols from phases three and four in *The Waste Land* (where we have to add four stages of Western culture, medieval, Renaissance, eighteenth-century, and contemporary). We may note that there is no cycle of air: the wind bloweth where it listeth, and images dealing with the movement of "spirit" are likely to be associated with the theme of unpredictability or sudden crisis.

In studying poems of immense scope, such as the *Commedia* or *Paradise Lost*, we find that we have to learn a good deal of cosmology. This cosmology is presented, quite correctly of course, as the science of its day, a schematism of correspondences which, after supplying us with a not too efficient calendar and a few words like "phlegmatic" and "jovial," became defunct as science. There are also other poems incorporating equally obsolete science, such as *The Purple Island, The Loves of the Plants, The Art of Preserving Health*, which survive chiefly as curiosities. A literary critic should not overlook the compliment to poetry implied by the existence of such poems, but still versified science, as such, keeps the descriptive structure of science, and so imposes a non-poetic form on poetry. To make it successful as poetry a great deal of tact is required, yet those most attracted to such themes are very apt to be tactless poets. Dante and Milton were certainly better poets than Darwin or Fletcher: perhaps, however, it would be more fruitful to say that it was their finer instincts and judgements that led them to cosmological, as distinct from scientific or descriptive, themes.

For the form of cosmology is clearly much closer to that of poetry, and the thought suggests itself that symmetrical cosmology may be a branch of myth. If so, then it would be, like myth, a structural principle of poetry, whereas in science itself, symmetrical cosmology is exactly what Bacon said it was, an idol of the theatre. Perhaps, then, this whole pseudo-scientific world of three spirits, four humors, five elements, seven planets, nine spheres, twelve zodiacal signs, and so on, belongs in fact, as it does in practice, to the grammar of literary imagery. It has long been noticed that the Ptolemaic universe provides a better framework of symbolism, with all the identities, associations, and correspondences that symbolism demands, than the Copernican one does. Perhaps it not only provides a framework of poetic symbols but *is* one, or at any rate becomes one after it loses its validity as science, just as Classical mythology became purely poetic after its oracles had ceased. The same principle would account for the attraction of poets in the last century or two to occult systems of correspondences, and to such constructs as Yeats's *Vision* and Poe's *Eureka*.

The conception of a heaven above, a hell beneath, and a cyclical cosmos or order of nature in between forms the ground plan, *mutatis mutandis*, of both Dante and Milton. The same plan is in paintings of the Last Judgement, where there is a rotary movement of the saved rising on the right and the damned falling on the left. We may apply this construct to our principle that there are two fundamental movements of narrative: a cyclical movement within the order of nature, and a dialectical movement from that order into the apocalyptic world above. (The movement to the demonic world below is very rare, because a constant rotation within the order of nature is demonic in itself.)

The top half of the natural cycle is the world of romance and the analogy of innocence; the lower half is the world of "realism" and the analogy of experience. There are thus four main types of mythical movement: within romance, within experience, down, and up. The downward movement is the tragic movement, the wheel of fortune falling from innocence toward hamartia, and from hamartia to catastrophe. The upward movement is the comic movement, from threatening complications to a happy ending and a general assumption of post-dated innocence in which everyone lives happily ever after. In Dante the upward movement is through purgatory.

We have thus answered the question: are there narrative categories of literature broader than, or logically prior to, the ordinary literary genres? There are four such categories: the romantic, the tragic, the comic, and the ironic or satiric. We get the same answer by inspection if we look at the ordinary meanings of these terms. Tragedy and comedy may have been originally names for two species of drama, but we also employ the terms to describe general characteristics of literary fictions, without regard to genre. It would be silly to insist that comedy can refer only to a certain type of stage play, and must never be employed in connection with Chaucer or Jane Austen. Chaucer himself would certainly have defined comedy, as his monk defines tragedy, much more broadly than that. If we are told that what we are about to read is tragic or comic, we expect a certain kind of structure and mood, but not necessarily a certain genre. The same is true of the word romance, and also of the words irony and satire, which are, as generally employed, elements of the literature of experience, and which we shall here adopt in place of "realism." We thus have four narrative pregeneric elements of literature which I shall call *mythoi* or generic plots.

If we think of our experience of these *mythoi*, we shall realize that they form two opposed pairs. Tragedy and comedy contrast rather than blend, and so do romance and irony, the champions respectively of the ideal and the actual. On the other hand, comedy blends insensibly into satire at one extreme and into romance at the other; romance may be comic or tragic; tragic extends from high romance to bitter and ironic realism.

THE MYTHOS OF SPRING: COMEDY

Dramatic comedy, from which fictional comedy is mainly descended, has been remarkably tenacious of its structural principles and character types. Bernard Shaw remarked that a comic dramatist could get a reputation for daring originality by stealing his method from Molière and his characters from Dickens: if we were to read Menander and Aristophanes for Molière and Dickens the statement would be hardly less true, at least as a general principle. The earliest extant European comedy, Aristophanes' *The Acharnians*, contains the *miles gloriosus* or military braggart who is still going strong in Chaplin's *Great Dictator*; the Joxer Daly of O'Casey's *Juno and the Paycock* has the same character and dramatic function as the parasites of twenty-five hundred years ago, and the audiences of vaudeville, comic strips, and television programs still laugh at the jokes that were declared to be outworn at the opening of *The Frogs*.

The plot structure of Greek New Comedy, as transmitted by Plautus and Terence, in itself less a form than a formula, has become the basis for most comedy, especially in its more highly conventionalized dramatic form, down to our own day. It will be most convenient to work out the theory of comic construction from drama, using illustrations from fiction only incidentally. What normally happens is that a young man wants a young woman, that his desire is resisted by some opposition, usually paternal, and that near the end of the play some twist in the plot enables the hero to have his will. In this simple pattern there are several complex elements. In the first place, the movement of comedy is usually a movement from one kind of society to another. At the beginning of the play the obstructing characters are in charge of the play's society, and the audience recognizes that they are usurpers. At the end of the play the device in the plot that brings hero and heroine together causes a new society to crystallize around the hero, and the moment when this crystallization occurs is the point of resolution in the action, the comic discovery, *anagnorisis* or *cognitio*.

The appearance of this new society is frequently signalized by some kind of party or festive ritual, which either appears at the end of the play or is assumed to take place immediately afterward. Weddings are most common, and sometimes so many of them occur, as in the quadruple wedding at the end of *As You Like It*, that they suggest also the wholesale pairing off that takes place in a dance, which is another common conclusion, and the normal one for the masque. The banquet at the end of *The Taming of the Shrew* has an ancestry that goes back to Greek Middle Comedy; in Plautus the audience is sometimes jocosely invited to an imaginary banquet afterwards; Old Comedy, like the modern Christmas pantomime, was more generous, and occasionally threw bits of food to the audience. As the final society reached by comedy is the one that the audience has recognized all along to be the proper and desirable state of affairs, an act of communion with the audience is in order. Tragic actors expect to be applauded as well as comic ones, but nevertheless the word "plaudite" at the end of a Roman comedy, the invitation to the audience to form part of the comic society, would seem rather out of place at the end of a tragedy. The resolution of comedy comes, so to speak, from the audience's side of the stage; in a tragedy it comes from some mysterious world on the opposite side. In the movie, where darkness permits a more erotically oriented audience, the plot usually moves toward an act which, like death in Greek tragedy, takes place offstage, and is symbolized by a closing embrace.

The obstacles to the hero's desire, then, form the action of the comedy, and the overcoming of them the comic resolution. The obstacles are usually parental, hence comedy often turns on a clash between a son's and a father's will. Thus the comic dramatist as a rule writes for the younger men in his audience, and the older members of almost any society are apt to feel that comedy has something subversive about it. This is certainly one element in the social persecution of drama, which is not peculiar to Puritans or even Christians, as Terence in pagan Rome met much the same kind of social opposition that Ben Jonson did. There is one scene in Plautus where a son and father are making love to the same courtesan, and the son asks his father pointedly if he really does love mother. One has to see this scene against the background of Roman family life to understand its importance as psychological release. Even in Shakespeare there are startling outbreaks of baiting older men, and in contemporary movies the triumph of youth is so relentless that the moviemakers find some difficulty in getting anyone over the age of seventeen into their audiences.

The opponent to the hero's wishes, when not the father, is generally someone who partakes of the father's closer relation to established society: that is, a rival with less youth and more money. In Plautus and Terence he is usually either the pimp who owns the girl, or a wandering soldier with a supply of ready cash. The fury with which these characters are baited and exploded from the stage shows that they are father-surrogates, and even if they were not, they would still be usurpers, and their claim to possess the girl must be shown up as somehow fraudulent. They are, in short, impostors, and the extent to which they have real power implies some criticism of the society that allows them their power. In Plautus and Terence this criticism seldom goes beyond the immorality of brothels and professional harlots, but in Renaissance dramatists, including Jonson, there is some sharp observation of the rising power of money and the sort of ruling class it is building up.

The tendency of comedy is to include as many people as possible in its final society: the blocking characters are more often reconciled or converted than simply repudiated. Comedy often includes a scapegoat ritual of expulsion which gets rid of some irreconcilable character, but exposure and disgrace make for pathos, or even tragedy. *The Merchant of Venice* seems almost an experiment in coming as close as possible to upsetting the comic balance. If the dramatic role of Shylock is ever so slightly exaggerated, as it generally is when the leading actor of the company takes the part, it is upset, and the play becomes the tragedy of the Jew of Venice with a comic epilogue. *Volpone* ends with a great bustle of sentences to penal servitude and the galleys, and one feels that the deliverance of society hardly needs so much hard labor; but then *Volpone* is exceptional in being a kind of comic imitation of a tragedy, with the point of Volpone's hybris carefully marked.

The principle of conversion becomes clearer with characters whose chief function is the amusing of the audience. The original *miles gloriosus* in Plautus is a son of Jove and Venus who has killed an elephant with his fist and seven thousand men in one day's fighting. In other words, he is trying to put on a good show: the exuberance of his boasting helps to put the play over. The convention says that the braggart must be exposed, ridiculed, swindled, and beaten. But why should a professional dramatist, of all people, want so to harry a character who is putting on a good show—*his* show at that? When we find Falstaff invited to the final feast in *The Merry Wives*, Caliban reprieved, attempts made to mollify Malvolio, and Angelo and Parolles allowed to live down their dis-

THIRD ESSAY: ARCHETYPAL CRITICISM

grace, we are seeing a fundamental principle of comedy at work. The tendency of the comic society to include rather than exclude is the reason for the traditional importance of the parasite, who has no business to be at the final festival but is nevertheless there. The word "grace," with all its Renaissance overtones from the graceful courtier of Castiglione to the gracious God of Christianity, is a most important thematic word in Shakespearean comedy.

The action of comedy in moving from one social center to another is not unlike the action of a lawsuit, in which plaintiff and defendant construct different versions of the same situation, one finally being judged as real and the other as illusory. This resemblance of the rhetoric of comedy to the rhetoric of jurisprudence has been recognized from earliest times. A little pamphlet called the *Tractatus Coislinianus*, closely related to Aristotle's *Poetics*, which sets down all the essential facts about comedy in about a page and a half, divides the *dianoia* of comedy into two parts, opinion (*pistis*) and proof (*gnosis*). These correspond roughly to the usurping and the desirable societies respectively. Proofs (i.e., the means of bringing about the happier society) are subdivided into oaths, compacts, witnesses, ordeals (or tortures), and laws—in other words the five forms of material proof in law cases listed in the *Rhetoric*. We notice how often the action of a Shakespearean comedy begins with some absurd, cruel, or irrational law: the law of killing Syracusans in the *Comedy of Errors*, the law of compulsory marriage in *A Midsummer Night's Dream*, the law that confirms Shylock's bond, the attempts of Angelo to legislate people into righteousness, and the like, which the action of the comedy then evades or breaks. Compacts are as a rule the conspiracies formed by the hero's society; witnesses, such as overhearers of conversations or people with special knowledge (like the hero's old nurse with her retentive memory for birthmarks), are the commonest devices for bringing about the comic discovery. Ordeals (*basanoi*) are usually tests or touchstones of the hero's character: the Greek word also means touchstones, and seems to be echoed in Shakespeare's Bassanio whose ordeal it is to make a judgement on the worth of metals.

There are two ways of developing the form of comedy: one is to throw the main emphasis on the blocking characters; the other is to throw it forward on the scenes of discovery and reconciliation. One is the general tendency of comic irony, satire, realism, and

166

studies of manners; the other is the tendency of Shakespearean and other types of romantic comedy. In the comedy of manners the main ethical interest falls as a rule on the blocking characters. The technical hero and heroine are not often very interesting people: the *adulescentes* of Plautus and Terence are all alike, as hard to tell apart in the dark as Demetrius and Lysander, who may be parodies of them. Generally the hero's character has the neutrality that enables him to represent a wish-fulfilment. It is very different with the miserly or ferocious parent, the boastful or foppish rival, or the other characters who stand in the way of the action. In Molière we have a simple but fully tested formula in which the ethical interest is focussed on a single blocking character, a heavy father, a miser, a misanthrope, a hypocrite, or a hypochondriac. These are the figures that we remember, and the plays are usually named after them, but we can seldom remember all the Valentins and Angeliques who wriggle out of their clutches. In *The Merry Wives* the technical hero, a man named Fenton, has only a bit part, and this play has picked up a hint or two from Plautus's *Casina*, where the hero and heroine are not even brought on the stage at all. Fictional comedy, especially Dickens, often follows the same practice of grouping its interesting characters around a somewhat dullish pair of technical leads. Even Tom Jones, though far more fully realized, is still deliberately associated, as his commonplace name indicates, with the conventional and typical.

Comedy usually moves toward a happy ending, and the normal response of the audience to a happy ending is "this should be," which sounds like a moral judgement. So it is, except that it is not moral in the restricted sense, but social. Its opposite is not the villainous but the absurd, and comedy finds the virtues of Malvolio as absurd as the vices of Angelo. Molière's misanthrope, being committed to sincerity, which is a virtue, is morally in a strong position, but the audience soon realizes that his friend Philinte, who is ready to lie quite cheerfully in order to enable other people to preserve their self-respect, is the more genuinely sincere of the two. It is of course quite possible to have a moral comedy, but the result is often the kind of melodrama that we have described as comedy without humor, and which achieves its happy ending with a self-righteous tone that most comedy avoids. It is hardly possible to imagine a drama without conflict, and it is hardly possible to imagine a conflict without some kind of enmity. But just as love, including sexual love, is a very different thing from lust, so enmity is a very different thing from hatred. In tragedy, of course, enmity almost always includes hatred; comedy is different, and one feels that the social judgement against the absurd is closer to the comic norm than the moral judgement against the wicked.

The question then arises of what makes the blocking character absurd. Ben Jonson explained this by his theory of the "humor," the character dominated by what Pope calls a ruling passion. The humor's dramatic function is to express a state of what might be called ritual bondage. He is obsessed by his humor, and his function in the play is primarily to repeat his obsession. A sick man is not a humor, but a hypochondriac is, because, *qua* hypochondriac, he can never admit to good health, and can never do anything inconsistent with the role that he has prescribed for himself. A miser can do and say nothing that is not connected with the hiding of gold or saving of money. In *The Silent Woman*, Jonson's nearest approach to Molière's type of construction, the whole action recedes from the humor of Morose, whose determination to eliminate noise from his life produces so loquacious a comic action.

The principle of the humor is the principle that unincremental repetition, the literary imitation of ritual bondage, is funny. In a tragedy—*Oedipus Tyrannus* is the stock example—repetition leads logically to catastrophe. Repetition overdone or not going anywhere belongs to comedy, for laughter is partly a reflex, and like other reflexes it can be conditioned by a simple repeated pattern. In Synge's *Riders to the Sea* a mother, after losing her husband and five sons at sea, finally loses her last son, and the result is a very beautiful and moving play. But if it had been a full-length tragedy plodding glumly through the seven drownings one after another, the audience would have been helpless with unsympathetic laughter long before it was over. The principle of repetition as the basis of humor both in Jonson's sense and in ours is well known to the creators of comic strips, in which a character is established as a parasite, a glutton (often confined to one dish), or a shrew, and who begins to be funny after the point has been made every day for several months. Continuous comic radio programs, too, are much more amusing to habitués than to neophytes. The girth of Falstaff and the hallucinations of Quixote are based on much the same comic laws. Mr. E. M. Forster speaks with disdain of Dickens's Mrs. Micawber, who never says anything except that she will never desert Mr. Micawber: a strong contrast is marked here between the refined writer too finicky for popular formulas, and the major one who exploits them ruthlessly.

The humor in comedy is usually someone with a good deal of social prestige and power, who is able to force much of the play's society into line with his obsession. Thus the humor is intimately connected with the theme of the absurd or irrational law that the action of comedy moves toward breaking. It is significant that the central character of our earliest humor comedy, *The Wasps*, is obsessed by law cases: Shylock, too, unites a craving for the law with the humor of revenge. Often the absurd law appears as a whim of a bemused tyrant whose will is law, like Leontes or the humorous Duke Frederick in Shakespeare, who makes some arbitrary decision or rash promise: here law is replaced by "oath," also mentioned in the *Tractatus*. Or it may take the form of a sham Utopia, a society of ritual bondage constructed by an act of humorous or pedantic will, like the academic retreat in *Love's Labor's Lost*. This theme is also as old as Aristophanes, whose parodies of Platonic social schemes in *The Birds* and *Ecclesiazusae* deal with it.

The society emerging at the conclusion of comedy represents, by contrast, a kind of moral norm, or pragmatically free society. Its ideals are seldom defined or formulated: definition and formulation belong to the humors, who want predictable activity. We are simply given to understand that the newly-married couple will live happily ever after, or that at any rate they will get along in a relatively unhumorous and clear-sighted manner. That is one reason why the character of the successful hero is so often left undeveloped: his real life begins at the end of the play, and we have to believe him to be potentially a more interesting character than he appears to be. In Terence's *Adelphoi*, Demea, a harsh father, is contrasted with his brother Micio, who is indulgent. Micio being more liberal, he leads the way to the comic resolution, and converts Demea, but then Demea points out the indolence inspiring a good deal of Micio's liberality, and releases him from a complementary humorous bondage.

Thus the movement from *pistis* to *gnosis*, from a society controlled by habit, ritual bondage, arbitrary law and the older characters to a society controlled by youth and pragmatic freedom is fundamentally, as the Greek words suggest, a movement from illusion to reality. Illusion is whatever is fixed or definable, and reality is best understood as its negation: whatever reality is, it's not *that*. Hence the importance of the theme of creating and dispelling illusion in comedy: the illusions caused by disguise, obsession, hypocrisy, or unknown parentage.

The comic ending is generally manipulated by a twist in the plot. In Roman comedy the heroine, who is usually a slave or courtesan, turns out to be the daughter of somebody respectable, so that the hero can marry her without loss of face. The *cognitio* in comedy, in which the characters find out who their relatives are, and who is left of the opposite sex not a relative, and hence available for marriage, is one of the features of comedy that have never changed much: *The Confidential Clerk* indicates that it still holds the attention of dramatists. There is a brilliant parody of a *cognitio* at the end of *Major Barbara* (the fact that the hero of this play is a professor of Greek perhaps indicates an unusual affinity to the conventions of Euripides and Menander), where Undershaft is enabled to break the rule that he cannot appoint his son-in-law as successor by the fact that the son-in-law's own father married his deceased wife's sister in Australia, so that the son-in-law is his own first cousin as well as himself. It sounds complicated, but the plots of comedy often are complicated because there is something inherently absurd about complications. As the main character interest in comedy is so often focussed on the defeated characters, comedy regularly illustrates a victory of arbitrary plot over consistency of character. Thus, in striking contrast to tragedy, there can hardly be such a thing as inevitable comedy, as far as the action of the individual play is concerned. That is, we may know that the convention of comedy will make some kind of happy ending inevitable, but still for each play the dramatist must produce a distinctive "gimmick" or "weenie," to use two disrespectful Hollywood synonyms for *anagnorisis*. Happy endings do not impress us as true, but as desirable, and they are brought about by manipulation. The watcher of death and tragedy has nothing to do but sit and wait for the inevitable end; but something gets born at the end of comedy, and the watcher of birth is a member of a busy society.

The manipulation of plot does not always involve metamorphosis of character, but there is no violation of comic decorum when it does. Unlikely conversions, miraculous transformations, and providential assistance are inseparable from comedy. Further, whatever emerges is supposed to be there for good: if the curmudgeon becomes lovable, we understand that he will not immediately relapse again into his ritual habit. Civilizations which stress the desirable rather than the real, and the religious as opposed to the scientific perspective, think of drama almost entirely in terms of comedy. In the classical drama of India, we are told, the tragic ending was regarded as bad taste, much as the manipulated endings of comedy are regarded as bad taste by novelists interested in ironic realism.

The total *mythos* of comedy, only a small part of which is ordinarily presented, has regularly what in music is called a ternary form: the hero's society rebels against the society of the *senex* and triumphs, but the hero's society is a Saturnalia, a reversal of social standards which recalls a golden age in the past before the main action of the play begins. Thus we have a stable and harmonious order disrupted by folly, obsession, forgetfulness, "pride and prejudice," or events not understood by the characters themselves, and then restored. Often there is a benevolent grandfather, so to speak, who overrules the action set up by the blocking humor and so links the first and third parts. An example is Mr. Burchell, the disguised uncle of the wicked squire, in *The Vicar of Wakefield*. A very long play, such as the Indian *Sakuntala*, may present all three phases; a very intricate one, such as many of Menander's evidently were, may indicate their outlines. But of course very often the first phase is not given at all: the audience simply understands an ideal state of affairs which it knows to be better than what is revealed in the play, and which it recognizes as like that to which the action leads. This ternary action is, ritually, like a contest of summer and winter in which winter occupies the middle action; psychologically, it is like the removal of a neurosis or blocking point and the restoring of an unbroken current of energy and memory. The Jonsonian masque, with the antimasque in the middle, gives a highly conventionalized or "abstract" version of it.

We pass now to the typical characters of comedy. In drama, characterization depends on function; what a character is follows from what he has to do in the play. Dramatic function in its turn depends on the structure of the play; the character has certain things to do because the play has such and such a shape. The structure of the play in its turn depends on the category of the play; if it is a comedy, its structure will require a comic resolution and a prevailing comic mood. Hence when we speak of typical characters, we are not trying to reduce lifelike characters to stock types, though we certainly are suggesting that the sentimental notion of an antithesis between the lifelike character and the stock type is a vulgar error. All lifelike characters, whether in drama or fiction, owe their consistency to the appropriateness of the stock type which belongs to their dramatic function. That stock type is not the character but it is as necessary to the character as a skeleton is to the actor who plays it.

With regard to the characterization of comedy, the *Tractatus* lists three types of comic characters: the *alazons* or impostors, the *eirons* or self-deprecators, and the buffoons (*bomolochoi*). This list is closely related to a passage in the *Ethics* which contrasts the first two, and then goes on to contrast the buffoon with a character whom Aristotle calls *agroikos* or churlish, literally rustic. We may reasonably accept the churl as a fourth character type, and so we have two opposed pairs. The contest of *eiron* and *alazon* forms the basis of the comic action, and the buffoon and the churl polarize the comic mood.

We have previously dealt with the terms *eiron* and *alazon*. The humorous blocking characters of comedy are nearly always impostors, though it is more frequently a lack of self-knowledge than simple hypocrisy that characterizes them. The multitudes of comic scenes in which one character complacently soliloquizes while another makes sarcastic asides to the audience show the contest of *eiron* and *alazon* in its purest form, and show too that the audience is sympathetic to the *eiron* side. Central to the *alazon* group is the *senex iratus* or heavy father, who with his rages and threats, his obsessions and his gullibility, seems closely related to some of the demonic characters of romance, such as Polyphemus. Occasionally a character may have the dramatic function of such a figure without his characteristics: an example is Squire Allworthy in *Tom Jones*, who as far as the plot is concerned behaves almost as stupidly as Squire Western. Of heavy-father surrogates, the *miles gloriosus* has been mentioned: his popularity is largely due to the fact that he is a man of words rather than deeds, and is consequently far more useful to a practising dramatist than any tight-lipped hero could ever be. The pedant, in Renaissance comedy often a student of the occult sciences, the fop or coxcomb, and similar humors, require no comment. The female *alazon* is rare: Katharina the shrew represents to some extent a female *miles gloriosus,* and the *précieuse ridicule* a female pedant, but the "menace" or siren who gets in the way of the true heroine is more often found as a sinister figure of melodrama or romance than as a ridiculous figure in comedy.

The *eiron* figures need a little more attention. Central to this group is the hero, who is an *eiron* figure because, as explained, the dramatist tends to play him down and make him rather neutral and unformed in character. Next in importance is the heroine, also often played down: in Old Comedy, when a girl accompanies a male hero in his triumph, she is generally a stage prop, a *muta persona* not previously introduced. A more difficult form of *cognitio* is achieved when the heroine disguises herself or through some other device brings about the comic resolution, so that the person whom the hero is seeking turns out to be the person who has sought him. The fondness of Shakespeare for this "she stoops to conquer" theme needs only to be mentioned here, as it belongs more naturally to the *mythos* of romance.

Another central *eiron* figure is the type entrusted with hatching the schemes which bring about the hero's victory. This character in Roman comedy is almost always a tricky slave (*dolosus servus*), and in Renaissance comedy he becomes the scheming valet who is so frequent in Continental plays, and in Spanish drama is called the *gracioso.* Modern audiences are most familiar with him in Figaro and in the Leporello of *Don Giovanni.* Through such intermediate nineteenth-century figures as Micawber and the Touchwood of Scott's *St. Ronan's Well,* who, like the gracioso, have buffoon affiliations, he evolves into the amateur detective of modern fiction. The Jeeves of P. G. Wodehouse is a more direct descendant. Female confidantes of the same general family are often brought in to oil the machinery of the well-made play. Elizabethan comedy had another type of trickster, represented by the Matthew Merrygreek of *Ralph Roister Doister,* who is generally said to be developed from the vice or iniquity of the morality plays: as usual, the analogy is sound enough, whatever historians decide about origins. The vice, to give him that name, is very useful to a comic dramatist because he acts from pure love of mischief, and can set a comic action going with the minimum of motivation. The vice may be as light-hearted as Puck or as malignant as Don John in *Much Ado,* but as a rule the vice's activity is, in spite of his name, benevolent.

One of the tricky slaves in Plautus, in a soliloquy, boasts that he is the *architectus* of the comic action: such a character carries out the will of the author to reach a happy ending. He is in fact the spirit of comedy, and the two clearest examples of the type in Shakespeare, Puck and Ariel, are both spiritual beings. The tricky slave often has his own freedom in mind as the reward of his exertions: Ariel's longing for release is in the same tradition.

The role of the vice includes a great deal of disguising, and the type may often be recognized by disguise. A good example is the Brainworm of Jonson's *Every Man in His Humour,* who calls the action of the play the day of his metamorphoses. Similarly Ariel has to surmount the difficult stage direction of "Enter invisible." The vice is combined with the hero whenever the latter is a cheeky, improvident young man who hatches his own schemes and cheats his rich father or uncle into giving him his patrimony along with the girl.

Another *eiron* type has not been much noticed. This is a character, generally an older man, who begins the action of the play by withdrawing from it, and ends the play by returning. He is often a father with the motive of seeing what his son will do. The action of *Every Man in His Humour* is set going in this way by Knowell Senior. The disappearance and return of Lovewit, the owner of the house which is the scene of *The Alchemist,* has the same dramatic function, though the characterization is different. The clearest Shakespearean example is the Duke in *Measure for Measure,* but Shakespeare is more addicted to the type than might appear at first glance. In Shakespeare the vice is rarely the real *architectus*: Puck and Ariel both act under orders from an older man, if one may call Oberon a man for the moment. In *The Tempest* Shakespeare returns to a comic action established by Aristophanes, in which an older man, instead of retiring from the action, builds it up on the stage. When the heroine takes the vice role in Shakespeare, she is often significantly related to her father, even when the father is not in the play at all, like the father of Helena, who gives her his medical knowledge, or the father of Portia, who arranges the scheme of the caskets. A more conventionally treated example of the same benevolent Prospero figure turned up recently in the psychiatrist of *The Cocktail Party,* and one may compare the mysterious alchemist who is the father of the heroine of *The Lady's Not for Burning.* The formula is not confined to comedy: Polonius, who shows so many of the disadvantages of a literary education, attempts the role of a retreating paternal *eiron* three times, once too often. *Hamlet* and *King Lear* contain subplots which are ironic versions of stock comic themes, Gloucester's story being the regular comedy theme of the gullible *senex* swindled by a clever and unprincipled son.

We pass now to the buffoon types, those whose function it is to increase the mood of festivity rather than to contribute to the plot. Renaissance comedy, unlike Roman comedy, had a great variety of such characters, professional fools, clowns, pages, singers, and incidental characters with established comic habits like malapropism or foreign accents. The oldest buffoon of this incidental nature is the parasite, who may be given something to do, as Jonson gives Mosca the role of a vice in *Volpone*, but who, *qua* parasite, does nothing but entertain the audience by talking about his appetite. He derives chiefly from Greek Middle Comedy, which appears to have been very full of food, and where he was, not unnaturally, closely associated with another established buffoon type, the cook, a conventional figure who breaks into comedies to bustle and order about and make long speeches about the mysteries of cooking. In the role of cook the buffoon or entertainer appears, not simply as a gratuitous addition like the parasite, but as something more like a master of ceremonies, a center for the comic mood. There is no cook in Shakespeare, though there is a superb description of one in the *Comedy of Errors*, but a similar role is often attached to a jovial and loquacious host, like the "mad host" of *The Merry Wives* or the Simon Eyre of *The Shoemakers Holiday*. In Middleton's *A Trick to Catch the Old One* the mad host type is combined with the vice. In Falstaff and Sir Toby Belch we can see the affinities of the buffoon or entertainer type both with the parasite and with the master of revels. If we study this entertainer or host role carefully we shall soon realize that it is a development of what in Aristophanic comedy is represented by the chorus, and which in its turn goes back to the *komos* or revel from which comedy is said to be descended.

Finally, there is a fourth group to which we have assigned the word *agroikos*, and which usually means either churlish or rustic, depending on the context. This type may also be extended to cover the Elizabethan gull and what in vaudeville used to be called the straight man, the solemn or inarticulate character who allows the humor to bounce off him, so to speak. We find churls in the miserly, snobbish, or priggish characters whose role is that of the refuser of festivity, the killjoy who tries to stop the fun, or, like Malvolio, locks up the food and drink instead of dispensing it. The melancholy Jaques of *As You Like It*, who walks out on the final festivities, is closely related. In the sulky and self-centered Bertram of *All's Well* there is a most unusual and ingenious combination of this type with the hero. More often, however, the churl belongs to the *alazon* group, all miserly old men in comedies, including Shylock, being churls. In *The Tempest* Caliban has much the same relation to the churlish type that Ariel has to the vice or tricky slave. But often, where the mood is more light-hearted, we may translate *agroikos* simply by rustic, as with the innumerable country squires and similar characters who provide amusement in the urban setting of drama. Such types do not refuse the mood of festivity, but they mark the extent of its range. In a pastoral comedy the idealized virtues of rural life may be represented by a simple man who speaks for the pastoral ideal, like Corin in *As You Like It*. Corin has the same *agroikos* role as the "rube" or "hayseed" of more citified comedies, but the moral attitude to the role is reversed. Again we notice the principle that dramatic structure is a permanent and moral attitude a variable factor in literature.

In a very ironic comedy a different type of character may play the role of the refuser of festivity. The more ironic the comedy, the more absurd the society, and an absurd society may be condemned by, or at least contrasted with, a character that we may call the plain dealer, an outspoken advocate of a kind of moral norm who has the sympathy of the audience. Wycherley's Manly, though he provides the name for the type, is not a particularly good example of it: a much better one is the Cléante of *Tartuffe*. Such a character is appropriate when the tone is ironic enough to get the audience confused about its sense of the social norm: he corresponds roughly to the chorus in a tragedy, which is there for a similar reason. When the tone deepens from the ironic to the bitter, the plain dealer may become a malcontent or railer, who may be morally superior to his society, as he is to some extent in Marston's play of that name, but who may also be too motivated by envy to be much more than another aspect of his society's evil, like Thersites, or to some extent Apemantus.

In tragedy, pity and fear, the emotions of moral attraction and repulsion, are raised and cast out. Comedy seems to make a more functional use of the social, even the moral judgement, than tragedy, yet comedy seems to raise the corresponding emotions, which are sympathy and ridicule, and cast them out in the same way. Comedy ranges from the most savage irony to the most dreamy wish-fulfilment romance, but its structural patterns and characterization are much the same throughout its range. This principle of the uniformity of comic structure through a variety of attitudes is clear in Aristophanes. Aristophanes is the most personal of writers, and his opinions on every subject are written all over his plays. We know that he wanted peace with Sparta and that he hated Cleon, so when his comedy depicts the attaining of peace and the defeat of Cleon we know that he approved and wanted his audience to approve. But in *Ecclesiazusae* a band of women in disguise railroad a communistic scheme through the Assembly which is a horrid parody of a Platonic republic, and proceed to inaugurate its sexual communism with some astonishing improvements. Presumably Aristophanes did not altogether endorse this, yet the comedy follows the same pattern and the same resolution. In *The Birds* the Peisthetairos who defies Zeus and blocks out Olympus with his Cloud-Cuckoo-Land is accorded the same triumph that is given to the Trygaios of the *Peace* who flies to heaven and brings a golden age back to Athens.

Let us look now at a variety of comic structures between the extremes of irony and romance. As comedy blends into irony and satire at one end and into romance at the other, if there are different phases or types of comic structure, some of them will be closely parallel to some of the types of irony and of romance. A somewhat forbidding piece of symmetry turns up in our argument at this point, which seems to have some literary analogy to the circle of fifths in music. I recognize six phases of each *mythos*, three being parallel to the phases of a neighboring *mythos*. The first three phases of comedy are parallel to the first three phases of irony and satire, and the second three to the second three of romance. The distinction between an ironic comedy and a comic satire, or between a romantic comedy and a comic romance, is tenuous, but not quite a distinction without a difference.

The first or most ironic phase of comedy is, naturally, the one in which a humorous society triumphs or remains undefeated. A good example of a comedy of this type is *The Alchemist*, in which the returning *eiron* Lovewit joins the rascals, and the plain dealer Surly is made a fool of. In *The Beggar's Opera* there is a similar twist to the ending: the (projected) author feels that the hanging of the hero is a comic ending, but is informed by the manager that the audience's sense of comic decorum demands a reprieve, whatever Macheath's moral status. This phase of comedy presents what Renaissance critics called *speculum consuetudinis*, the way of the world, *cosi fan tutte*. A more intense irony is achieved when the humorous society simply disintegrates without anything taking its place, as in *Heartbreak House* and frequently in Chekhov.

We notice in ironic comedy that the demonic world is never far away. The rages of the *senex iratus* in Roman comedy are directed mainly at the tricky slave, who is threatened with the mill, with being flogged to death, with crucifixion, with having his head dipped in tar and set on fire, and the like, all penalties that could be and were exacted from slaves in life. An epilogue in Plautus informs us that the slave-actor who has blown up in his lines will now be flogged; in one of the Menander fragments a slave is tied up and burned with a torch on the stage. One sometimes gets the impression that the audience of Plautus and Terence would have guffawed uproariously all through the Passion. We may ascribe this to the brutality of a slave society, but then we remember that boiling oil and burying alive ("such a *stuffy* death") turn up in *The Mikado*. Two lively comedies of the modern stage are *The Cocktail Party* and *The Lady's Not for Burning*, but the cross appears in the background of the one and the stake in the background of the other. Shylock's knife and Angelo's gallows appear in Shakespeare: in *Measure for Measure* every male character is at one time or another threatened with death. The action of comedy moves toward a deliverance from something which, if absurd, is by no means invariably harmless. We notice too how frequently a comic dramatist tries to bring his action as close to a catastrophic overthrow of the hero as he can get it, and then reverses the action as quickly as possible. The evading or breaking of a cruel law is often a very narrow squeeze. The intervention of the king at the end of *Tartuffe* is deliberately arbitrary: there is nothing in the action of the play itself to prevent Tartuffe's triumph. Tom Jones in the final book, accused of murder, incest, debt, and double-dealing, cast off by friends, guardian, and sweetheart, is a woeful figure indeed before all these turn into illusions. Any reader can think of many comedies in which the fear of death, sometimes a hideous death, hangs over the central character to the end, and is dispelled so quickly that one has almost the sense of awakening from nightmare.

Sometimes the redeeming agent actually is divine, like Diana in *Pericles*; in *Tartuffe* it is the king, who is conceived as a part of the audience and the incarnation of its will. An extraordinary number of comic stories, both in drama and fiction, seem to approach a potentially tragic crisis near the end, a feature that I may call the "point of ritual death"—a clumsy expression that I would gladly surrender for a better one. It is a feature not often noticed by critics, but when it is present it is as unmistakably present as a stretto in a fugue, which it somewhat resembles. In Smollett's *Humphry Clinker* (I select this because no one will suspect Smollett of deliberate mythopoeia but only of following convention, at least as far as his plot is concerned), the main characters are nearly drowned in an accident with an upset carriage; they are then taken to a nearby house to dry off, and a *cognitio* takes place, in the course of which their family relationships are regrouped, secrets of birth brought to light, and names changed. Similar points of ritual death may be marked in almost any story that imprisons the hero or gives the heroine a nearly mortal illness before an eventually happy ending.

Sometimes the point of ritual death is vestigial, not an element in the plot but a mere change of tone. Everyone will have noted in comic actions, even in very trivial movies and magazine stories, a point near the end at which the tone suddenly becomes serious, sentimental, or ominous of potential catastrophe. In Aldous Huxley's *Chrome Yellow*, the hero Denis comes to a point of self-evaluation in which suicide nearly suggests itself: in most of Huxley's later books some violent action, generally suicidal, occurs at the corresponding point. In *Mrs. Dalloway* the actual suicide of Septimus becomes a point of ritual death for the heroine in the middle of her party. There are also some interesting Shakespearean variations of the device: a clown, for instance, will make a speech near the end in which the buffoon's mask suddenly falls off and we look straight into the face of a beaten and ridiculed slave. Examples are the speech of Dromio of Ephesus beginning "I am an ass indeed" in the *Comedy of Errors*, and the speech of the Clown in *All's Well* beginning "I am a woodland fellow."

The second phase of comedy, in its simplest form, is a comedy in which the hero does not transform a humorous society but simply escapes or runs away from it, leaving its structure as it was before. A more complex irony in this phase is achieved when a society is constructed by or around a hero, but proves not sufficiently real or strong to impose itself. In this situation the hero is usually himself at least partly a comic humor or mental runaway, and we have either a hero's illusion thwarted by a superior reality or a clash of two illusions. This is the quixotic phase of comedy, a difficult phase for drama, though *The Wild Duck* is a fairly pure example of it, and in drama it usually appears as a subordinate theme of another phase. Thus in *The Alchemist* Sir Epicure Mammon's dream of what he will do with the philosopher's stone is, like Quixote's, a gigantic dream, and makes him an ironic parody of Faustus (who is mentioned in the play), in the same way that Quixote is an ironic parody of Amadis and Lancelot. When the tone is more light-hearted, the comic resolution may be strong enough to sweep over all quixotic illusions. In *Huckleberry Finn* the main theme is one of the oldest in comedy, the freeing of a slave, and the *cognitio* tells us that Jim had already been set free before his escape was bungled by Tom Sawyer's pedantries. Because of its unrivalled opportunities for double-edged irony, this phase is a favorite of Henry James: perhaps his most searching study of it is *The Sacred Fount*, where the hero is an ironic parody of a Prospero figure creating another society out of the one in front of him.

The third phase of comedy is the normal one that we have been discussing, in which a *senex iratus* or other humor gives way to a young man's desires. The sense of the comic norm is so strong that when Shakespeare, by way of experiment, tried to reverse the pattern in *All's Well*, in having two older people force Bertram to marry Helena, the result has been an unpopular "problem" play, with a suggestion of something sinister about it. We have noted that the *cognitio* of comedy is much concerned with straightening out the details of the new society, with distinguishing brides from sisters and parents from foster-parents. The fact that the son and father are so often in conflict means that they are frequently rivals for the same girl, and the psychological alliance of the hero's bride and the mother is often expressed or implied. The occasional "naughtiness" of comedy, as in the Restoration period, has much to do, not only with marital infidelity, but with a kind of comic

Oedipus situation in which the hero replaces his father as a lover. In Congreve's *Love for Love* there are two Oedipus themes in counterpoint: the hero cheats his father out of the heroine, and his best friend violates the wife of an impotent old man who is the heroine's guardian. A theme which would be recognized in real life as a form of infantile regression, the hero pretending to be impotent in order to gain admission to the women's quarters, is employed in Wycherley's *Country Wife*, where it is taken from Terence's *Eunuchus*.

The possibilities of incestuous combinations form one of the minor themes of comedy. The repellent older woman offered to Figaro in marriage turns out to be his mother, and the fear of violating a mother also occurs in *Tom Jones*. When in *Ghosts* and *Little Eyolf* Ibsen employed the old chestnut about the object of the hero's affections being his sister (a theme as old as Menander), his startled hearers took it for a portent of social revolution. In Shakespeare the recurring and somewhat mysterious father-daughter relationship already alluded to appears in its incestuous form at the beginning of *Pericles*, where it forms the demonic antithesis of the hero's union with his wife and daughter at the end. The presiding genius of comedy is Eros, and Eros has to adapt himself to the moral facts of society: Oedipus and incest themes indicate that erotic attachments have in their undisplaced or mythical origin a much greater versatility.

Ambivalent attitudes naturally result, and ambivalence is apparently the main reason for the curious feature of doubled characters which runs all through the history of comedy. In Roman comedy there is often a pair of young men, and consequently a pair of young women, of which one is often related to one of the men and exogamous to the other. The doubling of the *senex* figure sometimes gives us a heavy father for both the hero and the heroine, as in *The Winter's Tale*, sometimes a heavy father and benevolent uncle, as in Terence's *Adelphoi* and in *Tartuffe*, and so on. The action of comedy, like the action of the Christian Bible, moves from law to liberty. In the law there is an element of ritual bondage which is abolished, and an element of habit or convention which is fulfilled. The intolerable qualities of the *senex* represent the former and compromise with him the latter in the evolution of the comic *nomos*.

With the fourth phase of comedy we begin to move out of the

world of experience into the ideal world of innocence and romance. We said that normally the happier society established at the end of the comedy is left undefined, in contrast to the ritual bondage of the humors. But it is also possible for a comedy to present its action on two social planes, of which one is preferred and consequently in some measure idealized. At the beginning of Plato's *Republic* we have a sharp contest between the *alazon* Thrasymachus and the ironic Socrates. The dialogue could have stopped there, as several of Plato's dialogues do, with a negative victory over a humor and the kind of society he suggests. But in the *Republic* the rest of the company, including Thrasymachus, follow Socrates inside Socrates's head, so to speak, and contemplate there the pattern of the just state. In Aristophanes the comic action is often ironic, but in *The Acharnians* we have a comedy in which a hero with the significant name of Dicaeopolis (righteous city or citizen) makes a private peace with Sparta, celebrates the peaceful festival of Dionysos with his family, and sets up the pattern of a temperate social order on the stage, where it remains throughout the play, cranks, bigots, sharpers, and scoundrels all being beaten away from it. One of the typical comic actions is at least as clearly portrayed in our earliest comedy as it has ever been since.

Shakespeare's type of romantic comedy follows a tradition established by Peele and developed by Greene and Lyly, which has affinities with the medieval tradition of the seasonal ritual-play. We may call it the drama of the green world, its plot being assimilated to the ritual theme of the triumph of life and love over the waste land. In *The Two Gentlemen of Verona* the hero Valentine becomes captain of a band of outlaws in a forest, and all the other characters are gathered into this forest and become converted. Thus the action of the comedy begins in a world represented as a normal world, moves into the green world, goes into a metamorphosis there in which the comic resolution is achieved, and returns to the normal world. The forest in this play is the embryonic form of the fairy world of *A Midsummer Night's Dream*, the Forest of Arden in *As You Like It*, Windsor Forest in *The Merry Wives*, and the pastoral world of the mythical sea-coasted Bohemia in *The Winter's Tale*. In all these comedies there is the same rhythmic movement from normal world to green world and back again. In *The Merchant of Venice* the second world takes the form of Portia's mysterious house in Belmont, with its magic caskets and the wonderful cosmological harmonies that proceed from it in the fifth act. We notice too that this second world is absent from the more ironic comedies *All's Well* and *Measure for Measure*.

The green world charges the comedies with the symbolism of the victory of summer over winter, as is explicit in *Love's Labor's Lost*, where the comic contest takes the form of the medieval debate of winter and spring at the end. In *The Merry Wives* there is an elaborate ritual of the defeat of winter known to folklorists as "carrying out Death," of which Falstaff is the victim; and Falstaff must have felt that, after being thrown into the water, dressed up as a witch and beaten out of a house with curses, and finally supplied with a beast's head and singed with candles, he had done about all that could reasonably be asked of any fertility spirit.

In the rituals and myths the earth that produces the rebirth is generally a female figure, and the death and revival, or disappearance and withdrawal, of human figures in romantic comedy generally involves the heroine. The fact that the heroine often brings about the comic resolution by disguising herself as a boy is familiar enough. The treatment of Hero in *Much Ado*, of Helena in *All's Well*, of Thaisa in *Pericles*, of Fidele in *Cymbeline*, of Hermione in *The Winter's Tale*, show the repetition of a device in which progressively less care is taken of plausibility and in which in consequence the mythical outline of a Proserpine figure becomes progressively clearer. These are Shakespearean examples of the comic theme of ritual assault on a central female figure, a theme which stretches from Menander to contemporary soap operas. Many of Menander's plays have titles which are feminine participles indicating the particular indignity the heroine suffers in them, and the working formula of the soap opera is said to be to "put the heroine behind the eight-ball and keep her there." Treatments of the theme may be as light-hearted as *The Rape of the Lock* or as doggedly persistent as *Pamela*. However, the theme of rebirth is not invariably feminine in context: the rejuvenation of the *senex* in Aristophanes' *The Knights*, and a similar theme in *All's Well* based on the folklore motif of the healing of the impotent king, come readily to mind.

The green world has analogies, not only to the fertile world of ritual, but to the dream world that we create out of our own desires. This dream world collides with the stumbling and blinded follies of the world of experience, of Theseus' Athens with its idiotic marriage law, of Duke Frederick and his melancholy tyranny, of Leontes and his mad jealousy, of the Court Party with their plots and intrigues, and yet proves strong enough to impose the form of desire on it. Thus Shakespearean comedy illustrates, as clearly as any *mythos* we have, the archetypal function of literature in visualizing the world of desire, not as an escape from "reality," but as the genuine form of the world that human life tries to imitate.

In the fifth phase of comedy, some of the themes of which we have already anticipated, we move into a world that is still more romantic, less Utopian and more Arcadian, less festive and more pensive, where the comic ending is less a matter of the way the plot turns out than of the perspective of the audience. When we compare the Shakespearean fourth-phase comedies with the late fifth-phase "romances," we notice how much more serious an action is appropriate to the latter: they do not avoid tragedies but contain them. The action seems to be not only a movement from a "winter's tale" to spring, but from a lower world of confusion to an upper world of order. The closing scene of *The Winter's Tale* makes us think, not simply of a cyclical movement from tragedy and absence to happiness and return, but of bodily metamorphosis and a transformation from one kind of life to another. The materials of the *cognitio* of *Pericles* or *The Winter's Tale* are so stock that they would be "hooted at like an old tale," yet they seem both far-fetched and inevitably right, outraging reality and at the same time introducing us to a world of childlike innocence which has always made more sense than reality.

In this phase the reader or audience feels raised above the action, in the situation of which Christopher Sly is an ironic parody. The plotting of Cleon and Dionyza in *Pericles*, or of the Court Party in *The Tempest*, we look down on as generic or typical human behavior: the action, or at least the tragic implication of the action, is presented as though it were a play within a play that we can see in all dimensions at once. We see the action, in short, from the point of view of a higher and better ordered world. And as the forest in Shakespeare is the usual symbol for the dream world in conflict with and imposing its form on experience, so the usual symbol for the lower or chaotic world is the sea, from which the cast, or an important part of it, is saved. The group of "sea" comedies includes *A Comedy of Errors, Twelfth Night, Pericles,* and

The Tempest. A Comedy of Errors, though based on a Plautine original, is much closer to the world of Apuleius than to that of Plautus in its imagery, and the main action, moving from shipwreck and separation to reunion in a temple in Ephesus, is repeated in the much later play of *Pericles.* And just as the second world is absent from the two "problem" comedies, so in two of the "sea" group, *Twelfth Night* and *The Tempest,* the entire action takes place in the second world. In *Measure for Measure* the Duke disappears from the action and returns at the end; *The Tempest* seems to present the same type of action inside out, as the entire cast follows Prospero into his retreat, and is shaped into a new social order there.

These five phases of comedy may be seen as a sequence of stages in the life of a redeemed society. Purely ironic comedy exhibits this society in its infancy, swaddled and smothered by the society it should replace. Quixotic comedy exhibits it in adolescence, still too ignorant of the ways of the world to impose itself. In the third phase it comes to maturity and triumphs; in the fourth it is already mature and established. In the fifth it is part of a settled order which has been there from the beginning, an order which takes on an increasingly religious cast and seems to be drawing away from human experience altogether. At this point the undisplaced *commedia,* the vision of Dante's *Paradiso,* moves out of our circle of *mythoi* into the apocalyptic or abstract mythical world above it. At this point we realize that the crudest of Plautine comedy-formulas has much the same *structure* as the central Christian myth itself, with its divine son appeasing the wrath of a father and redeeming what is at once a society and a bride.

At this point too comedy proper enters its final or sixth phase, the phase of the collapse and disintegration of the comic society. In this phase the social units of comedy become small and esoteric, or even confined to a single individual. Secret and sheltered places, forests in moonlight, secluded valleys, and happy islands become more prominent, as does the *penseroso* mood of romance, the love of the occult and the marvellous, the sense of individual detachment from routine existence. In this kind of comedy we have finally left the world of wit and the awakened critical intelligence for the opposite pole, an oracular solemnity which, if we surrender uncritically to it, will provide a delightful *frisson.* This is the world of ghost stories, thrillers, and Gothic romances, and, on a more sophisticated level, the kind of imaginative withdrawal portrayed in Huysmans' *À Rebours*. The somberness of Des Esseintes' surroundings has nothing to do with tragedy: Des Esseintes is a dilettante trying to amuse himself. The comic society has run the full course from infancy to death, and in its last phase myths closely connected psychologically with a return to the womb are appropriate.

THE MYTHOS OF SUMMER: ROMANCE

The romance is nearest of all literary forms to the wish-fulfilment dream, and for that reason it has socially a curiously paradoxical role. In every age the ruling social or intellectual class tends to project its ideals in some form of romance, where the virtuous heroes and beautiful heroines represent the ideals and the villains the threats to their ascendancy. This is the general character of chivalric romance in the Middle Ages, aristocratic romance in the Renaissance, bourgeois romance since the eighteenth century, and revolutionary romance in contemporary Russia. Yet there is a genuinely "proletarian" element in romance too which is never satisfied with its various incarnations, and in fact the incarnations themselves indicate that no matter how great a change may take place in society, romance will turn up again, as hungry as ever, looking for new hopes and desires to feed on. The perennially childlike quality of romance is marked by its extraordinarily persistent nostalgia, its search for some kind of imaginative golden age in time or space. There has never to my knowledge been any period of Gothic English literature, but the list of Gothic revivalists stretches completely across its entire history, from the *Beowulf* poet to writers of our own day.

The essential element of plot in romance is adventure, which means that romance is naturally a sequential and processional form, hence we know it better from fiction than from drama. At its most naive it is an endless form in which a central character who never develops or ages goes through one adventure after another until the author himself collapses. We see this form in comic strips, where the central characters persist for years in a state of refrigerated deathlessness. However, no book can rival the continuity of the newspaper, and as soon as romance achieves a literary form, it tends to limit itself to a sequence of minor adventures leading up to a major or climacteric adventure, usually announced from the beginning, the completion of which rounds off the story. We may call this major adventure, the element that gives literary form to the romance, the quest.

The complete form of the romance is clearly the successful quest, and such a completed form has three main stages: the stage of the perilous journey and the preliminary minor adventures; the crucial struggle, usually some kind of battle in which either the hero or his foe, or both, must die; and the exaltation of the hero. We may call these three stages respectively, using Greek terms, the *agon* or conflict, the *pathos* or death-struggle, and the *anagnorisis* or discovery, the recognition of the hero, who has clearly proved himself to be a hero even if he does not survive the conflict. Thus the romance expresses more clearly the passage from struggle through a point of ritual death to a recognition scene that we discovered in comedy. A threefold structure is repeated in many features of romance—in the frequency, for instance, with which the successful hero is a third son, or the third to undertake the quest, or successful on his third attempt. It is shown more directly in the three-day rhythm of death, disappearance and revival which is found in the myth of Attis and other dying gods, and has been incorporated in our Easter.

A quest involving conflict assumes two main characters, a protagonist or hero, and an antagonist or enemy. (No doubt I should add, for the benefit of some readers, that I have read the article "Protagonist" in Fowler's *Modern English Usage*.) The enemy may be an ordinary human being, but the nearer the romance is to myth, the more attributes of divinity will cling to the hero and the more the enemy will take on demonic mythical qualities. The central form of romance is dialectical: everything is focussed on a conflict between the hero and his enemy, and all the reader's values are bound up with the hero. Hence the hero of romance is analogous to the mythical Messiah or deliverer who comes from an upper world, and his enemy is analogous to the demonic powers of a lower world. The conflict however takes place in, or at any rate primarily concerns, *our* world, which is in the middle, and which is characterized by the cyclical movement of nature. Hence the opposite poles of the cycles of nature are assimilated to the opposition of the hero and his enemy. The enemy is associated with winter, darkness, confusion, sterility, moribund life, and old age, and the hero with spring, dawn, order, fertility, vigor, and youth. As all the cyclical phenomena can be readily associated or identified, it follows that any attempt to prove that a romantic story does or does not resemble, say, a solar myth, or that its hero does or does not resemble a sun-god, is likely to be a waste of time. If it is a story within this general area, cyclical imagery is likely to be present, and solar imagery is normally prominent among cyclical images. If the hero of a romance returns from a quest disguised, flings off his beggar's rags, and stands forth in the resplendent scarlet cloak of the prince, we do not have a theme which has necessarily descended from a solar myth; we have the literary device of displacement. The hero does something which we may or may not, as we like, associate with the myth of the sun returning at dawn. If we are reading the story as critics, with an eye to structural principles, we shall make the association, because the solar analogy explains why the hero's act is an effective and conventional incident. If we are reading the story for fun, we need not bother: that is, some murky "subconscious" factor in our response will take care of the association.

We have distinguished myth from romance by the hero's power of action: in the myth proper he is divine, in the romance proper he is human. This distinction is much sharper theologically than it is poetically, and myth and romance both belong in the general category of mythopoeic literature. The attributing of divinity to the chief characters of myth, however, tends to give myth a further distinction, already referred to, of occupying a central *canonical* position. Most cultures regard certain stories with more reverence than others, either because they are thought of as historically true or because they have come to bear a heavier weight of conceptual meaning. The story of Adam and Eve in Eden has thus a canonical position for poets in our tradition whether they believe in its historicity or not. The reason for the greater profundity of canonical myth is not solely tradition, but the result of the greater degree of metaphorical identification that is possible is myth. In literary criticism the myth is normally the metaphorical key to the displacements of romance, hence the importance of the quest-myth of the Bible in what follows. But because of the tendency to expurgate and moralize in canonical myth, the less inhibited area of legend and folk tale often contains an equally great concentration of mythical meaning.

The central form of quest-romance is the dragon-killing theme exemplified in the stories of St. George and Perseus, already referred to. A land ruled by a helpless old king is laid waste by a sea-monster, to whom one young person after another is offered to be devoured, until the lot falls on the king's daughter: at that point the hero arrives, kills the dragon, marries the daughter, and succeeds to the kingdom. Again, as with comedy, we have a simple pattern with many complex elements. The ritual analogies of the myth suggest that the monster *is* the sterility of the land itself, and that the sterility of the land is present in the age and impotence of the king, who is sometimes suffering from an incurable malady or wound, like Amfortas in Wagner. His position is that of Adonis overcome by the boar of winter, Adonis's traditional thigh-wound being as close to castration symbolically as it is anatomically.

In the Bible we have a sea-monster usually named leviathan, who is described as the enemy of the Messiah, and whom the Messiah is destined to kill in the "day of the Lord." The leviathan is the source of social sterility, for it is identified with Egypt and Babylon, the oppressors of Israel, and is described in the Book of Job as "king over all the children of pride." It also seems closely associated with the natural sterility of the fallen world, with the blasted world of struggle and poverty and disease into which Job is hurled by Satan and Adam by the serpent in Eden. In the Book of Job God's revelation to Job consists largely of descriptions of the leviathan and a slightly less sinister land cousin named behemoth. These monsters thus apparently represent the fallen order of nature over which Satan has some control. (I am trying to make sense of the meaning of the Book of Job as we now have it, on the assumption that whoever was responsible for its present version had some reason for producing that version. Guesswork about what the poem may originally have been or meant is useless, as it is only the version we know that has had any influence on our literature.) In the Book of Revelation the leviathan, Satan, and the Edenic serpent are all identified. This identification is the basis for an elaborate dragon-killing metaphor in Christian symbolism in which the hero is Christ (often represented in art standing on a prostrate monster), the dragon Satan, the impotent old king Adam, whose son Christ becomes, and the rescued bride the Church.

Now if the leviathan is the whole fallen world of sin and death and tyranny into which Adam fell, it follows that Adam's children are born, live, and die inside his belly. Hence if the Messiah is to deliver us by killing the leviathan, he releases us. In the folk tale versions of dragon-killing stories we notice how frequently the previous victims of the dragon come out of him alive after he is killed. Again, if we are inside the dragon, and the hero comes to help us, the image is suggested of the hero going down the monster's open throat, like Jonah (whom Jesus accepted as a prototype of himself), and returning with his redeemed behind him. Hence the symbolism of the Harrowing of Hell, hell being regularly represented in iconography by the "toothed gullet of an aged shark," to quote a modern reference to it. Secular versions of journeys inside monsters occur from Lucian to our day, and perhaps even the Trojan horse had originally some links with the same theme. The image of the dark winding labyrinth for the monster's belly is a natural one, and one that frequently appears in heroic quests, notably that of Theseus. A less displaced version of the story of Theseus would have shown him emerging from the labyrinth at the head of a procession of the Athenian youths and maidens previously sacrificed to the Minotaur. In many solar myths, too, the hero travels perilously through a dark labyrinthine underworld full of monsters between sunset and sunrise. This theme may become a structural principle of fiction on any level of sophistication. One would expect to find it in fairy tales or children's stories, and in fact if we "stand back" from *Tom Sawyer* we can see a youth with no father or mother emerging with a maiden from a labyrinthine cave, leaving a bat-eating demon imprisoned behind him. But in the most complex and elusive of the later stories of Henry James, *The Sense of the Past*, the same theme is used, the labyrinthine underworld being in this case a period of past time from which the hero is released by the sacrifice of a heroine, an Ariadne figure. In this story, as in many folktales, the motif of the two brothers connected by sympathetic magic of some sort is also employed.

In the Old Testament the Messiah-figure of Moses leads his people out of Egypt. The Pharaoh of Egypt is identified with the leviathan by Ezekiel, and the fact that the infant Moses was rescued by Pharaoh's daughter gives to the Pharaoh something of the role of the cruel father-figure who seeks the hero's death, a role also taken by the raging Herod of the miracle plays. Moses and the Israelites wander through a labyrinthine desert, after which the reign of the law ends and the conquest of the Promised Land is achieved by Joshua, whose name is the same as that of Jesus. Thus when the angel Gabriel tells the Virgin to call her son Jesus, the typological meaning is that the era of the law is over, and the assault on the Promised Land is about to begin. There are thus two concentric quest-myths in the Bible, a Genesis-apocalypse myth and an Exodus-millennium myth. In the former Adam is cast out of Eden, loses the river of life and the tree of life, and wanders in the labyrinth of human history until he is restored to his original state by the Messiah. In the latter Israel is cast out of his inheritance and wanders in the labyrinths of Egyptian and Babylonian captivity until he is restored to his original state in the Promised Land. Eden and the Promised Land, therefore, are typologically identical, as are the tyrannies of Egypt and Babylon and the wilderness of the law. *Paradise Regained* deals with the temptation of Christ by Satan, which is, Michael tells us in *Paradise Lost*, the true form of the dragon-killing myth assigned to the Messiah. Christ is in the situation of Israel under the law, wandering in the wilderness: his victory is at once the conquest of the Promised Land typified by his namesake Joshua and the raising of Eden in the wilderness.

The leviathan is usually a sea-monster, which means metaphorically that he *is* the sea, and the prophecy that the Lord will hook and land the leviathan in Ezekiel is identical with the prophecy in Revelation that there shall be no more sea. As denizens of his belly, therefore, we are also metaphorically under water. Hence the importance of fishing in the Gospels, the apostles being "fishers of men" who cast their nets into the sea of this world. Hence, too, the later development, referred to in *The Waste Land*, of Adam or the impotent king as an ineffectual "fisher king." In the same poem the appropriate link is also made with Prospero's rescuing of a society out of the sea in *The Tempest*. In other comedies, too, ranging from *Sakuntala* to *Rudens*, something indispensable to the action or the *cognitio* is fished out of the sea, and many quest heroes, including Beowulf, achieve their greatest feats under water. The insistence on Christ's ability to command the sea belongs to the same aspect of symbolism. And as the leviathan, in his aspect as the fallen world, contains all forms of life imprisoned within himself, so as the sea he contains the imprisoned life-giving rain waters whose coming marks the spring. The monstrous animal who swallows all the water in the world and is then teased or tricked or forced into disgorging it is a favorite of folk tales, and a Mesopotamian version lies close behind the story of Creation in Genesis. In many solar myths the sun god is represented as sailing in a boat on the surface of our world.

Lastly, if the leviathan is death, and the hero has to enter the body of death, the hero has to die, and if his quest is completed the final stage of it is, cyclically, rebirth, and, dialectically, resurrection. In the St. George plays the hero dies in his dragon-fight and is brought to life by a doctor, and the same symbolism runs through all the dying-god myths. There are thus not three but four distinguishable aspects to the quest-myth. First, the *agon* or conflict itself. Second, the *pathos* or death, often the mutual death of hero and monster. Third, the disappearance of the hero, a theme which often takes the form of *sparagmos* or tearing to pieces. Sometimes the hero's body is divided among his followers, as in Eucharist symbolism: sometimes it is distributed around the natural world, as in the stories of Orpheus and more especially Osiris. Fourth, the reappearance and recognition of the hero, where sacramental Christianity follows the metaphorical logic: those who in the fallen world have partaken of their redeemer's divided body are united with his risen body.

The four *mythoi* that we are dealing with, comedy, romance, tragedy, and irony, may now be seen as four aspects of a central unifying myth. *Agon* or conflict is the basis or archetypal theme of romance, the radical of romance being a sequence of marvellous adventures. *Pathos* or catastrophe, whether in triumph or in defeat, is the archetypal theme of tragedy. *Sparagmos*, or the sense that heroism and effective action are absent, disorganized or foredoomed to defeat, and that confusion and anarchy reign over the world, is the archetypal theme of irony and satire. *Anagnorisis*, or recognition of a newborn society rising in triumph around a still somewhat mysterious hero and his bride, is the archetypal theme of comedy.

We have spoken of the Messianic hero as a redeemer of society, but in the secular quest-romances more obvious motives and rewards for the quest are more common. Often the dragon guards a hoard: the quest for buried treasure has been a central theme of romance from the Siegfried cycle to *Nostromo*, and is unlikely to be exhausted yet. Treasure means wealth, which in mythopoeic romance often means wealth in its ideal forms, power and wisdom. The lower world, the world inside or behind the guarding dragon, is often inhabited by a prophetic sybil, and is a place of oracles and secrets, such as Woden was willing to mutilate himself to obtain. Mutilation or physical handicap, which combines the themes of *sparagmos* and ritual death, is often the price of unusual wisdom or power, as it is in the figure of the crippled smith Weyland or Hephaistos, and in the story of the blessing of Jacob. The Arabian Nights are full of stories of what may be called the etiology of mutilation. Again, the reward of the quest usually is or includes a bride. This bride-figure is ambiguous: her psychological connection with the mother in an Oedipus fantasy is more insistent than in comedy. She is often to be found in a perilous, forbidden, or tabooed place, like Brunnhilde's wall of fire or the sleeping beauty's wall of thorns, and she is, of course, often rescued from the unwelcome embraces of another and generally older male, or from giants or bandits or other usurpers. The removal of some stigma from the heroine figures prominently in romance as in comedy, and ranges from the "loathly lady" theme of Chaucer's *Wife of Bath's Tale* to the forgiven harlot of the Book of Hosea. The "black but comely" bride of the Song of Songs belongs in the same complex.

The quest-romance has analogies to both rituals and dreams, and the rituals examined by Frazer and the dreams examined by Jung show the remarkable similarity in form that we should expect of two symbolic structures analogous to the same thing. Translated into dream terms, the quest-romance is the search of the libido or desiring self for a fulfilment that will deliver it from the anxieties of reality but will still contain that reality. The antagonists of the quest are often sinister figures, giants, ogres, witches and magicians, that clearly have a parental origin; and yet redeemed and emancipated paternal figures are involved too, as they are in the psychological quests of both Freud and Jung. Translated into ritual terms, the quest-romance is the victory of fertility over the waste land. Fertility means food and drink, bread and wine, body and blood, the union of male and female. The precious objects brought back from the quest, or seen or obtained as a result of it, sometimes combine the ritual and the psychological associations. The Holy Grail, for instance, is connected with Christian Eucharist symbolism; it is related to or descended from a miraculous food-provider like the cornucopia, and, like other cups and hollow vessels, it has female sexual affinities, its masculine counterpart being, we are told, the bleeding lance. The pairing of solid food and liquid refreshment recurs in the edible tree and the water of life in the Biblical apocalypse.

We may take the first book of *The Faerie Queene* as representing perhaps the closest following of the Biblical quest-romance theme in English literature: it is closer even than *The Pilgrim's Progress*, which resembles it because they both resemble the Bible. Attempts to compare Bunyan and Spenser without reference to the Bible, or to trace their similarities to a common origin in *secular* romance, are more or less perverse. In Spenser's account of the quest of St. George, the patron saint of England, the protagonist represents the Christian Church in England, and hence his quest is an imitation of that of Christ. Spenser's Redcross Knight is led by the lady Una (who is veiled in black) to the kingdom of her parents, which is being laid waste by a dragon. The dragon is of somewhat unusual size, at least allegorically. We are told that Una's parents held "all the world" in their control until the dragon "Forwasted all their land, and them expelled." Una's parents are Adam and Eve; their kingdom is Eden or the unfallen world, and the dragon, who is the entire fallen world, is identified with the leviathan, the serpent of Eden, Satan, and the beast of Revelation. Thus St. George's mission, a repetition of that of Christ, is by killing the dragon to raise Eden in the wilderness and restore England to the status of Eden. The association of an ideal England with Eden, assisted by legends of a happy island in the western ocean and by the similarity of the Hesperides story to that of Eden, runs through English literature at least from the end of Greene's *Friar Bacon* to Blake's "Jerusalem" hymn. St. George's wanderings with Una, or without her, are parallel to the wandering of the Israelites in the wilderness, between Egypt and the Promised Land, bearing the veiled ark of the covenant and yet ready to worship a golden calf.

The battle with the dragon lasts, of course, three days: at the end of each of the first two days St. George is beaten back and is strengthened, first by the water of life, then by the tree of life. These represent the two sacraments which the reformed church accepted; they are the two features of the garden of Eden to be restored to man in the apocalypse, and they have also a more general Eucharist connection. St. George's emblem is a red cross on a white ground, which is the flag borne by Christ in traditional iconography when he returns in triumph from the prostrate dragon of hell. The red and white symbolize the two aspects of the risen body, flesh and blood, bread and wine, and in Spenser they have a historical connection with the union of red and white roses in the reigning head of the church. The link between the sacramental and the sexual aspects of the red and white symbolism is indicated in alchemy, with which Spenser was clearly acquainted, in which a crucial phase of the production of the elixir of immortality is known as the union of the red king and the white queen.

The characterization of romance follows its general dialectic structure, which means that subtlety and complexity are not much favored. Characters tend to be either for or against the quest. If they assist it they are idealized as simply gallant or pure; if they obstruct it they are caricatured as simply villainous or cowardly. Hence every typical character in romance tends to have his moral opposite confronting him, like black and white pieces in a chess game. In romance the "white" pieces who strive for the quest correspond to the *eiron* group in comedy, though the word is no longer appropriate, as irony has little place in romance. Romance has a counterpart to the benevolent retreating *eiron* of comedy in its figure of the "old wise man," as Jung calls him, like Prospero, Merlin, or the palmer of Spenser's second quest, often a magician who affects the action he watches over. The Arthur of *The Faerie Queene*, though not an old man, has this function. He has a feminine counterpart in the sibylline wise mother-figure, often a potential bride like Solveig in *Peer Gynt*, who sits quietly at home waiting for the hero to finish his wanderings and come back to her. This latter figure is often the lady for whose sake or at whose bidding the quest is performed: she is represented by the Faerie Queene in Spenser and by Athene in the Perseus story. These are the king and queen of the white pieces, though their power of movement is of course reversed in actual chess. The disadvantage of making the queen-figure the hero's mistress, in anything more than a political sense, is that she spoils his fun with the distressed damsels he meets on his journey, who are often enticingly tied naked to rocks or trees, like Andromeda or Angelica in Ariosto. A polarization may thus be set up between the lady of duty and the lady of pleasure—we have already glanced at a late development of this in the light and dark heroines of Victorian romance. One simple way out is to make the former the latter's mother-in-law: a theme of reconciliation after enmity and jealousy most commonly results, as in the relations of Psyche and Venus in Apuleius. Where there is no reconciliation, the older female remains sinister, the cruel stepmother of folk tale.

The evil magician and the witch, Spenser's Archimago and Duessa, are the black king and queen. The latter is appropriately called by Jung the "terrible mother," and he associates her with the fear of incest and with such hags as Medusa who seem to have a suggestion of erotic perversion about them. The redeemed figures, apart from the bride, are generally too weak to be strongly characterized. The faithful companion or shadow figure of the hero has his opposite in the traitor, the heroine her opposite in the siren or beautiful witch, the dragon his opposite in the friendly or helping animals that are so conspicuous in romance, among which the horse who gets the hero to his quest has naturally a central place. The conflict of son and father that we noted in comedy recurs in romance: in the Bible the second Adam comes to the rescue of the first one, and in the Grail cycle the pure son Galahad accomplishes what his impure father Lancelot failed in.

The characters who elude the moral antithesis of heroism and villainy generally are or suggest spirits of nature. They represent partly the moral neutrality of the intermediate world of nature and partly a world of mystery which is glimpsed but never seen, and which retreats when approached. Among female characters of this type are the shy nymphs of Classical legends and the elusive half-wild creatures who might be called daughter-figures, and include Spenser's Florimell, Hawthorne's Pearl, Wagner's Kundry, and Hudson's Rima. Their male counterparts have a little more variety. Kipling's Mowgli is the best known of the wild boys; a green man lurked in the forests of medieval England, appearing as Robin Hood and as the knight of Gawain's adventure; the "salvage man," represented in Spenser by Satyrane, is a Renaissance favorite, and the awkward but faithful giant with unkempt hair has shambled amiably through romance for centuries.

Such characters are, more or less, children of nature, who can be brought to serve the hero, like Crusoe's Friday, but retain the inscrutability of their origin. As servants or friends of the hero, they impart the mysterious rapport with nature that so often marks the central figure of romance. The paradox that many of these children of nature are "supernatural" beings is not as distressing in romance as in logic. The helpful fairy, the grateful dead man, the wonderful servant who has just the abilities the hero needs in a crisis, are all folk tale commonplaces. They are romantic intensifications of the comic tricky slave, the author's *architectus*. In James Thurber's *The Thirteen Clocks* this character type is called the "Golux," and there is no reason why the word should not be adopted as a critical term.

In romance, as in comedy, there seem to be four poles of characterization. The struggle of the hero with his enemy corresponds to the comic contest of *eiron* and *alazon*. In the nature-spirits just referred to we find the parallel in romance to the buffoon or master of ceremonies in comedy: that is, their function is to intensify and provide a focus for the romantic mood. It remains to be seen if there is a character in romance corresponding to the *agroikos* type in comedy, the refuser of festivity or rustic clown.

Such a character would call attention to realistic aspects of life, like fear in the presence of danger, which threaten the unity of the romantic mood. St. George and Una in Spenser are accompanied by a dwarf who carries a bag of "needments." He is not a traitor, like the other bag-carrier Judas Iscariot, but he is "fearful," and urges retreat when the going is difficult. This dwarf with his needments represents, in the dream world of romance, the shrunken and wizened form of practical waking reality: the more realistic the story, the more important such a figure would become, until, when we reach the opposite pole in *Don Quixote*, he achieves his apotheosis as Sancho Panza. In other romances we find fools and jesters who are licensed to show fear or make realistic comments, and who provide a localized safety valve for realism without allowing it to disrupt the conventions of romance. In Malory a similar role is assumed by Sir Dinadan, who, it is carefully explained, is really a gallant knight as well as a jester: hence when he makes jokes "the king and Launcelot laughed that they might not sit"— the suggestion of excessive and hysterical laughter being psychologically very much to the point.

197

Romance, like comedy, has six isolatable phases, and as it moves from the tragic to the comic area, the first three are parallel to the first three phases of tragedy and the second three to the second three phases of comedy, already examined from the comic point of view. The phases form a cyclical sequence in a romantic hero's life.

The first phase is the myth of the birth of the hero, the morphology of which has been studied in some detail in folklore. This myth is often associated with a flood, the regular symbol of the beginning and the end of a cycle. The infant hero is often placed in an ark or chest floating on the sea, as in the story of Perseus; from there he drifts to land, as in the exordium to *Beowulf,* or is rescued from among reeds and bulrushes on a river bank, as in the story of Moses. A landscape of water, boat, and reeds appears at the beginning of Dante's journey up the mount of Purgatory, where there are many suggestions that the soul is in that stage a newborn infant. On dry land the infant may be rescued either from or by an animal, and many heroes are nurtured by animals in a forest during their nonage. When Goethe's Faust begins to look for his Helena, he searches in the reeds of the Peneus, and then finds a centaur who carried her to safety on his back when she was a child.

Psychologically, this image is related to the embryo in the womb, the world of the unborn often being thought of as liquid; anthropologically, it is related to the image of seeds of new life buried in a dead world of snow or swamp. The dragon's treasure hoard is closely linked with this mysterious infant life enclosed in a chest. The fact that the real source of wealth is potential fertility or new life, vegetable or human, has run through romance from ancient myths to Ruskin's *King of the Golden River,* Ruskin's treatment of wealth in his economic works being essentially a commentary on this fairy tale. A similar association of treasure hoard and infant life appears in more plausible guise in *Silas Marner.* The long literary history of the theme of mysterious parentage from Euripides to Dickens has already been mentioned.

In the Bible the end of a historical cycle and the birth of a new one is marked by parallel symbols. First we have a universal deluge and an ark, with the potency of all future life contained in it, floating on the waters; then we have the story of the Egyptian host drowned in the Red Sea and the Israelites set free to carry their ark through the wilderness, an image adopted by Dante as the basis of his purgatorial symbolism. The New Testament begins with an infant in a manger, and the tradition of depicting the world outside as sunk in snow relates the Nativity to the same archetypal phase. Images of returning spring soon follow: the rainbow in the Noah story, the bringing of water out of a rock by Moses, the baptism of Christ, all show the turning of the cycle from the wintry water of death to the reviving waters of life. The providential birds, the raven and dove in the Noah story, the ravens feeding Elijah in the wilderness, the dove hovering over Jesus, belong to the same complex.

Often, too, there is a search for the child, who has to be hidden away in a secret place. The hero being of mysterious origin, his true paternity is often concealed, and a false father appears who seeks the child's death. This is the role of Acrisius in the Perseus story, of the Cronos of Hesiodic myth who tries to swallow his children, of the child-killing Pharaoh in the Old Testament, and of Herod in the New. In later fiction he often modulates to the usurping wicked uncle who appears several times in Shakespeare. The mother is thus often the victim of jealousy, persecuted or calumniated like the mother of Perseus or like Constance in the *Man of Law's Tale*. This version is very close psychologically to the theme of the rivalry of the son and a hateful father for possession of the mother. The theme of the calumniated girl ordered out of the house with her child by a cruel father, generally into the snow, still drew tears from audiences of Victorian melodramas, and literary developments of the theme of the hunted mother in the same period extend from Eliza crossing the ice in *Uncle Tom's Cabin* to *Adam Bede* and *Far from the Madding Crowd*. The false mother, the celebrated cruel stepmother, is also common: her victim is of course usually female, and the resulting conflict is portrayed in many ballads and folktales of the Cinderella type. The true father is sometimes represented by a wise old man or teacher: this is the relation of Prospero to Ferdinand, as well as of Chiron the centaur to Achilles. The double of the true mother appears in the daughter of Pharaoh who adopts Moses. In more realistic modes the cruel parent speaks with the voice of, or takes the form of, a narrow-minded public opinion.

The second phase brings us to the innocent youth of the hero, a phase most familiar to us from the story of Adam and Eve in

Eden before the Fall. In literature this phase presents a pastoral and Arcadian world, generally a pleasant wooded landscape, full of glades, shaded valleys, murmuring brooks, the moon, and other images closely linked with the female or maternal aspect of sexual imagery. Its heraldic colors are green and gold, traditionally the colors of vanishing youth: one thinks of Sandburg's poem *Between Two Worlds*. It is often a world of magic or desirable law, and it tends to center on a youthful hero, still overshadowed by parents, surrounded by youthful companions. The archetype of erotic innocence is less commonly marriage than the kind of "chaste" love that precedes marriage; the love of brother for sister, or of two boys for each other. Hence, though in later phases it is often recalled as a lost happy time or Golden Age, the sense of being close to a moral taboo is very frequent, as it is of course in the Eden story itself. Johnson's *Rasselas*, Poe's *Eleanora*, and Blake's *Book of Thel* introduce us to a kind of prison-Paradise or unborn world from which the central characters long to escape to a lower world, and the same feeling of malaise and longing to enter a world of action recurs in the most exhaustive treatment of the phase in English literature, Keats's *Endymion*.

The theme of the sexual barrier in this phase takes many forms: the serpent of the Eden story recurs in *Green Mansions*, and a barrier of fire separates Amoret in Spenser from her lover Scudamour. At the end of the *Purgatorio* the soul reaches again its unfallen childhood or lost Golden Age, and Dante consequently finds himself in the garden of Eden, separated from the young girl Matelda by the river Lethe. The dividing river recurs in William Morris's curious story *The Sundering Flood*, where an arrow shot over it has to do for the symbol of sexual contact. In *Kubla Khan*, which is closely related both to the Eden story in *Paradise Lost* and to *Rasselas*, a "sacred river" is closely followed by the distant vision of a singing damsel. Melville's *Pierre* opens with a sardonic parody of this phase, the hero still dominated by his mother but calling her his sister. A good deal of the imagery of this world may be found in the sixth book of *The Faerie Queene*, especially in the stories of Tristram and Pastorella.

The third phase is the normal quest theme that we have been discussing, and needs no further comment at this point. The fourth phase corresponds to the fourth phase of comedy, in which the happier society is more or less visible throughout the action instead of emerging only in the last few moments. In romance the central theme of this phase is that of the maintaining of the integrity of the innocent world against the assault of experience. It thus often takes the form of a moral allegory, such as we have in Milton's *Comus*, Bunyan's *Holy War*, and many morality plays, including *The Castell of Perseveraunce*. The much simpler scheme of the *Canterbury Tales*, where the only conflict is to preserve the mood of holiday and festivity against bickering, seems for some reason to be less frequent.

The integrated body to be defended may be individual or social, or both. The individual aspect of it is presented in the allegory of temperance in the second book of *The Faerie Queene*, which forms a natural sequel to the first book, dealing as it does with the more difficult theme of consolidating heroic innocence in this world after the first great quest has been completed. Guyon, the knight of temperance, has as his main antagonists Acrasia, the mistress of the Bower of Bliss, and Mammon. These represent "Beauty and money," in their aspects as instrumental goods perverted into external goals. The temperate mind contains its good within itself, continence being its prerequisite, hence it belongs to what we have called the innocent world. The intemperate mind seeks its good in the external object of the world of experience. Both temperance and intemperance could be called natural, but one belongs to nature as an order and the other to nature as a fallen world. Comus's temptation of the Lady is based on a similar ambiguity in the meaning of nature. A central image in this phase of romance is that of the beleaguered castle, represented in Spenser by the House of Alma, which is described in terms of the economy of the human body.

The social aspect of the same phase is treated in the fifth book of *The Faerie Queene*, the legend of justice, where power is the prerequisite of justice, corresponding to continence in relation to temperance. Here we meet, in the vision of Isis and Osiris, the fourth-phase image of the monster tamed and controlled by the virgin, an image which appears episodically in Book One in connection with Una, who tames satyrs and a lion. The Classical prototype of it is the Gorgon's head on the shield of Athene. The theme of invincible innocence or virginity is associated with similar images in literature from the child leading the beasts of prey in Isaiah to Marina in the brothel in *Pericles*, and it reappears in later fictions in which an unusually truculent hero is brought to heel by the heroine. An ironic parody of the same theme forms the basis of Aristophanes' *Lysistrata*.

The fifth phase corresponds to the fifth phase of comedy, and like it is a reflective, idyllic view of experience from above, in which the movement of the natural cycle has usually a prominent place. It deals with a world very similar to that of the second phase except that the mood is a contemplative withdrawal from or sequel to action rather than a youthful preparation for it. It is, like the second phase, an erotic world, but it presents experience as comprehended and not as a mystery. This is the world of most of Morris's romances, of Hawthorne's *Blithedale Romance*, of the mature innocent wisdom of *The Franklin's Tale*, and of most of the imagery of the third book of *The Faerie Queene*. In this last, as well as in the late Shakespearean romances, notably *Pericles*, and even *The Tempest*, we notice a tendency to the moral stratification of characters. The true lovers are on top of a hierarchy of what might be called erotic imitations, going down through the various grades of lust and passion to perversion (Argante and Oliphant in Spenser; Antiochus and his daughter in *Pericles*). Such an arrangement of characters is consistent with the detached and contemplative view of society taken in this phase.

The sixth or *penseroso* phase is the last phase of romance as of comedy. In comedy it shows the comic society breaking up into small units or individuals; in romance it marks the end of a movement from active to contemplative adventure. A central image of this phase, a favorite of Yeats, is that of the old man in the tower, the lonely hermit absorbed in occult or magical studies. On a more popular and social level it takes in what might be called cuddle fiction: the romance that is physically associated with comfortable beds or chairs around fireplaces or warm and cosy spots generally. A characteristic feature of this phase is the tale in quotation marks, where we have an opening setting with a small group of congenial people, and then the real story told by one of the members. In *The Turn of the Screw* a large party is telling ghost stories in a country house; then some people leave, and a much smaller and more intimate circle gathers around the crucial tale. The opening dismissal of catechumens is thoroughly in the spirit and conventions of this phase. The effect of such devices is to present the story through a relaxed and contemplative haze as something that entertains us without, so to speak, confronting us, as direct tragedy confronts us.

Collections of tales based on a symposium device like the *Decameron* belong here. Morris's *Earthly Paradise* is a very pure example of the same phase: there a number of the great archetypal myths of Greek and Northern culture are personified as a group of old men who forsook the world during the Middle Ages, refusing to be made either kings or gods, and who now interchange their myths in an ineffectual land of dreams. Here the themes of the lonely old men, the intimate group, and the reported tale are linked. The calendar arrangement of the tales links it also with the symbolism of the natural cycle. Another and very concentrated treatment of the phase is Virginia Woolf's *Between the Acts*, where a play representing the history of English life is acted before a group. The history is conceived not only as a progression but as a cycle of which the audience is the end, and, as the last page indicates, the beginning as well.

From Wagner's *Ring* to science fiction, we may notice an increasing popularity of the flood archetype. This usually takes the form of some cosmic disaster destroying the whole fictional society except a small group, which begins life anew in some sheltered spot. The affinities of this theme to that of the cosy group which has managed to shut the rest of the world out are clear enough, and it brings us around again to the image of the mysterious newborn infant floating on the sea.

One important detail in poetic symbolism remains to be considered. This is the symbolic presentation of the point at which the undisplaced apocalyptic world and the cyclical world of nature come into alignment, and which we propose to call the point of epiphany. Its most common settings are the mountain-top, the island, the tower, the lighthouse, and the ladder or staircase. Folk tales and mythologies are full of stories of an original connection between heaven or the sun and earth. We have ladders of arrows, ropes pecked in two by mischievous birds, and the like: such stories are often analogues of the Biblical stories of the Fall, and survive in Jack's beanstalk, Rapunzel's hair, and even the curious bit of floating folklore known as the Indian rope trick. The movement from one world to the other may be symbolized by the golden fire that descends from the sun, as in the mythical basis of the Danae story, and by its human response, the fire kindled on the sacrificial altar. The "gold bug" in Poe's story, which reminds us that the Egyptian scarab was a solar emblem, is dropped from above on the end of a string through the eyehole of a skull on a tree and falls on top of a buried treasure: the archetype here is closely related to the complex of images we are dealing with, especially to some alchemical versions of it.

In the Bible we have Jacob's ladder, which in *Paradise Lost* is associated with Milton's cosmological diagram of a spherical cosmos hanging from heaven with a hole in the top. There are several mountain-top epiphanies in the Bible, the Transfiguration being the most notable, and the mountain vision of Pisgah, the end of the road through the wilderness from which Moses saw the distant Promised Land, is typologically linked. As long as poets accepted the Ptolemaic universe, the natural place for the point of epiphany was a mountain-top just under the moon, the lowest heavenly body. Purgatory in Dante is an enormous mountain with a path ascending spirally around it, on top of which, as the pilgrim gradually recovers his lost innocence and casts off his original sin, is the garden of Eden. It is at this point that the prodigious apocalyptic epiphany of the closing cantos of the *Purgatorio* is achieved. The sense of being between an apocalyptic world above and a cyclical world below is present too, as from the garden of Eden all seeds of vegetable life fall back into the world, while human life passes on.

In *The Faerie Queene* there is a Pisgah vision in the first book, when St. George climbs the mountain of contemplation and sees the heavenly city from a distance. As the dragon he has to kill is the fallen world, there is a level of the allegory in which his dragon is the space between himself and the distant city. In the corresponding episode of Ariosto the link between the mountain-top and the sphere of the moon is clearer. But Spenser's fullest treatment of the theme is the brilliant metaphysical comedy known as the *Mutabilitie Cantoes*, where the conflict of being and becoming, Jove and Mutability, order and change, is resolved at the sphere of the moon. Mutability's evidence consists of the cyclical movements of nature, but this evidence is turned against her and proved to be a principle of order in nature instead of mere change. In this poem the relation of the heavenly bodies to the apocalyptic world is not metaphorical identification, as it is, at least as a poetic convention, in Dante's *Paradiso*, but likeness: they are still within nature, and only in the final stanza of the poem does the real apocalyptic world appear.

The distinction of levels here implies that there may be analogous forms of the point of epiphany. For instance, it may be presented in erotic terms as a place of sexual fulfilment, where there is no apocalyptic vision but simply a sense of arriving at the summit of experience in nature. This natural form of the point of epiphany is called in Spenser the Gardens of Adonis. It recurs under that name in Keats's *Endymion* and is the world entered by the lovers at the end of Shelley's *Revolt of Islam*. The Gardens of Adonis, like Eden in Dante, are a place of seed, into which everything subject to the cyclical order of nature enters at death and proceeds from at birth. Milton's early poems are, like the *Mutabilitie Cantoes*, full of the sense of a distinction between nature as a divinely sanctioned order, the nature of the music of the spheres, and nature as a fallen and largely chaotic world. The former is symbolized by the Gardens of Adonis in *Comus*, from whence the attendant spirit descends to watch over the Lady. The central image of this archetype, Venus watching over Adonis, is (to use a modern distinction) the analogue in terms of Eros to the Madonna and Son in the context of Agape.

Milton picks up the theme of the Pisgah vision in *Paradise Regained*, which assumes an elementary principle of Biblical typology in which the events of Christ's life repeat those of the history of Israel. Israel goes to Egypt, brought down by Joseph, escapes a slaughter of innocents, is cut off from Egypt by the Red Sea, organizes into twelve tribes, wanders forty years in the wilderness, receives the law from Sinai, is saved by a brazen serpent on a pole, crosses the Jordan, and enters the Promised Land under "Joshua, whom the Gentiles Jesus call." Jesus goes to Egypt in infancy, led by Joseph, escapes a slaughter of innocents, is baptized and recognized as the Messiah, wanders forty days in the wilderness, gathers twelve followers, preaches the Sermon on the Mount, saves mankind by dying on a pole, and thereby conquers the Promised Land as the real Joshua. In Milton the temptation corresponds to the Pisgah vision of Moses, except that the gaze is turned in the opposite direction. It marks the climax of Jesus' obedience to the law, just before his active redemption of the world begins, and the sequence of temptations consolidates the world, flesh, and devil into the single form of Satan. The point of epiphany is here represented by the pinnacle of the temple, from which Satan falls away as Jesus remains motionless on top of it. The fall of Satan reminds us that the point of epiphany is also the top of the wheel of fortune, the point from which the tragic hero falls. This ironic use of the point of epiphany occurs in the Bible in the story of the Tower of Babel.

The Ptolemaic cosmos eventually disappeared, but the point of epiphany did not, though in more recent literature it is often ironically reversed, or brought to terms with greater demands for credibility. Allowing for this, one may still see the same archetype in the final mountain-top scene of Ibsen's *When We Dead Awaken* and in the central image of Virginia Woolf's *To the Lighthouse*. In the later poetry of Yeats and Eliot it becomes a central unifying image. Such titles as *The Tower* and *The Winding Stair* indicate its importance for Yeats, and the lunar symbolism and the apocalyptic imagery of *The Tower* and *Sailing to Byzantium* are both thoroughly consistent. In Eliot it is the flame reached in the fire sermon of *The Waste Land*, in contrast to the natural cycle which is symbolized by water, and it is also the "multifoliate rose" of *The Hollow Men*. *Ash Wednesday* brings us back again to the purgatorial winding stair, and *Little Gidding* to the burning rose, where there is a descending movement of fire symbolized by the Pentecostal tongues of flame and an ascending one symbolized by Hercules' pyre and "shirt of flame."

THE MYTHOS OF AUTUMN: TRAGEDY

Thanks as usual to Aristotle, the theory of tragedy is in considerably better shape than the other three *mythoi*, and we can deal with it more briefly, as the ground is more familiar. Without tragedy, all literary fictions might be plausibly explained as expressions of emotional attachments, whether of wish-fulfilment or of repugnance: the tragic fiction guarantees, so to speak, a disinterested quality in literary experience. It is largely through the tragedies of Greek culture that the sense of the authentic natural basis of human character comes into literature. In romance the characters are still largely dream-characters; in satire they tend to be caricatures; in comedy their actions are twisted to fit the demands of a happy ending. In full tragedy the main characters are emancipated from dream, an emancipation which is at the same time a restriction, because the order of nature is present. However thickly strewn a tragedy may be with ghosts, portents, witches, or oracles, we know that the tragic hero cannot simply rub a lamp and summon a genie to get him out of his trouble.

Like comedy, tragedy is best and most easily studied in drama, but it is not confined to drama, nor to actions that end in disaster. Plays that are usually called or classified with tragedies end in serenity, like *Cymbeline*, or even joy, like *Alcestis* or Racine's *Esther*, or in an ambiguous mood that is hard to define, like *Philoctetes*. On the other hand, while a predominantly sombre mood forms part of the unity of the tragic structure, concentrating on mood does not intensify the tragic effect: if it did, *Titus Andronicus* might well be the most powerful of Shakespeare's tragedies. The source of tragic effect must be sought, as Aristotle pointed out, in the tragic *mythos* or plot-structure.

It is a commonplace of criticism that comedy tends to deal with characters in a social group, whereas tragedy is more concentrated on a single individual. We have given reasons in the first essay for thinking that the typical tragic hero is somewhere between the divine and the "all too human." This must be true even of dying gods: Prometheus, being a god, cannot die, but he suffers for his sympathy with the "dying ones" (*brotoi*) or "mortal" men, and even suffering has something subdivine about it. The tragic hero is very great as compared with us, but there is something else, something on the side of him opposite the audience, compared to which he is small. This something else may be called God, gods, fate, accident, fortune, necessity, circumstance, or any combination of these, but whatever it is the tragic hero is our mediator with it.

The tragic hero is typically on top of the wheel of fortune, half-way between human society on the ground and the something greater in the sky. Prometheus, Adam, and Christ hang between heaven and earth, between a world of paradisal freedom and a world of bondage. Tragic heroes are so much the highest points in their human landscape that they seem the inevitable conductors of the power about them, great trees more likely to be struck by lightning than a clump of grass. Conductors may of course be instruments as well as victims of the divine lightning: Milton's Samson destroys the Philistine temple with himself, and Hamlet nearly exterminates the Danish court in his own fall. Something of Nietzsche's mountain-top air of transvaluation clings to the tragic hero: his thoughts are not ours any more than his deeds, even if, like Faustus, he is dragged off to hell for having them. Whatever eloquence or affability he may have, an inscrutable reserve lies behind it. Even sinister heroes—Tamburlaine, Macbeth, Creon—retain this reserve, and we are reminded that men will die loyally for a wicked or cruel man, but not for an amiable backslapper. Those who attract most devotion from others are those who are best able to suggest in their manner that they have no need of it, and from the urbanity of Hamlet to the sullen ferocity of Ajax, tragic heroes are wrapped in the mystery of their communion with that something beyond which we can see only through them, and which is the source of their strength and their fate alike. In the phrase which so fascinated Yeats, the tragic hero leaves his servants to do his "living" for him, and the center of tragedy is in the hero's isolation, not in a villain's betrayal, even when the villain is, as he often is, a part of the hero himself.

As for the something beyond, its names are variable but the form in which it manifests itself is fairly constant. Whether the context is Greek, Christian, or undefined, tragedy seems to lead up to an epiphany of law, of that which is and must be. It can hardly be an accident that the two great developments of tragic drama, in fifth-century Athens and in seventeenth-century Europe, were contemporary with the rise of Ionian and of Renaissance science. In such a world-view nature is seen as an impersonal process which human law imitates as best it can, and this direct relation of man and natural law is in the foreground. The sense in Greek tragedy that fate is stronger than the gods really implies that the gods exist primarily to ratify the order of nature, and that if any personality, even a divine one, possesses a genuine power of veto over law, it is most unlikely that he will want to exercise it. In Christianity much the same is true of the personality of Christ in relation to the inscrutable decrees of the Father. Similarly the tragic process in Shakespeare is natural in the sense that it simply happens, whatever its cause, explanation, or relationships. Characters may grope about for conceptions of gods that kill us for their sport, or for a divinity that shapes our ends, but the action of tragedy will not abide our questions, a fact often transferred to the personality of Shakespeare.

In its most elementary form, the vision of law (*dike*) operates as *lex talionis* or revenge. The hero provokes enmity, or inherits a situation of enmity, and the return of the avenger constitutes the catastrophe. The revenge-tragedy is a simple tragic structure, and like most simple structures can be a very powerful one, often retained as a central theme even in the most complex tragedies. Here the original act provoking the revenge sets up an antithetical or counterbalancing movement, and the completion of the movement resolves the tragedy. This happens so often that we may almost characterize the total *mythos* of tragedy as binary, in contrast to the three-part saturnalia movement of comedy.

We notice however the frequency of the device of making the revenge come from another world, through gods or ghosts or oracles. This device expands the conceptions of both nature and law beyond the limits of the obvious and tangible. It does not thereby transcend those conceptions, as it is still natural law that is manifested by the tragic action. Here we see the tragic hero as disturbing a balance in nature, nature being conceived as an order stretching over the two kingdoms of the visible and the invisible, a balance which sooner or later *must* right itself. The righting of the balance is what the Greeks called *nemesis*: again, the agent or instrument of *nemesis* may be human vengeance, ghostly vengeance, divine vengeance, divine justice, accident, fate or the logic of events, but the essential thing is that *nemesis* happens, and happens impersonally, unaffected, as *Oedipus Tyrannus* illustrates, by the moral quality of human motivation involved. In the *Oresteia* we are led from a series of revenge-movements into a final vision of natural law, a universal compact in which moral law is included and which the gods, in the person of the goddess of wisdom, endorse. Here *nemesis*, like its counterpart the Mosaic law in Christianity, is not abolished but fulfilled: it is developed from a mechanical or arbitrary sense of restored order, represented by the Furies, to the rational sense of it expounded by Athene. The appearance of Athene does not turn the *Oresteia* into a comedy, but clarifies its tragic vision.

There are two reductive formulas which have often been used to explain tragedy. Neither is quite good enough, but each is almost good enough, and as they are contradictory, they must represent extreme or limiting views of tragedy. One of these is the theory that all tragedy exhibits the omnipotence of an external fate. And, of course, the overwhelming majority of tragedies do leave us with a sense of the supremacy of impersonal power and of the limitation of human effort. But the fatalistic reduction of tragedy confuses the tragic condition with the tragic process: fate, in a tragedy, normally becomes external to the hero only *after* the tragic process has been set going. The Greek *ananke* or *moira* is in its normal, or pre-tragic, form the internal balancing condition of life. It appears as external or antithetical necessity only after it has been violated as a condition of life, just as justice is the internal condition of an honest man, but the external antagonist of the criminal. Homer uses a profoundly significant phrase for the theory of tragedy when he has Zeus speak of Aegisthus as going *hyper moron, beyond* fate.

The fatalistic reduction of tragedy does not distinguish tragedy from irony, and it is again significant that we speak of the irony of fate rather than of its tragedy. Irony does not need an exceptional central figure: as a rule, the dingier the hero the sharper the irony, when irony alone is aimed at. It is the admixture of heroism that gives tragedy its characteristic splendor and exhilaration. The tragic hero has normally had an extraordinary, often a nearly divine, destiny almost within his grasp, and the glory of that original vision never quite fades out of tragedy. The rhetoric of tragedy requires the noblest diction that the greatest poets can produce, and while catastrophe is the normal end of tragedy, this is balanced by an equally significant original greatness, a paradise lost.

The other reductive theory of tragedy is that the act which sets the tragic process going must be primarily a violation of *moral* law, whether human or divine; in short, that Aristotle's hamartia or "flaw" must have an essential connection with sin or wrongdoing. Again it is true that the great majority of tragic heroes do possess hybris, a proud, passionate, obsessed or soaring mind which brings about a morally intelligible downfall. Such hybris is the normal precipitating agent of catastrophe, just as in comedy the cause of the happy ending is usually some act of humility, represented by a slave or by a heroine meanly disguised. In Aristotle the hamartia of the tragic hero is associated with Aristotle's ethical conception of *proairesis*, or free choice of an end, and Aristotle certainly does tend to think of tragedy as morally, almost physically, intelligible. It has already been suggested, however, that the conception of catharsis, which is central to Aristotle's view of tragedy, is inconsistent with moral reductions of it. Pity and terror are moral feelings, and they are relevant but not attached to the tragic situation. Shakespeare is particularly fond of planting moral lightning-rods on both sides of his heroes to deflect the pity and terror: we have mentioned Othello flanked by Iago and Desdemona, but Hamlet is flanked by Claudius and Ophelia, Lear by his daughters, and even Macbeth by Lady Macbeth and Duncan. In all these tragedies there is a sense of some far-reaching mystery of which this morally intelligible process is only a part. The hero's act has thrown a switch in a larger machine than his own life, or even his own society.

All theories of tragedy as morally explicable sooner or later run into the question: is an innocent sufferer in tragedy (i.e., poetically innocent), Iphigeneia, Cordelia, Socrates in Plato's *Apology*, Christ in the Passion, not a tragic figure? It is not very convincing to try to provide crucial moral flaws for such characters. Cordelia shows a high spirit, perhaps a touch of wilfulness, in refusing to flatter her father, and Cordelia gets hanged. Joan of Arc in Schiller has a moment of tenderness for an English soldier, and Joan is burned alive, or would have been if Schiller had not decided to sacrifice the facts to save the face of his moral theory. Here we are getting away from tragedy, and close to a kind of insane cautionary tale, like Mrs. Pipchin's little boy who was gored to death by a bull for asking inconvenient questions. Tragedy, in short, seems to elude the antithesis of moral responsibility and arbitrary fate, just as it eludes the antithesis of good and evil.

In the third book of *Paradise Lost*, Milton represents God as arguing that he made man "Sufficient to have stood, though free to fall." God knew that Adam would fall, but did not compel him to do so, and on that basis he disclaims legal responsibility. This argument is so bad that Milton, if he was trying to escape refutation, did well to ascribe it to God. Thought and act cannot be so separated: if God had foreknowledge he must have known in the instant of creating Adam that he was creating a being who would fall. Yet the passage is a most haunting and suggestive one nonetheless. For *Paradise Lost* is not simply an attempt to write one more tragedy, but to expound what Milton believed to be the archetypal myth of tragedy. Hence the passage is another example of existential projection: the real basis of the relation of Milton's God to Adam is the relation of the tragic poet to his hero. The tragic poet knows that his hero will be in a tragic situation, but he exerts all his power to avoid the sense of having manipulated that situation for his own purposes. He exhibits his hero to us as God exhibits Adam to the angels. If the hero was not sufficient to have stood, the mode is purely ironic; if he was not free to fall, the mode is purely romantic, the story of an invincible hero who will conquer all his antagonists as long as the story is about him. Now most theories of tragedy take one great tragedy as their norm: thus Aristotle's theory is largely founded on *Oedipus Tyrannus*, and Hegel's on *Antigone*. In seeing the archetypal human tragedy in the story of Adam, Milton was, of course, in agreement with the whole Judaeo-Christian cultural tradition, and perhaps arguments drawn from the story of Adam may have better luck in literary criticism than in subjects compelled to assume Adam's real existence, either as fact or as a merely legal fiction. Chaucer's monk, who clearly understood what he was doing, began with Lucifer and Adam, and we may be well advised to follow his example.

Adam, then, is in a heroic human situation: he is on top of the wheel of fortune, with the destiny of the gods almost within his reach. He forfeits that destiny in a way which suggests moral responsibility to some and a conspiracy of fate to others. What he does is to exchange a fortune of unlimited freedom for the fate involved in the consequences of the act of exchange, just as, for a man who deliberately jumps off a precipice, the law of gravitation acts as fate for the brief remainder of his life. The exchange is presented by Milton as itself a free act or *proairesis*, a use of freedom to lose freedom. And just as comedy often sets up an arbitrary law and then organizes the action to break or evade it, so tragedy presents the reverse theme of narrowing a comparatively free life into a process of causation. This happens to Macbeth when he accepts the logic of usurpation, to Hamlet when he accepts the logic of revenge, to Lear when he accepts the logic of abdication. The discovery or *anagnorisis* which comes at the end of the tragic plot is not simply the knowledge by the hero of what has happened to him —*Oedipus Tyrannus*, despite its reputation as a typical tragedy, is rather a special case in that regard—but the recognition of the determined shape of the life he has created for himself, with an implicit comparison with the uncreated potential life he has forsaken. The line of Milton dealing with the fall of the devils, "O how unlike the place from whence they fell!", referring as it does both to Virgil's *quantum mutatus ab illo* and Isaiah's "How art thou fallen from heaven, O Lucifer son of the morning," combines the Classical and the Christian archetypes of tragedy—for Satan, of course, like Adam, possessed an original glory. In Milton the complement to the vision of Adam on top of the wheel of fortune and

falling into the world of the wheel is Christ standing on the pinnacle of the temple, urged by Satan to fall, and remaining motionless.

As soon as Adam falls, he enters his own created life, which is
also the order of nature as we know it. The tragedy of Adam, therefore, resolves, like all other tragedies, in the manifestation of natural law. He enters a world in which existence is itself tragic, not
existence modified by an act, deliberate or unconscious. Merely to
exist is to disturb the balance of nature. Every natural man is a
Hegelian thesis, and implies a reaction: every new birth provokes
the return of an avenging death. This fact, in itself ironic and now
called *Angst*, becomes tragic when a sense of a lost and originally
higher destiny is added to it. Aristotle's hamartia, then, is a condition of being, not a cause of becoming: the reason why Milton
ascribes his dubious argument to God is that he is so anxious to
remove God from a predetermined causal sequence. On one side
of the tragic hero is an opportunity for freedom, on the other the
inevitable consequence of losing that freedom. These two sides of
Adam's situation are represented in Milton by the speeches of
Raphael and Michael respectively. Even with an innocent hero or
martyr the same situation arises: in the Passion story it occurs in
Christ's prayer in Gethsemane. Tragedy seems to move up to an
Augenblick or crucial moment from which point the road to what
might have been and the road to what will be can be simultaneously
seen. Seen by the audience, that is: it cannot be seen by the hero
if he is in a state of hybris, for in that case the crucial moment is
for him a moment of dizziness, when the wheel of fortune begins
its inevitable cyclical movement downward.

In Adam's situation there is a feeling, which in Christian tradition can be traced back at least to St. Augustine, that time *begins*
with the fall; that the fall from liberty into the natural cycle also
started the movement of time as we know it. In other tragedies
too we can trace the feeling that *nemesis* is deeply involved with
the movement of time, whether as the missing of a tide in the affairs of men, as a recognition that the time is out of joint, as a
sense that time is the devourer of life, the mouth of hell at the
previous moment, when the potential passes forever into the actual,
or, in its ultimate horror, Macbeth's sense of it as simply one clock-
tick after another. In comedy time plays a redeeming role: it un-
covers and brings to light what is essential to the happy ending.

The subtitle of Greene's *Pandosto,* the source of *The Winter's Tale,* is "*The Triumph of Time,*" and it well describes the nature of Shakespeare's action, where time is introduced as a chorus. But in tragedy the *cognitio* is normally the recognition of the inevitability of a causal sequence in time, and the forebodings and ironic anticipations surrounding it are based on a sense of cyclical return.

In irony, as distinct from tragedy, the wheel of time completely encloses the action, and there is no sense of an original contact with a relatively timeless world. In the Bible the tragic fall of Adam is followed by its historical repetition, the fall of Israel into Egyptian bondage, which is, so to speak, its ironic confirmation. As long as the Geoffrey version of British history was accepted, the fall of Troy was the corresponding event in the history of Britain, and, as the fall of Troy began with an idolatrous misapplication of an apple, there were even symbolic parallels. Shakespeare's most ironic play, *Troilus and Cressida,* presents in Ulysses the voice of worldly wisdom, expounding with great eloquence the two primary categories of the perspective of tragic irony in the fallen world, time and the hierarchic chain of being. The extraordinary treatment of the tragic vision of time by Nietzsche's Zarathustra, in which the heroic acceptance of cyclical return becomes a glumly cheerful acceptance of a cosmology of identical recurrence, marks the influence of an age of irony.

Anyone accustomed to think archetypally of literature will recognize in tragedy a mimesis of sacrifice. Tragedy is a paradoxical combination of a fearful sense of rightness (the hero must fall) and a pitying sense of wrongness (it is too bad that he falls). There is a similar paradox in the two elements of sacrifice. One of these is communion, the dividing of a heroic or divine body among a group which brings them into unity with, and as, that body. The other is propitiation, the sense that in spite of the communion the body really belongs to another, a greater, and a potentially wrathful power. The ritual analogies to tragedy are more obvious than the psychological ones, for it is irony, not tragedy, that represents the nightmare or anxiety-dream. But, just as the literary critic finds Freud most suggestive for the theory of comedy, and Jung for the theory of romance, so for the theory of tragedy one naturally looks to the psychology of the will to power, as expounded in Adler and Nietzsche. Here one finds a "Dionysiac" aggressive will, intoxicated by dreams of its own omnipotence, impinging upon an "Apollonian" sense of external and immovable order. As a mimesis of ritual, the tragic hero is not really killed or eaten, but the corresponding thing in art still takes place, a vision of death which draws the survivors into a new unity. As a mimesis of dream, the inscrutable tragic hero, like the proud and silent swan, becomes articulate at the point of death, and the audience, like the poet in *Kubla Khan*, revives his song within itself. With his fall, a greater world beyond which his gigantic spirit had blocked out becomes for an instant visible, but there is also a sense of the mystery and remoteness of that world.

If we are right in our suggestion that romance, tragedy, irony and comedy are all episodes in a total quest-myth, we can see how it is that comedy can contain a potential tragedy within itself. In myth, the hero is a god, and hence he does not die, but dies and rises again. The ritual pattern behind the catharsis of comedy is the resurrection that follows the death, the epiphany or manifestation of the risen hero. In Aristophanes the hero, who often goes through a point of ritual death, is treated as a risen god, hailed as a new Zeus, or given the quasi-divine honors of the Olympic victor. In New Comedy the new human body is both a hero and a social group. The Aeschylean trilogy proceeds to the comic satyr-play, which is said to have affinities with spring festivals. Christianity, too, sees tragedy as an episode in the divine comedy, the larger scheme of redemption and resurrection. The sense of tragedy as a prelude to comedy seems almost inseparable from anything explicitly Christian. The serenity of the final double chorus in the St. Matthew Passion would hardly be attainable if composer and audience did not know that there was more to the story. Nor would the death of Samson lead to "calm of mind, all passion spent," if Samson were not a prototype of the rising Christ, associated at the appropriate moment with the phoenix.

This is an example of the way in which myths explain the structural principles behind familiar literary facts, in this case the fact that to make a sombre action end happily is easy enough, and to reverse the procedure almost impossible. (Of course we have a natural dislike of seeing pleasant situations turn out disastrously, but if a poet is working on a solid structural basis, our natural likes and dislikes have nothing to do with the matter.) Even Shakespeare, who can do anything, never does quite this. The action of *King Lear*, which seems heading for some kind of serenity, is suddenly wrenched into agony by the hanging of Cordelia, providing a conclusion which the stage refused to act for over a century, but none of Shakespeare's tragedies impresses us as a comedy gone wrong— *Romeo and Juliet* has a suggestion of such a structure, but it is only a suggestion. Hence while of course a tragedy may contain a comic action, it contains it only episodically as a subordinate contrast or underplot.

The characterization of tragedy is very like that of comedy in reverse. The source of *nemesis*, whatever it is, is an *eiron*, and may appear in a great variety of agents, from wrathful gods to hypocritical villains. In comedy we noticed three main types of *eiron* characters: a benevolent withdrawing and returning figure, the tricky slave or vice, and the hero and heroine. We have the tragic counterpart to the withdrawn *eiron* in the god who decrees the tragic action, like Athene in *Ajax* or Aphrodite in *Hippolytus*; a Christian example is God the Father in *Paradise Lost*. He may also be a ghost, like Hamlet's father; or it may not be a person at all but simply an invisible force known only by its effects, like the death that quietly seizes on Tamburlaine when the time has come for him to die. Often, as in the revenge-tragedy, it is an event previous to the action of which the tragedy itself is the consequence.

A tragic counterpart to the vice or tricky slave may be discerned in the soothsayer or prophet who foresees the inevitable end, or more of it than the hero does, like Teiresias. A closer example is the Machiavellian villain of Elizabethan drama, who, like the vice in comedy, is a convenient catalyzer of the action because he requires the minimum of motivation, being a self-starting principle of malevolence. Like the comic vice, too, he is something of an *architectus* or projection of the author's will, in this case for a tragic conclusion. "I limned this night-piece," says Webster's Lodovico, "and it was my best." Iago dominates the action of *Othello* almost to the point of being a tragic counterpart to the black king or evil magician of romance. The affinities of the Machiavellian villain with the diabolical are naturally close, and he may be an actual devil like Mephistopheles, but the sense of awfulness belonging to an agent of catastrophe can also make him something more like the high priest of a sacrifice. There is a touch of this in Webster's Bosola. *King Lear* has a Machiavellian villain in Edmund, and Edmund is contrasted with Edgar. Edgar, with his bewildering variety of disguises, his appearance to blind or mad people in different roles, and his tendency to appear on the third sound of the trumpet and to come pat like the catastrophe of the old comedy, seems to be an experiment in a new type, a kind of tragic "virtue," if I may coin this word by analogy, a counterpart in the order of nature to a guardian angel or similar attendant in romance.

The tragic hero usually belongs of course to the *alazon* group, an impostor in the sense that he is self-deceived or made dizzy by hybris. In many tragedies he begins as a semi-divine figure, at least in his own eyes, and then an inexorable dialectic sets to work which separates the divine pretence from the human actuality. "They told me I was everything," says Lear: " 'tis a lie; I am not ague-proof." The tragic hero is usually vested with supreme authority, but is often in the more ambiguous position of a *tyrannos* whose rule depends on his own abilities, rather than a purely hereditary or *de jure* monarch (*basileus*) like Duncan. The latter is more directly a symbol of the original vision or birthright, and is often a somewhat pathetic victim, like Richard II, or even Agamemnon. Parental figures in tragedy have the same ambivalence that they have in all other forms.

We found in comedy that the term *bomolochos* or buffoon need not be restricted to farce, but could be extended to cover comic characters who are primarily entertainers, with the function of increasing or focussing the comic mood. The corresponding contrasting type in tragedy is the suppliant, the character, often female, who presents a picture of unmitigated helplessness and destitution. Such a figure is pathetic, and pathos, though it seems a gentler and more relaxed mood than tragedy, is even more terrifying. Its basis is the exclusion of an individual from a group, hence it attacks the deepest fear in ourselves that we possess—a fear much deeper than the relatively cosy and sociable bogey of hell. In the figure of the suppliant pity and terror are brought to the highest possible pitch of intensity, and the awful consequences of rejecting the suppliant for all concerned is a central theme of Greek tragedy. Suppliant figures are often women threatened with death or rape, or children, like Prince Arthur in *King John*. The fragility of Shakespeare's Ophelia marks an affinity with the suppliant type. Often, too, the suppliant is in the structurally tragic position of having lost a place of greatness: this is the position of Adam and Eve in the tenth book of *Paradise Lost*, of the Trojan women after the fall

217

of Troy, of Oedipus in the Colonus play, and so on. A subordinate figure who plays the role of focussing the tragic mood is the messenger who regularly announces the catastrophe in Greek tragedy. In the final scene of comedy, when the author is usually trying to get all his characters on the stage at once, we often notice the introduction of a new character, generally a messenger bearing some missing piece of the *cognitio,* such as Jaques de Boys in *As You Like It* or the gentle astringer in *All's Well,* who represents the comic counterpart.

Finally, a tragic counterpart of the comic refuser of festivity may be discerned in a tragic type of plain dealer who may be simply the faithful friend of the hero, like Horatio in *Hamlet,* but is often an outspoken critic of the tragic action, like Kent in *King Lear* or Enobarbus in *Antony and Cleopatra.* Such a character is in the position of refusing, or at any rate resisting, the tragic movement toward catastrophe. Abdiel's role in the tragedy of Satan in *Paradise Lost* is similar. The familiar figures of Cassandra and Teiresias combine this role with that of the soothsayer. Such figures, when they occur in a tragedy without a chorus, are often called chorus characters, as they illustrate one of the essential functions of the tragic chorus. In comedy a society forms around the hero: in tragedy the chorus, however faithful, usually represents the society from which the hero is gradually isolated. Hence what it expresses is a social norm against which the hero's hybris may be measured. The chorus is not the voice of the hero's conscience by any means, but very seldom does it encourage him in his hybris or prompt him to disastrous action. The chorus or chorus character is, so to speak, the embryonic germ of comedy in tragedy, just as the refuser of festivity, the melancholy Jaques or Alceste, is a tragic germ in comedy.

In comedy the erotic and social affinities of the hero are combined and unified in the final scene; tragedy usually makes love and the social structure irreconcilable and contending forces, a conflict which reduces love to passion and social activity to a forbidding and imperative duty. Comedy is much concerned with integrating the family and adjusting the family to society as a whole; tragedy is much concerned with breaking up the family and opposing it to the rest of society. This gives us the tragic archetype of Antigone, of which the conflict of love and honor in Classical French drama, of *Neigung* and *Pflicht* in Schiller, of passion and authority in the Jacobeans, are all moralized simplifications. Again, just as the heroine of comedy often ties together the action, so it is obvious that the central female figure of a tragic action will often polarize the tragic conflict. Eve, Helen, Gertrude, and Emily in the *Knight's Tale* are some ready instances: the structural role of Briseis in the *Iliad* is similar. Comedy works out the proper relations of its characters and prevents heroes from marrying their sisters or mothers; tragedy presents the disaster of Oedipus or the incest of Siegmund. There is a great deal in tragedy about pride of race and birthright, but its general tendency is to isolate a ruling or noble family from the rest of society.

The phases of tragedy move from the heroic to the ironic, the first three corresponding to the first three phases of romance, the last three to the last three of irony. The first phase of tragedy is the one in which the central character is given the greatest possible dignity in contrast to the other characters, so that we get the perspective of a stag pulled down by wolves. The sources of dignity are courage and innocence, and in this phase the hero or heroine usually is innocent. This phase corresponds to the myth of the birth of the hero in romance, a theme which is occasionally incorporated into a tragic structure, as in Racine's *Athalie*. But owing to the unusual difficulty of making an interesting dramatic character out of an infant, the central and typical figure of this phase is the calumniated woman, often a mother the legitimacy of whose child is suspected. A whole series of tragedies based on a Griselda figure belong here, stretching from the Senecan *Octavia* to Hardy's *Tess*, and including the tragedy of Hermione in *The Winter's Tale*. If we are to read *Alcestis* as a tragedy, we have to see it as a tragedy of this phase in which Alcestis is violated by Death and then has her fidelity vindicated by being restored to life. *Cymbeline* belongs here too: in this play the theme of the birth of the hero appears offstage, for Cymbeline was the king of Britain at the time of the birth of Christ, and the halcyon peace in which the play concludes has a suppressed reference to this.

An even clearer example, and certainly one of the greatest in English literature, is *The Duchess of Malfi*. The Duchess has the innocence of abundant life in a sick and melancholy society, where the fact that she has "youth and a little beauty" is precisely why she is hated. She reminds us too that one of the essential characteristics of innocence in the martyr is an unwillingness to die. When Bosola comes to murder her he makes elaborate attempts to put her half in love with easeful death and to suggest that death is really a deliverance. The attempt is motivated by a grimly controlled pity, and is roughly the equivalent of the vinegar sponge in the Passion. When the Duchess, her back to the wall, says "I am the Duchess of Malfi still," "still" having its full weight of "always," we understand how it is that even after her death her invisible presence continues to be the most vital character in the play. *The White Devil* is an ironic parody-treatment of the same phase.

The second phase corresponds to the youth of the romantic hero, and is in one way or another the tragedy of innocence in the sense of inexperience, usually involving young people. It may be simply the tragedy of a youthful life cut off, as in the stories of Iphigeneia and Jephthah's daughter, of Romeo and Juliet, or, in a more complex situation, in the bewildered mixture of idealism and priggishness that brings Hippolytus to disaster. The simplicity of Shaw's Joan and her lack of worldly wisdom place her here also. For us however the phase is dominated by the archetypal tragedy of the green and golden world, the loss of the innocence of Adam and Eve, who, no matter how heavy a doctrinal load they have to carry, will always remain dramatically in the position of children baffled by their first contact with an adult situation. In many tragedies of this type the central character survives, so that the action closes with some adjustment to a new and more mature experience. "Henceforth I learn that to obey is best," says Adam, as he and Eve go hand in hand out to the world before them. A less clear cut but similar resolution occurs when Philoctetes, whose serpent-wound reminds us a little of Adam, is taken off his island to enter the Trojan war. Ibsen's *Little Eyolf* is a tragedy of this phase, and with the same continuing conclusion, in which it is the older characters who are educated through the death of a child.

The third phase, corresponding to the central quest-theme of romance, is tragedy in which a strong emphasis is thrown on the success or completeness of the hero's achievement. The Passion belongs here, as do all tragedies in which the hero is in any way related to or a prototype of Christ, like *Samson Agonistes*. The paradox of victory within tragedy may be expressed by a double perspective in the action. Samson is a buffoon of a Philistine carnival and simultaneously a tragic hero to the Israelites, but the tragedy ends in triumph and the carnival in catastrophe. Much the same is true of the mocked Christ in the Passion. But just as the second phase often ends in anticipation of greater maturity, so this one is often a sequel to a previous tragic or heroic action, and comes at the end of a heroic life. One of the greatest dramatic examples is *Oedipus at Colonus*, where we find the usual binary form of a tragedy conditioned by a previous tragic act, ending this time not in a second disaster, but in a full rich serenity that goes far beyond a mere resignation to Fate. In narrative literature we may cite Beowulf's last fight with the dragon, the pendant to his Grendel quest. Shakespeare's *Henry V* is a successfully completed romantic quest made tragic by its implicit context: everybody knows that King Henry died almost immediately and that sixty years of un-broken disaster followed for England—at least, if anyone in Shake-speare's audience did not know that, his ignorance was certainly no fault of Shakespeare's.

The fourth phase is the typical fall of the hero through hybris and hamartia that we have already discussed. In this phase we cross the boundary line from innocence to experience, which is also the direction in which the hero falls. In the fifth phase the ironic ele-ment increases, the heroic decreases, and the characters look further away and in a smaller perspective. *Timon of Athens* impresses us as more ironic and less heroic than the better known tragedies, not simply because Timon is a more middle-class hero who has to buy what authority he has, but because the feeling that Timon's suicide has somehow failed to make a fully heroic *point* is very strong. Timon is oddly isolated from the final action, in which the breach between Alcibiades and the Athenians closes up over his head, in striking contrast with the conclusions of most of the other trage-dies, where nobody is allowed to steal the show from the central character.

The ironic perspective in tragedy is attained by putting the char-acters in a state of lower freedom than the audience. For a Christian audience an Old Testament or pagan setting is ironic in this sense, as it shows its characters moving according to the conditions of a law, whether Jewish or natural, from which the audience has been, at least theoretically, redeemed. *Samson Agonistes*, though unique in English literature, presents a combination of Classical form and Hebrew subject-matter that the greatest contemporary trage-dian, Racine, also reached at the end of his life in *Athalie* and

221

Esther. Similarly the epilogue to Chaucer's *Troilus* puts a Courtly Love tragedy into its historical relation to "payens corsed olde rites." The events in Geoffrey of Monmouth's British history are supposed to be contemporary with those of the Old Testament, and the sense of life under the law is present everywhere in *King Lear.* The same structural principle accounts for the use of astrology and other fatalistic machinery connected with the turning wheels of fate or fortune. Romeo and Juliet are star-crossed, and Troilus loses Criseyde because every five hundred years Jupiter and Saturn meet the crescent moon in Cancer and claim another victim. The tragic action of the fifth phase presents for the most part the tragedy of lost direction and lack of knowledge, not unlike the second phase except that the context is the world of adult experience. *Oedipus Tyrannus* belongs here, and all tragedies and tragic episodes which suggest the existential projection of fatalism, and, like much of the Book of Job, seem to raise metaphysical or theological questions rather than social or moral ones.

Oedipus Tyrannus, however, is already moving into the sixth phase of tragedy, a world of shock and horror in which the central images are images of *sparagmos,* that is, cannibalism, mutilation, and torture. The specific reaction known as shock is appropriate to a situation of cruelty or outrage. (The secondary or false shock produced by the outrage done to some emotional attachment or fixation, as in the critical reception of *Jude the Obscure* or *Ulysses,* has no status in criticism, as false shock is a disguised resistance to the autonomy of culture.) Any tragedy may have one or more shocking scenes in it, but sixth-phase tragedy shocks as a whole, in its total effect. This phase is more common as a subordinate aspect of tragedy than as its main theme, as unqualified horror or despair makes a difficult cadence. *Prometheus Bound* is a tragedy of this phase, though this is partly an illusion due to its isolation from the trilogy to which it belongs. In such tragedies the hero is in too great agony or humiliation to gain the privilege of a heroic pose, hence it is usually easier to make him a villainous hero, like Marlowe's Barabas, although Faustus also belongs to the same phase. Seneca is fond of this phase, and bequeathed to the Elizabethans an interest in the gruesome, an effect which usually has some connection with mutilation, as when Ferdinand offers to shake hands with the Duchess of Malfi and gives her a dead man's hand. *Titus Andronicus* is an experiment in Senecan sixth-phase horror which makes a great deal of mutilation, and shows also a strong interest, from the opening scene on, in the sacrificial symbolism of tragedy.

At the end of this phase we reach a point of demonic epiphany, where we see or glimpse the undisplaced demonic vision, the vision of the *Inferno*. Its chief symbols, besides the prison and the madhouse, are the instruments of a torturing death, the cross under the sunset being the antithesis of the tower under the moon. A strong element of demonic ritual in public punishments and similar mob amusements is exploited by tragic and ironic myth. Breaking on the wheel becomes Lear's wheel of fire; bear-baiting is an image for Gloucester and Macbeth, and for the crucified Prometheus the humiliation of exposure, the horror of being watched, is a greater misery than the pain. *Derkou theama* (behold the spectacle; get your staring over with) is his bitterest cry. The inability of Milton's blind Samson to stare back is his greatest torment, and one which forces him to scream at Delilah, in one of the most terrible passages of all tragic drama, that he will tear her to pieces if she touches him.

THE MYTHOS OF WINTER: IRONY AND SATIRE

We come now to the mythical patterns of experience, the attempts to give form to the shifting ambiguities and complexities of unidealized existence. We cannot find these patterns merely in the mimetic or representational aspect of such literature, for that aspect is one of content and not form. As structure, the central principle of ironic myth is best approached as a parody of romance: the application of romantic mythical forms to a more realistic content which fits them in unexpected ways. No one in a romance, Don Quixote protests, ever asks who pays for the hero's accommodation.

The chief distinction between irony and satire is that satire is militant irony: its moral norms are relatively clear, and it assumes standards against which the grotesque and absurd are measured. Sheer invective or name-calling ("flyting") is satire in which there is relatively little irony: on the other hand, whenever a reader is not sure what the author's attitude is or what his own is supposed to be, we have irony with relatively little satire. Fielding's *Jonathan Wild* is satiric irony: certain flat moral judgements made by the narrator (as in the description of Bagshot in chapter twelve) are in accord with the decorum of the work, but would be out of key in,

say, *Madame Bovary*. Irony is consistent both with complete realism of content and with the suppression of attitude on the part of
the author. Satire demands at least a token fantasy, a content which
the reader recognizes as grotesque, and at least an implicit moral
standard, the latter being essential in a militant attitude to experience. Some phenomena, such as the ravages of disease, may be
called grotesque, but to make fun of them would not be very effective satire. The satirist has to select his absurdities, and the act of
selection is a moral act.

The argument of Swift's *Modest Proposal* has a brain-softening
plausibility about it: one is almost led to feel that the narrator is
not only reasonable but even humane; yet the "almost" can never
drop out of any sane man's reaction, and as long as it remains there
the modest proposal will be both fantastic and immoral. When in
another passage Swift suddenly says, discussing the poverty of Ireland, "But my Heart is too heavy to continue this Irony longer,"
he is speaking of satire, which breaks down when its content is too
oppressively real to permit the maintaining of the fantastic or
hypothetical tone. Hence satire is irony which is structurally close
to the comic: the comic struggle of two societies, one normal and
the other absurd, is reflected in its double focus of morality and
fantasy. Irony with little satire is the non-heroic residue of tragedy,
centering on a theme of puzzled defeat.

Two things, then, are essential to satire; one is wit or humor
founded on fantasy or a sense of the grotesque or absurd, the other
is an object of attack. Attack without humor, or pure denunciation,
forms one of the boundaries of satire. It is a very hazy boundary,
because invective is one of the most readable forms of literary art,
just as panegyric is one of the dullest. It is an established datum
of literature that we like hearing people cursed and are bored with
hearing them praised, and almost any denunciation, if vigorous
enough, is followed by a reader with the kind of pleasure that soon
breaks into a smile. To attack anything, writer and audience must
agree on its undesirability, which means that the content of a great
deal of satire founded on national hatreds, snobbery, prejudice,
and personal pique goes out of date very quickly.

But attack in literature can never be a pure expression of merely
personal or even social hatred, whatever the motivation for it may
be, because the words for expressing hatred, as distinct from enmity, have too limited a range. About the only ones we have are

224

derived from the animal world, but calling a man a swine or a skunk or a woman a bitch affords a severely restricted satisfaction, as most of the unpleasant qualities of the animal are human projections. As Shakespeare's Thersites says of Menelaus, "to what form, but that he is, should wit larded with malice, and malice forced with wit, turn him to? To an ass, were nothing; he is both ass and ox; to an ox, were nothing; he is both ox and ass." For effective attack we must reach some kind of impersonal level, and that commits the attacker, if only by implication, to a moral standard. The satirist commonly takes a high moral line. Pope asserts that he is "To Virtue only and her friends a friend," suggesting that that is what he is really being when he is reflecting on the cleanliness of the underwear worn by the lady who had jilted him.

Humor, like attack, is founded on convention. The world of humor is a rigidly stylized world in which generous Scotchmen, obedient wives, beloved mothers-in-law, and professors with presence of mind are not permitted to exist. All humor demands agreement that certain things, such as a picture of a wife beating her husband in a comic strip, are conventionally funny. To introduce a comic strip in which a husband beats his wife would distress the reader, because it would mean learning a new convention. The humor of pure fantasy, the other boundary of satire, belongs to romance, though it is uneasy there, as humor perceives the incongruous, and the conventions of romance are idealized. Most fantasy is pulled back into satire by a powerful undertow often called allegory, which may be described as the implicit reference to experience in the perception of the incongruous. The White Knight in Alice who felt that one should be provided for everything, and therefore put anklets around his horse's feet to guard against the bites of sharks, may pass as pure fantasy. But when he goes on to sing an elaborate parody of Wordsworth we begin to sniff the acrid, pungent smell of satire, and when we take a second look at the White Knight we recognize a character type closely related both to Quixote and to the pedant of comedy.

As in this *mythos* we have the difficulty of two words to contend with, it may be simplest, if the reader is now accustomed to our sequence of six phases, to start with them and describe them in order, instead of abstracting a typical form and discussing it first. The first three are phases of satire, and correspond to the first three or ironic phases of comedy.

The first phase corresponds to the first phase of ironic comedy in which there is no displacement of the humorous society. The sense of absurdity about such a comedy arises as a kind of back-fire or recall after the work has been seen or read. Once we have finished with it, deserts of futility open up on all sides, and we have, in spite of the humor, a sense of nightmare and a close proximity to something demonic. Even in very light-hearted comedy we may get a trace of this feeling: if the main theme of *Pride and Prejudice* had been the married life of Collins and Charlotte Lucas, one wonders how long Collins would continue to be funny. Hence it is in decorum for even a satire prevailingly light in tone, such as Pope's second Moral Essay on the characters of women, to rise to a terrifying climax of moral intensity.

The satire typical of this phase may be called the satire of the low norm. It takes for granted a world which is full of anomalies, injustices, follies, and crimes, and yet is permanent and undisplaceable. Its principle is that anyone who wishes to keep his balance in such a world must learn first of all to keep his eyes open and his mouth shut. Counsels of prudence, urging the reader in effect to adopt an *eiron* role, have been prominent in literature from Egyptian times. What is recommended is conventional life at its best: a clairvoyant knowledge of human nature in oneself and others, an avoidance of all illusion and compulsive behavior, a reliance on observation and timing rather than on aggressiveness. This is wisdom, the tried and tested way of life, which does not question the logic of social convention, but merely follows the procedures which in fact do serve to maintain one's balance from one day to the next. The *eiron* of the low norm takes an attitude of flexible pragmatism; he assumes that society will, if given any chance, behave more or less like Caliban's Setebos in Browning's poem, and he conducts himself accordingly. On all doubtful points of behavior convention is his deepest conviction. And however good or bad expertly conventional behavior may be thought to be, it is certainly the most difficult of all forms of behavior to satirize, just as anyone with a new theory of behavior, even if saint or prophet, is the easiest of all people to ridicule as a crank.

Hence the satirist may employ a plain, common-sense, conventional person as a foil for the various *alazons* of society. Such a person may be the author himself or a narrator, and he corresponds to the plain dealer in comedy or the blunt adviser in tragedy. When distinguished from the author, he is often a rustic with pastoral affinities, illustrating the connection of his role with the *agroikos* type in comedy. The kind of American satire that passes as folk humor, exemplified by the Biglow Papers, Mr. Dooley, Artemus Ward, and Will Rogers, makes a good deal of him, and this genre is closely linked with the North American development of the counsel of prudence in Poor Richard's Almanac and the Sam Slick papers. Other examples are easy enough to find, both where we expect them, as in Crabbe, whose tale *The Patron* also belongs to the counsel-of-prudence genre, and where we might not expect them, as in the Fish-Eater dialogue in Erasmus's *Colloquies*. Chaucer represents himself as a shy, demure, inconspicuous member of his pilgrimage, agreeing politely with everybody ("And I seyde his opinion was good"), and showing to the pilgrims none of the powers of observation that he displays to his reader. We are not surprised therefore to find that one of his "own" tales is in the counsel of prudence tradition.

The most elaborate form of low-norm satire is the encyclopaedic form favored by the Middle Ages, closely allied to preaching, and generally based on the encyclopaedic scheme of the seven deadly sins, a form which survived as late as Elizabethan times in Nashe's *Pierce Penilesse* and Lodge's *Wits Miserie*. Erasmus's *Praise of Folly* belongs to this tradition, in which the link with the corresponding comic phase, the view of an upside-down world dominated by humors and ruling passions, can be clearly seen. When adopted by a preacher, or even an intellectual, the low norm device is part of an implied *a fortiori* argument: if people cannot reach even ordinary common sense, or church porch virtue, there is little point in comparing them with any higher standards.

Where gaiety predominates in such satire, we have an attitude which fundamentally accepts social conventions but stresses tolerance and flexibility within their limits. Close to the conventional norm we find the lovable eccentric, the Uncle Toby or Betsey Trotwood who diversifies, without challenging, accepted codes of behavior. Such characters have much of the child about them, and a child's behavior is usually thought of as coming towards an accepted standard instead of moving away from it. Where attack predominates, we have an inconspicuous, unobtrusive *eiron* standard contrasted with the *alazons* or blocking humors who are in charge of society. This situation has for its archetype an ironic counterpart of the romance theme of giant-killing. For society to exist at all there must be a delegation of prestige and influence to organized groups such as the church, the army, the professions and the government, all of which consist of individuals given more than individual power by the institutions to which they belong. If a satirist presents, say, a clergyman as a fool or hypocrite, he is, *qua* satirist, attacking neither a man nor a church. The former has no literary or hypothetical point, and the latter carries him outside the range of satire. He is attacking an evil man protected by his church, and such a man is a gigantic monster: monstrous because not what he should be, gigantic because protected by his position and by the prestige of good clergymen. The cowl might make the monk if it were not for satire.

Milton says, "for a Satyr as it was born out of a Tragedy, so ought to resemble his parentage, to strike high, and adventure dangerously at the most eminent vices among the greatest persons." Apart from the etymology, this needs one qualification: a great vice does not need a great person to represent it. We have mentioned the gigantic size of Sir Epicure Mammon's dream in *The Alchemist*: the whole mystery of the corrupted human will is in it, yet the utter impotence of the dreamer is essential to the satire. Similarly, we miss much of the point of *Jonathan Wild* unless we take the hero seriously as a parody of greatness, or false social standards of valuation. But in general the principle may be accepted for the satirist's antagonists that the larger they come, the easier they fall. In low-norm satire the *alazon* is a Goliath encountered by a tiny David with his sudden and vicious stones, a giant prodded by a cool and observant but almost invisible enemy into a blind, stampeding fury and then polished off at leisure. This situation has run through satire from the stories of Polyphemus and Blunderbore to, in a much more ironic and equivocal context, the Chaplin films. Dryden transforms his victims into fantastic dinosaurs of bulging flesh and peanut brains; he seems genuinely impressed by the "goodly and great" bulk of Og and by the furious energy of the poet Doeg.

The figure of the low-norm *eiron* is irony's substitute for the hero, and when he is removed from satire we can see more clearly that one of the central themes of the *mythos* is the disappearance of the heroic. This is the main reason for the predominance in fictional satire of what may be called the Omphale archetype, the man bullied or dominated by women, which has been prominent in satire all through its history, and embraces a vast area of contemporary humor, both popular and sophisticated. Similarly, when the giant or monster is removed we can see that he is the mythical form of society, the hydra or fama full of tongues, Spenser's blatant beast which is still at large. And while the crank with his new idea is an obvious target for satire, still social convention is mainly fossilized dogma, and the standard appealed to by low-norm satire is a set of conventions largely invented by dead cranks. The strength of the conventional person is not in the conventions but in his common-sense way of handling them. Hence the logic of satire itself drives it on from its first phase of conventional satire on the unconventional to a second phase in which the sources and values of conventions themselves are objects of ridicule.

The simplest form of the corresponding second phase of comedy is the comedy of escape, in which a hero runs away to a more congenial society without transforming his own. The satiric counterpart of this is the picaresque novel, the story of the successful rogue who, from Reynard the Fox on, makes conventional society look foolish without setting up any positive standard. The picaresque novel is the social form of what with *Don Quixote* modulates into a more intellectualized satire, the nature of which needs some explanation.

Satire, according to Juvenal's useful if hackneyed formula, has an interest in anything men do. The philosopher, on the other hand, teaches a certain way or method of living; he stresses some things and despises others; what he recommends is carefully selected from the data of human life; he continually passes moral judgements on social behavior. His attitude is dogmatic; that of the satirist pragmatic. Hence satire may often represent the collision between a selection of standards from experience and the feeling that experience is bigger than any set of beliefs about it. The satirist demonstrates the infinite variety of what men do by showing the futility, not only of saying what they ought to do, but even of attempts to systematize or formulate a coherent scheme of what they do. Philosophies of life abstract from life, and an abstraction implies the leaving out of inconvenient data. The satirist brings up these inconvenient data, sometimes in the form of alternative and equally plausible theories, like the Erewhonian treatment of crime and disease or Swift's demonstration of the mechanical operation of spirit.

The central theme in the second or quixotic phase of satire, then, is the setting of ideas and generalizations and theories and dogmas over against the life they are supposed to explain. This theme is presented very clearly in Lucian's dialogue *The Sale of Lives*, in which a series of slave-philosophers pass in review, with all their arguments and guarantees, before a buyer who has to consider living with them. He buys a few, it is true, but as slaves, not as masters or teachers. Lucian's attitude to Greek philosophy is repeated in the attitude of Erasmus and Rabelais to the scholastics, of Swift and Samuel Butler I to Descartes and the Royal Society, of Voltaire to the Leibnitzians, of Peacock to the Romantics, of Samuel Butler II to the Darwinians, of Aldous Huxley to the behaviorists. We notice that low-norm satire often becomes *merely* anti-intellectual, a tendency that crops up in Crabbe (*vide The Learned Boy*) and even in Swift. The influence of low-norm satire in American culture has produced a popular contempt for longhairs and ivory towers, an example of what may be called a fallacy of poetic projection, or taking literary conventions to be facts of life. Anti-intellectual satire proper, however, is based on a sense of the comparative naivete of systematic thought, and should not be limited by such ready-made terms as skeptical or cynical.

Skepticism itself may be or become a dogmatic attitude, a comic humor of doubting plain evidence. Cynicism is a little closer to the satiric norm: Menippus, the founder of the Menippean satire, was a cynic, and cynics are generally associated with the role of intellectual Thersites. Lyly's play *Campaspe*, for instance, presents Plato, Aristotle, and Diogenes, but the first two are bores, and Diogenes, who is not a philosopher at all but an Elizabethan clown of the malcontent type, steals the show. But still cynicism is a philosophy, and one that may produce the strange spiritual pride of the Peregrinus of whom Lucian makes a searching and terrible analysis. In the *Sale of Lives* the cynic and the skeptic are auctioned in their turn, and the latter is the last to be sold, dragged off to have his very skepticism refuted, not by argument but by life. Erasmus and Burton called themselves Democritus Junior, followers of the philosopher who laughed at mankind, but Lucian's buyer considers that Democritus too has overdone his pose. Insofar as the satirist has a "position" of his own, it is the preference of practice to theory, experience to metaphysics. When Lucian goes to consult his master Menippus, he is told that the method of wisdom is to do the task that lies to hand, advice repeated in Voltaire's *Candide* and in the instructions given to the unborn in *Erewhon*. Thus philosophical pedantry becomes, as every target of satire eventually does, a form of romanticism or the imposing of over-simplified ideals on experience.

The satiric attitude here is neither philosophical nor anti-philosophical, but an expression of the hypothetical form of art. Satire on ideas is only the special kind of art that defends its own creative detachment. The demand for order in thought produces a supply of intellectual systems: some of these attract and convert artists, but as an equally great poet could defend any other system equally well, no one system can contain the arts as they stand. Hence a systematic reasoner, given the power, would be likely to establish hierarchies in the arts, or censor and expurgate as Plato wished to do to Homer. Satire on systems of reasoning, especially on the social effects of such systems, is art's first line of defence against all such invasions.

In the warfare of science against superstition, the satirists have done famously. Satire itself appears to have begun with the Greek *silloi* which were pro-scientific attacks on superstition. In English literature, Chaucer and Ben Jonson riddled the alchemists with a cross-fire of their own jargon; Nashe and Swift hounded astrologers into premature graves; Browning's *Sludge the Medium* annihilated the spiritualists, and a rabble of occultists, numerologists, Pythagoreans, and Rosicrucians lie sprawling in the wake of *Hudibras*. To the scientist it may seem little short of perverse that satire placidly goes on making fun of legitimate astronomers in *The Elephant in the Moon*, of experimental laboratories in *Gulliver's Travels*, of Darwinian and Malthusian cosmology in *Erewhon*, of conditioned reflexes in *Brave New World*, of technological efficiency in 1984. Charles Fort, one of the few who have continued the tradition of intellectual satire in this century, brings the wheel full circle by mocking the scientists for their very freedom from superstition itself, a rational attitude which, like all rational attitudes, still refuses to examine all the evidence.

Similarly with religion. The satirist may feel with Lucian that the eliminating of superstition would also eliminate religion, or with Erasmus that it would restore health to religion. But whether Zeus exists or not is a question; that men who think him vicious and stupid will insist that he change the weather is a fact, accepted by scoffer and devout alike. Any really devout person would surely welcome a satirist who cauterized hypocrisy and superstition as an ally of true religion. Yet once a hypocrite who sounds exactly like a good man is sufficiently blackened, the good man also may begin to seem a little dingier than he was. Those who would agree even with the theoretical parts of *Holy Willie's Prayer* in Burns look rather like Holy Willies themselves. One feels similarly that while the personal attitudes of Erasmus, Rabelais, Swift, and Voltaire to institutional religion varied a good deal, the effect of their satire varies much less. Satire on religion includes the parody of the sacramental life in English Protestantism that runs from Milton's divorce pamphlets to *The Way of All Flesh*, and the antagonism to Christianity in Nietzsche, Yeats, and D. H. Lawrence based on the conception of Jesus as another kind of romantic idealist.

The narrator in *Erewhon* remarks that while the real religion of most of the Erewhonians was, whatever they said it was, the acceptance of low-norm conventionality (the goddess Ydgrun), there was also a small group of "high Ydgrunites" who were the best people he found in Erewhon. The attitude of these people reminds us rather of Montaigne: they had the *eiron's* sense of the value of conventions that had been long established and were now harmless; they had the *eiron's* distrust of the ability of anyone's reason, including their own, to transform society into a better structure. But they were also intellectually detached from the conventions they lived with, and were capable of seeing their anomalies and absurdities as well as their stabilizing conservatism.

The literary form that high Ydgrunism produces in second-phase satire we may call the *ingenu* form, after Voltaire's dialogue of that name. Here an outsider to the society, in this case an American Indian, is the low norm: he has no dogmatic views of his own, but he grants none of the premises which make the absurdities of society look logical to those accustomed to them. He is really a pastoral figure, and like the pastoral, a form congenial to satire, he contrasts a set of simple standards with the complex rationalizations of society. But we have just seen that it is precisely the complexity of data in experience which the satirist insists on and the simple set of standards which he distrusts. That is why the *ingenu* is an outsider; he comes from another world which is either unattainable or associated with something else undesirable. Montaigne's cannibals have all the virtues we have not, if we don't mind being cannibals. More's Utopia is an ideal state except that to enter it we must give up the idea of Christendom. The Houyhnhnms live the life of reason and nature better than we, but Gulliver finds that he is born a Yahoo, and that such a life would be nearer the capacities of gifted animals than of humans. Whenever the "other world" appears in satire, it appears as an ironic counterpart to our own, a reversal of accepted social standards. This form of satire is represented in Lucian's *Kataplous* and *Charon*, journeys to the other world in which the eminent in this one are shown doing appropriate but unaccustomed things, a form incorporated in Rabelais, and in the medieval *danse macabre*. In the last named the simple equality of death is set against the complex inequalities of life.

Intellectual satire defends the creative detachment in art, but art too tends to seek out socially accepted ideas and become in its turn a social fixation. We have spoken of the idealized art of romance as in particular the form in which an ascendant class tends to express itself, and so the rising middle class in medieval Europe naturally turned to mock-romance. Other forms of satire have a similar function, whether so intended or not. The *danse macabre* and the *kataplous* are ironic reversals of the kind of romanticism that we have in the serious vision of the other world. In Dante, for instance, the judgements of the next world usually confirm the standards of this one, and in heaven itself nearly the whole available billeting is marked for officers only. The cultural effect of such satire is not to denigrate romance, but to prevent any group of conventions from dominating the whole of literary experience. Second-phase satire shows literature assuming a special function of analysis, of breaking up the lumber of stereotypes, fossilized beliefs, superstitious terrors, crank theories, pedantic dogmatisms, oppressive fashions, and all other things that impede the free movement (not necessarily, of course, the progress) of society. Such satire is the completion of the logical process known as the *reductio ad absurdum*, which is not designed to hold one in perpetual captivity, but to bring one to the point at which one can escape from an incorrect procedure.

The romantic fixation which revolves around the beauty of perfect form, in art or elsewhere, is also a logical target for satire. The word satire is said to come from *satura*, or hash, and a kind of parody of form seems to run all through its tradition, from the mixture of prose and verse in early satire to the jerky cinematic changes of scene in Rabelais (I am thinking of a somewhat archaic type of cinema). *Tristram Shandy* and *Don Juan* illustrate very clearly the constant tendency to self-parody in satiric rhetoric which prevents even the process of writing itself from becoming an oversimplified convention or ideal. In *Don Juan* we simultaneously read the poem and watch the poet at work writing it: we eavesdrop on his associations, his struggles for rhymes, his tentative and discarded plans, the subjective preferences organizing his choice of details (e.g.: "Her stature tall—I hate a dumpy woman"), his decisions whether to be "serious" or mask himself with humor. All of this and even more is true of *Tristram Shandy*. A deliberate rambling digressiveness, which in *A Tale of a Tub* reaches the point of including a digression in praise of digressions, is endemic in the narrative technique of satire, and so is a calculated bathos or art of sinking in its suspense, such as the quizzical mock-oracular conclusions in Apuleius and Rabelais and in the refusal of Sterne for hundreds of pages even to get his hero born. An extraordinary number of great satires are fragmentary, unfinished, or anonymous. In ironic fiction a good many devices turning on the difficulty of communication, such as having a story presented through an idiot mind, serve the same purpose. Virginia Woolf's *The Waves* is made up of speeches of characters constructed precisely out of what they do *not* say, but what their behavior and attitudes say in spite of them.

This technique of disintegration brings us well into the third phase of satire, the satire of the high norm. Second-phase satire may make a tactical defence of the pragmatic against the dogmatic, but here we must let go even of ordinary common sense as a standard. For common sense too has certain implied dogmas, notably that the data of sense experience are reliable and consistent, and that our customary associations with things form a solid basis for interpreting the present and predicting the future. The satirist cannot explore all the possibilities of his form without seeing what happens if he questions these assumptions. That is why he so often gives to ordinary life a logical and self-consistent shift of perspective. He will show us society suddenly in a telescope as posturing and dignified pygmies, or in a microscope as hideous and reeking giants, or he will change his hero into an ass and show us how humanity looks from an ass's point of view. This type of fantasy breaks down customary associations, reduces sense experience to one of many possible categories, and brings out the tentative, *als ob* basis of all our thinking. Emerson says that such shifts of perspective afford "a low degree of the sublime," but actually they afford something of far greater artistic importance, a high degree of the ridiculous. And, consistently with the general basis of satire as parody-romance, they are usually adaptations of romance themes: the fairyland of little people, the land of giants, the world of enchanted animals, the wonderlands parodied in Lucian's *True History*.

When we fall back from the outworks of faith and reason to the tangible realities of the senses, satire follows us up. A slight shift of perspective, a different tinge in the emotional coloring, and the solid earth becomes an intolerable horror. *Gulliver's Travels* shows us man as a venomous rodent, man as a noisome and clumsy pachyderm, the mind of man as a bear-pit, and the body of man as a compound of filth and ferocity. But Swift is simply following where his satiric genius leads him, and genius seems to have led practically every great satirist to become what the world calls obscene. Social convention means people parading in front of each other, and the preservation of it demands that the dignity of some men and the beauty of some women should be thought of apart from excretion, copulation, and similar embarrassments. Constant reference to these latter brings us down to a bodily democracy paralleling the democracy of death in the *danse macabre*. Swift's affinity with the *danse macabre* tradition is marked in his description of the Struldbrugs, and his *Directions to Servants* and his more unquotable poems are in the tradition of the medieval preachers who painted the repulsiveness of gluttony and lechery. For here as everywhere else in satire there is a moral reference: it is all very well to eat, drink, and be merry, but one cannot always put off dying until tomorrow.

In the riotous chaos of Rabelais, Petronius, and Apuleius satire plunges through to its final victory over common sense. When we have finished with their weirdly logical fantasies of debauch, dream, and delirium we wake up wondering if Paracelsus' suggestion is right that the things seen in delirium are really there, like stars in daytime, and invisible for the same reason. Lucius becomes initiated and slips evasively out of our grasp, whether he lied or told the truth, as St. Augustine says with a touch of exasperation; Rabelais promises us a final oracle and leaves us staring at an empty bottle; Joyce's HCE struggles for pages toward wakening, but just as we seem on the point of grasping something tangible we are swung around to the first page of the book again. The *Satyricon* is a torn fragment from what seems like a history of some monstrous Atlantean race that vanished in the sea, still drunk.

The first phase of satire is dominated by the figure of the giant-killer, but in this rending of the stable universe a giant power rears up in satire itself. When the Philistine giant comes out to battle with the children of light, he naturally expects to find someone his own size ready to meet him, someone who is head and shoulders over every man in Israel. Such a Titan would have to bear down his opponent by sheer weight of words, and hence be a master of that technique of torrential abuse which we call invective. The gigantic figures in Rabelais, the awakened forms of the bound or sleeping giants that meet us in *Finnegans Wake* and the opening of *Gulliver's Travels*, are expressions of a creative exuberance of which the most typical and obvious sign is the verbal tempest, the tremendous outpouring of words in catalogues, abusive epithets and erudite technicalities which since the third chapter of Isaiah (a satire on female ornament) has been a feature, and almost a monopoly, of third-phase satire. Its golden age in English literature was the age of Burton, Nashe, Marston, and Urquhart of Cromarty, the uninhibited translator of Rabelais, who in his spare time was what Nashe would call a "scholastical squitter-book," producing books with such titles as *Trissotetras, Pantochronochanon, Exkubalauron* and *Logopandecteison*. Nobody except Joyce has in modern English made much sustained effort to carry on this tradition of verbal exuberance: even Carlyle, from this point of view, is a sad comedown after Burton and Urquhart. In American culture it is represented by the "tall talk" of the folklore boaster, which has some literary congeners in the catalogues of Whitman and *Moby Dick*.

With the fourth phase we move around to the ironic aspect of tragedy, and satire begins to recede. The fall of the tragic hero, especially in Shakespeare, is so delicately balanced emotionally that we almost exaggerate any one element in it merely by calling attention to it. One of these elements is the elegiac aspect in which irony is at a minimum, the sense of gentle and dignified pathos, often symbolized by music, which marks the desertion of Antony by Hercules, the dream of the rejected Queen Catherine in *Henry VIII*, Hamlet's "absent thee from felicity awhile," and Othello's

Aleppo speech. One can of course find irony even here, as Mr. Eliot has found it in the last named, but the main emotional weight is surely thrown on the opposite side. Yet we are also aware that Hamlet dies in the middle of a frantically muddled effort at revenge which has taken eight lives instead of one, that Cleopatra fades away with great dignity after a careful search for easy ways to die, that Coriolanus is badly confused by his mother and violently resents being called a boy. Such tragic irony differs from satire in that there is no attempt to make fun of the character, but only to bring out clearly the "all too human," as distinct from the heroic, aspects of the tragedy. King Lear attempts to achieve heroic dignity through his position as a king and father, and finds it instead in his suffering humanity: hence it is in *King Lear* that we find what has been called the "comedy of the grotesque," the ironic parody of the tragic situation, most elaborately developed.

As a phase of irony in its own right, the fourth phase looks at tragedy from below, from the moral and realistic perspective of the state of experience. It stresses the humanity of its heroes, minimizes the sense of ritual inevitability in tragedy, supplies social and psychological explanations for catastrophe, and makes as much as possible of human misery seem, in Thoreau's phrase, "superfluous and evitable." This is the phase of most sincere, explicit realism: it is in general Tolstoy's phase, and also that of a good deal of Hardy and Conrad. One of its central themes is Stein's answer to the problem of the "romantic" Lord Jim in Conrad: "in the destructive element immerse." This remark, without ridiculing Jim, still brings out the quixotic and romantic element in his nature and criticizes it from the point of view of experience. The chapter on watches and chronometers in Melville's *Pierre* takes a similar attitude.

The fifth phase, corresponding to fatalistic or fifth-phase tragedy, is irony in which the main emphasis is on the natural cycle, the steady unbroken turning of the wheel of fate or fortune. It sees experience, in our terms, with the point of epiphany closed up, and its motto is Browning's "there may be heaven; there must be hell." Like the corresponding phase of tragedy, it is less moral and more generalized and metaphysical in its interest, less melioristic and more stoical and resigned. The treatment of Napoleon in *War and Peace* and in *The Dynasts* affords a good contrast between the fourth and fifth phases of irony. The refrain in the Old English *Complaint of Deor*: "Thaes ofereode; thisses swa maeg" (freely

237

translatable as "Other people got through things; maybe I can") expresses a stoicism not of the "invictus" type, which maintains a romantic dignity, but rather a sense, found also in the parallel second phase of satire, that the practical and immediate situation is likely to be worthy of more respect than the theoretical explanation of it.

The sixth phase presents human life in terms of largely unrelieved bondage. Its settings feature prisons, madhouses, lynching mobs, and places of execution, and it differs from a pure inferno mainly in the fact that in human experience suffering has an end in death. In our day the chief form of this phase is the nightmare of social tyranny, of which 1984 is perhaps the most familiar. We often find, on this boundary of the *visio malefica*, the use of parody-religious symbols suggesting some form of Satan or Antichrist worship. In Kafka's *In the Penal Colony* a parody of original sin appears in the officer's remark, "Guilt is never to be doubted." In 1984 the parody of religion in the final scenes is more elaborate: there is a parody of the atonement, for instance, when the hero is tortured into urging that the torments be inflicted on the heroine instead. The assumption is made in this story that the lust for sadistic power on the part of the ruling class is strong enough to last indefinitely, which is precisely the assumption one has to make about devils in order to accept the orthodox picture of hell. The "telescreen" device brings into irony the tragic theme of *derkou theama*, the humiliation of being constantly watched by a hostile or derisive eye.

The human figures of this phase are, of course, *desdichado* figures of misery or madness, often parodies of romantic roles. Thus the romantic theme of the helpful servant giant is parodied in *The Hairy Ape* and *Of Mice and Men*, and the romantic presenter or Prospero figure is parodied in the Benjy of *The Sound and the Fury* whose idiot mind contains, without comprehending, the whole action of the novel. Sinister parental figures naturally abound, for this is the world of the ogre and the witch, of Baudelaire's black giantess and Pope's goddess Dullness, who also has much of the parody deity about her ("Light dies before thy uncreating word!"), of the siren with the imprisoning image of shrouding hair, and, of course, of the *femme fatale* or malignant grinning female, "older than the rocks among which she sits," as Pater says of her.

This brings us around again to the point of demonic epiphany, the dark tower and prison of endless pain, the city of dreadful night in the desert, or, with a more erudite irony, the *tour abolie*, the goal of the quest that isn't there. But on the other side of this blasted world of repulsiveness and idiocy, a world without pity and without hope, satire begins again. At the bottom of Dante's hell, which is also the center of the spherical earth, Dante sees Satan standing upright in the circle of ice, and as he cautiously follows Virgil over the hip and thigh of the evil giant, letting himself down by the tufts of hair on his skin, he passes the center and finds himself no longer going down but going up, climbing out on the other side of the world to see the stars again. From this point of view, the devil is no longer upright, but standing on his head, in the same attitude in which he was hurled downward from heaven upon the other side of the earth. Tragedy and tragic irony take us into a hell of narrowing circles and culminate in some such vision of the source of all evil in a personal form. Tragedy can take us no farther; but if we persevere with the *mythos* of irony and satire, we shall pass a dead center, and finally see the gentlemanly Prince of Darkness bottom side up.

FOURTH ESSAY

Rhetorical Criticism: Theory of Genres

Fourth Essay

RHETORICAL CRITICISM: THEORY OF GENRES

INTRODUCTION

THE PRESENT BOOK employs a diagrammatic framework that has been used in poetics ever since Plato's time. This is the division of "the good" into three main areas, of which the world of art, beauty, feeling, and taste is the central one, and is flanked by two other worlds. One is the world of social action and events, the other the world of individual thought and ideas. Reading from left to right, this threefold structure divides human faculties into will, feeling, and reason. It divides the mental constructs which these faculties produce into history, art, and science and philosophy. It divides the ideals which form compulsions or obligations on these faculties into law, beauty, and truth. Poe gives his version of the diagram (right to left) as Pure Intellect, Taste, and the Moral Sense. "I place Taste in the middle," said Poe, "because it is just this position which in the mind it occupies." Until someone can refute this admirable explanation, we shall retain the traditional structure. True, we have hinted that there may be another way of looking at it in which the middle world is not simply one of three but a trinity containing them all. But as yet the simpler conception has by no means exhausted its usefulness for us.

Similarly, we have portrayed the poetic symbol as intermediate between event and idea, example and precept, ritual and dream, and have finally displayed it as Aristotle's *ethos*, human nature and the human situation, between and made up of *mythos* and *dianoia*, which are verbal imitations of action and thought respectively. There is however still another aspect of the same diagram. The world of social action and event, the world of time and process, has a particularly close association with the ear. The ear listens, and the ear translates what it hears into practical conduct. The world of individual thought and idea has a correspondingly close association with the eye, and nearly all our expressions for thought, from the Greek *theoria* down, are connected with visual metaphors. Further, not only does art as a whole seem to be central to events and ideas, but literature seems in a way to be central to the arts.

It appeals to the ear, and so partakes of the nature of music, but music is a much more concentrated art of the ear and of the imaginative perception of time. Literature appeals to at least the inner eye, and so partakes of the nature of the plastic arts, but the plastic arts, especially painting, are much more concentrated on the eye and on the spatial world. We notice that Aristotle gives a list of *six* elements of poetry, three of which, *mythos*, *ethos* and *dianoia*, we have been considering. The other three, *melos*, *lexis*, and *opsis* (spectacle), deal with this second aspect of the same diagram. Considered as a verbal structure, literature presents a *lexis* which combines two other elements: *melos*, an element analogous to or otherwise connected with music, and *opsis*, which has a similar connection with the plastic arts. The word *lexis* itself may be translated "diction" when we are thinking of it as a narrative sequence of sounds caught by the ear, and as "imagery" when we are thinking of it as forming a simultaneous pattern of meaning apprehended in an act of mental "vision." This second or rhetorical aspect of literature we must now turn to examine. It is an aspect which returns us to the "literal" level of narrative and meaning, the context that Ezra Pound has in mind when he speaks of the three qualities of poetic creation as *melopoeia*, *logopoeia*, and *phanopoeia*. The terms musical and pictorial are often employed figuratively in literary criticism, and we shall attempt among other things to see how much genuine sense they make as critical terms.

The word "rhetoric" reminds us of yet another triad: the traditional division of studies based on words into a "trivium" of grammar, rhetoric, and logic. While grammar and logic have become the names of specific sciences, they also retain something of a more general connection with the narrative and significant aspects respectively of all verbal structures. As grammar may be called the art of ordering words, there is a sense—a literal sense—in which grammar and narrative are the same thing; as logic may be called the art of producing meaning, there is a sense in which logic and meaning are the same thing. The second part of this sentence is more traditional, and hence more familiar. There is no historical justification for the first part, as the art of constructing narrative ("invention," "disposition," and the like) has traditionally formed a part of rhetoric. Let us, however, in spite of history, begin with an association between narrative and grammar, grammar being understood primarily as syntax or getting words in the right (narrative) order, and between logic and meaning, logic being understood primarily as words arranged in a pattern with significance. Grammar is the linguistic aspect of a verbal structure; logic is the "sense" which is the permanent common factor in translation.

What we have been calling assertive, descriptive, or factual writing tends to be, or attempts to be, a direct union of grammar and logic. An argument cannot be logically correct unless it is verbally correct, the right words chosen and the proper syntactical relations among them established. Nor does a verbal narrative communicate anything to a reader unless it has continuous significance. In assertive writing, therefore, there seems to be little place for any such middle term as rhetoric, and in fact we often find that among philosophers, scientists, jurists, critics, historians, and theologians, rhetoric is looked upon with some distrust.

Rhetoric has from the beginning meant two things: ornamental speech and persuasive speech. These two things seem psychologically opposed to each other, as the desire to ornament is essentially disinterested, and the desire to persuade essentially the reverse. In fact ornamental rhetoric is inseparable from literature itself, or what we have called the hypothetical verbal structure which exists for its own sake. Persuasive rhetoric is applied literature, or the use of literary art to reinforce the power of argument. Ornamental rhetoric acts on its hearers statically, leading them to admire its own beauty or wit; persuasive rhetoric tries to lead them kinetically toward a course of action. One articulates emotion; the other manipulates it. And whatever we decide about the ultimate literary status of oratory, there seems little doubt that ornamental rhetoric is the *lexis* or verbal texture of poetry. Aristotle remarks, when he comes to *lexis* in the *Poetics*, that that subject belongs more properly to rhetoric. We may, then, adopt the following tentative postulate: that if the direct union of grammar and logic is characteristic of non-literary verbal structures, literature may be described as the rhetorical organization of grammar and logic. Most of the features characteristic of literary form, such as rhyme, alliteration, metre, antithetical balance, the use of exempla, are also rhetorical schemata.

The psychology of creation is not our theme, but it must happen very rarely that a writer sits down to write without *any* notion of what he proposes to produce. In the poet's mind, then, some kind of controlling and coordinating power, what Coleridge called the "initiative," establishes itself very early, gradually assimilates everything to itself, and finally reveals itself to be the containing form of the work. This initiative is clearly not a unit but a complex of factors. The theme is one such factor; the sense of the unity of mood which makes certain images appropriate and others not is another. If what is produced is to be a poem in a regular metre, the metre will be a third: if not, some other integrating rhythm will be present. We remarked earlier, too, that the poet's intention to produce a poem normally includes the genre, the intention of producing a specific kind of verbal structure. The poet thus is incessantly deciding that certain things, whether they can be critically accounted for by himself or not, belong in his structure, and that what he cuts out in revising does not, though it may be good enough in itself to belong somewhere else. But as the structure is complex, so these decisions relate to a variety of poetic elements, or a *group* of initiatives. Of these, theme and the choice of images engaged our attention in the previous essay; genre and the integrating rhythm concern us here.

We complained in our introduction that the theory of genres was an undeveloped subject in criticism. We have the three generic terms drama, epic, and lyric, derived from the Greeks, but we use the latter two chiefly as jargon or trade slang for long and short (or shorter) poems respectively. The middle-sized poem does not even have a jargon term to describe it, and any long poem gets to be called an epic, especially if it is divided into a dozen or so parts, like Browning's *Ring and the Book*. This poem takes a dramatic structure, a triangle of jealous husband, patient wife, and chivalrous lover involved in a murder trial with courtroom and death-house scenes, and works it all out through the soliloquies of the characters. It is an astounding *tour de force*, but we can fully appreciate this only when we see it as a generic experiment in drama, a drama turned inside out, as it were. Similarly, we call Shelley's *Ode to the West Wind* a lyric, perhaps because it is a lyric; if we hesitate to call *Epipsychidion* a lyric, and have no idea what it is, we can always call it the product of an essentially lyrical genius. It is shorter than the *Iliad*, and there's an end of it.

However, the origin of the words drama, epic, and lyric suggests that the central principle of genre is simple enough. The basis of generic distinctions in literature appears to be the radical of presen-

246

tation. Words may be acted in front of a spectator; they may be spoken in front of a listener; they may be sung or chanted; or they may be written for a reader. Criticism, we note resignedly in passing, has no word for the individual member of an author's audience, and the word "audience" itself does not really cover all genres, as it is slightly illogical to describe the readers of a book as an audience. The basis of generic criticism in any case is rhetorical, in the sense that the genre is determined by the conditions established between the poet and his public.

We have to speak of the *radical* of presentation if the distinctions of acted, spoken, and written word are to mean anything in the age of the printing press. One may print a lyric or read a novel aloud, but such incidental changes are not enough in themselves to alter the genre. For all the loving care that is rightfully expended on the printed texts of Shakespeare's plays, they are still radically acting scripts, and belong to the genre of drama. If a Romantic poet gives his poem a dramatic form, he may not expect or even want any stage representation; he may think entirely in terms of print and readers; he may even believe, like many Romantics, that the stage drama is an impure form because of the limitations it puts on individual expression. Yet the poem is still being referred back to some kind of theatre, however much of a castle in the air. A novel is written, but when Conrad employs a narrator to help him tell his story, the genre of the written word is being assimilated to that of the spoken one.

The question of how we are to classify such a novel is less important than the recognition of the fact that two different radicals of presentation exist in it. It might be thought simpler, instead of using the term radical, to say that the generic distinctions are among the ways in which literary works are *ideally* presented, whatever the actualities are. But Milton, for example, seems to have no ideal of reciter and audience in mind for *Paradise Lost*; he seems content to leave it, in practice, a poem to be read in a book. When he uses the convention of invocation, thus bringing the poem into the genre of the spoken word, the significance of the convention is to indicate what tradition his work primarily belongs to and what its closest affinities are with. The purpose of criticism by genres is not so much to classify as to clarify such traditions and affinities, thereby bringing out a large number of literary relationships that would

247

not be noticed as long as there were no context established for them.

The genre of the spoken word and the listener is very difficult to describe in English, but part of it is what the Greeks meant by the phrase *ta epe*, poems intended to be recited, not necessarily epics of the conventional jumbo size. Such "epic" material does not have to be in metre, as the prose tale and the prose oration are important spoken forms. The difference between metre and prose is evidently not in itself a generic difference, as the example of drama shows, though it tends to become one. In this essay I use the word *"epos"* to describe works in which the radical of presentation is oral address, keeping the word epic for its customary use as the name of the form of the *Iliad, Odyssey, Aeneid,* and *Paradise Lost. Epos* thus takes in all literature, in verse or prose, which makes some attempt to preserve the convention of recitation and a listening audience.

The Greeks gave us the names of three of our four genres: they did not give us a word for the genre that addresses a reader through a book, and naturally we have not invented one of our own. The nearest to it is "history," but this word, in spite of *Tom Jones,* has gone outside literature, and the Latin "scripture" is too specialized in meaning. As I have to have some word, I shall make an arbitrary choice of "fiction" to describe the genre of the printed page. I know that I used this word in the first essay in a different context, but it seems better to compromise with the present confused terminology than to increase the difficulties of this book by introducing too many new terms. The analogy of the keyboard in music may illustrate the difference between fiction and other genres which for practical purposes exist in books. A book, like a keyboard, is a mechanical device for bringing an entire artistic structure under the interpretive control of a single person. But just as it is possible to distinguish genuine piano music from the piano score of an opera or symphony, so we may distinguish genuine "book literature" from books containing the reduced textual scores of recited or acted pieces.

The connection between a speaking poet and a listening audience, which may be actual in Homer or Chaucer, soon becomes increasingly theoretical, and as it does so *epos* passes insensibly into fiction. One may even suggest, not quite seriously, that the legendary figure of the blind bard, which is used so effectively by Milton, indicates that the drift toward an unseen audience sets in very early. But whenever the same material does duty for both genres, the distinction between the genres becomes immediately apparent. The chief distinction, though not a simple one of length, is involved with the fact that *epos* is episodic and fiction continuous. The novels of Dickens are, as books, fiction; as serial publications in a magazine designed for family reading, they are still fundamentally fiction, though closer to *epos*. But when Dickens began to give readings from his own works, the genre changed wholly to *epos*; the emphasis was then thrown on immediacy of effect before a visible audience.

In drama, the hypothetical or internal characters of the story confront the audience directly, hence the drama is marked by the concealment of the author from his audience. In very spectacular drama, such as we get in many movies, the author is of relatively little importance. Drama, like music, is an ensemble performance for an audience, and music and drama are most likely to flourish in a society with a strong consciousness of itself as a society, like Elizabethan England. When a society becomes individualized and competitive, like Victorian England, music and drama suffer accordingly, and the written word almost monopolizes literature. In *epos*, the author confronts his audience directly, and the hypothetical characters of his story are concealed. The author is still theoretically there when he is being represented by a rhapsode or minstrel, for the latter speaks as the poet, not as a character in the poem. In written literature both the author and his characters are concealed from the reader.

The fourth possible arrangement, the concealment of the poet's audience from the poet, is presented in the lyric. There is, as usual, no word for the audience of the lyric: what is wanted is something analogous to "chorus" which does not suggest simultaneous presence or dramatic context. The lyric is, to go back to Mill's aphorism referred to at the beginning of this book, preeminently the utterance that is overheard. The lyric poet normally pretends to be talking to himself or to someone else: a spirit of nature, a Muse (note the distinction from *epos*, where the Muse speaks *through* the poet), a personal friend, a lover, a god, a personified abstraction, or a natural object. The lyric is, as Stephen Dedalus says in Joyce's *Portrait*, the poet presenting the image in relation to himself: it is to *epos*, rhetorically, as prayer is to sermon. The radical of presentation in the lyric is the hypothetical form of what in religion is called the "I-Thou" relationship. The poet, so to speak, turns his back on his listeners, though he may speak for them, and though they may repeat some of his words after him.

Epos and fiction make up the central area of literature, and are flanked by the drama on one side and by the lyric on the other. Drama has a peculiarly intimate connection with ritual, and lyric with dream or vision, the individual communing with himself. We said at the beginning of this book that there is no such thing as direct address in literature, but direct address is natural communication, and literature may imitate it as it may imitate anything else in nature. In *epos*, where the poet faces his audience, we have a *mimesis* of direct address. *Epos* and fiction first take the form of scripture and myth, then of traditional tales, then of narrative and didactic poetry, including the epic proper, and of oratorical prose, then of novels and other written forms. As we progress historically through the five modes, fiction increasingly overshadows *epos*, and as it does, the mimesis of direct address changes to a mimesis of assertive writing. This in its turn, with the extremes of documentary or didactic prose, becomes actual assertion, and so passes out of literature.

The lyric is an internal mimesis of sound and imagery, and stands opposite the external mimesis, or outward representation of sound and imagery, which is drama. Both forms avoid the mimesis of direct address. The characters in a play talk to each other, and are theoretically talking to themselves in an aside or soliloquy. Even if they are conscious of an audience, they are not speaking for the poet, except in special cases like the parabasis of Old Comedy or the prologues and epilogues of the rococo theatre, where there is an actual generic change from drama to *epos*. In Bernard Shaw the comic parabasis is transferred from the middle of the play to a separate prose preface, which is a change from drama to fiction.

In *epos* some kind of comparatively regular metre tends to predominate: even oratorical prose shows many metrical features, both in its syntax and in its punctuation. In fiction prose tends to predominate, because only prose has the continuous rhythm appropriate for the continuous form of the book. Drama has no controlling rhythm peculiar to itself, but it is most closely related to *epos* in the earlier modes and to fiction in the later ones. In the lyric a rhythm which is poetic but not necessarily metrical tends to predominate. We proceed to examine each genre in turn with a view to discovering what its chief features are. As in what immediately follows we are largely concerned with diction and linguistic elements, we must limit our survey mainly to a specific language, which will be English: this means that a good deal of what we say will be true only of English, but it is hoped that the main principles can be adapted to other languages as well.

THE RHYTHM OF RECURRENCE: EPOS

The regular pulsating metre that traditionally distinguishes verse from prose tends to become the organizing rhythm in *epos* or extended oratorical forms. Metre is an aspect of recurrence, and the two words for recurrence, rhythm and pattern, show that recurrence is a structural principle of all art, whether temporal or spatial in its primary impact. Besides metre itself, quantity and accent (or stress) are elements in poetic recurrence, though quantity is not an element of regular recurrence in modern English, except in experiments in which the poet has to make up his own rules as he goes along. The relation of accent or stress to metre needs, perhaps, a different kind of explanation from what is usually given it.

A four-stress line seems to be inherent in the structure of the English language. It is the prevailing rhythm of the earlier poetry, though it changes its scheme from alliteration to rhyme in Middle English; it is the common rhythm of popular poetry in all periods, of ballads and of most nursery rhymes. In the ballad, the eight-six-eight-six quatrain is a continuous four-beat line, with a "rest" at the end of every other line. This principle of the rest, or a beat coming at a point of actual silence, was already established in Old English. The iambic pentameter provides a field of syncopation in which stress and metre can to some extent neutralize one another. If we read many iambic pentameters "naturally," giving the important words the heavy accent that they do have in spoken English, the old four-stress line stands out in clear relief against its metrical background. Thus:

> To bé, or nót to be: thát is the quéstion.
> Whéther 'tis nóbler in the mínd to súffer
> The slíngs and árrows of outrágeous fórtune,
> Or táke up árms against a séa of tróubles . . .

Of mán's fírst disobédience, and the frúit
Of that forbídden trée, whose mórtal táste
Brought déath into the wórld and áll our wóe,
With lóss of Éden, till one gréater Mán
Restóre us, and regáin the blíssful séat . . .

The stopped couplet of Dryden and Pope, as we should expect, has
a higher percentage of five-stress lines, but any rhythmical license
such as a feminine caesura is likely to bring back the old beat:

Forgét their hátred, and consént to féar.   (Waller)

Nor héll a fúry, like a wóman scórn'd.   (Congreve)

A líttle leárning is a dángerous thíng.   (Pope)

Any period of metrical uncertainty or transition will illustrate
the native strength of the four-stress line. After the death of Chaucer and the change from middle to modern English, we find ourselves in the strange metrical world of Lydgate, in which we are
strongly tempted to apply to Lydgate himself what the Minstrel
says to Death in the *Danse Macabre*:

This newe daunce   /   is to me so straunge
Wonder dyverse   /   and passyngli contrarie
The dredful fotynge   /   doth so ofte chaunge
And the mesures   /   so ofte sithes varie.

But there is a dance there all the same: let us look at the preceding
stanza, Death's speech to the Minstrel:

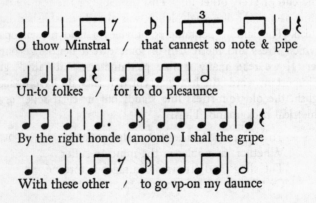

O thow Minstral   /   that cannest so note & pipe

Un-to folkes   /   for to do plesaunce

By the right honde (anoone) I shal the gripe

With these other   /   to go vp-on my daunce

Ther is no scape / nowther a-voydaunce

On no side / to contrarie my sentence

For yn musik / be crafte & accordaunce

Who maister is / shew his science.

This stanza will give us a bad time if we try to analyze it as a pentameter stanza of Chaucer's *ABC* type: the last line, for instance, is not a pentameter at all. Read as a continuous four-beat line, it is fairly simple; and such a reading will bring out what the prosodic analysis could never do, the grotesque, leaping-skeleton lilt of the voice of Death ending in the measured irony of the last line. I do not claim to know the details of Lydgate's prosody, what e's he might have preferred to pronounce or elide or what foreign words he might have accented differently. It is possible that neither Lydgate nor the fifteenth-century reader was entirely clear on all such points either; but a line with four main stresses and a variable number of syllables between the stresses is the obvious device for getting over such problems, as a good deal can be left to the individual reader's choice. In any case I am not indicating how the passage is to be read so much as how it may most easily be scanned: as with metrical scansion, every reader will make his own modification of the pattern.

The "Skeltonic" line is also usually a four-beat line: the spirited prelude to *Philip Sparowe* is a quick-march rhythm, with more rests and more accented beats coming close together than we found in Lydgate:

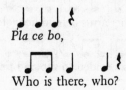

Pla ce bo,

Who is there, who?

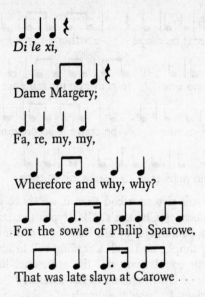

Di le xi,

Dame Margery;

Fa, re, my, my,

Wherefore and why, why?

For the sowle of Philip Sparowe,

That was late slayn at Carowe . . .

In short, the "new principle" on which Coleridge constructed *Christabel* was about as new as principles usually are in literature. It is clear too that the Finnish inspiration of *Hiawatha* was no more fundamentally exotic than such inspirations usually are. *Hiawatha* fits the four-stress pattern of English very snugly, which explains perhaps why it is one of the easiest poems in the language to parody. Meredith's *Love in the Valley*, also, is most easily scanned as a four-stress line very similar in its rhythmical make-up to Lydgate's:

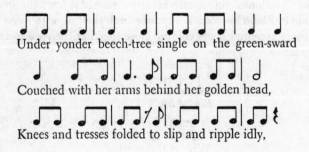

Under yonder beech-tree single on the green-sward

Couched with her arms behind her golden head,

Knees and tresses folded to slip and ripple idly,

Lies my young love sleeping in the shade.

These examples have, perhaps, begun to illustrate already something of what the word "musical," Aristotle's *melos*, really means as a term in modern literary criticism. In the music contemporary with English poetry since Lydgate's time, we have had almost uniformly a stress accent, the stresses marking rhythmical units (measures) within which a variable number of notes is permitted. When in poetry we have a predominating stress accent and a variable number of syllables between two stresses (usually four stresses to a line, corresponding to "common time" in music), we have musical poetry, that is, poetry which resembles in its structure the music contemporary with it. We are speaking now of *epos* or extended poetry in a continuous metre: the music most closely analogous to such poetry is music in its more extended instrumental forms, in which the organizing rhythm has descended more directly from dance than from song.

This technical use of the word musical is very different from the sentimental fashion of calling any poetry musical if it sounds nice. In practice the technical and the sentimental uses are often directly opposed, as the sentimental term would be applied to, for example, Tennyson, and withdrawn from, for example, Browning. Yet if we ask the external but relevant question: Which of these two poets knew more about music, and was *a priori* more likely to be influenced by it? the answer is certainly not Tennyson. Here is a passage from Tennyson's *Oenone*:

> O mother Ida, many-fountain'd Ida,
> Dear mother Ida, harken ere I die.
> I waited underneath the dawning hills,
> Aloft the mountain lawn was dewy-dark,
> And dewy dark aloft the mountain pine:
> Beautiful Paris, evil-hearted Paris,
> Leading a jet-black goat white-horn'd, white-hooved,
> Came up from reedy Simois all alone.

And here is a passage from Browning's *The Flight of the Duchess*:

> I could favour you with sundry touches
> Of the paint-smutches with which the Duchess

255

Heightened the mellowness of her cheek's yellowness
(To get on faster) until at last her
Cheek grew to be one master-plaster
Of mucus and fucus from mere use of ceruse:
In short, she grew from scalp to udder
Just the object to make you shudder.

In the Browning passage speed is a positive factor: one has the sense of a metronome beat. Tennyson has tried to minimize the sense of movement; his passage should be read slowly and with much dwelling on the vowels. Both passages repeat sounds obtrusively, but the repetitions in Tennyson are there to slow down the advance of ideas, to compel the rhythm to return on itself, and to elaborate what is essentially a *pattern* of sound. In Browning the rhymes sharpen the accentuation of the beat and help to build up a cumulative rhythm. The speed and the sharp accent in Browning's poetry are musical features in it, and it is difficult to see what the words in parentheses can be except a musical direction, an English translation of *più mosso*.

Such phrases as "smooth musical flow" or "harsh unmusical diction" belong to the sentimental use of the word musical, and are perhaps derived from the fact that the word "harmony" in ordinary English, apart from music, means a stable and permanent relationship. In this figurative sense of the word harmony, music is not a sequence of harmonies at all, but a sequence of discords ending in a harmony, the only stable and permanent "harmony" in music being the final resolving tonic chord. It is more likely to be the harsh, rugged, dissonant poem (assuming of course some technical competence in the poet) that will show in poetry the tension and the driving accented impetus of music. When we find a careful balancing of vowels and consonants and a dreamy sensuous flow of sound, we are probably dealing with an unmusical poet. Pope, Keats, and Tennyson are all unmusical. This term, I need hardly observe, is not pejorative: *The Rape of the Lock* is unmusical, just as it is a bad example of blank verse, because it is something else altogether. When we find sharp barking accents, crabbed and obscure language, mouthfuls of consonants, and long lumbering polysyllables, we are probably dealing with *melos*, or poetry which shows an analogy to music, if not an actual influence from it.

The musical diction is better fitted for the grotesque and hor-

256

rible, or for invective and abuse. It is congenial to a gnarled intel-
lectualism of the so-called "metaphysical" type. It is irregular in
metre (because of the syncopation against stress), leans heavily
on enjambement, and employs a long cumulative rhythm sweeping
the lines up into larger rhythmical units such as the paragraph. The
fact that Shakespeare shows an increasing use of *melos* as he goes
on is the principle employed for dating his plays on internal evidence. When Milton says that rhymed heroic verse is "of no true
musical delight," because musical poetry must have "the sense
variously drawn out from one verse into another," he is using the
word musical in its technical sense. When Samuel Johnson speaks
of "the old manner of continuing the sense ungracefully from verse
to verse," he is speaking from his own consistently anti-musical
point of view. *The Heretic's Tragedy* is a musical poem; *Thyrsis* is
not. *The Jolly Beggars* is; the *Ode on a Grecian Urn* is not. Pope's
Messiah is not musical, but Smart's *Song to David*, with its pounding thematic words and the fortissimo explosion of its coda, is a
musical *tour de force*. Crashaw's hymns and Cowley's Pindarics are
musical, with their fluent, variable, prevailingly four-stress lines and
their relentless pushing enjambement; Herbert's stanzaic poems
and Gray's Pindarics are not. Skelton, Wyatt, and Dunbar are musical; Gavin Douglas and Surrey are not. Alliterative verse is usually accentual and musical; elaborate stanza forms usually are not.
The use of *melos* in poetry does not, of course, necessarily imply
any technical knowledge of music on the part of the poet, but it
often goes with it. Such a technically musical poem as Crashaw's
Musicks Duell (a Baroque aria with instrumental accompaniment)
is an example.

And occasionally it is at least conceivable that some exposure
to music would have guided a tendency to *melos* in verse. One
feels that Southey, for instance, never quite clarified his remarkable
experiments in *epos* rhythm: if so, it may be instructive to set be-
side Milton's incisive list of the musical qualities of poetry the
stammer and mumble of the preface to *Thalaba*: "I do not wish
the *improvisatorè* tune;—but something that denotes the sense of
harmony, something like the accent of feeling,—like the tone which
every poet necessarily gives to poetry." The conception of *melos*,
too, may throw more light on what Wordsworth was trying to do
in *Peter Bell* and *The Idiot Boy*. Wordsworth's remarks about
metre as the source of excitement in verse apply more particularly

to accent, in which the physical pulsation of the dance is present. What metre in itself gives is rather the pleasure of seeing a relatively predictable pattern filling up with the inevitably felicitous words. Pope's "What oft was thought, but ne'er so well expressed" is a metrical conception: as we listen to his couplets, we have a sense of fulfilled expectation which is the opposite of obviousness. The greater violence in the imagery of Donne's satires is appropriate to the greater energy of a more accentually-conceived rhythm.

If we turn to the contrasting group of what we have called the unmusical poets, Spenser, Pope, Keats, Tennyson, we find slower and more resonant rhythms. Four-stress lines are much rarer in *The Faerie Queene* than in *Paradise Lost*, and the opposite tendency is marked by the recurrent Alexandrine. The practice of this group of poets is finely expressed by Johnson in his anti-musical dictum: "The musick of the English heroic line strikes the ear so faintly that it is easily lost, unless all the syllables of every line co-operate together; this co-operation can be obtained only by the preservation of every verse unmingled with another, as a distinct system of sounds." The implication is that as the only musical elements in poetry that Johnson is considering have been lost for good with the loss of pitch accent and quantity, English poetry should think in terms of sound-pattern rather than cumulative rhythm.

The relations between poetry and the visual arts are perhaps more far-fetched than those between poetry and music. Unmusical poets are often "pictorial" in a general sense: they frequently use their more meditative rhythms to build up, detail by detail, a static picture, as in the careful description of the nude Venus in *Oenone* or in the elaborate tapestry-like pageants in *The Faerie Queene*. Where we do have something really analogous to *opsis*, however, is in the rhetorical device known as imitative harmony or onomatopoeia, as described and exemplified by Pope in the *Essay on Criticism*:

'Tis not enough no harshness gives offence,
The sound must seem an echo to the sense . . .
When Ajax strives some rock's vast weight to throw,
The line too labours, and the words move slow;
Not so, when swift Camilla scours the plain,
Flies o'er th' unbending corn, and skims along the main.

258

This device is easy to recognize, and has been remarked on ever since Aristotle, in his treatise on rhetoric, illustrated in Homer's line about the stone of Sisyphus the sound of a large stone rolling downhill:

αὖτις ἔπειτα πέδονδε κυλίνδετο λᾶας ἀναιδής

Pope's translation renders this line "Thunders impetuous down, and smoaks along the ground," and won for once the approval of Johnson, Johnson being in general very doubtful about imitative harmony. He ridicules it in one of the *Idler* papers in the figure of Dick Minim the critic, who points out that the words bubble and trouble cause "a momentary inflation of the cheeks by the retention of the breath, which is afterwards forcibly emitted, as in the practice of blowing bubbles." All that the ridicule really illustrates, however, is that onomatopoeia is a linguistic as well as a poetic tendency, and that the poet takes advantage of whatever his language offers as a matter of course. The English language has many excellent sound-effects, though it has lost a few: in Old English *The Wanderer* can express cold weather as a modern poem cannot:

Hreosan hrim ond snaw   hagle gemenged

But because such devices are linguistic as well as literary, they are continually being recreated in colloquial speech. Colloquial speech, when good, is frequently called "picturesque" or "colorful," both words being pictorial metaphors. The narrative passages of *Huckleberry Finn* have an imitative flexibility about them that the narrative passages of *Tom Sawyer*, for instance, hardly attain to:

. . . Then there was a racket of ripping and tearing and smashing, and down she goes, and the front wall of the crowd begins to roll in like a wave.

The most remarkably sustained mastery of verbal *opsis* in English, perhaps, is exhibited in *The Faerie Queene*, which we have to read with a special kind of attention, an ability to catch visualization through sound. Thus in

The Eugh obedient to the bender's will,

the line has a number of weak syllables in the middle that makes it sag out in a bow shape. When Una goes astray the rhythm goes astray with her:

And Una wandring farre in woods and forrests . . .

Part of the effect of this line is due to the weak rhyme of "forrests" against "guests." When the subject is wreckage, the rhythm is wrecked with the same kind of disappointment-rhyme:

> For else my feeble vessell crazd, and crackt
>   Through thy strong buffets and outrageous blowes,
>   Cannot endure, but needs it must be wrackt
>   On the rough rocks, or on the sandy shallowes.

When Florimell finds her way difficult to scan, so does the reader:

> Through the tops of the high trees she did descry . . .

When the subject is harmony in music, we have an identical rhyme on one of the few appropriate words in the language:

> To th' instruments diuine respondence meet:
>   The siluer sounding instruments did meet . . .

When the subject is a "perillous Bridge," we have:

> Streight was the passage like a ploughed ridge,
>   That if two met, the one mote needes fall ouer the lidge.

Renaissance readers had been put on the alert for such effects by their school training in rhetoric: a harmless looking line from Spenser's *January*, for instance, is promptly sandbagged by E. K. as "a prety Epanorthosis . . . and withall a Paronomasia." The source of Pope's passage quoted above is Vida's *Art of Poetry*, which is earlier than Spenser. After Spenser the poet who showed the most consistent—or persistent—interest in imitative harmony was Cowley, who uses it so freely in *Davideis* as to draw a hoarse growl from Johnson that he saw no reason why a pine tree should be taller in Alexandrines than in pentameters. Some of Cowley's effects however are interesting enough, such as his use of the oracular hemistich. Here, for instance, three feet of a pentameter line are assigned to silent contemplation:

> O who shall tell, who shall describe thy Throne,
>   Thou great Three-One?

The first line in the passage quoted from Pope (" 'Tis not enough no harshness gives offence") implies that a sharp discord or apparent bungle in the writing may often be interpreted as imitative decorum. Pope uses such intentional discords in the same poem when he gives horrible examples of practices he disapproves of, and Addison's discussion of the passage in *Spectator* 253 shows how lively an interest such devices still aroused. Here, for example, is the way that Pope describes constipated genius:

> And strains, from hard-bound brains, eight lines a year.

Spenser, naturally, employs the same device constantly. A tasteless misuse of alliteration marks a speaker (Braggadocchio) as a liar and hypocrite:

> But minds of mortall men are muchell mard,
> And mou'd amisse with massie mucks vnmeet regard.

and when the false Duessa tempts St. George, the grammar, rhythm, and assonance could hardly be worse: the worthy knight's ear should have warned him that all was not well:

> Yet thus perforce he bids me do, or die.
> Die is my dew; yet rew my wretched state
> You . . .

Certain imitative devices become standardized in every language, and most of them in English are too familiar to need recapitulation here: beheaded lines increase speed, trochaic rhythms suggest falling movement, and so on. The native stock of English words consists largely of monosyllables, and a monosyllable always demands a separate accent, however slight. Hence long Latin words, if skilfully used, have the rhythmical function of lightening the metre, in contrast to the sodden unrhythmical roar that results "When ten low words oft creep in one dull line." A by-product of this latter phenomenon in English is more useful: the so-called broken-backed line with a spondee in the middle has since Old English times (when it was Sievers' type C) been most effective for suggesting the ominous and foreboding:

> Thy wishes then dare not be told.   (Wyatt)

> Depending from on high, dreadful to sight.   (Spenser)

> Which tasted works knowledge of good and evil.   (Milton)

Imitative harmony may of course be employed occasionally in any form of writing, but as a continuous effect it seems to adhere most naturally to *epos* in verse, where it takes the form of variants from a sustained normal pattern. Dramatists and prose writers use it very sparingly: in Shakespeare it occurs only for some definite reason, as when Lear calls to the storm on the heath in the accents of the storm itself. In lyrics its introduction has the effect of a *tour de force* which absorbs most of the interest and turns the poem into an epigram. An example is the brilliant little fourteenth-century poem *The Blacksmiths*, which uses the alliterative line to represent hammering:

> Swarte smekyd smethes smateryd wyth smoke
> Dryue me to deth wyth den of here dyntes . . .

Recurrently in the history of rhetoric some theory of a "natural" relation between sound and sense turns up. It is unlikely that there is any such natural relation, but that there is an onomatopoeic element in language which is developed and exploited by the poet is obvious enough. It is simpler to think rather of imitative harmony as a special application of a rhetorical feature which is analogous to Classical quantity, but would be better described as "quality": the patterns of assonance made by vowels and consonants. It is not difficult to distinguish *epos* with a continuous "quality" or sound-pattern, such as *Hyperion*, from the *epos* of, say, *Red Cotton Night-cap Country*, where the sound exists primarily for the sake of the sense, and is consequently felt to be closer to prose. We have an indication that there is *no* consistent sound-pattern when there are two equally satisfactory versions of the same poem differing in texture, as in the Prologue to Chaucer's *Legend of Good Women*.

The main reason for the confused use of the term musical in literary criticism is that when critics think of music in poetry, they seldom think of the actual music contemporary with the poetry they are discussing, with its stress accent and dance rhythm, but of the (very largely unknown) structure of Classical music, which was presumably closer to song and to pitch accent. We have stressed imitative harmony because it illustrates the principle that while in Classical poetry sound-pattern or quantity, being an element of recurrence, is part of the *melos* of the poetry, it is part of the *opsis* in ours.

THE RHYTHM OF CONTINUITY: PROSE

In every poem we can hear at least two distinct rhythms. One is the recurring rhythm, which we have shown to be a complex of accent, metre, and sound-pattern. The other is the semantic rhythm of sense, or what is usually felt to be the prose rhythm. Exaggerating the former, in speaking poetry aloud, will produce sing-song; exaggerating the latter will produce "insanely pompous prose," to quote a remark of Bernard Shaw on the speaking of Shakespeare in his day. We have verse *epos* when the recurrent rhythm is the primary or organizing one, and prose when the semantic rhythm is primary. Literary prose results from the use within literature of the form used for discursive or assertive writing. Treatises in verse, however "unpoetical," are invariably classified as literary.

The sixteenth century was a period of experiment, mainly in verse *epos* or running rhythm, to use Hopkins's term. The influence of *melos* developed blank verse; the influence of *opsis* the Spenserian stanza and Drayton's hexameter (the fact that *Polyolbion* is a descriptive poem may account for Drayton's choice of this metre). As in all experimental periods, there were some comparative failures, such as poulterer's measure, which had a vogue and were then dropped. Prose *epos*, that is, prose which is conceived primarily as oratorical prose, reflects the cultural domination of *epos*: it is normally thought of as a subsidiary form of spoken expression, of which the highest form is verse. It is assigned to the low or at best the middle style, such metaphors as Milton's "sitting here below in the cool element of prose" being typical. Hence any attempt to give literary dignity to prose is likely to give it some of the characteristics of verse.

Jeremy Bentham is reputed to have distinguished prose from verse by the fact that in prose all the lines run to the end of the page. Like many simple-minded observations, this has a truth that the myopia of knowledgeability is more apt to overlook. The rhythm of prose is continuous, not recurrent, and the fact is symbolized by the purely mechanical breaking of prose lines on a printed page. Of course every prose writer knows that the writing of prose is not as mechanical as the printing of it, and that it is possible for printing to injure or even spoil the rhythm of a sentence by putting an emphatic word at the end of a line instead of at the beginning of the next one, by hyphenating a strongly stressed word, and so on.

FOURTH ESSAY: RHETORICAL CRITICISM

But the prose writer is largely the prisoner of his luck, unless he is willing to make the kind of revolt against luck illustrated by Mallarmé's *Coup des Dés*. The characteristics of Renaissance oratorical prose, with the many recurrent features in its rhythm, are often concealed by the continuous printing of typography. The antiphonal chant in which the character books are written is a good example.

> He distastes religion as a sad thing,
>> and is six years elder for a thought of heaven.
> He scorns and fears, and yet hopes for old age,
>> but dare not imagine it with wrinkles . . .
> He offers you his blood today in kindness,
>> and is ready to take yours tomorrow.
> He does seldom anything which he wishes not to do again,
>> and is only wise after a misfortune . . .

Euphuism, again, employs every device known to the rhetoric books, including rhyme, metrical balance, and alliteration, which are usually thought of as the prerogative of verse. Ciceronian prose was based on a periodic rhythm and a balancing of clauses that was often a quasi-metrical balance. In prose works which are deliberate rhetorical exercises, such as Browne's *Urn Burial*, one can pick out recurring units of rhythm like the *clausulae* of Cicero: "handsome enclosure in glasses," "revengeful contentions of Rome," are anapestic examples. The 1611 Bible is frequently printed with each verse a separate paragraph: this is doubtless done primarily for the convenience of preachers, but it also gives a clearer idea of its prose rhythm than conventionally printed prose would do. The rhythm of some of Bacon's essays, especially the earlier and more aphoristic ones, would also emerge more clearly if each sentence were a separate paragraph.

By the seventeenth century the period of experiment in running rhythm had run its course, and a period of experiment in prose succeeded. This begins with the "Senecan amble" or Attic prose, the revolt in the direction of a natural speaking style against the formal half-metrical rhetoric of the Ciceronians. In Dryden the emancipating of prose from the domination of metre and the liberating of the distinctive semantic rhythm of prose is an accomplished fact. Thus Matthew Arnold was right in calling the period of Dryden and Pope an age of prose and reason, not because its poetry is prosaic, but because its prose is fully realized prose. One of the curious facts of literary history is that M. Jourdain's celebrated discovery in fact *is* a discovery, and one that a literature seems most often to make at a well advanced point in its development.

In saying that the distinctive rhythm of prose emerges more clearly from Dryden's time on, we are not, of course, saying that *better* prose was then written, though perhaps the reader needs no further warnings against premature value-judgements. But it becomes obvious that prose by itself is a transparent medium: it is at its purest—that is, at its furthest from *epos* and other metrical influences—when it is least obtrusive and presents its subject-matter like plate glass in a shop window. It goes without saying that such neutral clarity is far from dullness, as dullness is invariably opaque. Hence, while there is no *literary* reason why prose should not be as rhetorical as the writer pleases, rhetorical prose often becomes a disadvantage when prose is used for non-literary purposes. Something of this is expressed by the remark that it is impossible to tell the truth in Macaulay's style—not that Macaulay is the best writer to attach the remark to. A highly mannered prose is not sufficiently flexible to do the purely descriptive work of prose: it continually oversimplifies and over-symmetrizes its material. Even Gibbon is not above sacrificing a necessary qualification of a fact to an antithesis. Something of the same principle can be seen within literature itself: in studying the euphuist romances, for example, one becomes aware of how difficult it is to get a story told in euphuist prose. Euphuism grew out of oratorical forms, and remains best adapted to harangue: the euphuist writer seizes every chance for relapsing into monologue that he can get.

Rhetorical prose, in short, is naturally best adapted to the two purposes of rhetoric, ornament and persuasion. But as these two purposes are a psychological contrast, persuasive prose is often neutralized in its effect by the very ornament that makes it delightfully persuasive. The beauty of Jeremy Taylor's devotional writing is a disinterested factor in it which has kept him in the permanent confines of literature instead of in the transient stream of kinetic persuasion. The principle involved is by no means confined to Taylor: even in the Anglo-Saxon congregation of Wulfstan there must have been a few secular-minded highbrows who were thinking less of their sins than of the preacher's mastery of alliterative rhythm:

265

Her syndan mannslagan ond maegslagan ond maesserbanan ond mynsterhatan, ond her syndan mansworan ond morthorwyrhtan, ond her syndan myltestran ond bearnmyrthran ond fule forlegene horingas manege, ond her syndan wiccan ond waelcyrian, ond her syndan ryperas ond reaferas ond worolstruderas, ond, hraedest is to cwethenne, mana ond misdaeda ungerim ealra.

We are concerned here with literary prose: an account of non-literary prose rhythm will be given later in the essay. A tendency to long sentences made up of short phrases and coordinate clauses, to emphatic repetition combined with a driving linear rhythm, to invective, to exhaustive catalogues, and to expressing the process or movement of thought instead of the logical word-order of achieved thought, are among the signs of prose *melos*. Rabelais is one of the greatest masters of *melos* in prose: the wonderful drinking party in the fifth chapter of the first book seems to me to be technically musical, Jannequin set to words, so to speak. In English we have Burton, who is said to have amused himself by going down to the Isis and listening to the bargemen swear. Perhaps his visits were professional, for the qualities of his style are essentially the qualities of good swearing: a swinging sense of rhythm, a love of invective and of catalogue, an unlimited vocabulary, a tendency to think in short accentual units, and an encyclopaedic knowledge of the two subjects relevant to swearing, theology and personal hygiene. All of these except the last are musical characteristics.

The prose of Milton, like his verse, is at its best full of "true musical delight," though of course of a very different kind. The enormous periodic sentences with their short barking phrases, the variations of speed within these sentences, the rhetorical accumulation of emotionally charged epithets, the roaring Beethovenish-coda perorations, are some of its features. Sterne, however, is the chief master of prose *melos* before the development of "stream of consciousness" techniques for presenting thought as a process revived it in our own day. In Proust this technique takes the form of a Wagnerian intertwining of leitmotifs. In Gertrude Stein a deliberate prolixity of language gives to the words something of the capacity for repetition that music has. But it is of course Joyce who has made the most elaborate experiments in *melos*, and the bar-room scene in *Ulysses* (the one called "Sirens" in the Stuart Gilbert commentary) is, if somewhat acrobatic, still good evidence that the prose techniques just discussed have an analogy to music which is not purely fanciful. The analogy is accepted in Wyndham Lewis, for example, whose *Men Without Art* is evidently intended as a manifesto in favor of *opsis*. Here and there we can discern a tendency to *melos* even in normally unmusical writers. When in the rhetoric of *Sartor Resartus*, for instance, we run across such a passage as "From amid these confused masses of Eulogy and Elegy, with their mad Petrarchan and Werterean ware lying madly scattered among all sorts of quite extraneous matter," we can see that some of the devices of euphuism are being used for linear accentuation instead of for parallel balance, as they would be in actual euphuism.

In prose, as in verse, the writers most frequently called musical in the sentimental sense are usually the ones most remote from actual music. The tendency to *opsis* in De Quincey, Pater, Ruskin, and Morris, to name a few at random, often includes a tendency to elaborate pictorial description and long decorative similes, but the second tendency does not define the first: we cannot judge a quality of style by choice of subject-matter. The real difference is rather in the conception of the sentence. The long sentences in the later novels of Henry James are *containing* sentences: all the qualifications and parentheses are fitted in to a pattern, and as one point after another is made, there emerges not a linear process of thought but a simultaneous comprehension. What explained is turned around and viewed from all aspects, but it is completely there, so to speak, from the beginning. In Conrad, too, the dislocations in the narrative—working backwards and forwards, as he put it—are designed to make us shift our attention from listening to the story to looking at the central situation. His phrase "above all to make you see" contains a visual metaphor with much of its original meaning left in it. The dislocations of narrative in *Tristram Shandy* have the opposite effect: they take our attention away from looking at the external situation to listening to the process of its coming into being in the author's mind.

As prose is by itself a transparent medium, relatively few prose writers show a pronounced leaning to one side or the other. In general, when we are most conscious of a marked "style," or rhetorical idiosyncrasy of verbal structure, we are most likely to be in contact with either *melos* or *opsis*. Browne and Jeremy Taylor are as much inclined to *opsis* as Burton and Milton are to *melos*: the comment on Taylor made by a character in an O. Henry story, "Why doesn't someone write words to it?", refers to something analogous, not to music, but to a Tennysonian sound-pattern.

One may perhaps risk the generalization that the main weight of Classical influence falls on the *opsis* side, for the reason that an inflected language permits greater freedom in word order than Modern English or French, and so one tends to think of the sentence as containing all its parts at once. Even in Cicero, who is an orator, we are intensely aware of "balance," and balance implies a neutralizing of linear movement. In later Latin a new kind of linear propulsion begins to be perceptible, and one feels closer to the new Teutonic civilization with its alliterative line and its embryonic stress-accent music. Thus in Cassiodorus thematic words and alliterative accents echo and call and respond through the turgid sentences:

> Hinc etiam appellatam aestimamus chordam, quod facile corda moveat: ubi tenta vocum collecta est sub diversitate concordia, ut vicina chorda pulsata alteram faciat sponte contremiscere, quam nullam contigit attigisse.

THE RHYTHM OF DECORUM: DRAMA

In all literary structures we are aware of a quality that we may call the quality of a verbal personality or a speaking voice—something different from direct address, though related to it. When this quality is felt to be the voice of the author himself, we call it style: *le style c'est l'homme* is a generally accepted axiom. The conception of style is based on the fact that every writer has his own rhythm, as distinctive as his handwriting, and his own imagery, ranging from a preference for certain vowels and consonants to a preoccupation with two or three archetypes. Style exists in all literature, of course, but may be seen at its purest in thematic prose: in fact it is the chief literary term applied to works of prose generally classified as non-literary. Style had its great period in late Victorian times, when the primary connection between writing and personality was a fundamental principle of criticism.

In a novel we are aware of a more complicated problem: dialogue has to speak with the voice of the internal characters, not the author, and sometimes dialogue and narrative are so far apart as to divide the book into two different languages. The suiting of style to an internal character or subject is known as decorum or appropriateness of style to content. Decorum is in general the poet's *ethical* voice, the modification of his own voice to the voice of a character or to the vocal tone demanded by subject or mood. And as style is at its purest in discursive prose, so decorum is obviously at its purest in drama, where the poet does not appear in person. Drama might be described, from our present point of view, as *epos* or fiction absorbed by decorum.

Drama is a mimesis of dialogue or conversation, and the rhetoric of conversation obviously has to be a very fluid one. It may range from a set speech to the kind of thrust and parry which is called stichomythia when its basis is metrical; and it has the double difficulty of expressing the speaker's character and speech rhythm and yet modifying them to the situation and the moods of other speakers. In Elizabethan drama the center of gravity, so to speak, is somewhere between verse *epos* and prose, so that it can move easily from one to the other depending on the requirements of decorum, which are chiefly the social rank of the character and the genre of the play. Comedy and lower ranks run to prose, and in later centuries, as *epos* gives way before fiction, comedy and prose exhibit a power of adaptation to the changed conditions that tragedy and verse *epos* conspicuously lack.

Yet even in prose comedy, where the lofty style of rhetoric demanded by ruling-class figures has largely disappeared, there still remains the technical problem of representing in prose the features that a verse drama would express by verse: such features as dignity, passion, witty imagery (probably the most important), and pathos. Prose comedy often meets such requirements by developing a mannered epigrammatic prose style, in which something of the antithetical and repetitive structure of rhetorical prose reappears. Nearly all the great writers of English comedy from Congreve to O'Casey have been Irishmen, and the rhetorical tradition survived longer in Ireland. The dramatic prose of Synge also ranks as literary mannerism, even if it does reproduce the speech rhythms of Irish peasantry. By contrast a verse rhythm like that of Browning in the nineteenth century or that of Eliot and Fry in this one seems to straddle the gap between *epos* and prose with much less effort. One wonders if there is not something to be said for Shaw's contention that it is actually easier to write a play in blank verse than in prose. The feeling of unnaturalness and strain in a good deal of modern verse drama would in that case be the result of attempting an inappropriate kind of rhetoric, one which is too far out of touch with normal conversational rhythms, in a way that Elizabethan drama, however elaborately stylized, very seldom is.

The attempt to find verse forms for conversational rhythms did not interest very many of the Romantics or Victorians. Students of English are often urged, in Romantic fashion, to use as many short words of native origin as possible, on the ground that they make one's vocabulary concrete, but a style founded on simple native words can be the most artificial of all styles. Samuel Johnson at his most bumbling is still colloquial and conversational compared to a William Morris romance. Standard educated English speech today, with its many long abstract and technical words and the heavy accent of its short ones, is a polysyllabic clatter which is much easier to fit to prose than to verse. Blake's Prophetic Books represent one of the few successful efforts to tackle conversational rhythm in verse—so successful that many critics are still wondering if they are "real poetry." Blake's view that a longer line than the pentameter was needed to represent educated colloquial speech in verse may be compared with the experiments of Clough and Bridges in hexameters, which are also attempts to capture the same kind of rhythm, though at least in Clough one feels that a strict adherence to the metre gives a somewhat roller-coaster quality to the accent. In the verse rhythm of *The Cocktail Party*, which perhaps most clearly foreshadows the development of a new rhythmical center of gravity between verse and prose in modern speech, we go back to a rhythm very close to the old four-accent line. Perhaps what is taking shape here is a long six-or-seven-beat accentual line finally made practicable for spoken dialogue by being split in two.

The question of *melos* and *opsis* in drama is easily dealt with: *melos* is actual music and *opsis* visible scenery and costume.

THE RHYTHM OF ASSOCIATION: LYRIC

In the historical sequence of modes, each genre in turn seems to rise to some degree of ascendancy. Myth and romance express themselves mainly in *epos*, and in the high mimetic the rise of a new national consciousness and an increase of secular rhetoric bring the drama of the settled theatre into the foreground. The low mimetic brings fiction and an increasing use of prose, the rhythm of which finally begins to influence verse. Wordsworth's theory that apart from metre the *lexis* of poetry and of prose are identical is a low mimetic manifesto. The lyric is the genre in which the poet, like the ironic writer, turns his back on his audience. It is also the genre which most clearly shows the hypothetical core of literature, narrative and meaning in their literal aspects as word-order and word-pattern. It looks as though the lyric genre has some peculiarly close connection with the ironic mode and the literal level of meaning.

Let us take a line of poetry at random, say the beginning of Claudio's great speech in *Measure for Measure*:

> Ay, but to die, and go we know not where:

We can hear of course the metrical rhythm, an iambic pentameter spoken as a four-stress line. We can hear the semantic or prose rhythm, and we hear what we may call the rhythm of decorum, the verbal representation of the horror of a man facing death. But we can also, if we listen to the line very attentively, make out still another rhythm in it, an oracular, meditative, irregular, unpredictable, and essentially discontinuous rhythm, emerging from the coincidences of the sound-pattern:

> Ay:
> But to die . . .
>
> > and go
> > we know
> >
> > > not where . . .

Just as the semantic rhythm is the initiative of prose, and as the metrical rhythm is the initiative of *epos*, so this oracular rhythm seems to be the predominating initiative of lyric. The initiative of prose normally has its center of gravity in the conscious mind: the discursive writer writes deliberately, and the literary prose writer imitates a deliberative process. In verse *epos* the choice of a metre prescribes the form of rhetorical organization: the poet develops an unconscious habitual skill in thinking in this metre, and is thereby set free to do other things, such as tell stories, expound ideas, or make the various modifications demanded by decorum. Neither of these by itself seems quite to get down to what we think of as typically the poetic creation, which is an associative rhetorical process, most of it below the threshold of consciousness, a chaos of paronomasia, sound-links, ambiguous sense-links, and memory-links very like that of the dream. Out of this the distinctively lyrical union of sound and sense emerges. Like the dream, verbal association is subject to a censor, which (or whom) we may call the "plausibility-principle," the necessity of shaping itself into a form acceptable to the poet's and his reader's waking consciousness, and of adapting itself to the sign-meanings of assertive language well enough to be communicable to that consciousness. But associative rhythm seems to retain a connection with dream corresponding to the drama's connection with ritual. The associative rhythm, no less than the others, can be found in all writing: Yeats's typographical rearrangement of Pater which begins *The Oxford Book of Modern Verse* illustrates how it may be extracted from prose.

The most natural unit of the lyric is the discontinuous unit of the stanza, and in earlier periods most lyrics tended to be fairly regular strophic patterns, reflecting the ascendancy of *epos*. Stanzaic *epos*, such as we find in medieval romance, is usually much closer to the atmosphere of a dream world than linear *epos*. With the Romantic movement a sense that the "true voice of feeling" was unpredictable and irregular in its rhythm began to increase. Poe's *Poetic Principle* maintains that poetry is *essentially* oracular and discontinuous, that the poetic *is* the lyrical, and that verse *epos* consists really of lyrical passages stuck together with versified prose. This is a manifesto of the ironic age, as Wordsworth's preface was a low mimetic one, and announces the arrival of a third period of technical experiment in English literature, in which the object is to liberate the distinctive rhythm of lyric. The aim of "free" verse is not simply revolt against metre and *epos* conventions, but the articulation of an independent rhythm equally distinct from metre and from prose. If we do not recognize this third rhythm, we shall have no answer for the naive objection that when poetry loses regular metre it becomes prose.

The loosening of rhyme in Emily Dickinson and of stanzaic structure in Yeats are intended, not to make the metrical pattern more irregular, but to make the lyric rhythm more precise. Hopkins's term "sprung rhythm," too, has as close an affinity with lyric as running rhythm has with *epos*. Pound's theories and techniques, from his early imagism to the discontinuous pastiche of the *Cantos* (preceded by a half-century of French and English experiment in the "fragmentation" or lyricizing of *epos*), are lyric-centered theories and techniques. The rhetorical analysis founded on ambiguity in new criticism is a lyric-centered criticism which tends, often explicitly, to extract the lyrical rhythm from all the genres. The most admired and advanced poets of the twentieth century are chiefly those who have most fully mastered the elusive, meditative, resonant, centripetal word-magic of the emancipated lyrical rhythm. In the course of this development the associative rhythm has become more flexible, and has consequently moved from its Romantic basis in style to a new kind of subjectivized decorum.

The traditional associations of lyric are chiefly with music. The Greeks spoke of lyrics as *ta mele*, usually translated as "poems to be sung"; in the Renaissance, lyric was constantly associated with the lyre and the lute, and Poe's essay just referred to lays an emphasis on the importance of music in poetry which makes up in strength what it lacks in precision. We should remember, however, that when a poem is "sung," at least in the modern musical sense, its rhythmical organization has been taken over by music. The words of a "singable" lyric are generally neutral and conventional words, and modern song has the stress accent of music, with little if anything left of the pitch accent that marks the domination of music by poetry. We should therefore get a clearer impression of the lyric if we translated *ta mele* as "poems to be chanted," for chanting, or what Yeats called cantillation, is an emphasis on words as words. Modern poets who, like Yeats, want their poems chanted are often precisely those who are most suspicious of musical settings.

The history of music shows a recurrent tendency to develop elaborate contrapuntal structures which, in vocal music, almost annihilate the words. There has also been a recurrent tendency to reform and simplify musical structures in order to give the words more prominence. This has sometimes been the result of religious pressure, but literary influences have been at work too. We may take the madrigal, perhaps, as representing something close to a limit of the subservience of poetry to music. In the madrigal the poetic rhythm disappears as the words are tossed from voice to voice, and the imagery in the words is expressed by the devices of what is usually called program music. We may find long passages filled up with nonsense words, or the whole collection may bear the subtitle "apt for voices or viols," indicating that the words can be dispensed with altogether. The dislike of poets for this trituration of

273

their words can be seen in the support they gave to the seventeenth-century style of isolating the words on a single melodic line, the style which made the opera possible. This certainly brings us closer to poetry, though music still predominates in the rhythm. But the closer the composer moves toward emphasizing the verbal rhythm of the poem, the closer he comes to the chanting which is the real rhythmical basis of lyric. Henry Lawes made some experiments in this direction which won the applause of Milton, and the admiration that so many *symbolistes* expressed for Wagner was evidently based on the notion (if so erroneous a notion can be said to be a base) that he was also trying to identify, or at least closely associate, the rhythm of music and the rhythm of poetry.

But now that we have music on one boundary of lyric, and the purely verbal emphasis of cantillation in the center, we can see that lyric has a relation to the pictorial on the other side which is equally important. Something of this is present in the typographical appearance of a lyric on a printed page, where it is, so to speak, overseen as well as overheard. The arrangement of stanzas and indentations gives a visible pattern to a lyric which is quite distinct from *epos*, where the lines have approximately the same length, as well as of course from prose. In any case there are thousands of lyrics so intently focussed on visual imagery that they are, as we may say, set to pictures. In the emblem an actual picture appears, and the poet-painter Blake, whose engraved lyrics are in the emblem tradition, has a role in the lyric analogous to that of the poet-composers Campion and Dowland on the musical side. The movement called imagism made a great deal of the pictorial element in the lyric, and many imagistic poems could almost be described as a series of captions to invisible pictures.

In such emblems as Herbert's *The Altar* and *Easter Wings*, where the pictorial shape of the subject is suggested in the shape of the lines of the poem, we begin to approach the pictorial boundary of the lyric. The absorption of words by pictures, corresponding to the madrigal's absorption of words by music, is picture-writing, of the kind most familiar to us in comic strips, captioned cartoons, posters, and other emblematic forms. A further stage of absorption is represented by Hogarth's *Rake's Progress* and similar narrative sequences of pictures, in the scroll pictures of the Orient, or in the novels in woodcuts that occasionally appear. Pictorial arrangements of the visible basis of literature, which is alphabetical writing, have had a more fitful and sporadic existence, ranging from capitals in illuminated manuscripts to surrealist experiments in collage, and have not had much specifically literary importance. They would have had more, of course, if our writing had remained in the hieroglyphic stage, as in hieroglyphics writing and drawing are much the same art. We have previously glanced at Pound's comparison of the imagistic lyric to the Chinese ideogram.

We should expect that during the last century there would have been a good deal said about the relation of poetry to music on the one hand, and to painting on the other. In fact the attempts to bring words as near as possible to the more repetitive and emphatic rhythm of music or the more concentrated stasis of painting make up the main body of what is usually called experimental writing. It would make for clearer thinking if these developments were regarded as lateral explorations of a single phase of rhetoric, not, through a false analogy with science, as "new directions" portending a general advance of literary technique on all fronts. The reverse movement of the same progressive fallacy gives us the moral indignation that talks about "decadence." A question on which little has yet been said is the extent to which poetry may, so to speak, disappear into painting or music and come back with a different rhythm. This happened for example in the emergence of the "prosa" out of the sequence in medieval music, and it happens in a different way when a song becomes a kind of rhythmical reservoir for a number of different lyrics.

The two elements of subconscious association which form the basis for lyrical *melos* and *opsis* respectively have never been given names. We may call them, if the terms are thought dignified enough, babble and doodle. In babble, rhyme, assonance, alliteration, and puns develop out of sound-associations. The thing that gives shape to the associating is what we have been calling the rhythmical initiative, though in a free verse poem it would be rather a sense of the oscillations of rhythm within an area which gradually becomes defined as the containing form. We can see from the revisions poets make that the rhythm is usually prior, either in inspiration or in importance or both, to the selection of words to fill it up. This phenomenon is not confined to poetry: in Beethoven's notebooks, too, we often see how he knows that he wants a cadence at a certain bar before he has worked out any melodic sequence to reach it. One can see a similar evolution in

children, who start with rhythmical babble and fill in the appropriate words as they go along. The process is also reflected in nursery
rhymes, college yells, work songs, and the like, where rhythm is a
physical pulsation close to the dance, and is often filled up with
nonsense words. An obvious priority of rhythm to sense is a regular
feature of popular poetry, and verse, like music, is called "light"
whenever it has the rhythmical accentuation of a railway coach
with a flat wheel.

When babble cannot rise into consciousness, it remains on the
level of uncontrolled association. This latter is often a literary way
of representing insanity, and Smart's *Jubilate Agno*, parts of which
are usually considered mentally unbalanced, shows the creative
process in an interesting formative stage:

> For the power of some animal is predominant in every language.
> For the power and spirit of a CAT is in the Greek.
> For the sound of a cat is in the most useful preposition κατ᾽ εὐ-
> χεν . . .
> For the Mouse (Mus) prevails in the Latin.
> For edi-mus, bibi-mus, vivi-mus—ore-mus . . .
> For two creatures the Bull & the Dog prevail in the English,
> For all the words ending in ble are in the creature.
> Invisi-ble, Incomprehensi-ble, ineffa-ble, A-ble . . .
> For there are many words under Bull . . .
> For Brook is under Bull. God be gracious to Lord Bolingbroke.

It is possible that similar sputters and sparks of the fusing intellect
take place in all poetic thinking. The puns in this passage impress
the reader as both outrageous and humorous, which is consistent
with Freud's view of wit as the escape of impulse from the control
of the censor. In creation the impulse is the creative energy itself,
and the censor is what we have called the plausibility-principle.
Paronomasia is one of the essential elements of verbal creation,
but a pun introduced into a conversation turns its back on the sense
of the conversation and sets up a self-contained verbal sound-sense
pattern in its place.

There is a perilous balance in paronomasia between verbal wit
and hypnotic incantation. In Poe's line "the viol, the violet and the
vine," we have a fusion of two opposed qualities. Wit makes us
laugh, and is addressed to the awakened intelligence; incantation
by itself is humorlessly impressive. Wit detaches the reader; the

oracle absorbs him. In dream-poems like Arthur Benson's *The Phoenix*, or in poems intended to represent dreaming or drowsy states, like the medieval *Pearl* and many passages in Spenser and Tennyson, we notice a similar insistence on hypnotically recurrent sound-patterns. If we were to laugh at the wit in such a line as Poe's, we should break the spell of his poem, yet the line is witty, just as *Finnegans Wake* is a very funny book, although it never leaves the oracular solemnity of the dream world. In the latter, of course, the researches of Freud and Jung into the mechanisms of both dream and wit have been extensively drawn upon. There may well be buried in it some such word as "vinolent," intended to express everything in Poe's line at once. In fiction the associative process ordinarily shows itself chiefly in the names the author invents for his characters. Thus "Lilliputian" and "Ebenezer Scrooge" are associative names for midgets and misers respectively, because one suggests "little" and "puny" and the other "squeeze," "screw" and perhaps "geezer." Spenser says that a character of his has been named Malfont:

> Eyther for th' euill, which he did therein,
> Or that he likened was to a welhed,

which implies that the second syllable of his name is to be derived both from *fons* and from *facere*. We may call this kind of associative process poetic etymology, and we shall say more about it later.

The characteristics of babble are again present in doggerel, which is also a creative process left unfinished through lack of skill or patience, though the psychological conditions are of the opposite kind from those of *Jubilate Agno*. Doggerel is not necessarily stupid poetry; it is poetry that begins in the conscious mind and has never gone through the associative process. It has a prose initiative, but tries to make itself associative by an act of will, and it reveals the same difficulties that great poetry has overcome at a subconscious level. We can see in doggerel how words are dragged in because they rhyme or scan, how ideas are dragged in because they are suggested by a rhyme-word, and so on. Deliberate doggerel, as we have it in *Hudibras* or German *knittelvers*, can be a source of brilliant rhetorical satire, and one which involves a kind of parody of poetic creation itself, just as malapropism is a parody of poetic etymology. The difficulties in the way of giving prose itself something of the associative concentration of poetry are enormous, and not many prose writers, apart from Flaubert and Joyce, have consistently and resolutely faced them.

The first rough sketches of verbal design ("doodle") in the creative process are hardly separable from associative babble. Phrases are scribbled in notebooks to be used later; a first stanza may suddenly "come" and then other stanzas of the same shape have to be designed to go with it, and all the ingenuity that Freud has traced in the dream has to be employed in putting words into patterns. The elaborateness of conventional forms—the sonnet and its less versatile congeners the ballade, villanelle, sestina, and the like, together with all the other conventions that the individual lyric poet invents for himself—indicates how far removed the lyrical initiative really is from whatever a *cri de coeur* is supposed to be. Poe's essay on his own *The Raven* is a perfectly accurate account of what he did in that poem, whether he did it on the conscious mental level that the essay suggests or not, and this essay, like *The Poetic Principle*, anticipates the critical techniques of a new mode.

We may note that although of course lyrics in all ages are addressed to the ear, the rise of fiction and the printing press develops an increasing tendency to address the ear through the eye. The visual patterns of E. E. Cummings are obvious examples, but do not by any means stand alone. A poem of Marianne Moore's, *Camellia Sabina*, employs an eight-line stanza in which the rhyming words are at the end of the first line, at the end of the eighth line, and at the third syllable of the seventh line. I doubt if the most attentive listener could pick this last rhyme up merely from hearing the poem read aloud: one sees it first on the page, and then translates the visual structural pattern to the ear.

We are now in a position to find more acceptable words for babble and doodle, the radicals of lyrical *melos* and *opsis* respectively. The radical of *melos* is *charm*: the hypnotic incantation that, through its pulsing dance rhythm, appeals to involuntary physical response, and is hence not far from the sense of magic, or physically compelling power. The etymological descent of charm from *carmen*, song, may be noted. Actual charms have a quality that is imitated in popular literature by work songs of various kinds, especially lullabies, where the drowsy sleep-inducing repetition shows the underlying oracular or dream pattern very clearly. Invective or flyting, the literary imitation of the spell-binding curse, uses similar

278

incantatory devices for opposite reasons, as in Dunbar's *Flyting with Kennedy*:

> Mauch mutton, byt buttoun, peilit gluttoun, air to Hilhous;
> Rank beggar, ostir dregar, foule fleggar in the flet;
> Chittirlilling, ruch rilling, like schilling in the milhous;
> Baird rehator, theif of natour, fals tratour, feyindis gett . . .

From here the line of descent is easy to the *melos* of physical absorption in sound and rhythm, the pounding movement and clashing noise which the heavy accentuation of English makes possible. Lindsay's *The Congo* and *Sweeney Agonistes* are modern examples of a tendency to ragtime in English poetry that can be traced back through Poe's *Bells* and Dryden's *Alexander's Feast* to Skelton and to Dunbar's *Ane Ballat of our Lady*. A more refined aspect of *melos* is exhibited in lyrics which combine accentual repetition with variations in speed. Thus Wyatt's sonnet:

> I abide and abide and better abide,
>> And, after the olde proverbe, the happie daye:
>> And ever my ladye to me dothe saye,
>> "Let me alone and I will provyde."
> I abide and abide and tarrye the tyde
>> And with abiding spede well ye maye:
>> Thus do I abide I wott allwaye,
>> Nother obtayning nor yet denied.
> Aye me! this long abidyng
>> Semithe to me as who sayethe
>> A prolonging of a dieng dethe,
> Or a refusing of a desyred thing.
>> Moche ware it bettre for to be playne,
>> Then to saye abide and yet shall not obtayne.

This lovely sonnet is intensely musical in its conception: there is the repeated clang of "abide" and the musical, though poetically very audacious, sequential repetition of the first line in the fifth. Then as hope follows expectancy, doubt hope, and despair doubt, the lively rhythm gradually slows down and collapses. On the other hand, Skelton, like Scarlatti after him, gets fidgety in a slow rhythm and is more inclined to speed up. Here is an *accelerando* in a rhyme royal stanza from *The Garland of Laurell*:

That long tyme blew a full tymorous blaste,
Like to the Boriall wyndes, whan they blowe,
That towres and tounes and trees downe cast,
Drove clouds together like dryftes of snowe;
The dredful dinne drove all the route on a row;
Som trembled, som girned, som gasped, som gased,
As people half pevissh or men that were mased.

In the same poem there is a curious coincidental link with music: the verses to Margery Wentworth, Margaret Hussey, and Gertrude Statham are miniature musical rondos of the *abaca* type.

We have several times noticed the close relation between the visual and the conceptual in poetry, and the radical of *opsis* in the lyric is *riddle*, which is characteristically a fusion of sensation and reflection, the use of an object of sense experience to stimulate a mental activity in connection with it. Riddle was originally the cognate object of read, and the riddle seems intimately involved with the whole process of reducing language to visible form, a process which runs through such by-forms of riddle as hieroglyphic and ideogram. The actual riddle-poems of Old English include some of its finest lyrics, and belong to a culture in which such a phrase as "curiously inwrought" is a favorite aesthetic judgement. Just as the charm is not far from a sense of magical compulsion, so the curiously wrought object, whether sword-hilt or illuminated manuscript, is not far from a sense of enchantment or magical imprisonment. Closely parallel to the riddle in Old English is the figure of speech known as the kenning or oblique description which calls the body the bone-house and the sea the whale-road.

In all ages of poetry the fusion of the concrete and the abstract, the spatial and the conceptual aspects of *dianoia*, has been a central feature of poetic imagery in every genre, and the kenning has had a long line of descent. In the fifteenth century we have "aureate diction," the use of abstract terms in poetry, then thought of as "colors" of rhetoric. When such words were new and the ideas represented by them exciting, aureate diction must have sounded far less dull and bumbling than it generally does to us, and have had much more of the sense of intellectual precision that we feel in such phrases as Eliot's "piaculative pence" or Auden's "cerebrotonic Cato." The seventeenth century gave us the conceit or intellectualized image of "metaphysical" poetry, typically Baroque in its ability to express an exuberant sense of design combined with a witty and paradoxical sense of the stress and tension underlying the design. The eighteenth century showed its respect for the categorizing power of abstract thought in its poetic diction, in which fish appear as the finny tribe. In the low mimetic period a growing prejudice against convention made poets less aware of the conventional phrases they used, but the technical problems of poetical imagery did not thereby disappear, nor did conventional figures of speech.

Two of these connected with the matter under discussion, the fusion of the concrete with the abstract, may be noted. An abstract noun in the possessive case followed by an adjective and a concrete noun ("death's dateless night" is a Shakespearean example) is a nineteenth-century favorite. In J. R. Lowell's Harvard Commemoration Ode of 1865 this figure is employed nineteen times, "life's best oil," "Oblivion's subtle wrong" and "Fortune's fickle moon" being three examples. In the twentieth century it was succeeded in favor by another phrase of "the adjective noun of noun" type, in which the first noun is usually concrete and the second abstract. Thus: "the pale dawn of longing," "the broken collar-bone of silence," "the massive eyelids of time," "the crimson tree of love." I have made these up myself, and they are free to any poet who wants them, but on examining a volume of twentieth-century lyrics I find, counting all the variants, thirty-eight phrases of this type in the first five poems.

The fusion of the concrete and abstract is a special case, though a very important one, of a general principle that the technical development of the last century has exposed to critical view. All poetic imagery seems to be founded on metaphor, but in the lyric, where the associative process is strongest and the ready-made descriptive phrases of ordinary prose furthest away, the unexpected or violent metaphor that is called catachresis has a peculiar importance. Much more frequently than any other genre does the lyric depend for its main effect on the fresh or surprising image, a fact which often gives rise to the illusion that such imagery is radically new or unconventional. From Nashe's "Brightness falls from the air" to Dylan Thomas's "A grief ago," the emotional crux of the lyric has over and over again tended to be this "sudden glory" of fused metaphor.

SPECIFIC FORMS OF DRAMA

We have now to see whether this expansion of perspective, which enables us to consider the relation of the *lexis* or verbal pattern to music and spectacle, gives us any new light on the traditional classifications within the genres. The division of dramas into tragedies and comedies, for instance, is a conception based entirely on verbal drama, and does not include or account for types of drama, such as the opera or masque, in which music and scenery have a more organic place. Yet verbal drama, whether tragic or comic, has clearly developed a long way from the primitive idea of drama, which is to present a powerful sensational focus for a community. The scriptural plays of the Middle Ages are primitive in this sense: they present to the audience a myth already familiar to and significant for that audience, and they are designed to remind the audience of their communal possession of this myth.

The scriptural play is a form of a spectacular dramatic genre which we may provisionally call a "myth-play." It is a somewhat negative and receptive form, and takes on the mood of the myth it represents. The crucifixion play in the Towneley cycle is tragic because the Crucifixion is; but it is not a tragedy in the sense that *Othello* is a tragedy. It does not, that is, make a tragic *point*; it simply presents the story because it is familiar and significant. It would be nonsense to apply such tragic conceptions as hybris to the figure of Christ in that play, and while pity and terror are raised, they remain attached to the subject, and there is no catharsis of them. The characteristic mood and resolution of the myth-play are pensive, and pensiveness, in this context, implies a continuing imaginative subjection to the story. The myth-play emphasizes dramatically the symbol of spiritual and corporeal communion. The scriptural plays themselves were associated with the festival of Corpus Christi, and Calderon's religious plays are explicitly *autos sacramentales* or Eucharist plays. The appeal of the myth-play is a curious mixture of the popular and the esoteric; it is popular for its immediate audience, but those outside its circle have to make a conscious effort to appreciate it. In a controversial atmosphere it disappears, as it cannot deal with controversial issues unless it selects its audience. In view of the ambiguities attaching to the word myth, we shall speak of this genre as the *auto*.

When there is no clear-cut distinction between gods and heroes in a society's mythology, or between the ideals of the nobility and the priesthood, the *auto* may present a legend which is secular and sacred at once. An example is the No drama of Japan, which with its unification of chivalric and otherworldly symbols and its dreamy un-tragic, un-comic mood so strongly attracted Yeats. It is interesting to see how Yeats, both in his theory of the *anima mundi* and in his desire to get his play as physically close to the audience as possible, reverts to the archaic idea of corporeal communion. In Greek drama, too, there is no sharp boundary line between the divine and the heroic protagonist. But in Christian societies we can see glimpses of a secular *auto*, a romantic drama presenting the exploits of a hero, which is closely related to tragedy, the end of a hero's exploit being eventually his death, but which in itself is neither tragic nor comic, being primarily spectacular.

Tamburlaine is such a play: there the relation between the hero's hybris and his death is more casual than causal. This genre has had varying luck: more in Spain, for instance, than in France, where the establishing of tragedy was part of an intellectual revolution. The two attempts in France to move tragedy back towards heroic romance, *Le Cid* and *Hernani*, each precipitated a big row. In Germany, on the other hand, it is clear that the actual genre of many plays by Goethe and Schiller is the heroic romance, however much affected they have been by the prestige of tragedy. In Wagner, who expands the heroic form all the way back to a sacramental drama of gods, the symbol of communion again occupies a conspicuous place, negatively in *Tristan*, positively in *Parsifal*. In proportion as it moves closer to tragedy and further from the sacred *auto*, drama tends to make less use of music. If we look at the earliest extant play of Aeschylus, *The Suppliants*, we can see that close behind it is a predominantly musical structure of which the modern counterpart would normally be the oratorio—it is perhaps possible to describe Wagner's operas as fermented oratorios.

In Renaissance England the audience was too bourgeois for a chivalric drama to get firmly established, and the Elizabethan secular *auto* eventually became the history-play. With the history-play we move from spectacle to a more purely verbal drama, and the symbols of communion become much attenuated, although they are still there. The central theme of Elizabethan history is the unifying of the nation and the binding of the audience into the myth as the inheritors of that unity, set over against the disasters of civil war and weak leadership. One may even recognize a secular Eucharist symbol in the red and white rose, just as one may recognize in the plays that end by pointing to Elizabeth, like Peele's *Arraignment of Paris*, a secular counterpart of a mystery play of the Virgin. But the emphasis and characteristic resolution of the history play are in terms of continuity and the closing up both of tragic catastrophe and (as in the case of Falstaff) of the comic festival. One may compare Shaw's "chronicle play" of *Saint Joan*, where the end of the play is a tragedy, followed by an epilogue in which the rejection of Joan is, like the rejection of Falstaff, historical, suggesting continuity rather than a rounded finish.

The history merges so gradually into tragedy that we often cannot be sure when communion has turned into catharsis. *Richard II* and *Richard III* are tragedies insofar as they resolve on those defeated kings; they are histories insofar as they resolve on Bolingbroke and Richmond, and the most one can say is that they lean toward history. *Hamlet* and *Macbeth* lean toward tragedy, but Fortinbras and Malcolm, the continuing characters, indicate the historical element in the tragic resolution. There seems to be a far less direct connection between history and comedy: the comic scenes in the histories are, so to speak, subversive. *Henry V* ends in triumph and marriage, but an action that kills Falstaff, hangs Bardolph and debases Pistol is not related to comedy in the way that *Richard II* is related to tragedy.

We are here concerned only with tragedy as a species of drama. Tragic drama derives from the *auto* its central heroic figure, but the association of heroism with downfall is due to the simultaneous presence of irony. The nearer the tragedy is to *auto*, the more closely associated the hero is with divinity; the nearer to irony, the more human the hero is, and the more the catastrophe appears to be a social rather than a cosmological event. Elizabethan tragedy shows a historical development from Marlowe, who presents his heroes more or less as demigods moving in a kind of social ether, to Webster, whose tragedies are almost clinical analyses of a sick society. Greek tragedy never broke completely from the *auto*, and so never developed a social form, though there are tendencies to it in Euripides. But whatever the proportions of heroism and irony, tragedy shows itself to be primarily a vision of the supremacy of the event or *mythos*. The response to tragedy is "this must be," or, perhaps more accurately, "this does happen": the event is primary, the explanation of it secondary and variable.

As tragedy moves over towards irony, the sense of inevitable event begins to fade out, and the sources of catastrophe come into view. In irony catastrophe is either arbitrary and meaningless, the impact of an unconscious (or, in the pathetic fallacy, malignant) world on conscious man, or the result of more or less definable social and psychological forces. Tragedy's "this must be" becomes irony's "this at least is," a concentration on foreground facts and a rejection of mythical superstructures. Thus the ironic drama is a vision of what in theology is called the fallen world, of simple humanity, man as natural man and in conflict with both human and non-human nature. In nineteenth-century drama the tragic vision is often identical with the ironic one, hence nineteenth-century tragedies tend to be either *Schicksal* dramas dealing with the arbitrary ironies of fate, or (clearly the more rewarding form) studies of the frustrating and smothering of human activity by the combined pressure of a reactionary society without and a disorganized soul within. Such irony is difficult to sustain in the theatre because it tends toward a stasis of action. In those parts of Chekhov, notably the last act of *The Three Sisters*, where the characters one by one withdraw from each other into their subjective prison-cells, we are coming about as close to pure irony as the stage can get.

The ironic play passes through a dead center of complete realism, a pure mime representing human life without comment and without imposing any sort of dramatic form beyond what is required for simple exhibition. This idolatrous form of mimesis is rare, but the thin line of its tradition can be traced from Classical mime-writers like Herodas to their *tranche-de-vie* descendants in recent times. The mime is somewhat commoner as an individual performance, and, outside the theatre, the Browning monodrama is a logical development of the isolating and soliloquizing tendencies of ironic conflict. In the theatre we usually find that the spectacle of "all too human" life is either oppressive or ridiculous, and that it tends to pass directly from one to the other. Irony, then, as it moves away from tragedy, begins to merge into comedy.

Ironic comedy presents us of course with "the way of the world," but as soon as we find sympathetic or even neutral characters in a comedy, we move into the more familiar comic area where we have a group of humors outwitted by the opposing group. Just as tragedy

285

is a vision of the supremacy of *mythos* or thing done, and just as irony is a vision of *ethos*, or character individualized against environment, so comedy is a vision of *dianoia*, a significance which is ultimately social significance, the establishing of a desirable society. As an imitation of life, drama is, in terms of *mythos*, conflict; in terms of *ethos*, a representative image; in terms of *dianoia*, the final harmonic chord revealing the tonality under the narrative movement, it is community. The further comedy moves from irony, the more it becomes what we here call ideal comedy, the vision not of the way of the world, but of what you will, life as you like it. Shakespeare's main interest is in getting away from the son-father conflict of ironic comedy towards a vision of a serene community, a vision most prominent in *The Tempest*. Here the action is polarized around a younger and an older man working in harmony together, a lover and a benevolent teacher.

The next step brings us to the extreme limit of social comedy, the symposium, the structure of which is, as we should expect, clearest in Plato, whose Socrates is both teacher and lover, and whose vision moves toward an integration of society in a form like that of the symposium itself, the dialectic festivity which, as is explained in the opening of the *Laws*, is the controlling force that holds society together. It is easy to see that Plato's dialogue form is dramatic and has affinities with comedy and mime; and while there is much in Plato's thought that contradicts the spirit of comedy as we have outlined it, it is significant that he contradicts it directly, tries to kidnap it, so to speak. It seems almost a rule that the more he does this, the further he moves into pure exposition or dictatorial monologue and away from drama. The most dramatic of his dialogues, such as *Euthydemus*, are regularly the most indecisive in philosophical "position."

In our own day Bernard Shaw has tried hard to keep the symposium in the theatre. His early manifesto, *The Quintessence of Ibsenism*, states that a play should be an intelligent discussion of a serious problem, and in his preface to *Getting Married* he remarks approvingly on the fact that it observes the unities of time and place. For comedy of Shaw's type tends to a symposium form which occupies the same amount of time in its action that the audience consumes in watching it. However, Shaw discovered in practice that what emerges from the theatrical symposium is not a dialectic that compels to a course of action or thought, but one that emancipates from formulated principles of conduct. The shape of such a comedy is very clear in the bright little sketch *In Good King Charles's Golden Days*, where even the most highly developed human types, the saintly Fox and the philosophical Newton, are shown to be comic humors by the mere presence of other types of people. Yet the central symposium figure of the haranguing lover bulks formidably in *Man and Superman*, and even the renunciation of love for mathematics at the end of *Back to Methusaleh* is consistent with the symposium spirit.

The view of poetry which sees it as intermediate between history and philosophy, its images combining the temporal events of the one with the timeless ideas of the other, seems to be still involved in this exposition of dramatic forms. We can now see a mimetic or verbal drama stretching from the history-play to the philosophy-play (the act-play and the scene-play), with the mime, the pure image, halfway between. These three are specialized forms, cardinal points of drama rather than generic areas. But the whole mimetic area is only a part, a semicircle, let us say, of all drama. In the misty and unexplored region of the other semicircle of spectacular drama we have identified a quadrant that we have called the *auto*, and we have now to chart the fourth quadrant that lies between the *auto* and comedy, and establish the fourth cardinal point where it meets the *auto* again. When we think of the clutter of forms that belong here, we are strongly tempted to call our fourth area "miscellaneous" and let it go; but it is precisely here that new generic criticism is needed.

The further comedy moves from irony, and the more it rejoices in the free movement of its happy society, the more readily it takes to music and dancing. As music and scenery increase in importance, the ideal comedy crosses the boundary line of spectacular drama and becomes the masque. In Shakespeare's ideal comedies, especially *A Midsummer Night's Dream* and *The Tempest*, the close affinity with the masque is not hard to see. The masque—or at least the kind of masque that is nearest to comedy, and which we shall here call the ideal masque—is still in the area of *dianoia*: it is usually a compliment to the audience, or an important member of it, and leads up to an idealization of the society represented by that audience. Its plots and characters are fairly stock, as they exist only in relation to the significance of the occasion.

It thus differs from comedy in its more intimate attitude to the audience: there is more insistence on the connection between the audience and the community on the stage. The members of a masque are ordinarily disguised members of the audience, and there is a final gesture of surrender when the actors unmask and join the audience in a dance. The ideal masque is in fact a myth-play like the *auto*, to which it is related much as comedy is to tragedy. It is designed to emphasize, not the ideals to be achieved by discipline or faith, but ideals which are desired or considered to be already possessed. Its settings are seldom remote from magic and fairyland, from Arcadias and visions of earthly Paradise. It uses gods freely, like the *auto*, but possessively, and without imaginative subjection. In Western drama, from the Renaissance to the end of the eighteenth century, masque and ideal comedy make great use of Classical mythology, which the audience is not obliged to accept as "true."

The rather limited masque throws some light on the structure and characteristics of its two far more important and versatile neighbors. For the masque is flanked on one side by the musically organized drama which we call opera, and on the other by a scenically organized drama, which has now settled in the movie. Puppet-plays and the vast Chinese romances where, as in the movie, the audience enters and leaves unpredictably, are examples of pre-camera scenic masques. Both opera and movie are, like the masque, proverbial for lavish display, and part of the reason for it in the movie is that many movies are actually bourgeois myth-plays, as half a dozen critics suddenly and almost simultaneously discovered a few years ago. The predominance of the private life of the actor in the imaginations of many moviegoers may perhaps have some analogy with the consciously assumed disguise of the masque.

Opera and movie possess, unlike the masque, the power of producing spectacular imitations of mimetic drama. The opera can only do this by simplifying its musical organization, otherwise its dramatic structure will be blurred by the distortion of acting which the highly repetitive structure of music makes necessary. The movie similarly must simplify its spectacle. In proportion as it follows its natural bent for scenic organization, the movie reveals its affinities with other forms of scenic masque: with the puppet-play in Chaplin and others, with the commedia dell' arte in recent Italian films, with the ballet and pantomime in musical comedies. When the movie succeeds in imitating a mimetic drama, the distinction between the two forms is not worth making, but the generic difference shows itself in other ways. Mimetic drama works towards an end which illuminates, by being logically connected with, the beginning: hence the parabola shape of the typical five-act mimetic structure, and hence the teleological quality in drama expressed by the term discovery. Spectacular drama, on the other hand, is by nature processional, and tends to episodic and piecemeal discovery, as we can see in all forms of pure spectacle, from the circus parade to the revue. In the *auto* too, on the other side of spectacular drama, the same processional structure appears in the long continued stories of Shakespearean history and scriptural pageant. In the rotating performance and casual attendance of the movie, and the sequence of arias forcibly linked to dramatic structure by recitative in the opera, one can see the strong native tendency to linear movement in spectacular forms. In Shakespeare's first experimental romance, *Pericles*, the movement toward processional structure, a sequence of scenes "dispersedly in various countries," is very clear.

The essential feature of the ideal masque is the exaltation of the audience, who form the goal of its procession. In the *auto*, drama is at its most objective; the audience's part is to accept the story without judgement. In tragedy there is judgement, but the source of the tragic discovery is on the other side of the stage; and whatever it is, it is stronger than the audience. In the ironic play, audience and drama confront each other directly; in the comedy the source of the discovery has moved across to the audience itself. The ideal masque places the audience in a position of superiority to discovery. The verbal action of *Figaro* is comic and that of *Don Giovanni* tragic; but in both cases the audience is exalted by the music above the reach of tragedy and comedy, and, though as profoundly moved as ever, is not emotionally involved with the discovery of plot or characters. It looks at the downfall of Don Juan as spectacular entertainment, much as the gods are supposed to look at the downfall of Ajax or Darius. The same sense of viewing the dramatic mimesis through a haze of spectacular exhilaration is also of central importance in the movie, as it is even more obviously in the puppet-play from which the movie is chiefly descended. We move from ironic to ideal comedy through the symposium, and we note that at the conclusion of Plato's *Symposium* the prophecy is made that the same poet should be able to write both tragedy and comedy, though the ones who have done so most successfully are those who, like Shakespeare and Mozart, have had a strong interest in spectacular forms.

For our next step we must return to the masque proper. The further comedy moves from irony, the less social power is allowed to the humors. In the masque, where the ideal society is still more in the ascendant, the humors become degraded into the uncouth figures of the Jonsonian antimasque, who are said to be descended from a dramatic form far older than the rest of the masque. Farce, being a non-mimetic form of comedy, has a natural place in the masque, though in the ideal masque its natural place is that of a rigorously controlled interlude. In *The Tempest*, a comedy so profound that it seems to draw the whole masque into itself, Stephano and Trinculo are comic humors and Caliban an antimasque figure, and the group shows the transition very clearly. The main theme of the masque involves gods, fairies, and personifications of virtues; the figures of the antimasque thus tend to become demonic, and dramatic characterization begins to split into an antithesis of virtue and vice, god and devil, fairy and monster. The tension between them partly accounts for the importance of the theme of magic in the masque. At the comic end this magic is held by the benevolent side, as in *The Tempest*; but as we move further away from comedy, the conflict becomes increasingly serious, and the antimasque figures less ridiculous and more sinister, possessed in their turn of powers of enchantment. This is the stage represented by *Comus*, which is very close to the open conflict of good and evil in the morality play. With the morality play we pass into another area of masque which we shall here call the archetypal masque, the prevailing form of most twentieth-century highbrow drama, at least in continental Europe, as well as of many experimental operas and unpopular movies.

The ideal masque tends to individualize its audience by pointing to the central member of it: even the movie audience, sitting in the dark in small units (usually of two), is a relatively individualized one. A growing sense of loneliness is noticeable as we move away from comedy. The archetypal masque, like all forms of spectacular drama, tends to detach its settings from time and space, but instead of the Arcadias of the ideal masque, we find ourselves frequently in a sinister limbo, like the threshold of death in *Everyman*, the sealed underworld crypts of Maeterlinck, or the nightmares of the future in expressionist plays. As we get nearer the rationale of the form, we see that the *auto* symbol of communion in one body is reappearing, but in a psychological and subjective form, and without gods. The action of the archetypal masque takes place in a world of human types, which at its most concentrated becomes the interior of the human mind. This is explicit even in the old moralities, like *Mankynd* and *The Castell of Perseveraunce*, and at least implicit in a good deal of Maeterlinck, Pirandello, Andreyev, and Strindberg.

Naturally, with such a setting, characterization has to break down into elements and fragments of personality. This is why I call the form the archetypal masque, the word archetype being in this context used in Jung's sense of an aspect of the personality capable of dramatic projection. Jung's persona and anima and counsellor and shadow throw a great deal of light on the characterization of modern allegorical, psychic, and expressionist dramas, with their circus barkers and wraith-like females and inscrutable sages and obsessed demons. The abstract entities of the morality play and the stock types of the commedia dell' arte (this latter representing one of the primitive roots of the genre) are similar constructions.

A sense of confusion and fear accompanies the sense of loneliness: Maeterlinck's early plays are almost dedicated to fear, and the constant undermining of the distinction between illusion and reality, as mental projections become physical bodies and vice versa, splits the action up into a kaleidoscopic chaos of reflecting mirrors. The mob scenes of German expressionist plays and the mechanical fantasies of the Capeks show the same disintegration at work in a social context. From the generic point of view, one of the most interesting archetypal plays is Andreyev's powerful *The Black Maskers*, in which its author saw reflected not only the destruction of an individual's *nobile castello*, which is its explicit theme, but the whole social collapse of modern Russia. This play distinguishes two groups of dissociative elements of personality, one group connected with self-accusation and the other with the death-wish, and it exhibits the human soul as a castle possessed by a legion of demons. It is evident that the further the archetypal masque gets from the ideal masque, the more clearly it reveals itself as the emancipated antimasque, a revel of satyrs who have got out of control. The progress of sophisticated drama appears to be towards an *anagnorisis* or recognition of the most primitive of all dramatic forms.

At the far end of the archetypal masque, where it joins the *auto*, we reach the point indicated by Nietzsche as the point of the birth of tragedy, where the revel of satyrs impinges on the appearance of a commanding god, and Dionysos is brought into line with Apollo. We may call this fourth cardinal point of drama the epiphany, the dramatic apocalypse or separation of the divine and the demonic, a point directly opposite the mime, which presents the simply human mixture. This point is the dramatic form of the point of epiphany, most familiar as the point at which the Book of Job, after describing a complete circuit from tragedy through symposium, finally ends. Here the two monsters behemoth and leviathan replace the more frequent demonic animals.

The Classical critics, from Aristotle to Horace, were puzzled to understand why a disorganized ribald farce like the satyr-play should be the source of tragedy, though they were clear that it was. In medieval drama, where the progression through sacred and heroic *auto* to tragedy is so much less foreshortened, the development is plainer. The most clearly epiphanic form of scriptural drama is the Harrowing of Hell play, which depicts the triumph of a divine redeemer over demonic resistance. The devils of that play are the Christian forms of figures very like the Greek satyrs, and dramatic groups generically very close to the satyrs are never far from any scriptural play that deals directly with Christ, whether tamed and awed as in the *Secunda Pastorum*, or triumphantly villainous, as in the crucifixion and Herod plays. And just as Greek tragedy retained and developed the satyr-play, so Elizabethan tragedy retains a satyric counterpoint in its clown scenes and the farcical underplots of *Faustus* and many later tragedies. The same element provides those superb episodes of the porter in *Macbeth*, the grave-diggers in *Hamlet*, and the serpent-bearer in *Antony and Cleopatra*, which so baffled Classically-minded critics who had forgotten about the satyr-play. Perhaps we could make more dramatic sense out of *Titus Andronicus* if we could see it as an unharrowed hell, a satyr-play of obscene and gibbering demons.

The two nodes of the scriptural play are Christmas and Easter: the latter presents the triumphant god, the former the quiet virgin mother who gathers to herself the processional masque of the kings and shepherds. This figure is at the opposite end of the masque from the watching queen or peeress of an ideal masque, with the virtuous but paralyzed Lady of *Comus* halfway between.

A female figure symbolizing some kind of reconciling unity and order appears dimly at the end of the great panoramic masques of *Faust* and *Peer Gynt*, the "eternal feminine" of the former having some of its traditional links. Modern examples of the same epiphanic form range from Claudel's Annunciation play to Yeats's *Countess Cathleen*, where the heroine is really a female and Irish Jesus, sacrificing herself for her people and then cheating the devils by the purity of her nature, very much as in the pre-Anselm theory of the atonement. As Yeats remarks in a note, the story represents one of the supreme parables of the world.

SPECIFIC THEMATIC FORMS (LYRIC AND EPOS)

We said that the drama was an external and the lyric an internal mimesis of sound and imagery, both genres avoiding the mimesis of direct address. Again, in the terms of our first essay, drama tends to be a fictional and lyric a thematic mode. We found it most convenient to survey the specific forms of drama as a cycle of fictions, and this gave us a rough but possibly useful classification of the species of drama as well. We propose now to make a survey of a corresponding cycle of themes, and apply the survey to the lyric, along with such *epos* forms, including oratorical prose, as are sufficiently thematic or close to the lyric to belong here. Purely narrative poems, being fictions, will, if episodic, correspond to the species of drama; if continuous, to the species of prose fiction to be examined later.

The lyric, however, can obviously be on any subject and of any shape. It is not conventionalized by its audience, like the drama, or by a fixed radical of presentation, such as the drama has in the theatre. Consequently this survey will not give, and is not intended to give, a classification of specific forms of lyric: what it attempts to give is an account of the chief conventional themes of lyric and *epos*. Once more, the object is not to "fit" poems into categories, but to show empirically how conventional archetypes get embodied in conventional genres.

Let us start with the oracular associative process that we identified as one of the initiatives of lyric, and which corresponds to what we called the epiphany in drama. One of the most direct products of this is a type of religious poetry marked by a concentration of sound and ambiguity of sense, of which the most familiar modern example is the poetry of Hopkins. In religious poetry with elaborate stanzaic patterns, such as the *Pearl* and many poems of Herbert, we realize that the discipline of finding rhymes and arranging words in intricate patterns is appropriate to the sense of chastened wit, a type of *sacrificium intellectus*, that goes with the form. Such intricate verbal patterns go back through the acrostics of Aldhelm at the very beginning of poetry in England to the Hebrew psalms themselves.

We notice that a good deal of sacred literature is written in a style full of puns and verbal echoes, in which the distinction in rhythm between verse and prose is often hard to feel consistently. The English translations of the Bible, especially the 1611, preserve this oracular prose-verse rhythm admirably; the Hebrew puns of course are another matter. The curious sing-song chant of the Koran is a very pure example of oracular style, and the poetic ambiguities of the Classical oracles are in the same convention. Such features survive vestigially throughout religious poetry: in English from Anglo-Saxon times to the opening of the fifth section of *Ash Wednesday*. From what has been said it is clear that the oracle is the germ or growing point of an oratorical prose rhythm as well. The most obvious result of this is prayer, and prayer seems to require a rhetoric of parataxis, short phrases strung together in a rhythm close to free verse.

In the more public type of religious lyric represented by the Apollonian paean, the Hebrew psalm, the Christian hymn, or the Hindu Vedas, the rhythms become more stately, simple, and dignified, the "I" of the poem is one of a visible community of worshippers, and the syntax and diction become less ambiguous. Here the emphasis is usually thrown on the objectivity and ascendancy of the god, and the lyric reflects the sense of an external and social discipline.

The narrative *epos* form corresponding to the psalm or hymn presents a more connected account of the god. This myth has two main parts: legend, recounting the god's biography or his former dealings with his people; and the description of the ritual he requires. Often the first leads up to, and provides an explanation for, the second. The Homeric hymns are largely concerned with legend; the Vedic hymns tend to subordinate the past legend to the present ritual. One may compare the "P" narrative of creation with which the Bible opens, and which, in the strophic form given it by the seven days of creation, has many of the characteristics of a hymn: here the account of creation has the establishing of the Sabbath as its climax. In contrast to the more rhapsodic or dithyrambic forms that we shall deal with later, the desire of the worshipper in the paean or psalm is not so much to be identified *with* his god as to be identified *as* his worshipper.

Closely related to the hymn is the panegyrical ode to a human representative of deity, whether hero or king. In some of the Hebrew psalms, notably the 45th, the king is the intermediary figure out of which the Messiah, the son of David who reaches the extreme both of exaltation and of suffering for his people, develops. In Greek literature, the Pindaric ode focusses on the victorious athlete who, though a human figure, has the ritual link with deity brought out by the mythology and legend incorporated into the ode. In Roman times the honors paid to the Emperor and the state provided another focus for mythological panegyric, which continues in the fourth eclogue of Virgil, the first of Calpurnius, and the *Carmen Saeculare* of Horace. Later the chief form of panegyric becomes the poem in praise of the Courtly Love mistress. The panegyric is also one of the rhetorical prose forms, not one with a very impressive literary record when its subject is a human being, but capable of some flexibility in more impersonal directions. Prose panegyrics of virtues or aspects of culture, notably poetry, appear from time to time, often in the quasi-legal aspect of the apology or defence. In poetry itself we have such forms as the St. Cecilia ode, the panegyric of music. The epithalamium, the triumph, and similar poems of festivity or procession are also species of panegyric. As it is naturally a public convention, the panegyric is often in an extended form which combines both lyric and *epos* characteristics.

In the panegyric the poet invites his reader to gaze with him at something else. If this something else is not visibly present, we have the poem of community, such as we get in patriotic verse of all kinds. The poem of community brings us to the next cardinal point of the lyric, defined earlier as the charm or response to some kind of physical or quasi-physical compulsion—perhaps propulsion is the word. One's education in this type of charm begins with nursery rhymes, where the infant is swung or bounced to the rhythm, or where the theme includes some form of affectionate assault on the child. It continues through college yells, sing-songs, and similar forms of *participation mystique*. The national anthem is another form which illustrates the close relationship to the poem of community. In earlier societies we find work songs in peace and battle songs in war, both with the same characteristics. Of *epos* developments, the best known is the ballad, many features of which, such as incremental repetition and the demand for attention with which it often begins, are so close to the poem of community as to have led some scholars to believe that its origin was in communal composition. The cardinal point of oratorical prose corresponding to the charm is the commandment or exhortation, and of the longer prose forms founded on the exhortation the most highly developed in Western literature is the sermon. Other forms will be mentioned later.

Participation mystique is essentially spasmodic: in primitive communities it may be sustained for hours by dance, and in decadent ones by oratory, but in a state of culture it falls into the background. For literature, the disappearance of the visible presence of panegyric usually means the invisible presence of death. With the panegyrical funeral ode we move from the conventions corresponding to the dramatic *auto* to those corresponding to tragedy. Here we meet first of all the elegy or threnody on the death of a hero, friend, leader or mistress. Threnodies also show a strong tendency to mythological expansion: the subject is not only idealized but often exalted into a nature-spirit or dying god. The pastoral elegy, which traditionally identifies its subject with Adonis, forms the conventional center of the threnody. Some of Wordsworth's Lucy poems indicate the capacity of even a very brief and simple elegy to absorb such imagery. The corresponding form in oratorical prose is the *oraison funèbre*, which survives in some forms of modern obituary: here, as is natural for a prose medium, mythological expansion is less marked, and is often replaced by doctrinal or conceptual expansion. A rare and difficult *epos* form, the tragic panegyric, in which a hero is presented as a tragic figure as well as a conquering hero, is represented by Marvell's ode on Cromwell and by its prototype, the Regulus ode of Horace.

We come to a more isolated form of elegy in the convention of the epitaph, in which the whole shape of a life is frequently indicated. Epitaphs may vary in tone from the panegyrical to the ribald, but even in the Greek Anthology they retain something of their original function as markers, as something visibly set up to arrest the passer-by and compel him to read. The corresponding *epos* form is the historical epitaph, the meditation over a vanished past which has the same relation to the ruin that the individual epitaph has to the gravestone. In prose there is the rhetorical elegiac meditation represented in English by Browne's *Urn Burial*.

Still closer to irony is the complaint, the poem of exile, neglect or protest at cruelty. Here the individual demanding attention, unlike the corpse in the epitaph, is able to speak for himself, and is of course usually represented as the poet himself. This theme takes up most of the Courtly Love convention, where the central archetype is the scornful and unrelenting mistress. Such a figure is an ironic reversal of the original form of pastoral elegy. The most logical person to lament the death of Adonis is Venus, though she seldom does so in literature unless that specific myth is the theme; but in most Courtly Love poetry the mistress is responsible for all the lover's sufferings, including his death. We shall meet this ambivalent female figure later in the essay. The complaint is easily extended into *epos* forms, including narrative tragedies in which the emotional focus is not the catastrophe but the lament following the catastrophe, as in the two narrative poems of Shakespeare.

The phase of tragic irony is represented by the poem of melancholy in its extreme form of accidia or ennui, where the individual is so isolated as to feel his existence a living death. In Baudelaire's *géante* the scornful mistress takes on a more deeply sinister tone, and the theme of death is presented in terms of simple physical dissolution: "earth upon earth," as a medieval poem has it. The appropriate *epos* form of this phase is the *danse macabre*, the poem of the dying community.

Our next cardinal point is difficult to name: we might almost parody Hopkins's term and call it the poem of "outscape." It is the lyrical counterpart of what in drama we call the mime, the center of the irony which is common to tragedy and comedy. It is a convention of pure projected detachment, in which an image, a situation, or a mood is observed with all the imaginative energy thrown outward to it and away from the poet. The word epigram in its broadest sense defines some of its characteristics, except that epigram as ordinarily used leans strongly in the direction of comedy and satire. The lyrical poetry of China and Japan appears to be based very largely on this convention, in striking contrast to Western poetry, where epigram shows much more of a tendency to attach emotions or make out a rhetorical case. Some of Shakespeare's sonnets, such as "The expense of spirit in a waste of shame," are exceptions.

The corresponding cardinal point of prose is the proverb or aphorism, the germ of such forms as the wisdom literature of the Bible. Here we are close to the counsel-of-prudence type of satire, and at the opposite pole from the oracle. The proverb is a secular or purely human oracle: it usually has the same rhetorical features, alliteration, assonance, parallelism, that we find in the oracle, but it is addressed to the detached consciousness and the critical wit. Its authority comes from experience: for it, wisdom is the tried and tested way; only folly seeks what is new, and the essential virtues are prudence and moderation. The proverbs in Blake's *Marriage of Heaven and Hell* are parody-proverbs, written from the oracular or epiphanic point of view.

As we move into the conventions of satire, either in the lyric forms of Hardy and Housman or the *epos* form of Dryden and Pope, the features of epigram and proverb persist. Such poets produce brilliance and clarity rather than mystery or magic, and their technique is concerned with concentration of sense. Two things are essential to this: one is a tight metrical framework of words stepping along in a sharply outlined order; the other is a clear statement of what sound-patterns we may expect, such as the full ring of the rhyming couplet. Additional or unexpected sound-patterns, such as alliteration or assonance within the line, are kept to a minimum, and the poetry follows Wordsworth's precept in being, except for the metre, very like non-rhetorical prose in its diction. The *epos* and prose forms of this phase, such as the epistle and the formal satire, are naturally very close together.

In satire observation is still primary, but as the observed phenomena move from the sinister to the grotesque, they grow more illusory and unsubstantial. We note among *epos* forms a comic counterpart of the *danse macabre*: the "testament" poem, of which the best known English example is Swift's poem on his death. Closely related to the testament convention are Donne's Anniversaries, where the death of a girl expands into a general satire or "anatomy"—this term will also meet us later.

We are now in the area corresponding to comedy, and still within the vision of experience. The convention that marks a slight removal from satire is the poem of paradox, i.e., the poem in which some form of paradox is the theme and not simply an incidental feature of the technique. Naturally we find many of this type in the "metaphysical" poetry which makes a regular use of a deliberately forced and consequently humorous conceit. Donne and Herbert provide examples, and so does Emily Dickinson. The paradox is among other things often a paradox of feeling as well, so that we are sometimes in doubt whether to "take" the poem seriously or humorously. The paradox poem belongs in the comedy of experience, near satire, because paradox in poetry is usually an ironic treatment of quixotic love or religion, like the stylized Petrarchan code of which Donne remarks "May barren angels love so," or the vaunting virtue that ignominiously collapses into human nature in some poems of Herbert. Another paradoxical treatment of the Courtly Love convention is the pastourelle, or deadlocked love dialogue. A closely related *epos* form, recalling the association of comedy with law courts, is the debate, in which two sides of a question are argued at length and then submitted to an umpire, who often postpones or puts off the decision. Examples include *The Owl and the Nightingale*, Chaucer's *Parliament of Fowls*, and Spenser's Mutability Cantos.

A less ambiguous form of lyrical comedy is represented by the *carpe diem* poem based on a moment of pleasure in experience. The mood of such a poem is one of detachment, both subjective and objective. The poet is usually, even when drunk, in full conscious control, and the moment of pleasure itself is detached from time. Most unqualified poems of joy are associated with some kind of innocent vision, as in Blake: the great Epicurean poets, from Horace to Herrick, accept the limitations of joy in experience, its transience in an abyss of "endless night." Even in Herrick there are many features, such as the love of folklore and the imagery of clothes, jewels and perfumes, which indicate an affinity with masque rather than comedy. The limits of ordinary experience in lyrical comedy are reached by the poem of the quiet mind, the triumphant *eiron* or "settled low content," the serenity which adjusts itself to experience and renounces the emotionally quixotic. Wordsworth's formula of tranquil recollection marks his tendency to remain within the state of experience, in contrast to most Romantics. The *epos* expression of serenity is frequently the descriptive poem, where the poet climbs a hill and surveys a landscape below, an imitation in experience of the point of epiphany. The poem of the quiet mind, if it has a subject beyond recommending itself, attempts to communicate to the reader a private and secret possession, which brings us to the next cardinal point, the riddle.

The idea of the riddle is descriptive containment: the subject is not described but circumscribed, a circle of words drawn around it. In simple riddles, the central subject is an image, and the reader feels impelled to guess, that is, to equate the poem to the name or sign-symbol of its image. A slightly more complicated form of riddle is the emblematic vision, probably one of the oldest forms of human communication, where an example will be briefer than description:

And the Lord said unto me, Amos, what seest thou? And I said, A plumbline. Then said the Lord, Behold, I will set a plumbline in the midst of my people Israel.

Other prophets are represented as carrying symbolic apparatus around with them, like Diogenes' lantern, a rhetorical device surviving as late as Burke's dagger. Literary developments of the same form include the emblem itself, to the tradition of which Blake's tiger and sunflower and sick rose belong, and such pictorial conceit-poems as Herbert's *Pulley*. The connection of the emblematic vision with the heraldic image of modern fiction is easy to see. In *symbolisme* we have a third form of riddle where it is normally a mood rather than an object that is contained. Here, too, as usually happens in sophisticated developments, simpler elements in the same tradition survive vestigially, like the riddling "ptyx" in Mallarmé.

The riddle and emblematic vision are closely related to the corresponding cardinal point of prose, which is the parable or fable, both of which are of course *epos* forms as well. The fable is the simpler of the two forms, and nearer the simple riddle, the providing of the moral in the fable being the counterpart of guessing the riddle. The parable is a more highly developed form with a greater tendency to contain its own moral. In the fable, mythical stylizing (talking animals and the like) is a regular feature of the narrative; in the parable the stylizing is less obvious. Of the parables of Jesus, only the parable of the sheep and goats, which is an apocalypse, makes much use of material outside the realistic range of credibility.

In Herrick's poems on primroses and daffodils we are still very close to the fable and emblem tradition: so close that there is no incongruity in "reading a lecture" from the primroses. Nevertheless Herrick's daffodils, unlike Wordsworth's, are directly confronted, and the confronted image readily becomes personified. Here we are in the area corresponding to the masque in drama, and the innocent vision and the fairyland of animistic romance return. The poem of imaginative confrontation, where a close connection between the poet's mood and the imagery is expressed by the personifying of the imagery, is the genre of the Keats ode, the Grecian Urn being the nearest to the emblem poem. The next step takes us into the pastoral, where we come back to the mode of romance mentioned in the first essay, pity and terror becoming modes of pleasure, usually the beautiful and the sublime respectively. These are generally thought of as a contrast, as they are in Milton's wonderful diptych of idyllic and pensive moods, but occasionally, as in some of the "green" poems of Marvell, we have a poetry of absorption so complete that the two moods seem blended into one.

But when the vision of innocence becomes unified, the contrasting vision of experience often reappears, in a convention that we might call the poem of expanded consciousness, where the poet balances the catharsis of his view of experience with the ecstasis of his view of a spiritual, invisible, or imaginative world. Here, as in the corresponding forms of drama, we have not a direct mimesis of life but a spectacular mimesis of it, able to look down on experience because of the simultaneous presence of another kind of vision. In drama this spectacular mimesis is attained by the help of music as well as spectacle. Music and painting cannot express the tragic or comic, which are verbal conceptions only: they express moods which we may fit to tragedy or comedy if we have some literary program ready for them. In our day the most impressive examples of the poem of expanded consciousness are the Eliot quartets and the Duino elegies of Rilke, and the musical references of the one and the pictorial images of the other express the close affinity of the genre with arts which, much more obviously than poetry, do not speak.

The next convention we might call the recognition poem, the poem which reverses the usual associations of dream and waking, so that it is experience that seems to be the nightmare and the vision that seems to be reality. The *epos* form of this convention includes the medieval love vision, where we have again a *spectacle* of a direct personal relation, attained by being placed in an extraordinary world. Of lyrical forms, a very pure modern example, generically speaking, is Eliot's *Marina*, which is close to the corresponding dramatic forms. Many of Rilke's Orpheus sonnets belong to it; it is also the central convention of Vaughan and Traherne. This theme is rare and difficult to handle in the rhythm of prose, but we have it in the *Centuries of Meditation*, especially the famous "The corn was orient and immortal wheat" passage.

A very important group of recognition poems are the poems of self-recognition, where the poet himself is involved in the awakening from experience into a visionary reality. Examples include Collins's *Ode on the Poetical Character*, Coleridge's *Kubla Khan*, and Yeats's *Tower* and *Sailing to Byzantium*. This genre is near the boundary line of our next and last group of themes, which bring us back to the oracle again. These are the dithyrambic or rhapsodic forms, where the poet feels taken possession of by some internal and quasi-personal force. Nearest the poem of recognition is the poem of iconic response, such as we have in some of the odes of Crashaw; in Romantic times a more subjective and dithyrambic form became very popular. Shelley's *Ode to the West Wind*, a good deal of Swinburne, of Victor Hugo, of Nietzsche (who makes the curious statement that he invented the dithyramb), of Blake's prophecies, especially the ninth night of *The Four Zoas*, and the two great poems of Smart, are examples. Most of these are *epos* forms: the dithyrambic lends itself readily to recurring metre. Of lyric forms, we may note the convention of the mad song, which we have in Edgar's songs in *King Lear*, in Yeats's Crazy Jane poems, and sporadically in a few other poets, including Scott. As the singer of a mad song is usually a vagrant, he suggests a closer rapport with mysterious beings and forces, such as nature-spirits, than normal people have. On a more sophisticated level, where the poet suggests the breaking of autonomous visions into his own mind, the *illuminations* of Rimbaud may be mentioned.

As we come nearer to the oracular rhythm with which we began, the rhythms of verse and prose begin to merge once more. We notice in Whitman, for example, that there is a strong pause at the end of every line—naturally enough, for where the rhythm is irregular there is no point in a run-on line. The rhythm is approaching a form in which the lyrical associative rhythm, the *epos* line and the prose sentence are becoming much the same unit, a tendency that we can observe in dithyrambic poetry as naive as Ossian's or as sophisticated as the modern French developments of it that follow the *Saison en Enfer*.

SPECIFIC CONTINUOUS FORMS
(PROSE FICTION)

In assigning the term fiction to the genre of the written word, in which prose tends to become the predominating rhythm, we collide with the view that the real meaning of fiction is falsehood or unreality. Thus an autobiography coming into a library would be classified as non-fiction if the librarian believed the author, and as fiction if she thought he was lying. It is difficult to see what use such a distinction can be to a literary critic. Surely the word fiction, which, like poetry, means etymologically something made for its own sake, could be applied in criticism to any work of literary art in a radically continuous form, which almost always means a work of art in prose. Or, if that is too much to ask, at least some protest can be entered against the sloppy habit of identifying fiction with the one genuine form of fiction which we know as the novel.

Let us look at a few of the unclassified books lying on the boundary of "non-fiction" and "literature." Is *Tristram Shandy* a novel? Nearly everyone would say yes, in spite of its easygoing disregard of "story values." Is *Gulliver's Travels* a novel? Here most would demur, including the Dewey decimal system, which puts it under "Satire and Humor." But surely everyone would call it fiction, and if it is fiction, a distinction appears between fiction as a genus and the novel as a species of that genus. Shifting the ground to fiction, then, is *Sartor Resartus* fiction? If not, why not? If it is, is *The Anatomy of Melancholy* fiction? Is it a literary form or only a work of "non-fiction" written with "style"? Is Borrow's *Lavengro* fiction? Everyman's Library says yes; the World's Classics puts it under "Travel and Topography."

The literary historian who identifies fiction with the novel is greatly embarrassed by the length of time that the world managed to get along without the novel, and until he reaches his great deliverance in Defoe, his perspective is intolerably cramped. He is compelled to reduce Tudor fiction to a series of tentative essays in the novel form, which works well enough for Deloney but makes nonsense of Sidney. He postulates a great fictional gap in the seventeenth century which exactly covers the golden age of rhetorical prose. He finally discovers that the word novel, which up to about 1900 was still the name of a more or less recognizable form, has since expanded into a catchall term which can be applied to practically any prose book that is not "on" something. Clearly, this novel-centered view of prose fiction is a Ptolemaic perspective which is now too complicated to be any longer workable, and some more relative and Copernican view must take its place.

When we start to think seriously about the novel, not as fiction, but as a form of fiction, we feel that its characteristics, whatever they are, are such as make, say, Defoe, Fielding, Austen, and James central in its tradition, and Borrow, Peacock, Melville, and Emily Bronte somehow peripheral. This is not an estimate of merit: we may think *Moby Dick* "greater" than *The Egoist* and yet feel that Meredith's book is closer to being a typical novel. Fielding's conception of the novel as a comic epic in prose seems fundamental to the tradition he did so much to establish. In novels that we think of as typical, like those of Jane Austen, plot and dialogue are closely linked to the conventions of the comedy of manners. The conventions of *Wuthering Heights* are linked rather with the tale and the ballad. They seem to have more affinity with tragedy, and the tragic emotions of passion and fury, which would shatter the balance of tone in Jane Austen, can be safely accommodated here. So can the supernatural, or the suggestion of it, which is difficult to get into a novel. The shape of the plot is different: instead of manoeuvering around a central situation, as Jane Austen does, Emily Bronte tells her story with linear accents, and she seems to need the help of a narrator, who would be absurdly out of place in Jane Austen. Conventions so different justify us in regarding *Wuthering Heights* as a different form of prose fiction from the novel, a form which we shall here call the romance. Here again we have to use the same word in several different contexts, but romance seems on the whole better than tale, which appears to fit a somewhat shorter form.

The essential difference between novel and romance lies in the conception of characterization. The romancer does not attempt to create "real people" so much as stylized figures which expand into psychological archetypes. It is in the romance that we find Jung's libido, anima, and shadow reflected in the hero, heroine, and villain respectively. That is why the romance so often radiates a glow of subjective intensity that the novel lacks, and why a suggestion of allegory is constantly creeping in around its fringes. Certain elements of character are released in the romance which make it naturally a more revolutionary form than the novel. The novelist deals with personality, with characters wearing their *personae* or social masks. He needs the framework of a stable society, and many of our best novelists have been conventional to the verge of fussiness. The romancer deals with individuality, with characters *in vacuo* idealized by revery, and, however conservative he may be, something nihilistic and untamable is likely to keep breaking out of his pages.

The prose romance, then, is an independent form of fiction to be distinguished from the novel and extracted from the miscellaneous heap of prose works now covered by that term. Even in the other heap known as short stories one can isolate the tale form used by Poe, which bears the same relation to the full romance that the stories of Chekhov or Katherine Mansfield do to the novel. "Pure" examples of either form are never found; there is hardly any modern romance that could not be made out to be a novel, and vice versa. The forms of prose fiction are mixed, like racial strains in human beings, not separable like the sexes. In fact the popular demand in fiction is always for a mixed form, a romantic novel just romantic enough for the reader to project his libido on the hero and his anima on the heroine, and just novel enough to keep these projections in a familiar world. It may be asked, therefore, what is the use of making the above distinction, especially when, though undeveloped in criticism, it is by no means unrealized. It is no surprise to hear that Trollope wrote novels and William Morris romances.

The reason is that a great romancer should be examined in terms of the conventions he chose. William Morris should not be left on the side lines of prose fiction merely because the critic has not learned to take the romance form seriously. Nor, in view of what has been said about the revolutionary nature of the romance, should his choice of that form be regarded as an "escape" from his social attitude. If Scott has any claims to be a romancer, it is not good criticism to deal only with his defects as a novelist. The romantic qualities of *The Pilgrim's Progress*, too, its archetypal characterization and its revolutionary approach to religious experience, make it a well-rounded example of a literary form: it is not merely a book swallowed by English literature to get some religious bulk in its diet. Finally, when Hawthorne, in the preface to *The House of the Seven Gables,* insists that his story should be read as romance and not as novel, it is possible that he meant what he said, even though he indicates that the prestige of the rival form has induced the romancer to apologize for not using it.

Romance is older than the novel, a fact which has developed the historical illusion that it is something to be outgrown, a juvenile and undeveloped form. The social affinities of the romance, with its grave idealizing of heroism and purity, are with the aristocracy (for the apparent inconsistency of this with the revolutionary nature of the form just mentioned, see the introductory comment on the *mythos* of romance in the previous essay). It revived in the period we call Romantic as part of the Romantic tendency to archaic feudalism and a cult of the hero, or idealized libido. In England the romances of Scott and, in less degree, the Brontes, are part of a mysterious Northumbrian renaissance, a Romantic reaction against the new industrialism in the Midlands, which also produced the poetry of Wordsworth and Burns and the philosophy of Carlyle. It is not surprising, therefore, that an important theme in the more bourgeois novel should be the parody of the romance and its ideals. The tradition established by *Don Quixote* continues in a type of novel which looks at a romantic situation from its own point of view, so that the conventions of the two forms make up an ironic compound instead of a sentimental mixture. Examples range from *Northanger Abbey* to *Madame Bovary* and *Lord Jim.*

The tendency to allegory in the romance may be conscious, as in *The Pilgrim's Progress,* or unconscious, as in the very obvious sexual mythopoeia in William Morris. The romance, which deals with heroes, is intermediate between the novel, which deals with men, and the myth, which deals with gods. Prose romance first appears as a late development of Classical mythology, and the prose Sagas of Iceland follow close on the mythical Eddas. The novel tends rather to expand into a fictional approach to history. The soundness of Fielding's instinct in calling *Tom Jones* a history is confirmed by the general rule that the larger the scheme of a novel becomes, the more obviously its historical nature appears. As it is creative history, however, the novelist usually prefers his material in a plastic, or roughly contemporary state, and feels cramped by a fixed historical pattern. *Waverley* is dated about sixty years back from the time of writing and *Little Dorrit* about forty years, but the historical pattern is fixed in the romance and plastic in the novel, suggesting the general principle that most "historical novels" are romances. Similarly a novel becomes more romantic in its appeal when the life it reflects has passed away: thus the novels of Trollope were read primarily as romances during the Second World War. It is perhaps the link with history and a sense of temporal context that has confined the novel, in striking contrast to the world-wide romance, to the alliance of time and Western man.

Autobiography is another form which merges with the novel by a series of insensible gradations. Most autobiographies are inspired by a creative, and therefore fictional, impulse to select only those events and experiences in the writer's life that go to build up an integrated pattern. This pattern may be something larger than himself with which he has come to identify himself, or simply the coherence of his character and attitudes. We may call this very important form of prose fiction the confession form, following St. Augustine, who appears to have invented it, and Rousseau, who established a modern type of it. The earlier tradition gave *Religio Medici*, *Grace Abounding*, and Newman's *Apologia* to English literature, besides the related but subtly different type of confession favored by the mystics.

Here again, as with the romance, there is some value in recognizing a distinct prose form in the confession. It gives several of our best prose works a definable place in fiction instead of keeping them in a vague limbo of books which are not quite literature because they are "thought," and not quite religion or philosophy because they are Examples of Prose Style. The confession, too, like the novel and the romance, has its own short form, the familiar essay, and Montaigne's *livre de bonne foy* is a confession made up of essays in which only the continuous narrative of the longer form is missing. Montaigne's scheme is to the confession what a work of fiction made up of short stories, such as Joyce's *Dubliners* or Boccaccio's *Decameron*, is to the novel or romance.

After Rousseau—in fact in Rousseau—the confession flows into the novel, and the mixture produces the fictional autobiography, the *Künstler-roman*, and kindred types. There is no literary reason why the subject of a confession should always be the author himself, and dramatic confessions have been used in the novel at least since *Moll Flanders*. The "stream of consciousness" technique permits of a much more concentrated fusion of the two forms, but even here the characteristics peculiar to the confession form show up clearly. Nearly always some theoretical and intellectual interest in religion, politics, or art plays a leading role in the confession. It is his success in integrating his mind on such subjects that makes the author of a confession feel that his life is worth writing about. But this interest in ideas and theoretical statements is alien to the genius of the novel proper, where the technical problem is to dissolve all theory into personal relationships. In Jane Austen, to take a familiar instance, church, state, and culture are never examined except as social data, and Henry James has been described as having a mind so fine that no idea could violate it. The novelist who cannot get along without ideas, or has not the patience to digest them in the way that James did, instinctively resorts to what Mill calls a "mental history" of a single character. And when we find that a technical discussion of a theory of aesthetics forms the climax of Joyce's *Portrait*, we realize that what makes this possible is the presence in that novel of another tradition of prose fiction.

The novel tends to be extroverted and personal; its chief interest is in human character as it manifests itself in society. The romance tends to be introverted and personal: it also deals with characters, but in a more subjective way. (Subjective here refers to treatment, not subject-matter. The characters of romance are heroic and therefore inscrutable; the novelist is freer to enter his characters' minds because he is more objective.) The confession is also introverted, but intellectualized in content. Our next step is evidently to discover a fourth form of fiction which is extroverted and intellectual.

We remarked earlier that most people would call *Gulliver's Travels* fiction but not a novel. It must then be another form of fiction, as it certainly has a form, and we feel that we are turning from the novel to this form, whatever it is, when we turn from Rousseau's *Emile* to Voltaire's *Candide*, or from Butler's *The Way of All Flesh* to the Erewhon books, or from Huxley's *Point Counterpoint* to *Brave New World*. The form thus has its own traditions, and, as the examples of Butler and Huxley show, has preserved some integrity even under the ascendancy of the novel. Its existence is easy enough to demonstrate, and no one will challenge the statement that the literary ancestry of *Gulliver's Travels* and *Candide* runs through Rabelais and Erasmus to Lucian. But while much has been said about the style and thought of Rabelais, Swift, and

Voltaire, very little has been made of them as craftsmen working in a specific medium, a point no one dealing with a novelist would ignore. Another great writer in this tradition, Huxley's master Peacock, has fared even worse, for, his form not being understood, a general impression has grown up that his status in the development of prose fiction is that of a slapdash eccentric. Actually, he is as exquisite and precise an artist in his medium as Jane Austen is in hers.

The form used by these authors is the Menippean satire, also more rarely called the Varronian satire, allegedly invented by a Greek cynic named Menippus. His works are lost, but he had two great disciples, the Greek Lucian and the Roman Varro, and the tradition of Varro, who has not survived either except in fragments, was carried on by Petronius and Apuleius. The Menippean satire appears to have developed out of verse satire through the practice of adding prose interludes, but we know it only as a prose form, though one of its recurrent features (seen in Peacock) is the use of incidental verse.

The Menippean satire deals less with people as such than with mental attitudes. Pedants, bigots, cranks, parvenus, virtuosi, enthusiasts, rapacious and incompetent professional men of all kinds, are handled in terms of their occupational approach to life as distinct from their social behavior. The Menippean satire thus resembles the confession in its ability to handle abstract ideas and theories, and differs from the novel in its characterization, which is stylized rather than naturalistic, and presents people as mouthpieces of the ideas they represent. Here again no sharp boundary lines can or should be drawn, but if we compare a character in Jane Austen with a similar character in Peacock we can immediately feel the difference between the two forms. Squire Western belongs to the novel, but Thwackum and Square have Menippean blood in them. A constant theme in the tradition is the ridicule of the *philosophus gloriosus*, already discussed. The novelist sees evil and folly as social diseases, but the Menippean satirist sees them as diseases of the intellect, as a kind of maddened pedantry which the *philosophus gloriosus* at once symbolizes and defines.

Petronius, Apuleius, Rabelais, Swift, and Voltaire all use a loose-jointed narrative form often confused with the romance. It differs from the romance, however (though there is a strong admixture of romance in Rabelais), as it is not primarily concerned with the ex-

309

ploits of heroes, but relies on the free play of intellectual fancy and the kind of humorous observation that produces caricature. It differs also from the picaresque form, which has the novel's interest in the actual structure of society. At its most concentrated the Menippean satire presents us with a vision of the world in terms of a single intellectual pattern. The intellectual structure built up from the story makes for violent dislocations in the customary logic of narrative, though the appearance of carelessness that results reflects only the carelessness of the reader or his tendency to judge by a novel-centered conception of fiction.

The word "satire," in Roman and Renaissance times, meant either of two specific literary forms of that name, one (this one) prose and the other verse. Now it means a structural principle or attitude, what we have called a *mythos*. In the Menippean satires we have been discussing, the name of the form also applies to the attitude. As the name of an attitude, satire is, we have seen, a combination of fantasy and morality. But as the name of a form, the term satire, though confined to literature (for as a *mythos* it may appear in any art, a cartoon, for example), is more flexible, and can be either entirely fantastic or entirely moral. The Menippean adventure story may thus be pure fantasy, as it is in the literary fairy tale. The Alice books are perfect Menippean satires, and so is *The Water-Babies*, which has been influenced by Rabelais. The purely moral type is a serious vision of society as a single intellectual pattern, in other words a Utopia.

The short form of the Menippean satire is usually a dialogue or colloquy, in which the dramatic interest is in a conflict of ideas rather than of character. This is the favorite form of Erasmus, and is common in Voltaire. Here again the form is not invariably satiric in attitude, but shades off into more purely fanciful or moral discussions, like the *Imaginary Conversations* of Landor or the "dialogue of the dead." Sometimes this form expands to full length, and more than two speakers are used: the setting then is usually a *cena* or symposium, like the one that looms so large in Petronius. Plato, though much earlier in the field than Menippus, is a strong influence on this type, which stretches in an unbroken tradition down through those urbane and leisurely conversations which define the ideal courtier in Castiglione or the doctrine and discipline of angling in Walton. A modern development produces the country-house weekends in Peacock, Huxley, and their imitators in which the opinions and ideas and cultural interests expressed are as important as the love-making.

The novelist shows his exuberance either by an exhaustive analysis of human relationships, as in Henry James, or of social phenomena, as in Tolstoy. The Menippean satirist, dealing with intellectual themes and attitudes, shows his exuberance in intellectual ways, by piling up an enormous mass of erudition about his theme or in overwhelming his pedantic targets with an avalanche of their own jargon. A species, or rather sub-species, of the form is the kind of encyclopaedic farrago represented by Athenaeus' *Deipnosophists* and Macrobius' *Saturnalia*, where people sit at a banquet and pour out a vast mass of erudition on every subject that might conceivably come up in a conversation. The display of erudition had probably been associated with the Menippean tradition by Varro, who was enough of a polymath to make Quintilian, if not stare and gasp, at any rate call him *vir Romanorum eruditissimus*. The tendency to expand into an encyclopaedic farrago is clearly marked in Rabelais, notably in the great catalogues of torcheculs and epithets of codpieces and methods of divination. The encyclopaedic compilations produced in the line of duty by Erasmus and Voltaire suggest that a magpie instinct to collect facts is not unrelated to the type of ability that has made them famous as artists. Flaubert's encyclopaedic approach to the construction of *Bouvard et Pecuchet* is quite comprehensible if we explain it as marking an affinity with the Menippean tradition.

This creative treatment of exhaustive erudition is the organizing principle of the greatest Menippean satire in English before Swift, Burton's *Anatomy of Melancholy*. Here human society is studied in terms of the intellectual pattern provided by the conception of melancholy, a symposium of books replaces dialogue, and the result is the most comprehensive survey of human life in one book that English literature had seen since Chaucer, one of Burton's favorite authors. We may note in passing the Utopia in his introduction and his "digressions," which when examined turn out to be scholarly distillations of Menippean forms: the digression of air, of the marvellous journey; the digression of spirits, of the ironic use of erudition; the digression of the miseries of scholars, of the satire on the *philosophus gloriosus*. The word "anatomy" in Burton's title means a dissection or analysis, and expresses very accurately the intellectualized approach of his form. We may as well adopt it as a

311

convenient name to replace the cumbersome and in modern times rather misleading "Menippean satire."

The anatomy, of course, eventually begins to merge with the novel, producing various hybrids including the *roman à these* and novels in which the characters are symbols of social or other ideas, like the proletarian novels of the thirties in this century. It was Sterne, however, the disciple of Burton and Rabelais, who combined them with greatest success. *Tristram Shandy* may be, as was said at the beginning, a novel, but the digressing narrative, the catalogues, the stylizing of character along "humor" lines, the marvellous journey of the great nose, the symposium discussions, and the constant ridicule of philosophers and pedantic critics are all features that belong to the anatomy.

A clearer understanding of the form and traditions of the anatomy would make a good many elements in the history of literature come into focus. Boethius' *Consolation of Philosophy*, with its dialogue form, its verse interludes and its pervading tone of contemplative irony, is a pure anatomy, a fact of considerable importance for the understanding of its vast influence. *The Compleat Angler* is an anatomy because of its mixture of prose and verse, its rural *cena* setting, its dialogue form, its deipnosophistical interest in food, and its gentle Menippean raillery of a society which considers everything more important than fishing and yet has discovered very few better things to do. In nearly every period of literature there are many romances, confessions, and anatomies that are neglected only because the categories to which they belong are unrecognized. In the period between Sterne and Peacock, for example, we have, among romances, *Melmoth the Wanderer*; among confessions, Hogg's *Confessions of a Justified Sinner*; among anatomies, Southey's *Doctor*, Amory's *John Buncle*, and the *Noctes Ambrosianae*.

To sum up then: when we examine fiction from the point of view of form, we can see four chief strands binding it together, novel, confession, anatomy, and romance. The six possible combinations of these forms all exist, and we have shown how the novel has combined with each of the other three. Exclusive concentration on one form is rare: the early novels of George Eliot, for instance, are influenced by the romance, and the later ones by the anatomy. The romance-confession hybrid is found, naturally, in the autobiography of a romantic temperament, and is represented in English by the extroverted George Borrow and the introverted De Quincey. The romance-anatomy one we have noticed in Rabelais; a later example is *Moby Dick*, where the romantic theme of the wild hunt expands into an encyclopaedic anatomy of the whale. Confession and anatomy are united in *Sartor Resartus* and in some of Kierkegaard's strikingly original experiments in prose fiction form, including *Either/Or*. More comprehensive fictional schemes usually employ at least three forms: we can see strains of novel, romance, and confession in *Pamela*, of novel, romance, and anatomy in *Don Quixote*, of novel, confession, and anatomy in Proust, and of romance, confession, and anatomy in Apuleius.

I deliberately make this sound schematic in order to suggest the advantage of having a simple and logical explanation for the form of, say, *Moby Dick* or *Tristram Shandy*. The usual critical approach to the form of such works resembles that of the doctors in Brobdingnag, who after great wrangling finally pronounced Gulliver a *lusus naturae*. It is the anatomy in particular that has baffled critics, and there is hardly any fiction writer deeply influenced by it who has not been accused of disorderly conduct. The reader may be reminded here of Joyce, for describing Joyce's books as monstrous has become a nervous tic. I find "demogorgon," "behemoth," and "white elephant" in good critics; the bad ones could probably do much better. The care that Joyce took to organize *Ulysses* and *Finnegans Wake* amounted nearly to obsession, but as they are not organized on familiar principles of prose fiction, the impression of shapelessness remains. Let us try our formulas on him.

If a reader were asked to set down a list of the things that had most impressed him about *Ulysses*, it might reasonably be somewhat as follows. First, the clarity with which the sights and sounds and smells of Dublin come to life, the rotundity of the character-drawing, and the naturalness of the dialogue. Second, the elaborate way that the story and characters are parodied by being set against archetypal heroic patterns, notably the one provided by the *Odyssey*. Third, the revelation of character and incident through the searching use of the stream-of-consciousness technique. Fourth, the constant tendency to be encyclopaedic and exhaustive both in technique and in subject matter, and to see both in highly intellectualized terms. It should not be too hard for us by now to see that these four points describe elements in the book which relate to the novel, romance, confession, and anatomy respectively. *Ulysses*, then, is a complete prose epic with all four forms employed in it, all of practically equal importance, and all essential to one another, so that the book is a unity and not an aggregate.

This unity is built up from an intricate scheme of parallel contrasts. The romantic archetypes of Hamlet and Ulysses are like remote stars in a literary heaven looking down quizzically on the shabby creatures of Dublin obediently intertwining themselves in the patterns set by their influences. In the "Cyclops" and "Circe" episodes particularly there is a continuous parody of realistic patterns by romantic ones which reminds us, though the irony leans in the opposite direction, of *Madame Bovary*. The relation of novel and confession techniques is similar; the author jumps into his characters' minds to follow their stream of consciousness, and out again to describe them externally. In the novel-anatomy combination, too, found in the "Ithaca" chapter, the sense of lurking antagonism between the personal and intellectual aspects of the scene accounts for much of its pathos. The same principle of parallel contrast holds good for the other three combinations: of romance and confession in "Nausicaa" and "Penelope," of confession and anatomy in "Proteus" and "The Lotos-Eaters," of romance and anatomy (a rare and fitful combination) in "Sirens" and parts of "Circe."

In *Finnegans Wake* the unity of design goes far beyond this. The dingy story of the sodden HCE and his pinched wife is not contrasted with the archetypes of Tristram and the divine king: HCE is himself Tristram and the divine king. As the setting is a dream, no contrast is possible between confession and novel, between a stream of consciousness inside the mind and the appearances of other people outside it. Nor is the experiential world of the novel to be separated from the intelligible world of the anatomy. The forms we have been isolating in fiction, and which depend for their existence on the commonsense dichotomies of the daylight consciousness, vanish in *Finnegans Wake* into a fifth and quintessential form. This form is the one traditionally associated with scriptures and sacred books, and treats life in terms of the fall and awakening of the human soul and the creation and apocalypse of nature. The Bible is the definitive example of it; the Egyptian Book of the Dead and the Icelandic Prose Edda, both of which have left deep imprints on *Finnegans Wake*, also belong to it.

SPECIFIC ENCYCLOPAEDIC FORMS

We met in the first essay the principle that in every age of literature there tends to be some kind of central encyclopaedic form, which is normally a scripture or sacred book in the mythical mode, and some "analogy of revelation," as we called it, in the other modes. In our culture the central sacred book is the Christian Bible, which is also probably the most systematically constructed sacred book in the world. To say that the Bible is "more" than a work of literature is merely to say that other methods of approaching it are possible. No book could have had its influence on literature without itself having literary qualities, and the Bible is a work of literature as long as it is being examined by a literary critic.

The absence of any genuinely literary criticism of the Bible in modern times (until very recently) has left an enormous gap in our knowledge of literary symbolism as a whole, a gap which all the new knowledge brought to bear on it is quite incompetent to fill. I feel that historical scholarship is without exception "lower" or analytic criticism, and that "higher" criticism would be a quite different activity. The latter seems to me to be a purely literary criticism which would see the Bible, not as the scrapbook of corruptions, glosses, redactions, insertions, conflations, misplacings, and misunderstandings revealed by the analytic critic, but as the typological unity which all these things were originally intended to help construct. The tremendous cultural influence of the Bible is inexplicable by any criticism of it which stops where it begins to look like something with the literary form of a specialist's stamp collection. A genuine higher criticism of the Bible, therefore, would be a synthetizing process which would start with the assumption that the Bible is a definitive myth, a single archetypal structure extending from creation to apocalypse. Its heuristic principle would be St. Augustine's axiom that the Old Testament is revealed in the New and the New concealed in the Old: that the two testaments are not so much allegories of one another as metaphorical identifications of one another. We cannot trace the Bible back, even historically, to a time when its materials were not being shaped into a typological unity, and if the Bible is to be regarded as inspired in any sense, sacred or secular, its editorial and redacting processes must be regarded as inspired too.

This is the only way in which we can deal with the Bible as

the major informing influence on literary symbolism which it actually has been. Such an approach would be a conservative criticism recovering and re-establishing the traditional typologies based on the assumption of its figurative unity. The historical critic of the Song of Songs, for instance, is largely concerned with fertility cults and village festivals: the cultural criticism of it would concern itself mainly with the developments of its symbolism in Dante, Bernard of Clairvaux and other mystics and poets, for whom it represented the love of Christ for his Church. This latter is not an allegory inappropriately stuck on to the poem, but the larger archetypal or cultural context of interpretation into which it has been fitted. There is no need to choose between the two types of criticism; no need to regard the book's literary career as the result of a prudish distortion or over-imaginative mistake; no need to treat the view of it as a voluptuous *orientale* as a modern and an ironic discovery.

Once our view of the Bible comes into proper focus, a great mass of literary symbols from *The Dream of the Rood* to *Little Gidding* begins to take on meaning. We are concerned at present with the heroic quest of the central figure called the Messiah, who is associated with various royal figures in the Old Testament and identified with Christ in the New. The stages and symbols of this quest have been dealt with under the *mythos* of romance. A mysterious birth is followed by an epiphany or recognition as God's son; symbols of humiliation, betrayal, and martyrdom, the so-called suffering servant complex, follow, and in their turn are succeeded by symbols of the Messiah as bridegroom, as conqueror of a monster, and as the leader of his people into their rightful home. The oracles of the original prophets appear to have been mainly if not entirely denunciatory, but they have been furnished with "post-exilic" sequels which help to infuse the whole Bible with the rhythm of the total cyclical *mythos* in which disaster is followed by restoration, humiliation by prosperity, and which we find in epitome in the stories of Job and the prodigal son.

The Bible as a whole, therefore, presents a gigantic cycle from creation to apocalypse, within which is the heroic quest of the Messiah from incarnation to apotheosis. Within this again are three other cyclical movements, expressed or implied: individual from birth to salvation; sexual from Adam and Eve to the apocalyptic wedding; social from the giving of the law to the established kingdom of the law, the rebuilt Zion of the Old Testament and the millennium of the New. These are all completed or dialectic cycles, where the movement is first down and then up to a permanently redeemed world. In addition there is the ironic or "all too human" cycle, the *mere* cycle of human life without redemptive assistance, which goes recurrently through the "same dull round," in Blake's phrase, from birth to death. Here the final cadence is one of bondage, exile, continuing war, or destruction by fire (Sodom, Babylon) or water (the flood). These two forms of cyclical movement supply us with two epic frameworks: the epic of return and the epic of wrath. The fact that the cycle of life and death and rebirth is closely analogous in its symbolism to the Messianic cycle of pre-existence, life-in-death and resurrection gives us a third type of analogical epic. A fourth type is the contrast-epic, where one pole is the ironic human situation and the other the origin or continuation of a divine society.

Even in myth the full apocalyptic cadence is rare, though it occurs in Northern mythology, in the Eddas and the *Muspilli*, and the last book of the *Mahabharata* is an entry into heaven. There are myths of apotheosis, as in the legend of Hercules, and of salvation, as in the Osiris symbolism of the Book of the Dead, but the main concern of most sacred books is to lay down the law, chiefly of course the ceremonial law. The resulting shape is an embryonic form of contrast-epic: myths accounting for the origin of law, including creation myths, are at one pole and human society under the law is at the other. The antiquity of the contrast-epic is indicated by the epic of Gilgamesh, where the hero's search for immortality leads him only to hear about the end of the natural cycle, symbolized here, as in the Bible, by a flood. The collections of myth made by Hesiod and Ovid are based on the same form: here the poet himself, a victim of injustice or exile, has a prominent place at the human pole. The same structure is carried on through Boethius, where the two poles are the lost golden age and the poet in prison falsely accused, into medieval times.

Romantic encyclopaedic forms use human or sacramental imitations of the Messianic myth, like the quest of Dante in the *Commedia*, of St. George in Spenser, and of the knights of the Holy Grail. The *Commedia* reverses the usual structure of the contrast-epic, as it starts with the ironic human situation and ends with divine vision. The human nature of Dante's quest is established by the fact that he is unable to overcome or even to face the monsters who confront him at the beginning: his quest thus begins in a retreat from the conventional knight-errant role. In Langland's great vision we have the first major English treatment of the contrast-epic. At one pole is the risen Christ and the salvation of Piers: at the other is the somber vision of human life which presents at the end of the poem something very like a triumph of Antichrist. *The Faerie Queene* was to have ended with an epithalamium, which would probably have been filled with Biblical bridegroom imagery, but as we have it the poem ends with the Blatant Beast of calumny still at large and the poet a victim of it.

In the high mimetic we reach the structure that we think of as typically epic, the form represented by Homer, Virgil, and Milton. The epic differs from the narrative in the encyclopaedic range of its theme, from heaven to the underworld, and over an enormous mass of traditional knowledge. A narrative poet, a Southey or a Lydgate, may write any number of narratives, but an epic poet normally completes only one epic structure, the moment when he decides on his theme being the crisis of his life.

The cyclical form of the Classical epic is based on the natural cycle, a mediterranean known world in the middle of a boundlessness (*apeiron*) and between the upper and the lower gods. The cycle has two main rhythms: the life and death of the individual, and the slower social rhythm which, in the course of years (*periplomenon eniauton* in Homer, *volvibus* or *labentibus annis* in Virgil), brings cities and empires to their rise and fall. The steady vision of the latter movement is possible only to gods. The convention of beginning the action *in medias res* ties a knot in time, so to speak. The total action in the background of the *Iliad* moves from the cities of Greece through the ten-year siege of Troy back to Greece again; the total action of the *Odyssey* is a specialized example of the same thing, moving from Ithaca back to Ithaca. The *Aeneid* moves with the household gods of Priam, from Troy to New Troy.

The foreground action begins at a point described in the *Odyssey* as *hamothen*, "somewhere": actually, it is far more carefully chosen. All three epics begin at a kind of nadir of the total cyclical action: the *Iliad*, at a moment of despair in the Greek camp; the *Odyssey*, with Odysseus and Penelope furthest from one another, both wooed by importunate suitors; the *Aeneid*, with its hero ship-

318

wrecked on the shores of Carthage, citadel of Juno and enemy of Rome. From there, the action moves both backward and forward far enough to indicate the general shape of the historical cycle. The discovery of the epic action is the sense of the end of the total action as like the beginning, and hence of a consistent order and balance running through the whole. This consistent order is not a divine fiat or fatalistic causation, but a stability in nature controlled by the gods, and extended to human beings if they accept it. The sense of this stability is not necessarily tragic, but it is the kind of sense that makes tragedy possible.

It does so in the *Iliad,* for example. The number of valid reasons for praising the *Iliad* would fill a bigger book than this, but the relevant reason for us here is the fact that its theme is *menis,* a song of wrath. It is hardly possible to overestimate the importance for Western literature of the *Iliad's* demonstration that the fall of an enemy, no less than of a friend or leader, is tragic and not comic. With the *Iliad,* once for all, an objective and disinterested element enters into the poet's vision of human life. Without this element, poetry is merely instrumental to various social aims, to propaganda, to amusement, to devotion, to instruction: with it, it acquires the authority that since the *Iliad* it has never lost, an authority based, like the authority of science, on the vision of nature as an impersonal order.

The *Odyssey* begins the other tradition of the epic of return. The story is a romance of a hero escaping safely from incredible perils and arriving in the nick of time to claim his bride and baffle the villains, but our central feeling about it is a much more prudent sense, rooted in all our acceptance of nature, society, and law, of the proper master of the house coming to reclaim his own. The *Aeneid* develops the theme of return into one of rebirth, the end in New Troy being the starting-point renewed and transformed by the hero's quest. The Christian epic carries the same themes into a wider archetypal context. The action of the Bible, from the poetic point of view, includes the themes of the three great epics: the theme of the destruction and captivity of the city in the *Iliad,* the theme of the *nostos* or return home in the *Odyssey,* and the theme of the building of the new city in the *Aeneid.* Adam is, like Odysseus, a man of wrath, exiled from home because he angered God by going *hyper moron,* beyond his limit as a man. In both stories the provoking act is symbolized by the eating of food reserved for deity. As with Odysseus, Adam's return home is contingent on the appeasing of divine wrath by divine wisdom (Poseidon and Athene reconciled by the will of Zeus in Homer; the Father reconciled with man in the Christian atonement). Israel carries its ark from Egypt to the Promised Land just as Aeneas carries his household goods from the fallen Troy to the eternally established one.

Hence there is, as we go from the Classical to the Christian epic, a progress in completeness of theme (not in any kind of value), as Milton indicates in such phrases as "Beyond the Aonian mount." In Milton the foreground action of the epic is again the nadir of the total cyclical action, the fall of Satan and Adam. From there the action works backward through the speech of Raphael, and forward through the speech of Michael, to the beginning and end of the total action. The beginning is God's presence among the angels before the Son is manifested to them; the end comes after the apocalypse when God again is "all in all," but the beginning and end are the same point, the presence of God, renewed and transformed by the heroic quest of Christ. As a Christian, Milton has to reconsider the epic theme of heroic action, to decide what in Christian terms a hero is and what an act is. Heroism for him consists in obedience, fidelity and perseverance through ridicule or persecution, and is exemplified by Abdiel, the faithful angel. Action for him means positive or creative act, exemplified by Christ in the creation of the world and the recreation of man. Satan thus takes over the traditional qualities of martial heroism: he is the wrathful Achilles, the cunning Ulysses, the knight-errant who achieves the perilous quest of chaos; but he is from God's point of view a mock-hero, what man in his fallen state naturally turns to with admiration as the idolatrous form of the kingdom, the power, and the glory.

In the low mimetic period the encyclopaedic structure tends to become either subjective and mythological, or objective and historical. The former is usually expressed in *epos* and the latter in prose fiction. The main attempts to combine the two were made, somewhat unexpectedly, in France, and extend from the fragments left by Chenier to Victor Hugo's *Légendes des Siècles*. Here the theme of heroic action is transferred, consistently with low mimetic conventions, from the leader to humanity as a whole. Hence the fulfilment of the action is conceived mainly as social improvement in the future.

In the traditional epic the gods affect the action from a continuous present: Athene and Venus appear epiphanically, on definite occasions, to illuminate or cheer the hero at that moment. To gain information about the future, or what is "ahead" in terms of the lower cycle of life, it is normally necessary to descend to a lower world of the dead, as is done in the nekyia, or katabasis, in the eleventh book of the *Odyssey* and the sixth of the *Aeneid*. Similarly in Dante the damned know the future but not the present, and in Milton the forbidden knowledge which "brought death into the world" is actualized in the form of Michael's prophecy of the future. We are thus not surprised to find a great increase, in the low mimetic period of future hopes, of a sense of Messianic powers as coming from "underneath" or through esoteric and hermetic traditions. *Prometheus Unbound* is the most familiar English example: the attempt to insert a katabasis into the second part of *Faust*, first as the descent to the "mothers" and then as the Classical Walpurgis Night, was evidently one of the most baffling structural problems in that work. Sometimes, however, the katabasis is combined with and complemented by the more traditional point of epiphany. Keats's Endymion goes "down" in search of truth and "up" in search of beauty, discovering, not surprisingly for Keats, that truth and beauty are the same. In *Hyperion* some alignment between a Dionysian "below" and an Apollonian "above" was clearly on the agenda. Eliot's *Burnt Norton* is founded on the principle that "the way up and the way down are the same," which resolves this dichotomy in Christian terms. Time in this world is a horizontal line, and God's timeless presence is a vertical one crossing it at right angles, the crossing point being the Incarnation. The rose garden and subway episodes outline the two semi-circles of the cycle of nature, the upper one the romantic mythopoeic fantasy world of innocence and the lower the world of experience. But if we go further up than the rose garden and further down than the subway we reach the same point.

Comedy and irony supply us with parody-symbolism, of which the relation of the bound Gulliver in Lilliput to Prometheus, of the staggering hod-carrier in *Finnegans Wake* to Adam, of the madeleine cake in Proust to the Eucharist, are examples on varying levels of seriousness. Here too belongs the kind of use of archetypal structure made in *Absalom and Achitophel*, where the resemblance between the story and its Old Testament model is treated as a series of witty coincidences. The theme of encyclopaedic parody is endemic in satire, and in prose fiction is chiefly to be found in the anatomy, the tradition of Apuleius and Rabelais and Swift. Satires and novels show a relation corresponding to that of epics and narratives: the more novels a novelist writes the more successful he is, but Rabelais, Burton, and Sterne build their creative lives around one supreme effort. Hence it is in satire and irony that we should look for the continuing encyclopaedic tradition, and we should expect that the containing form of the ironic or satiric epic would be the pure cycle, in which every quest, however successful or heroic, has sooner or later to be made over again.

In Blake's poem *The Mental Traveller* we have a vision of the cycle of human life, from birth to death to rebirth. The two characters of the poem are a male and a female figure, moving in opposite directions, one growing old as the other grows young, and vice versa. The cyclical relation between them runs through four cardinal points: a son-mother phase, a husband-wife phase, a father-daughter phase, and a fourth phase of what Blake calls spectre and emanation, terms corresponding roughly to Shelley's alastor and epipsyche. None of these phases is quite true: the mother is only a nurse, the wife merely "bound down" for the male's delight, the daughter a changeling, and the emanation does not "emanate," but remains elusive. The male figure represents humanity, and therefore includes women—the "female will" in Blake becomes associated with women only when women dramatize or mimic the above relation in human life, as they do in the Courtly Love convention. The female figure represents the natural environment which man partially but never wholly subdues. The controlling symbolism of the poem, as the four phases suggest, is lunar.

To the extent that the encyclopaedic form concerns itself with the cycle of human life, an ambivalent female archetype appears in it, sometimes benevolent, sometimes sinister, but usually presiding over and confirming the cyclical movement. One pole of her is represented by an Isis figure, a Penelope or Solveig who is the fixed point on which the action ends. The goddess who frequently begins and ends the cyclical action is closely related. This figure is Athene in the *Odyssey* and Venus in the *Aeneid*; in Elizabethan literature, for political reasons, usually some variant of Diana, like the Faerie Queen in Spenser. The *alma Venus* who suffuses Lucretius' great vision of life balanced in the order of nature is another version. Beatrice in Dante presides over not a cycle but a sacramental spiral leading up to deity, as does, in a far less concrete way, the *Ewig-Weibliche* of *Faust*. At the opposite pole is a figure— Calypso or Circe in Homer, Dido in Virgil, Cleopatra in Shakespeare, Duessa in Spenser, sometimes a "terrible mother" but often sympathetically treated—who represents the opposite direction from the heroic quest. Eve in Milton, who spirals man downward into the Fall, is the contrasting figure to Beatrice.

In the ironic age there are naturally a good many visions of a cycle of experience, often presided over by a female figure with lunar and femme fatale affiliations. Yeats's *Vision*, which Yeats was quite right in associating with *The Mental Traveller*, is based on this symbolism, and more recently Mr. Robert Graves' *The White Goddess* has expounded it with even greater learning and ingenuity. In Eliot's *Waste Land* the figure in the background is less "the lady of situations" than the androgynous Teiresias, and although there is a fire sermon and a thunder sermon, both with apocalyptic overtones, the natural cycle of water, the Thames flowing into the sea and returning through death by water in the spring rains, is the containing form of the poem. In Joyce's *Ulysses* a female figure at once maternal, marital, and meretricious, a Penelope who embraces all her suitors, merges in her sleep with the drowsy spinning earth, constantly affirming but never forming, and taking the whole book with her.

But it is *Finnegans Wake* which is the chief ironic epic of our time. Here again the containing structure is cyclical, as the end of the book swings us around to the beginning again. Finnegan never really wakes up, because HCE fails to establish any continuity between his dreaming and waking worlds. The central figure is ALP, but we notice that ALP, although she has very little of the Beatrice or Virgin Mary about her, has even less of the femme fatale. She is a harried but endlessly patient and solicitous wife and mother: she runs through her natural cycle and achieves no quest herself, but she is clearly the kind of being who makes a quest possible. Who then is the hero who achieves the permanent quest in *Finnegans Wake*? No character in the book itself seems a likely candidate; yet one feels that this book gives us something more than the merely irresponsible irony of a turning cycle. Eventually it dawns on us that it is the *reader* who achieves the quest, the reader who, to the extent that he masters the book of Doublends Jined, is able to look down on its rotation, and see its form as something more than rotation.

In encyclopaedic forms, such as the epic and its congeners, we see how the conventional themes, around which lyrics cluster, reappear as *episodes* of a longer story. Thus the panegyric reappears in the *klea andron* or heroic contests, the poem of community action in the convention of the games, the elegy in heroic death, and so on. The reverse development occurs when a lyric on a conventional theme achieves a concentration that expands it into a miniature epic: if not the historical "little epic" or epyllion, something very like it generically. Thus *Lycidas* is a miniature scriptural epic extending over the whole range covered by *Paradise Lost*, the death of man and his redemption by Christ. Spenser's *Epithalamion* also probably contains in miniature as much symbolic range as the unwritten conclusion to his epic would have had. In modern times the miniature epic becomes a very common form: the later poems of Eliot, of Edith Sitwell, and many cantos of Pound belong to it.

Often too, in illustration of our general principle, a miniature epic actually forms part of a bigger one. The prophecy of Michael in *Paradise Lost* presents the whole Bible as a miniature contrastepic, with one pole at the apocalypse and the other at the flood. The Bible itself contains the Book of Job, which is a kind of microcosm of its total theme, and is cited by Milton as the model for the "brief" epic.

Similarly, oratorical prose develops into the more continuous forms of prose fiction, and similarly too the growing points of prose, so to speak, which we called the commandment, parable, aphorism, and oracle, reappear as the kernels of scriptural forms. In many types of prose romance verse or characteristics of verse are prominent: the old Irish epics, euphuism in Elizabethan romance, the rhyming prose of the Arabian Nights, the use of poems for cultivated dialogue in the Japanese *Tale of Genji*, are random examples showing how universal the tendency is. But as *epos* grows into epic, it conventionalizes and unifies its metre, while prose goes its own way in separate forms. In the low mimetic period the gap between the subjective mythological epic and the objective historical one is increased by the fact that the former seems to belong by its decorum to verse and the latter to prose. In prose satire, however, we notice a strong tendency on the part of prose to reabsorb verse. We have mentioned the frequency of the verse interlude in the anatomy tradition, and in the *melos* of Rabelais, Sterne and Joyce the tendency is carried much farther. In scriptural forms, we have seen, the gap between prose and verse is very narrow, and sometimes hardly exists at all.

We come back to where we started this section, then, to the Bible, the only form which unites the architectonics of Dante with the disintegration of Rabelais. From one point of view, the Bible presents an epic structure of unsurpassed range, consistency and completeness; from another, it presents a seamy side of bits and pieces which makes the *Tale of a Tub, Tristram Shandy,* and *Sartor Resartus* look as homogeneous as a cloudless sky. Some mystery is here which literary criticism might find it instructive to look into.

When we do look into it, we find that the sense of unified continuity is what the Bible has as a work of fiction, as a definitive myth extending over time and space, over invisible and visible orders of reality, and with a parabolic dramatic structure of which the five acts are creation, fall, exile, redemption, and restoration. The more we study this myth, the more its descriptive or sigmatic aspect seems to fall into the background. For most readers, myth, legend, historical reminiscence, and actual history are inseparable in the Bible; and even what is historical fact is not there because it is "true" but because it is mythically significant. The begats in Chronicles may be authentic history; the Book of Job is clearly an imaginative drama, but the Book of Job is more important, and closer to Christ's practice of revelation through parable. The priority of myth to fact is religious as well as literary; in both contexts the significance of the flood story is in its imaginative status as an archetype, a status which no layer of mud on top of Sumeria will ever account for. When we apply this principle to the gospels, with all the variations in their narratives, the descriptive aspect of them too dissolves. The basis of their form is something other than biography, just as the basis of the Exodus story is something other than history.

At this point the analytic view of the Bible begins to come into focus as the thematic aspect of it. In proportion as the continuous fictional myth begins to look illusory, as the text breaks down into smaller and smaller fragments, it takes on the appearance of a sequence of epiphanies, a discontinuous but rightly ordered series of significant moments of apprehension or vision. The Bible may thus be examined from an aesthetic or Aristotelian point of view as a single form, as a story in which pity and terror, which in this context are the knowledge of good and evil, are raised and cast out. Or it may be examined from a Longinian point of view as a series of ecstatic moments or points of expanding apprehension—this approach is in fact the assumption on which every selection of a text for a sermon is based. Here we have a critical principle which we can take back to literature and apply to anything we like, a principle in which the "holism," as it has been called, of Coleridge and the discontinuous theories of Poe, Hulme, and Pound are reconciled. Yet the Bible is "more" than a work of literature, so perhaps the principle has a wider range of extension even than literature. In any case we have gone as far as we can within literature, and the remainder of this book will be concerned with the literary aspect of verbal structures generally called non-literary.

THE RHETORIC OF NON-LITERARY PROSE

Prose is, unlike verse, used also for non-literary purposes: it extends not only to the literary boundaries of *melos* and *opsis*, but to the outer worlds of *praxis* and *theoria*, social action and individual thought themselves. Renaissance critics used to argue about what the greatest form for poetry was, and whether it was epic or tragedy. There is probably no answer to such a question, but one can learn a good deal about literary form by discussing it. Now if we ask the question: What is the greatest possible *prose* form? there is probably no answer to that question either, but the moment we ask it, a great number of works, the Bible, the dialogues of Plato, the meditations of Pascal—in fact, all "great books" usually placed outside literature—leap into a new literary significance. It is thus necessary for us at this point to consider what literary elements are involved in the verbal structures in which the literary or hypothetical intention is not the primary one.

We are still thinking of literature as facing the world of social action on one side, and of individual thought on the other, so that the rhetoric of non-literary prose would tend to emphasize emotion and the appeal to action through the ear in the former area, and intellect and the appeal to contemplation based predominantly on visual metaphors in the latter. Let us begin with that extensive suburb of prose that is concerned with the technique of social or oratorical persuasion.

The most concentrated examples of this are to be found in the pamphlet or speech that catches the rhythm of history, that seizes on a crucial event or phase of action, interprets it, articulates the emotions concerned with it, or in some means employs a verbal structure to insulate and conduct the current of history. *Areopagitica*, Johnson's letter to Chesterfield, some sermons in the period between Latimer and the Commonwealth, some of Burke's speeches, Lincoln's Gettysburg address, Vanzetti's death speech, Churchill's 1940 speeches, are a few examples that come readily to mind. None of these were designed with a primarily literary intention, and would have failed of their original purpose if they had been, but they are literary now, and data for the critic. Nearly all of them are marked by the emphatic patterns of repetition and anaphora characteristic of rhetorical prose.

The measured cadences of these historical oracles represent a kind of strategic withdrawal from action: they marshal and review the ranks of familiar but deeply-held ideas. The rhetoric of persuasion to action itself, which is the next stage of prose as we proceed from literature outwards into social life, is considerably stepped up in its rhythm. Here the repetitions are hypnotic and incantatory, aimed at breaking down customary associations of ideas and habitual responses, and at excluding any alternative line of action. Such a rhetoric may be heard in its purest form in the speech rhythms of a boy talking to a dog, with the object of persuading him to sit up or shake hands or otherwise move out of the normal line of canine endeavor. When addressed to a human audience, such rhetoric must follow the dialectic of rhetoric: it must have either a rallying point or a point of attack, or both. The rhetoric of attack or invective is exemplified in the pulpit's crusade against sin and in the prosecutor's summing-up in the courtroom. The latter has produced the by-form of the philippic, the indictment of a social enemy. The rhetoric of eulogy, the so-called epideictic rhetoric of the Classical world, is in our day most clearly seen in advertising and publicity, although it has a more genuinely literary form in the type of "purple

327

passage" prose, usually with a descriptive content, that attempts to communicate some kind of wordless emotion.

As these examples show, we are moving rapidly away from literature towards the direct verbal expression of kinetic emotion. The further we go in this direction, the more likely the author is to be, or to pretend to be, emotionally involved with his subject, so that what he exhorts us to embrace or avoid is in part a projection from his own emotional life. As this increases, a certain automatism comes into the writing: the verbal expression of infantile-centered hatreds, fears, loves, and objects of adoration. When Swinburne speaks of "the yelling Yahoos whom the scandalous and senseless license of our own day allows to run and roar about the country unmuzzled and unwhipped," we may not know what he is referring to, but a glance at the prose structure, with its automatic alliteration and doubling of adjectives, makes it clear that whatever it is we hardly need to take it seriously. Such writing is a familiar and easily recognized phenomenon: it is tantrum prose, the prose of so much Victorian criticism, of several acres of Carlyle and Ruskin, of clerical denunciations of heresies or secular amusements, of totalitarian propaganda, and in fact of nearly all rhetoric in which we feel that the author's pen is running away from him, setting up a mechanical for an imaginative impetus. The metaphor of "intoxication" is often employed for the breakdown of rhetorical control.

The more incoherent this kind of rhetoric becomes, the more clearly it shows itself to be an attempt to express emotion apart from or without intellect. At this point we enter the area of emotional jargon, which consists largely in an obsessive repetition of verbal formulas. Not far removed is the kind of vulgar inarticulateness that uses one word, generally unprintable, for the whole rhetorical ornament of the sentence, including adjectives, adverbs, epithets, and punctuation. Finally, words disappear altogether, and we are back to a primitive language of screams and gestures and sighs. The whole sequence can of course be imitated within literature, Shakespeare giving us everything from Henry V's address before the walls of Harfleur to Othello's "goats and monkeys" speech. The imitation of emotional rhetoric in literary prose is a feature making for *melos* in the latter. Similarly in literature we occasionally run across a writer who uses such rhetorical material without being able to absorb or assimilate it: the result is pathological, a kind of literary diabetes, and may be studied in the novels of Amanda Ros.

The expression of conceptual thought in prose exhibits a parallel sequence of phenomena, moving in the opposite direction. Philosophy is assertive or propositional writing, and we notice in the history of philosophy a persistent attempt to isolate the rhythm of the proposition. Philosophy begins in proverbs and axioms, and at various times it has produced the dialectic dialogue of Plato and the Upanishads, the closely related question-objection-answer scheme of St. Thomas, the quasi-mathematical arrangements of ideas in Spinoza, the aphorisms of Bacon (who remarks that aphorisms are a sign of vitality in philosophy), and, in our day, the numbered propositions of Wittgenstein's *Tractatus*. All of these are clearly at least in part endeavors to purify verbal communication of the emotional content of rhetoric; all of them, however, impress the literary critic as being themselves rhetorical devices.

The implication is that there is a conceptual rhetoric aimed, like persuasive rhetoric, at separating emotion and intellect, but attempting to throw away the emotional half. It seeks the book and the individual reader as its fellow seeks the audience; its goal is understanding as the goal of persuasion is action or emotional response. A good deal of the strategy of teaching is rhetorical strategy, choosing words and images with great care in order to evoke the response: "I never thought of it that way before," or "Now that you put it that way, I can see it." What distinguishes, not simply the epigram, but profundity itself from platitude is very frequently rhetorical wit. In fact it may be doubted whether we ever really call an idea profound unless we are pleased with the wit of its expression. Teaching, like persuasion, employs a dissociative rhetoric aimed at breaking down habitual response: the maddening prolixity of Oriental sutras results from this, and there are passages in the New Testament almost as dissociative as Gertrude Stein:

> That which was from the beginning, which we have heard, which we have seen with our eyes, which we have looked upon, and our hands have handled, of the Word of life; (For the life was manifested, and we have seen it, and bear witness, and shew unto you that eternal life, which was with the Father, and was manifested unto us;) That which we have seen and heard declare we unto you . . .

Without trying to suggest that only good writers can be good philosophers, we may still observe that much of the *difficulty* in a philosophical style is rhetorical in origin, resulting from a feeling that it is necessary to detach and isolate the intellect from the emotions. A sentence from James Mill's *Essay on Government* will illustrate what I mean:

> One caution, first of all, we should take along with us, and it is this: that all those persons who hold the powers of government without having an identity of interests with the community, and all those persons who share in the profits which are made by the abuse of those powers, and all those persons whom the example and representations of the two first classes influence, will be sure to represent the community, or a part having an identity of interest with the community, as incapable in the highest degree of acting according to their own interest; it being clear that they who have not an identity of interest with the community ought to hold the power of government no longer, if those who have that identity of interest could be expected to act in any tolerable conformity with their interest.

This is finally discovered to mean, after one has worked it all out like a crossword puzzle, that those who have a stake in one form of government are likely to resist the introduction of another. The critic, searching for the reasons why, if James Mill meant that, he could not have said it, eventually realizes that the style is motivated by a perverse, bristly intellectual honesty. *He* will not condescend to employ any of the pretty arts of persuasion, sugar-coated illustrations or emotionally-loaded terms; he will appeal only to the cold logic of reason itself—reinforced, to be sure, by a peculiarly Victorian sense that the more difficult the style, the tougher the moral and intellectual fibre one develops in wrestling with it.

We note that the basis of James Mill's rhetoric is the imitation of legal style, with its careful qualifying inclusiveness. The long containing sentences of the later Henry James already mentioned illustrate the literary use of similar devices. Passing over some intermediate stages, we eventually arrive, in this pursuit of non-emotional rhetoric, at conceptual jargon, otherwise known as gobble-dygook or officialese. This is a naive intensification of Mill's desire to speak with the voice, not of personality, but of Reason itself. The jargon of government reports, inter-office memoranda, and military instructions is motivated by a wish to be as impersonal as possible, to represent verbally the Institution or some anonymous cybernetic deity functioning in a state of "normalcy." What it actually utters, of course, is the voice of the lonely crowd, the anxiety of the outward-directed conformist. Such jargon may be called, borrowing a term from medicine, benign jargon: it is unmistakably a disease of language, but not—yet—a cancerous disease like a demagogue's oratory. It is found in most aspects of journalism and is the dress uniform of a large amount of professional writing, including that of humanists. That it could become malignant is indicated in 1984, where a further stage of it is caricatured as "Newspeak," a pseudo-logical simplification of language which has, like emotional jargon, complete automatism as its goal. We are not surprised to find that the further we depart from literature, or the use of language to express the completely integrated state of emotional consciousness we call imagination, the nearer we come to the use of language as the expression of reflex. Whether we go in the emotional or in the intellectual direction, we arrive at much the same point, a point antipodal to literature in which language is a running commentary on the unconscious, like a squirrel's chatter.

If there is such a thing as conceptual rhetoric, which is likely to increase in proportion as the discursive writer tries to avoid it, it seems as though the direct union of grammar and logic, which we suggested at the beginning of this essay might be the characteristic of the non-literary verbal structure, does not, in the long run, exist. Anything which makes a functional use of words will always be involved in all the technical problems of words, including rhetorical problems. The only road from grammar to logic, then, runs through the intermediate territory of rhetoric.

We notice in the first place that attempts to reduce grammar to logic, or logic to grammar, have not had the success they should have had if there were a large and important non-rhetorical common factor on which non-literary writing could be built. For a long time the prestige of the discursive reason fostered the notion that logic was the formal cause of language, that universal grammars on logical principles were possible, and that the entire resources of linguistic expression could be categorized. We are now more accustomed to think of reasoning as one of many things that man does with words, a specialized function of language. There seems

331

to be no evidence whatever that man learned to speak primarily because he wanted to speak logically.

The attempts to reduce logic to grammar are more recent, but not much more successful. Logic grows out of grammar, the unconscious or potential logic inherent in language, and we often find that the containing forms of conceptual thought are of grammatical origin, the stock example being the subject and predicate of Aristotelian logic. The fluid primitive linguistic conceptions often mentioned by anthropologists, such as the Polynesian *mana* or the Iroquois *orenda*, are participial or gerundive conceptions: they belong in a world where energy and matter have not been clearly separated, either in thought or into the verbs and nouns of our own less flexible language-structure. As energy and matter are not clearly separated in nuclear physics either, we might do worse than to return to such "primitive" words ourselves. The words atom and light, for example, being nouns, may be too material and static to be adequate symbols for what they now mean, and when they pass from the equations of a physicist into the linguistic apparatus of contemporary social consciousness, the grammatical difficulties in the translation show up clearly.

But there is still the scholar's mate in the argument for reducing logic to grammar: the fallacy of thinking that we have explained the nature of something by accounting for its origin in something else. Logic may have grown out of grammar, but to grow out of something is in part to outgrow it. For grammar may also be a hampering force in the development of logic, and a major source of logical confusions and pseudo-problems. These confusions extend much further than even the enormous brood of fallacies spawned by paronomasia, which is, like so many of our phenomena, a structural principle in literature and an obstacle in discursive writing. For instance, many long arguments may be annihilated by a grammatical change from definite articles and statements of identity to indefinite articles and active verbs. To say "reason is *a* function of the mind" is unlikely to lead to dispute; to say "reason is *the* function of the mind" involves one in a pointless struggle for the exclusive possession of an essence. To say "art communicates" is similarly to be content with an obvious plurality of functions: to say "art is communication" forces us into circular wrangling around a metaphor taken as an assertion. It is no wonder, then, that many logicians tend to think of grammar as something of a logical disease, some of them even maintaining that mathematics is the real source of coherence in logic. I have no opinion on this, except to repeat that anything which makes a functional use of words will always be involved in all the problems of words.

Grammar and logic both seem to develop through internal conflict. The humanist tradition has always, and rightly, stressed the importance of linguistic conflict in training the mind: if we do not know another language, we have missed the best and simplest opportunity of getting our ideas disentangled from the swaddling clothes of their native syntax. Similarly logic cannot develop properly without dialectic, the principle of opposition in thought. Now when people speaking different languages come into contact, an *ideogrammatic* structure is built up out of the efforts at communication. The figure 5 is an ideogram, because it means the same number to people who call it five, cinq, cinque, fünf, and a dozen other things. Similarly, the purely linguistic associations of English "time" and French "temps" are different, but it is quite practicable to translate Proust or Bergson on time into English without serious risk of misunderstanding the meaning. When two languages are in different cultural orbits, like English and Zulu, the ideogrammatic structure is more difficult to build up, but it always seems to be more or less possible. There are French equivalents for all English words and ideas, but obviously one cannot walk into a Polynesian or Iroquois society and ask: "What are *your* words for God, the soul, reality, knowledge?" They may have no such words or concepts, nor can we give them our equivalents for *mana* and *orenda*. Yet it seems clear that we can eventually, with patient and sympathetic study, find out what is going on in a Polynesian or Iroquois mind. The problems of communication between two people speaking the same language may in some respects be even greater, because more difficult to become aware of, but even they can be ultimately surmounted. It is out of such ideogrammatic inner structures, whether produced linguistically between two languages, or psychologically between two people speaking the same language, that the capacity to assimilate language to rational thought develops.

This ideogrammatic middle ground between two languages, or between two personal structures of meaning in the same language, must itself be a symbolic structure, not simply a bilingual dictionary. Hence the ideogram is neither purely grammatical nor purely logical: it is both at once, and rhetorical as well, for, like rhetoric, it brings an *audience* into being, and reinforces the language of consciousness with that of association. The ideogram, in short, is a metaphor, the identification of two things of which each retains its own form, the realization that what you mean by X in this context is what I mean by Y. Such an ideogram may differ from the purely hypothetical metaphor of the poem, but the mental leap of metaphor away from the simple "this means that" sign is present in it.

Whether the reader agrees with all this or not, he may at any rate be willing to admit the possibility of links between grammar and rhetoric, and between rhetoric and logic, that have a neglected but crucial importance. Let us take the link of grammar and rhetoric first.

We remember that a good deal of verbal creation begins in associative babble, in which sound and sense are equally involved. The result of this is poetic ambiguity, the fact that, as remarked earlier, the poet does not define his words but establishes their powers by placing them in a great variety of contexts. Hence the importance of poetic etymology, or the tendency to associate words similar in sound or sense. For many centuries this tendency passed itself off as genuine etymology, and the student was taught to think in terms of verbal association. He learned to think of snow as coming etymologically as well as physically from clouds (*nix a nubes*), and of dark groves as derived from sunlight (the derivation by opposites which produced the famous *lucus a non lucendo*). When real etymology developed, this associative process was discarded as mumbo-jumbo, which it is from one point of view, but it remains a factor of great importance in criticism. Here again we meet the principle that an analogy between A and B (in this case two words) may still be important even if the view that A is the source of B is dropped. Whether or not one is etymologically justified in associating Prometheus with forethought or Odysseus with wrath, the poets have accepted such associations and they are data for the critic. Whether or not "new" critics make mistakes or anachronisms in explicating the texture of earlier poetry, the principle involved is defensible historically as well as psychologically.

We soon become aware, moreover, that verbal association is still a factor of importance even in rational thought. One of the most effective methods of conveying meaning in translation, for instance, is to leave a key word untranslated, so that the reader has to pick up its contextual associations in the original language from his own. Again, in trying to understand the thought of a philosopher, one often starts by considering a single word, say nature in Aristotle, substance in Spinoza, or time in Bergson, in the total range of its connotations. One often feels that a full understanding of such a word would be a key to the understanding of the whole system. If so, it would be a metaphorical key, as it would be a set of identifications made by the thinker with the word. The attempt to regard such connotative terms as invariably fallacious does not get us very far. Students are often graduated from college armed only with complaints that people will not define their terms, reason clearly, or argue about freedom or order without emotional attachments to those words. It is perhaps more useful to shift our attention from what verbal communication is not to what it is, and what is communicated is usually some ambiguous and emotionally charged complex. In any case the notion that it is possible to reduce language to sign-language, to make one word invariably mean one thing, is an illusion. After one has removed associative ambiguity from verbs and nouns, one has then the problem of adjectives and adverbs, which are universals by their very nature, and finally prepositions and conjunctions, which, being pure connectives, will always display a disconcerting semantic versatility. A glance at the N.E.D. entries for "to," "for," and "in" should discourage the brashest of verbal atomizers.

The link between rhetoric and logic is "doodle" or associative diagram, the expression of the conceptual by the spatial. A great number of prepositions are spatial metaphors, most of them derived from the orientation of the human body. Every use of "up," "down," "besides," "on the other hand," "under" implies a subconscious diagram in the argument, whatever it is. If a writer says "But on the other hand there is a further consideration to be brought forward in support of the opposing argument," he may be writing normal (if wordy) English, but he is also doing precisely what an armchair strategist does when he scrawls plans of battle on a tablecloth. Very often a "structure" or "system" of thought can be reduced to a diagrammatic pattern—in fact both words are to some extent synonyms of diagram. A philosopher is of great assistance to his reader when he realizes the presence of such a diagram and extracts it, as Plato does in his discussion of the divided

335

line. We cannot go far in any argument without realizing that there is some kind of graphic formula involved. All division and categorization, the use of chapters, the topotropism (if I have constructed this correctly) signalled by "let us now turn to" or "reverting to the point made earlier," the sense of what "fits" the argument, the feeling that one point is "central" and another peripheral, has some kind of geometrical basis.

It used to be said that, as all abstract words were originally concrete metaphors, something of the latter will always adhere to the word through all its semantic history. This view is discredited now, but it still has much truth in it: I question whether it is really possible to make B depend on A without in some measure hanging it on, or involve B with A without in some measure wrapping them up. The only fallacy in it, I think, is the assumption that the attached metaphor must necessarily be the one implied in the etymology of the word. Of course a writer may give a word a meaning which has no recognizable connection with its origin. But it looks as though abstract words and ideas were on loan, so to speak, from a latent concrete formulation which is to be found, not in the history of the word used, but in the structure of the argument into which the word is fitted.

As soon as one starts to think of the role of association and diagram in argument, one begins to realize how extraordinarily pervasive they are. I once heard a preacher advocate religion on the ground that science was too cold and dry to serve as a guide to life, while the heat of revolutionary zeal still left one thirsting for something more. The figures seemed commonplace, yet it was clear that the ancient diagram of the four principles of substance, hot, cold, moist, and dry, was the graphic formula of his argument, and that religion meant something wet to him, a fertilizing moisture that would warm the scientists and cool the radicals. The same principle of a graphic formula is found in such assumptions as: that the intellect is cool and sober and the emotions warm and drunk; that the practical sense walks and the imaginative one leaps; that facts are solid ("stubborn"), hypotheses liquid ("covering" facts), and theories gaseous; that whatever is "inside" the mind is dimly lit and whatever is "outside" it clear, and so on. Also in value-assumptions: that the concrete is better than the abstract, the active better than the passive, the dynamic better than the static, the unified better than the multiple, the simple better than the complex. Religious people think of heaven as "up"; psychologists think of the subconscious as "underneath" the consciousness, both words being obviously spatial metaphors.

We could go on for a long time, but by now it is surely clear that it is wiser simply to become aware of metaphor than to try to eradicate it. Attempts to analyze metaphor solely to debunk an argument or suggest that it is "nothing but" a metaphor are not to be encouraged. What is to be encouraged is the analysis itself, in which there is, I think, an activity of considerable and increasing importance for literary critics, as the conclusion of this book will suggest.

The discursive reason has traditionally been given the place of honor in Western culture. In religion, no poetry outside Scripture is given the authority of the theologian's propositions; in philosophy, the reason is the high priest of reality (unless there are special features in the philosophy giving a peculiar importance to the arts, as there are in Schelling's); in science the same hierarchical diagram is even clearer. Hence the arts have been traditionally regarded as forms of "accommodation," their function being to establish a link between reason and whatever is put "below" it on the assumed diagram, such as the emotions or the senses. It is thus no surprise to find "accommodation" in verbal structures aimed at rousing emotion or at some form of kinetic persuasion. Such accommodation has been recognized for centuries, as it is consistent with the traditional subordinating of rhetoric to dialectic. The notion of a *conceptual* rhetoric raises new problems, as it suggests that nothing built out of words can transcend the nature and conditions of words, and that the nature and conditions of *ratio*, so far as *ratio* is verbal, are contained by *oratio*.

337

TENTATIVE CONCLUSION

Tentative Conclusion

THE PRESENT BOOK has dealt with a variety of critical techniques and approaches, most of them already used in contemporary scholarship. We have tried to show where the archetypal or mythical critic, the aesthetic form critic, the historical critic, the medieval four-level critic, the text-and-texture critic, belong in a comprehensive view of criticism. Whether the comprehensive view is right or not, I hope some sense has been communicated of what folly it would be to try to exclude any of these groups from criticism. As was said at the beginning, the present book is not designed to suggest a new program for critics, but a new perspective on their existing programs, which in themselves are valid enough. The book attacks no methods of criticism, once that subject has been defined: what it attacks are the barriers between the methods. These barriers tend to make a critic confine himself to a single method of criticism, which is unnecessary, and they tend to make him establish his primary contacts, not with other critics, but with subjects outside criticism. Hence the number of essays, not large but too large, in mythical criticism that read like bad comparative religion, in rhetorical criticism that read like bad semantics, in aesthetic criticism that read like bad metaphysics, and so on.

In this process of breaking down barriers I think archetypal criticism has a central role, and I have given it a prominent place. One element in our cultural tradition which is usually regarded as fantastic nonsense is the allegorical explanations of myths which bulk so large in medieval and Renaissance criticism and continue sporadically (e.g., Ruskin's *Queen of the Air*) to our own time. The allegorization of myth is hampered by the assumption that the explanation "is" what the myth "means." A myth being a centripetal structure of meaning, it can be made to mean an indefinite number of things, and it is more fruitful to study what in fact myths have been made to mean.

The term myth may have, and obviously does have, different meanings in different subjects. These meanings are doubtless reconcilable in the long run, but the task of reconciling them lies in the future. In literary criticism myth means ultimately *mythos*, a structural organizing principle of literary form. Commentary, we remember, is allegorization, and any great work of literature may carry an infinite amount of commentary. This fact often depresses the critic and makes him feel that everything to be said about *Hamlet*, for instance, must already have been said many times. To what has occurred to the learned and astute minds of A and B in reading *Hamlet* is added what occurs to the learned and astute minds of C, D, E, and so on, until out of sheer self-preservation most of it is left unread, or (much the same thing culturally) is assigned to specialists. Commentary which has no sense of the archetypal shape of literature as a whole, then, continues the tradition of allegorized myth, and inherits its characteristics of brilliance, ingenuity, and futility.

The only cure for this situation is the supplementing of allegorical with archetypal criticism. Things become more hopeful as soon as there is a feeling, however dim, that criticism has an end in the structure of literature as a total form, as well as a beginning in the text studied. It is not sufficient to use the text as a check on commentary, like a string tied to a kite, for one may develop a primary body of commentary around the obvious meaning, then a secondary body about the unconscious meaning, then a third body around the conventions and external relations of the poem, and so on indefinitely. This practice is not confined to modern critics, for the interpretation of Virgil's Fourth Eclogue as Messianic also assumed that Virgil was "unconsciously" prophesying the Messiah. But the poet unconsciously meant the whole corpus of his possible commentary, and it is simpler merely to say that Virgil and Isaiah use the same type of imagery dealing with the myth of the hero's birth, and that because of this similarity the Nativity Ode, for instance, is able to use both. This procedure helps to distribute the commentary, and prevents each poem from becoming a separate center of isolated scholarship.

The theory of criticism embraces the "humanities," in their educational aspect, according to our principle that it is criticism and not literature which is directly taught and learned. Hence a sense of bewilderment about the theory of criticism is readily projected as a concern over the "fate" or "plight" of the humanities. The breaking down of barriers within criticism would therefore have the long-run effect of making critics more aware of the external relations of criticism as a whole with other disciplines. This last subject is one on which I make a few final comments only because it seems to me that it would be an excess of prudence, in fact hardly honest, to shrink altogether from the larger issues of the questions here discussed.

The production of art is usually described in the "creative" metaphors of organic life. There is a curious tendency in human life to imitate some of the aspects of "lower" forms of existence, like the rituals which imitate the subtle synchronizations with the rhythms of the turning year that vegetable life makes. It is not in itself unreasonable that human culture would unconsciously assume the rhythms of an organism. Artists tend to imitate their predecessors in a slightly more sophisticated way, thus producing a tradition of cultural *aging* which goes on until some large change interrupts the process and starts it over again. Hence the containing form of historical criticism may well be some quasi-organic rhythm of cultural aging, such as is postulated in one form or another by most of the philosophical historians of our time, most explicitly by Spengler. The conception of our own time as a "late" phase of a "Western" culture of which the Middle Ages was the youth, and as a phase resembling the Roman phase of an earlier Classical culture, is in practice taken for granted by everyone today, and seems to be one of the inevitable categories of the contemporary outlook. The progression of modes traced in the first essay seems to have some analogy to this view of cultural history.

Any such view, if adopted, could be decorated metaphysically to suit the tenant: but there is no reason why it should be "fatalistic," unless it is fatalism to say that one gets older every year, nor why it should include any theory of inevitable cycles in history or a pre-ordained future. Certainly it should not be perverted into a basis for rhetorical value-judgements. We get these, for instance, in the sentimental view of medieval culture which sees it as a gigantic synthesis followed by a progressive disintegration which has subdivided and specialized until it has finally landed us all in the Pretty Pass which we are in today. A movement which will restore something of the unity of medieval culture to the modern world, or some other qualities of it, has been hailed in one form or other in nearly every generation since the middle of the eighteenth century. Subsidiary forms of the same view are present in the people who cannot listen with pleasure to any music later than Mozart, or whatever terminal they choose; in the Marxists who speak of the decadence of capitalist culture; in the alarmists who speak of a return to a new Dark Ages, and so on. All these have a more or less muddled version of some quasi-organic theory of history as their basis.

It is a commonplace of criticism that art does not evolve or improve: it produces the classic or model. One can still buy books narrating the "development" of painting from the Stone Age to Picasso, but they show no development, only a series of mutations in skill, Picasso being on much the same level as his Magdalenian ancestors. Every once in a while we experience in the arts a feeling of definitive revelation. This, we may feel after a Palestrina motet or a Mozart divertimento, is the voice of music itself: this is the kind of thing that music was invented to say. Here is a simplicity which makes us realize that the simple is the opposite of the commonplace, a feeling that the boundaries of possible expression in the art have been reached for all time. This feeling belongs to direct experience, not to criticism, but it suggests the critical principle that the profoundest experiences possible to obtain in the arts are available in the art already produced.

What does improve in the arts is the comprehension of them, and the refining of society which results from it. It is the consumer, not the producer, who benefits by culture, the consumer who becomes humanized and liberally educated. There is no reason why a great poet should be a wise and good man, or even a tolerable human being, but there is every reason why his reader should be improved in his humanity as a result of reading him. Hence while the production of culture may be, like ritual, a half-involuntary imitation of organic rhythms or processes, the response to culture is, like myth, a revolutionary act of consciousness. The contemporary development of the technical ability to study the arts, represented by reproductions of painting, the recording of music, and modern libraries, forms part of a cultural revolution which makes the humanities quite as pregnant with new developments as the sciences. For the revolution is not simply in technology, but in spiritual productive power. The humanistic tradition itself arose, in its modern form, with the invention of the printing press, the immediate effect of which was not to stimulate new culture so much as to codify the heritage of the past.

Nearly every work of art in the past had a social function in its own time, a function which was often not primarily an aesthetic function at all. The whole conception of "works of art" as a classification for all pictures, statues, poems, and musical compositions is a relatively modern one. We can see an aesthetic impulse at work in Peruvian textiles, palaeolithic drawings, Scythian horse ornaments, or Kwakiutl masks, but in doing so we make a sophisticated abstraction which may well have been outside the mental habits of the people who produced them. Thus the question of whether a thing "is" a work of art or not is one which cannot be settled by appealing to something in the nature of the thing itself. It is convention, social acceptance, and the work of criticism in the broadest sense that determines where it belongs. It may have been originally made for use rather than pleasure, and so fall outside the general Aristotelian conception of art, but if it now exists for our pleasure it is what *we* call art.

When anything is reclassified in this way, it loses much of its original function. Even the most fanatical historical critic is bound to see Shakespeare and Homer as writers whom we admire for reasons that would have been largely unintelligible to them, to say nothing of their societies. But we can hardly be satisfied with an approach to works of art which simply strips from them their original function. One of the tasks of criticism is that of the recovery of function, not of course the restoration of an original function, which is out of the question, but the recreation of function in a new context.

Kierkegaard has written a fascinating little book called *Repetition*, in which he proposes to use this term to replace the more traditional Platonic term anamnesis or recollection. By it he apparently means, not the simple repeating of an experience, but the recreating of it which redeems or awakens it to life, the end of the process, he says, being the apocalyptic promise: "Behold, I make all things new." The preoccupation of the humanities with the past is sometimes made a reproach against them by those who forget that we face the past: it may be shadowy, but it is all that is there. Plato draws a gloomy picture of man staring at the flickering shapes made on the wall of the objective world by a fire behind us like the sun. But the analogy breaks down when the shadows are those of the past, for the only light we can see them by is the Promethean fire within us. The substance of these shadows can only be in ourselves, and the goal of historical criticism, as our metaphors about it often indicate, is a kind of self-resurrection, the vision of a valley of dry bones that takes on the flesh and blood of our own vision.

The culture of the past is not only the memory of mankind, but our own buried life, and study of it leads to a recognition scene, a discovery in which we see, not our past lives, but the total cultural form of our present life. It is not only the poet but his reader who is subject to the obligation to "make it new."

Without this sense of "repetition," historical criticism tends to remove the products of culture from our own sphere of interest. It must be counterpoised, as it is in all genuine historical critics, by a sense of the contemporary relevance of past art. But it is natural that this sense of contemporary relevance should often be confined to a specific issue in the present; that it should be thought of, not as expanding the perspective of present life, but as supporting a cause or thesis in the present.

If we cut through history at any point, including our own, and study a cross-section of it, we get a class structure. Culture may be employed by a social or intellectual class to increase its prestige; and in general, moral censors, selectors of great traditions, apologists of religious or political causes, aesthetes, radicals, codifiers of great books, and the like, are expressions of such class tensions. We soon realize, in studying their pronouncements, that the only really consistent moral criticism of this type would be the kind which is harnessed to an all-round revolutionary philosophy of society, such as we find not only in Marxism but in Nietzsche and in some of the rationalizations of oligarchic values in nineteenth-century Britain and twentieth-century America. In all these culture is treated as a human productive power which in the past has been, like other productive powers, exploited by other ruling classes and is now to be revalued in terms of a better society. But as this ideal society exists only in the future, the present valuation of culture is in terms of its interim revolutionary effectiveness.

This revolutionary way of looking at culture is also as old as Plato, the selected tradition being always some version of the argument about poets in the *Republic*. As soon as we make culture a definite image of a future and perhaps attainable society, we start selecting and purging a tradition, and all the artists who don't fit (an increasing number as the process goes on) have to be thrown out. So, just as historical criticism uncorrected relates culture only to the past, ethical criticism uncorrected relates culture only to the future, to the ideal society which may eventually come if we take sufficient pains to guard the educating of our youth. For all such lines of thought end in indoctrinating the next generation, just as the moral version of Victorian progressivism led to Podsnap and the blushing cheeks of the young person.

The body of work done in society, or civilization, both maintains and undermines the class structure of that society. The social energy which maintains the class structure produces perverted culture in its three chief forms: mere upper-class culture, or ostentation, mere middle-class culture, or vulgarity, and mere lower-class culture, or squalor. These three classes are called by Matthew Arnold respectively, in so far as they are classes, the barbarians, the philistines, and the populace. Revolutionary action, of whatever kind, leads to the dictatorship of one class, and the record of history seems clear that there is no quicker way of destroying the benefits of culture. If we attach our vision of culture to the conception of ruler-morality, we get the culture of barbarians; if we attach it to the conception of a proletariat, we get the culture of the populace; if we attach it to any kind of bourgeois Utopia, we get the culture of philistinism.

Whatever one thinks of dialectic materialism as a philosophy, it is certainly true that when men behave or pretend to behave like material bodies they do behave dialectically. If England goes to war with France, all the weaknesses in the English case and all the virtues in the French case are ignored in England; not only is the traitor the lowest of criminals, but it is indignantly denied that any traitor can be honestly motivated. In war, the physical or idolatrous substitute for the real dialectic of the spirit, one lives by half-truths. The same principle applies to the verbal or mimic wars made out of "points of view," which are usually the ghosts of some kind of social conflict.

It seems better to try to get clear of all such conflicts, attaching ourselves to Arnold's other axiom that "culture seeks to do away with classes." The ethical purpose of a liberal education is to liberate, which can only mean to make one capable of conceiving society as free, classless, and urbane. No such society exists, which is one reason why a liberal education must be deeply concerned with works of imagination. The imaginative element in works of art, again, lifts them clear of the bondage of history. Anything that emerges from the total experience of criticism to form part of a liberal education becomes, by virtue of that fact, part of the emancipated and humane community of culture, whatever its original reference. Thus liberal education liberates the works of culture them-

347

selves as well as the mind they educate. The corruption out of which human art has been constructed will always remain in the art, but the imaginative quality of the art preserves it in its corruption, like the corpse of a saint. No discussion of beauty can confine itself to the formal relations of the isolated work of art; it must consider, too, the participation of the work of art in the vision of the goal of social effort, the idea of complete and classless civilization. This idea of complete civilization is also the implicit moral standard to which ethical criticism always refers, something very different from any system of morals.

The idea of the free society implied in culture can never be formulated, much less established as a society. Culture is a present social ideal which we educate and free ourselves by trying to attain, and never do attain. It teaches, with the endless patience of the book which always presents the same words whenever we open it, but it is not possessed, for the experiences and meanings attached to the words are always new. No society can plan for its own culture unless it restricts the output of culture to socially predictable standards. The goal of ethical criticism is transvaluation, the ability to look at contemporary social values with the detachment of one who is able to compare them in some degree with the infinite vision of possibilities presented by culture. One who possesses such a standard of transvaluation is in a state of intellectual freedom. One who does not possess it is a creature of whatever social values get to him first: he has only the compulsions of habit, indoctrination, and prejudice. The current tendency to insist that man cannot be a spectator of his own life seems to me to be one of those lethal half-truths that arise in response to some kind of social malaise. Most ethical action is a mechanical reflex of habit: to get any principle of freedom in it we need some kind of theory of action, theory in the sense of *theoria*, a withdrawn or detached vision of the means and end of action which does not paralyze action, but makes it purposeful by enlightening its aims.

The two great classics of the theory of liberty in the modern world, *Areopagitica* and Mill's *Essay on Liberty*, deal of course with liberty in different contexts. For Milton culture is potential prophecy, set in judgement over against the kind of social acceptance of sanctioned error represented by the censor, whereas for Mill culture is a social critique. But allowing for this, both essays insist that liberty can begin only with an immediate and present guarantee of the autonomy of culture. In Mill unlimited liberty of thought and discussion is not only the best way of developing liberty of action, but the best way of controlling it, because it is the only means of preventing impulsive or stampeded action. In Milton liberty of conscience is not the freedom to listen to the compulsions acquired in childhood which make up the greater part of what we ordinarily call conscience, but the freedom to listen to the Word of God, which, as it is a message from an infinite mind to a finite one, can never be definitively understood by the latter.

At this point the theory of criticism seems ready to settle quietly into the larger humanistic principle that the freedom of man is inseparably bound up with his acceptance of his cultural heritage. The writer believes this, of course, and so probably do most of those who will read his book; but there may still be a residue from the parasite fallacy of criticism, which all our arguments may not yet have dispelled. This is the feeling that as criticism is based on cultural products, the more important the critic claims his work to be, the more he tends to magnify the normal pleasure that a cultivated person finds in the arts into something awful and portentous, replacing culture with aesthetic superstition, literature with bardolatry, of however sophisticated a kind.

This would be true if in fact the aesthetic or contemplative aspect of art were the final resting place for either art or criticism. Here again it is archetypal criticism that comes to our aid. We tried to show in the second essay that the moment we go from the individual work of art to the sense of the total form of the art, the art becomes no longer an object of aesthetic contemplation but an ethical instrument, participating in the work of civilization. In this shift to the ethical, criticism as well as poetry is involved, though some of the ways in which it is involved are not commonly recognized as aspects of criticism. It is obvious, for instance, that one major source of order in society is an established pattern of words. In religion this may be a scripture, a liturgy, or a creed; in politics it may be a written constitution or a set of ideological directives like the pamphlets of Lenin in present-day Russia. Such verbal patterns may remain fixed for centuries: the meanings attached to them will change out of all recognition in that time, but the feeling that the verbal structure must remain unchanged, and the consequent necessity of reinterpreting it to suit the changes of history, bring the operations of criticism into the center of society.

But we then had to complete our argument by removing all external goals from literature, thus postulating a self-contained literary universe. Perhaps in doing so we merely restored the aesthetic view on a gigantic scale, substituting Poetry for a mass of poems, aesthetic mysticism for aesthetic empiricism. The argument of our last essay, however, led to the principle that all structures in words are partly rhetorical, and hence literary, and that the notion of a scientific or philosophical verbal structure free of rhetorical elements is an illusion. If so, then our literary universe has expanded into a verbal universe, and no aesthetic principle of self-containment will work.

I am not wholly unaware that at every step of this argument there are extremely complicated philosophical problems which I am incompetent to solve as such. I am aware also, however, of something else. That something else is the confused swirl of new intellectual activities today associated with such words as communication, symbolism, semantics, linguistics, metalinguistics, pragmatics, cybernetics, and the ideas generated by and around Cassirer, Korzybsky, and dozens of others in fields as remote (as they seemed until recently) as prehistory and mathematics, logic and engineering, sociology and physics. Many of these movements were instigated by a desire to free the modern mind from the tyranny of emotional rhetoric, from the advertising and propaganda that try to pervert thought by a misuse of irony into conditioned reflex. Many of them have also moved in the direction of conceptual rhetoric, reducing the content of many arguments to their ambiguous or diagrammatic structures. My knowledge of most of the books dealing with this new material is largely confined, like Moses' knowledge of God in the mount, to gazing at their spines, but it is clear to me that literary criticism has a central place in all this activity, and from the point of view of literary criticism I offer an admittedly very speculative suggestion.

We have several times hinted at an analogy between literature and mathematics. Mathematics appears to begin in the counting and measuring of objects, as a numerical commentary on the outside world. But the mathematician does not think of his subject so: for him it is an autonomous language, and there is a point at which it becomes in a measure independent of that common field of experience which we call the objective world, or nature, or existence, or reality, according to our mood. Many of its terms, such as irrational numbers, have no direct connection with the common field of experience, but depend for their meaning solely on the interrelations of the subject itself. Irrational numbers in mathematics may be compared to prepositions in verbal languages, the centripetal character of which we have noted. When we distinguish pure from applied mathematics, we are thinking of the former as a disinterested conception of numerical relationships, concerned more and more with its inner integrity, and less and less with its reference to external criteria.

We think also of literature at first as a commentary on an external "life" or "reality." But just as in mathematics we have to go from three apples to three, and from a square field to a square, so in reading a novel we have to go from literature as reflection of life to literature as autonomous language. Literature also proceeds by hypothetical possibilities, and though literature, like mathematics, is constantly useful—a word which means having a continuing relationship to the common field of experience—pure literature, like pure mathematics, contains its own meaning.

Both literature and mathematics proceed from postulates, not facts; both can be applied to external reality and yet exist also in a "pure" or self-contained form. Both, furthermore, drive a wedge between the antithesis of being and non-being that is so important for discursive thought. The symbol neither is nor is not the reality which it manifests. The child beginning geometry is presented with a dot and is told, first, that that is a point, and second, that it is not a point. He cannot advance until he accepts both statements at once. It is absurd that that which is no number can also be a number, but the result of accepting the absurdity was the discovery of zero. The same kind of hypothesis exists in literature, where Hamlet and Falstaff neither exist nor do not exist, and where an airy nothing is confidently located and named. We notice that rhetoric differs sharply from logic in that it invariably gives some positive quality to a negative statement. Logic counts the negatives in a statement and calls it affirmative if there is an even number, but no one in the history of communication ever took "I hain't got no money" to mean that the speaker *did* have money. Similarly in literature: Iago's urging Othello to beware of jealousy is designed to plant jealousy in Othello's mind; the negatives at the beginning of *Gerontion* mean logically that Gerontion is not a hero, but rhetorically they build up a contrasting picture of sacrifice and

351

endurance. If the poet never affirmeth, he never denies either; and in this respect Aristotle's opening statement about rhetoric, that it is the *antistrophos* or answering chorus of dialectic, breaks down.

In the final chapter of Sir James Jeans' *The Mysterious Universe*, the author speaks of the failure of physical cosmology in the nineteenth century to conceive of the universe as ultimately mechanical, and suggests that a mathematical approach to it may have better luck. The universe cannot be a machine, but it may be an interlocking set of mathematical formulas. What this means is surely that pure mathematics exists in a mathematical universe which is no longer a commentary on an outside world, but contains that world within itself. Mathematics is at first a form of understanding an objective world regarded as its content, but in the end it conceives of the content as being itself mathematical in form, and when a conception of a mathematical universe is reached, form and content become the same thing. Mathematics relates itself indirectly to the common field of experience, then, not to avoid it, but with the ultimate design of swallowing it. It appears to be a kind of informing or constructive principle in the natural sciences: it continually gives shape and coherence to them without being itself dependent on external proof or evidence, and yet finally the physical or quantitative universe appears to be contained by mathematics. The occult or mystical sound of Jeans' chapter, which nevertheless expresses a dream that has haunted mathematicians at least since Pythagoras, may be compared with the religious terminology we found ourselves compelled to use as soon as we reached the corresponding conception of a literary or verbal universe.

Other points in this analogy strike one: the curious similarity in form, for instance, between the units of literature and of mathematics, the metaphor and the equation. Both of these are, in the expanded sense of the term employed by many logicians, tautologies. But if the analogy is to hold, the question of course arises: is literature like mathematics in being substantially useful, and not just incidentally so? That is, is it true that the verbal structures of psychology, anthropology, theology, history, law, and everything else built out of words have been informed or constructed by the same kind of myths and metaphors that we find, in their original hypothetical form, in literature?

The possibility that seems to me suggested by the present discussion is as follows. Discursive verbal structures have two aspects, one descriptive, the other constructive, a content and a form. What is descriptive is sigmatic: that is, it establishes a verbal replica of external phenomena, and its verbal symbolism is to be understood as a set of representative signs. But whatever is constructive in any verbal structure seems to me to be invariably some kind of metaphor or hypothetical identification, whether it is established among different meanings of the same word or by the use of a diagram. The assumed metaphors in their turn become the units of the myth or constructive principle of the argument. While we read, we are aware of a sequence of metaphorical identifications; when we have finished, we are aware of an organizing structural pattern or conceptualized myth.

It looks now as though Freud's view of the Oedipus complex were a psychological conception that throws some light on literary criticism. Perhaps we shall eventually decide that we have got it the wrong way round: that what happened was that the myth of Oedipus informed and gave structure to some psychological investigations at this point. Freud would in that case be exceptional only in having been well read enough to spot the source of the myth. It looks now as though the psychological discovery of an oracular mind "underneath" the conscious one forms an appropriate allegorical explanation of a poetic archetype that has run through literature from the cave of Trophonius to our own day. Perhaps it was the archetype that informed the discovery: it is after all considerably older, and to explain it in this way would involve us in less anachronism. The informing of metaphysical and theological constructs by poetic myths, or by associations and diagrams analogous to poetic myths, is even more obvious.

Such an approach need not be distorted into a poetic determinism, for, as has been said, it would be silly to use a reductive rhetoric to try to prove that theology, metaphysics, law, the social sciences, or whichever one or group of these we happen to dislike, are based on "nothing but" metaphors or myths. Any such proof, if we are right, would have the same kind of basis itself. Criticisms of truth or adequacy, then, are mainly criticism of content, not form. Rousseau says that the original society of nature and reason has been overlaid by the corruptions of civilization, and that a sufficiently courageous revolutionary act could reestablish it. It is nothing either for or against this argument to say that it is informed by the myth of the sleeping beauty. But we cannot agree or disagree with Rousseau until we fully understand what he does say, and while of course we can understand him well enough without extracting the myth, there is much to be gained by extracting the myth if the myth is in fact, as we are suggesting here, the source of the coherence of his argument. Such a view of the relation of myth to argument would take us very close to Plato, for whom the ultimate acts of apprehension were either mathematical or mythical.

Literature, like mathematics, is a language, and a language in itself represents no truth, though it may provide the means for expressing any number of them. But poets and critics alike have always believed in some kind of imaginative truth, and perhaps the justification for the belief is in the containment by the language of what it can express. The mathematical and the verbal universes are doubtless different ways of conceiving the same universe. The objective world affords a provisional means of unifying experience, and it is natural to infer a higher unity, a sort of beatification of common sense. But it is not easy to find any language capable of expressing the unity of this higher intellectual universe. Metaphysics, theology, history, law, have all been used, but all are verbal constructs, and the further we take them, the more clearly their metaphorical and mythical outlines show through. Whenever we construct a system of thought to unite earth with heaven, the story of the Tower of Babel recurs: we discover that after all we can't quite make it, and that what we have in the meantime is a plurality of languages.

If I have read the last chapter of *Finnegans Wake* correctly, what happens there is that the dreamer, after spending the night in communion with a vast body of metaphorical identifications, wakens and goes about his business forgetting his dream, like Nebuchadnezzar, failing to use, or even to realize that he can use, the "keys to dreamland." What he fails to do is therefore left for the reader to do, the "ideal reader suffering from an ideal insomnia," as Joyce calls him, in other words the critic. Some such activity as this of reforging the broken links between creation and knowledge, art and science, myth and concept, is what I envisage for criticism. Once more, I am not speaking of a change of direction or activity in criticism: I mean only that if critics go on with their own business, this will appear to be, with increasing obviousness, the social and practical result of their labors.

354

NOTES

GLOSSARY

INDEX

NOTES

p. 5, line 7   "John Stuart Mill." "Thoughts on Poetry and its Varieties," *Dissertations and Discussions*, Series I.

p. 9, line 24   "Matthew Arnold." "The Literary Influence of Academies," *Essays in Criticism*, First Series.

p. 15, line 7   "whatever it is now." This phrase expresses, not a contempt for aesthetics, but a conviction that it is time for aesthetics to get out from under philosophy, as psychology has already done. Most philosophers deal with aesthetic questions only as a set of analogies to their logical and metaphysical views, hence it is difficult to use, say, Kant or Hegel on the arts without getting into a Kantian or Hegelian "position." Aristotle is the only philosopher known to me who not only talks specifically about poetics when he is aware of larger aesthetic problems, but who assumes that such poetics would be the organon of an independent discipline. Consequently a critic can use the *Poetics* without involving himself in Aristotelianism (though I know that some Aristotelian critics do not think so).

p. 15, line 9   "state of naive induction." I am indebted here to a passage in Susanne K. Langer, *The Practice of Philosophy* (1930).

p. 18, line 38   "better critics of all ages." Shelley, for example, speaks in A *Defence of Poetry* of "that great poem, which all poets, like the co-operating thoughts of one great mind, have built up since the beginning of the world."

p. 21, line 22   "Arnold's 'touchstone' theory." "The Study of Poetry," *Essays in Criticism*, Second Series.

p. 37, line 1   "Beowulf." The precise meaning of "enta geweorc" (2717) does not affect the illustration.

p. 37, line 19   "central position of high mimetic tragedy." Cf. Louis L. Martz, "The Saint as Tragic Hero," *Tragic Themes in Western Literature*, ed. Cleanth Brooks (1955), 176.

p. 41, line 7   "Coleridge." See *Coleridge's Miscellaneous Criticism*, ed. T. M. Raysor (1936), 294; I have expanded what Coleridge says in order to bring out the critical principle involved.

p. 46, line 8   "deliverance from the unpleasant." Cf. Max Eastman, *Enjoyment of Laughter* (1936), which also provides some illuminating comments on the *eiron* and *alazon* roles.

p. 46, line 13   "suggested for Old Comedy." See Francis M. Cornford, *The Origin of Attic Comedy* (1934).

p. 53, line 23   "named after its plot." See R. S. Crane, "The Concept of Plot and the Plot of *Tom Jones*," *Critics and Criticism*, ed. R. S. Crane (1952), 616 ff.

p. 61, line 8   "*Augenblick* of modern German thought." The *Erkennung* of Rilke's *Sonnets to Orpheus* (II, xii) is a less vague example; it also illustrates the conception of thematic discovery or recognition (p. 52; cf. p. 302).

p. 61, line 37   "One study." Sir George Rostrevor Hamilton, *The Tell-Tale Article* (1949).

p. 71, line 1   "lack of a technical vocabulary." The revival of the technical language of rhetoric would not only provide us with useful terms, but in many cases would revive the conceptions themselves which have been forgotten along with their names. It may be true that, as Samuel Butler said:

> . . . all a rhetorician's rules
> Teach nothing but to name his tools

but if a critic cannot name his tools, the world is unlikely to concede much authority to his craft. We should not entrust our cars to a mechanic who lived entirely in a world of gadgets and doohickeys.

p. 76, line 30   "Dante says." *Epistola* X, to Can Grande (*Opere*, ed. Moore and Toynbee, 4th ed., 416). See also *Il Convivio*, II, i (*op. cit.*, 251-252).

p. 82, line 2   "What is now called 'new criticism.'" The account of literal meaning given here depends on I. A. Richards, Richard Blackmur, William Empson (ambiguity), Cleanth Brooks (literal irony), and John Crowe Ransom (texture) in particular.

p. 82, line 26   "the word form." For the theory of the formal phase, I have been considerably indebted to R. S. Crane, *The Languages of Criticism and the Structure of Poetry* (1953), as well as to *Critics and Criticism* (1952), edited by him.

p. 86, line 21   "'the intentional fallacy.'" See W. K. Wimsatt, Jr., and Monroe Beardsley, *The Verbal Icon* (1954), Ch. 1. I have taken the word "holism" (p. 326) from the same book, p. 238.

p. 93, line 9   "Yeats and Sturge Moore." See *W. B. Yeats and T. Sturge Moore; Their Correspondence, 1901-1937* (1953).

p. 95, line 18   "convention and genre." The conception of the autonomy of form in art is essential to the argument of André Malraux, *The Voices of Silence*, tr. Stuart Gilbert (1953). In modern English criticism the archetypal approach is highly developed in both theory and practice. In theory, the books of Maud Bodkin, Kenneth Burke, Gaston Bachelard, Francis Fergusson, and Philip Wheelwright are of obvious and exceptional usefulness. See the excellent bibliographies in René Wellek and Austin Warren, *Theory of Literature* (1942), Ch. xv.

p. 98, line 1   "remark of Mr. Eliot." In his essay on Philip Massinger.

p. 99 line 34   "literary adaptation of the ritual of the Adonis lament." This phrase should be understood in the light of the general principle that "ritual" refers to content rather than source.

p. 101, line 34   "clueless." My only point is that there may not be any point, but as Rose Armiger is a sister to dragons rather than knights errant, there is a faint possibility of parody-symbolism, discussed below.

p. 103, line 16   "*topoi*." For these see E. R. Curtius, *European Literature and the Latin Middle Ages*, tr. Willard Trask (1953), 79 ff. An example of the point made in the text is the relation of

Milton's first prolusion, "Whether Day is more excellent than Night," to *L'Allegro* and *Il Penseroso*.

p. 105, line 6   "the work of the dream." Throughout this book "dream" is used in an extended sense to mean, not simply the fantasies of the sleeping mind, but the whole interpenetrating activity of desire and repugnance in shaping thought.

p. 111, line 23   "actual content, its *dianoia*." The expression here is careless, as *dianoia* refers to form.

p. 113, line 32   "its own object." I have taken this phrase from an oral lecture by M. Jacques Maritain.

p. 122, line 8   "a letter of Rilke." Letter to Ellen Delp, October 27, 1915.

p. 122, line 22   "universal human body." To these should be added the great meditation on time in the second part of *Le Temps Retrouvé*. One wonders if there is anything more than doubtful puns connecting the anagogic perspective in literature with Kant's conception of "transcendental aesthetic" as the *a priori* consciousness of space and time.

p. 125, line 10   "Coleridge." *Coleridge's Miscellaneous Criticism*, ed. T. M. Raysor (1936), 343.

p. 135, line 10   "credible facts." I pass over the point that the younger brother is warned of his danger by the elder brother's cow.

p. 140, line 27   "hero descending." The statement that Hamlet descends into the grave is expendable, but the contrast in his mood before and after the scene indicates some kind of *rite de passage*.

p. 141, line 21   "grammar of apocalyptic imagery." For Biblical typology a useful book is Austin Farrer, *A Rebirth of Images* (1949). See also Alan W. Watts, *Myth and Ritual in Christianity* (1954).

p. 142, line 5   " 'figura.' " See Erich Auerbach, *Mimesis*, tr. Willard Trask (1953), 73.

p. 144, line 1   "Of birds." Several poems by Wallace Stevens, including "The Dove in the Belly," employ this symbolism. Other favored members of the animal kingdom include the fish and the dolphin, traditionally Christian in contrast to the leviathan, and among insects the bee, so beloved of Virgil, whose sweetness and light are a contrast to the devouring spider. Cf. Dame Edith Sitwell's poem, "The Bee Oracles." The old theory of "primates" in the various kingdoms is connected with this symbolic use of typical representatives.

p. 145, line 37   "burning man." Cf. D. H. Lawrence's remarks on vermilion paint in *Etruscan Places*, Ch. III.

p. 146, line 4   "In alchemy." For alchemical symbolism see Herbert Silberer, *Problems of Mysticism and its Symbolism*, tr. Smith Ely Jelliffe (1917), and C. G. Jung, *Psychology and Alchemy*, tr. R. F. C. Hull (1953). Allegorical alchemy, Rosicrucianism, Cabbalism, Freemasonry, and the Tarot pack are all typological constructs based on paradigms similar to those given here. For the literary critic they are simply reference tables: the atmosphere of oracular harrumph about them, which recurs in some forms of archetypal criticism, is not much to the point.

pp. 159-160   "Animal lives." Hence the relation of animal symbolism to the phase of the cycle is characterized by the choice of animal rather than by its age. We expect to find deer in romances and rats in *The Waste Land*.

p. 165, line 28   "carefully marked." *Volpone*, V, ii, 12-14.

p. 166, line 14   "*Tractatus Coislinianus*." See Lane Cooper, *An Aristotelian Theory of Comedy* (1922).

p. 168, line 39   "Mr. E. M. Forster." *Aspects of the Novel* (1927), Ch. I. It would perhaps be better to draw the contrast between a fictional repetition like Mrs. Micawber's formula, and a thematic repetition, like Matthew Arnold's deliberate echoing *ad nauseam* of fatuous phrases used by his opponents. For the role of such thematic repetitions in Forster's own work, see E. K. Brown, *Rhythm in the Novel* (1950).

p. 171, line 28   "occupies the middle action." Hence the archetype of the blocking character in comedy is the "interrex" or deputy ruler: see Theodor H. Gaster, *Thespis* (1950), 34. Angelo in *Measure for Measure* is the clearest example.

p. 173, line 28   "amateur detective of modern fiction." This is his naive incarnation; in more sophisticated comedy a popular form of *gracioso* is the dandy, a disengaged figure whose epigrams are largely inverted clichés, whose attitude is that of comic scorn for sentimentality as described on p. 48, and who is normally a conservative, opposed to a group of humors who feel that they are progressive because they all face in the same direction. He is well exhibited in Wilde's *An Ideal Husband*. In the twenties the dandy revived, both fictionally and thematically, in Firbank, Huxley, Waugh, the Knickerbocker figure of *The New Yorker*, and elsewhere.

p. 178, line 34   "and then reverses the action." The impetus of irony or "realism" is toward a conclusion which remains within the state of experience; the impetus of comedy is toward a lift out of that state. Which conclusion the author chooses is often a matter of a sentence or two, like a piece of music in a minor key which may or may not end on the parallel major chord. Besides *The Beggar's Opera*, Dickens's *Great Expectations* and Charlotte Bronte's *Villette* go to the length of providing alternative endings, one conventionally comic, the other more equivocal.

p. 183, line 30   " 'behind the eight-ball.' " I forget where I read this, but perhaps the reader will excuse the reference.

p. 186, line 32   "endless form." This endless form has many literary manifestations: in the sequence of stories based on the same formula, like *The Monk's Tale* in Chaucer and its slower-witted descendants in Lydgate and *The Mirror for Magistrates*; in the arbitrarily determined number of stories to be told in a given situation, like the thousand and one that Scheherezade tells for dear life; in the curiously muted conclusion of Lady Murasaki's *Tale of Genji*, which, though a

logical enough conclusion, would hardly have precluded the
author from starting again. For its appearance in drama, see
the note to p. 289. The principle of discovery, which brings
the end into line with the beginning, gives to the symmetrical plot its characteristic parabola shape.

p. 187, line 10 "using Greek terms." That is, using the terms employed by
Sir Gilbert Murray in his Excursus in Jane Harrison, *Themis*,
2nd ed. (1927), 341 ff.

p. 188, line 18 " 'subconscious' factor." It should also be said, however,
that archetypal criticism, which can do nothing but abstract
and typify and reduce to convention, has only a "subconscious" role in the direct experience of literature, where
uniqueness is everything. In direct experience we are dimly
aware of familiar conventions, but as a rule we are consciously aware of them only when we are bored or disap-
pointed, and feel that there is nothing new here. Hence the
usual confusion between direct experience and criticism may
well lead to the feeling that archetypal criticism is simply
bad criticism, as in some pronouncements of Mr. Wyndham Lewis.

p. 191, line 17 "*Paradise Regained.*" See "The Typology of *Paradise Regained*," *Modern Philology* (1956), 227 ff.

p. 192, line 26 "central unifying myth." Cf. Joseph Campbell, *The Hero
with a Thousand Faces* (1949); Lord Raglan, *The Hero*
(1936); C. G. Jung, *Wandlungen und Symbole der Libido*,
soon to be retranslated in the Bollingen series as *Symbols
of Transformation*, and the account of the "eniautos-dai-
mon" in Jane Harrison, *Themis*. To these perhaps I may
add my own account of Blake's Orc symbolism in *Fearful
Symmetry* (1947), Ch. VII.

p. 194, line 6 "we are told." Jessie Weston, *From Ritual to Romance*
(1920).

p. 194, line 25 "identified." The Biblical identification is in Rev. 12:9,
from which the phrase "that old dragon" in the head verse
to Canto XI comes.

p. 198, line 8 "studied in some detail." See Otto Rank, *The Myth of the
Birth of the Hero* (1910); also C. G. Jung and C. Kerenyi,
Essays toward a Science of Mythology, tr. R. F. C. Hull
(1949).

p. 201, line 13 "natural sequel to the first book." The archetype is that of
the building of a habitation for the god or hero after his triumph: cf. Theodor H. Gaster, *Thespis*, 163. The phrase
"Beauty and money" is from *Faerie Queene*, II, xi. For the
distinctions between temperance and continence and the two
levels of nature, see A. S. P. Woodhouse, "Nature and
Grace in *The Faerie Queene*," *ELH* (1949), 194 ff. and
"The Argument of Milton's *Comus*," *University of Toronto
Quarterly* (1941), 46 ff. .

p. 203, line 35 "analogues of the Biblical stories of the Fall." See Apollodo-
rus, *Bibliotheca*, ed. Frazer (Loeb Classical Library, 1921);

Sir James Frazer, *Folk Lore in the Old Testament*, Vol. I (1918); Leo Frobenius, *The Childhood of Man*, tr. A. H. Keane (1909).

p. 204, line 2   "'gold bug' in Poe's story." This example will not please the oh-come-now school of criticism, but is added because it illustrates the principle that logical construction, in a popular tale, is a matter of the linking of archetypes. The use of the gold bug to discover the treasure is, from the irrelevant point of view of plausibility, unnecessary, and only the lamest excuse is given for it in the dialogue.

p. 208, line 23   "rise of Ionian and of Renaissance science." Cf. A. N. Whitehead, *Science and the Modern World* (1925), Ch. 1.

p. 214, line 20   "treatment of the tragic vision." See *Also Sprach Zarathustra*, III, lvii. Zarathustra is at the point of epiphany, with the cyclical world below him; as his vision is primarily that of the tragic hero, his natural movement is downward into the cycle. Like the Father's speech in Milton, to which it affords an instructive parallel, the argument itself may be unconvincing, but the reason for its being there is plain enough. Eliot's *Ash Wednesday* and Yeats's *Dialogue of Self and Soul*, which deal with the same archetype from directly opposed points of view, are much clearer in structure.

p. 228, line 17   "does not need a great person." Chaucer's pardoner is a perhaps better example.

p. 231, line 31   "Charles Fort." See *The Books of Charles Fort* (1941), 435.

p. 235, line 3   "Emerson says." *Nature*, vi.

p. 237, line 7   "Coriolanus." See Wyndham Lewis, *The Lion and the Fox* (1927).

p. 244, line 20   "Ezra Pound." *ABC of Reading*, Ch. iv. *Melopoiia* is actually Aristotle's word: I use *melos* because it is short.

p. 245, line 40   "Coleridge." From the Essay on Method in *The Friend*, iv. I do not claim that I am correctly interpreting Coleridge's term, but the necessity of being a terminological buccaneer should be clear enough by now.

p. 250, line 37   "no controlling rhythm." No specifically *verbal* rhythm, that is: the controlling rhythm of drama is the rhythm of its production on the stage.

p. 253, line 24   "his own modification." I should modify it myself to make the beat "on no side" begin with an eighth rest.

p. 258, line 13   "recurrent Alexandrine." Also by a number of six-stress pentameters; see "Lexis and Melos," *Sound and Poetry* (*English Institute Essays* 1956; forthcoming).

p. 259, line 2   "treatise on rhetoric." *Rhetoric* III, xi; but the actual use of the line (*Od.* xi, 598) as a blackboard example of imitative harmony comes rather from Dionysius of Halicarnassus.

p. 261, line 26   "'ten low words.'" *Essay on Criticism*, 347; what is wrong with the line, of course, is not too many monosyllables, but too many stressed accents.

p. 264, line 32   "'Senecan amble.'" See the book of that title by George Williamson (1951).

p. 265, line 37   "Wulfstan." Another text of the *Sermo Lupi ad Anglos* adds two more alliterative pairs to the quotation given, indicating a certain *ad libitum* quality in such rhetoric.

p. 268, line 13   "Cassiodorus." Quoted from W. P. Ker, *The Dark Ages* (1911), 119.

p. 269, line 33   "literary mannerism." Cf. T. S. Eliot, *Poetry and Drama* (1951).

p. 272, line 19   " 'true voice of feeling.' " See the book of that title by Sir Herbert Read (1953).

p. 275, line 20   "little has yet been said." See however the conception of "parody" in Frederick W. Sternfeld, *Goethe and Music* (1954).

p. 278, line 23   "*Camellia Sabina*." See Marianne Moore, *Selected Poems* (1935); the scheme of the poem is altered in later editions.

p. 281, line 25   "thirty-eight phrases." The book examined was Oscar Williams, *The Man Coming Toward You* (1940); the only point made by the count is that modern diction is as conventionalized as any other diction.

p. 284, line 1   "secular Eucharist symbol." We may glance in passing at the conclusion of *Richard III* (V, iv, 31-32):

> And then, as we have ta'en the sacrament,
> We will unite the white rose and the red.

p. 286, line 34   "preface to *Getting Married*." More exactly, in a prefatory note separated from the preface.

p. 289, line 14   "tendency to linear movement." For this processional structure, so much disliked by Aristotle, cf. the note to p. 186. The hypothesis that Shakespeare may have used a collaborator in *Pericles* does not affect my statements about it.

p. 290, line 7   "said to be descended." See Enid Welsford, *The Court Masque* (1927).

p. 293, line 21   "along with such *epos* forms." An extremely complicated problem, the problem of the intervening generic stages between lyric and *epos*, has had to be omitted from this discussion.

p. 317, line 10   "two epic frameworks." In G. R. Levy, *The Sword from the Rock* (1954), three types of epic structure are recognized: mythical epics, quest-epics, and conflict-epics. As far as the epic material used is concerned, these correspond roughly to our mythical, romantic and high mimetic encyclopaedic forms.

p. 320, line 36   "in France." See H. J. Hunt, *The Epic in Nineteenth-Century France* (1941).

p. 326, line 8   "a Longinian point of view." This conception of Aristotelian aesthetic catharsis and Longinian psychological ecstasis as complementary to one another (cf. p. 66) is explained perhaps more coherently in "Towards Defining an Age of Sensibility," *ELH* (1956), 144ff., in connection with eighteenth-century English literature.

p. 328, line 10   "Swinburne." The passage, if it matters, comes from his introduction to the Mermaid Series edition of Middleton, ed. Havelock Ellis (1887).

p. 334, line 10   "possibility of links." For a criticism of some of the views here advanced, see Donald Davie, *Articulate Energy* (1955), 130 ff.

p. 341, line 24   "allegorical explanations of myths." See Jean Seznec, *The Survival of the Pagan Gods*, tr. Barbara Sessions (1953), Bk. II.

p. 349, line 40   "center of society." Cf. Ezra Pound's conception of the "unwobbling pivot."

p. 353, line 5   "some kind of metaphor." The critic would of course need to distinguish an explicit metaphor from a metaphorical verbal construct. "X has a bee in his bonnet about Y" is an explicit metaphor; "X has got the notion Y into his head" is the verbal frame of the same metaphor, but for ordinary purposes it would pass as a simply descriptive statement.

p. 354, line 7   "either mathematical or mythical." It is difficult to see how aesthetic theory can get much further without recognizing the creative element in mathematics. The arts might be more clearly understood if they were thought of as forming a circle, stretching from music through literature, painting and sculpture to architecture, with mathematics, the missing art, occupying the vacant place between architecture and music. The feeling that mathematics belongs to science rather than art is largely due to the fact that mathematics is an art that we know how to use. The difference between mathematics and literature on this point will be greatly reduced when criticism achieves its proper form of the theory of the use of words.

GLOSSARY

(This glossary omits the regular Aristotelian, rhetorical, and critical terms which are also employed in this book.)

ALAZON: A deceiving or self-deceived character in fiction, normally an object of ridicule in comedy or satire, but often the hero of a tragedy. In comedy he most frequently takes the form of a *miles gloriosus* or a pedant.

ANAGOGIC: Relating to literature as a total order of words.

ANATOMY: A form of prose fiction, traditionally known as the Menippean or Varronian satire and represented by Burton's *Anatomy of Melancholy*, characterized by a great variety of subject-matter and a strong interest in ideas. In shorter forms it often has a *cena* or symposium setting and verse interludes.

APOCALYPTIC: The thematic term corresponding to "myth" in fictional literature: metaphor as pure and potentially total identification, without regard to plausibility or ordinary experience.

ARCHETYPE: A symbol, usually an image, which recurs often enough in literature to be recognizable as an element of one's literary experience as a whole.

AUTO: A form of drama in which the main subject is sacred or sacrosanct legend, such as miracle plays, solemn and processional in form but not strictly tragic. Name taken from Calderon's *Autos Sacramentales*.

CONFESSION: Autobiography regarded as a form of prose fiction, or prose fiction cast in the form of autobiography.

DIANOIA: The meaning of a work of literature, which may be the total pattern of its symbols (literal meaning), its correlation with an external body of propositions or facts (descriptive meaning), its theme, or relation as a form of imagery to a potential commentary (formal meaning), its significance as a literary convention or genre (archetypal meaning), or its relation to total literary experience (anagogic meaning).

DISPLACEMENT: The adaptation of myth and metaphor to canons of morality or plausibility.

EIRON: A self-deprecating or unobtrusively treated character in fiction, usually an agent of the happy ending in comedy and of the catastrophe in tragedy.

ENCYCLOPAEDIC FORM: A genre presenting an anagogic form of symbolism, such as a sacred scripture, or its analogues in other modes. The term includes the Bible, Dante's *Commedia*, the great epics, and the works of Joyce and Proust.

EPOS: The literary genre in which the radical of presentation is the author or minstrel as oral reciter, with a listening audience in front of him.

ETHOS: The internal social context of a work of literature, comprising the characterization and setting of fictional literature and the relation of the author to his reader or audience in thematic literature.

FICTION: Literature in which the radical of presentation is the printed or written word, such as novels and essays.

FICTIONAL: Relating to literature in which there are internal characters, apart from the author and his audience; opposed to thematic. (*N.B.*

The use of this term is regrettably inconsistent with the preceding one, as noted on p. 248.)

HIGH MIMETIC: A mode of literature in which, as in most epics and trage-dies, the central characters are above our own level of power and au-thority, though within the order of nature and subject to social criti-cism.

IMAGE: A symbol in its aspect as a formal unit of art with a natural content.

INITIATIVE: A primary consideration governing the process of composition, such as the metre selected for a poem; taken from Coleridge.

IRONIC: A mode of literature in which the characters exhibit a power of action inferior to the one assumed to be normal in the reader or audi-ence, or in which the poet's attitude is one of detached objectivity.

IRONY: The mythos (sense 2) of the literature concerned primarily with a "realistic" level of experience, usually taking the form of a parody or contrasting analogue to romance. Such irony may be tragic or comic in its main emphasis; when comic it is normally identical with the usual meaning of satire.

LEXIS: The verbal "texture" or rhetorical aspect of a work of literature, in-cluding the usual meanings of the terms "diction" and "imagery."

LOW MIMETIC: A mode of literature in which the characters exhibit a power of action which is roughly on our own level, as in most comedy and realistic fiction.

LYRIC: A literary genre characterized by the assumed concealment of the audience from the poet and by the predominance of an associational rhythm distinguishable both from recurrent metre and from semantic or prose rhythm.

MASQUE: A species of drama in which music and spectacle play an important role and in which the characters tend to be or become aspects of hu-man personality rather than independent characters.

MELOS: The rhythm, movement, and sound of words; the aspect of litera-ture which is analogous to music, and often shows some actual relation to it. From Aristotle's *melopoiia*.

METAPHOR: A relation between two symbols, which may be simple juxta-position (literal metaphor), a rhetorical statement of likeness or simi-larity (descriptive metaphor), an analogy of proportion among four terms (formal metaphor), an identity of an individual with its class (concrete universal or archetypal metaphor), or statement of hypo-thetical identity (anagogic metaphor).

MODE: A conventional power of action assumed about the chief characters in fictional literature, or the corresponding attitude assumed by the poet toward his audience in thematic literature. Such modes tend to succeed one another in a historical sequence.

MONAD: A symbol in its aspect as a center of one's total literary experience; related to Hopkins's term "inscape" and to Joyce's term "epiphany."

MOTIF: A symbol in its aspect as a verbal unit in a work of literary art.

MYTH: A narrative in which some characters are superhuman beings who do things that "happen only in stories"; hence, a conventionalized or stylized narrative not fully adapted to plausibility or "realism."

MYTHOS: (1) The narrative of a work of literature, considered as the gram-mar or order of words (literal narrative), plot or "argument" (descrip-tive narrative), secondary imitation of action (formal narrative), imitation of generic and recurrent action or ritual (archetypal narrative), or imitation of the total conceivable action of an omnipotent god or human society (anagogic narrative). (2) One of the four archetypal narratives, classified as comic, romantic, tragic, and ironic.

NAIVE: Primitive or popular, in the sense given those terms of an ability to communicate in time and space more readily than other types of literature.

OPSIS: The spectacular or visible aspect of drama; the ideally visible or pictorial aspect of other literature.

PHARMAKOS: The character in an ironic fiction who has the role of a scapegoat or arbitrarily chosen victim.

PHASE: (1) One of the five contexts in which the narrative and meaning of a work of literature may be considered, classified as literal, descriptive, formal, archetypal, and anagogic. (2) One of six distinguishable stages of a mythos (sense 2).

POINT OF EPIPHANY: An archetype presenting simultaneously an apocalyptic world and a cyclical order of nature, or sometimes the latter alone. Its usual symbols are ladders, mountains, lighthouses, islands, and towers.

ROMANCE: (1) The mythos of literature concerned primarily with an idealized world. (2) A form of prose fiction practised by Scott, Hawthorne, William Morris, etc., distinguishable from the novel.

ROMANTIC: (1) A fictional mode in which the chief characters live in a world of marvels (naive romance), or in which the mood is elegiac or idyllic and hence less subject to social criticism than in the mimetic modes. (2) The general tendency to present myth and metaphor in an idealized human form, midway between undisplaced myth and "realism."

SIGN: A symbol in its aspect as a verbal representative of a natural object or concept.

SYMBOL: Any unit of any work of literature which can be isolated for critical attention. In general usage restricted to the smaller units, such as words, phrases, images, etc.

THEMATIC: Relating to works of literature in which no characters are involved except the author and his audience, as in most lyrics and essays, or to works of literature in which internal characters are subordinated to an argument maintained by the author, as in allegories and parables; opposed to fictional.

INDEX

Works will be found under the author's name.

379

Atheneum Paperbacks

HISTORY

HISTORY—AMERICAN

Atheneum Paperbacks

Atheneum Paperbacks

Atheneum Paperbacks

PSYCHOLOGY AND SOCIOLOGY

LITERATURE AND THE ARTS

PHYSICAL SCIENCES AND MATHEMATICS

Atheneum Paperbacks

LIFE SCIENCES AND ANTHROPOLOGY

THE WORLDS OF NATURE AND MAN